Kimuak: The Seeds of Basque Cinema

Occasional Papers Series No. 30

Kimuak
The Seeds of Basque Cinema

Ainhoa Fernandez de Arroyabe Olaortua,
Nekane E. Zubiaur Gorozika,
Iñaki Lazkano Arrillaga

Center for Basque Studies
University of Nevada, Reno
2018

Occasional Papers Series No. 30
Series Editor: Joseba Zulaika

William A. Douglass Center for Basque Studies
University of Nevada, Reno
Reno, Nevada 89557

Editors:
Ainhoa Fernandez de Arroyabe,
Nekane E. Zubiaur and Iñaki Lazkano

Translated by Mariann Vaczi

http://basque.unr.edu

ISBN-13: 978-1-935709-99-2
ISBN-10: 1-935709-99-2

Copyright © 2018 by the Center for Basque Studies and the
University of Nevada, Reno
All rights reserved. Printed in the United States of America

Library of Congress Cataloging-in-Publication Data forthcoming

Contents

Before the Prologue 7

Introduction 11

Fifteen Years of Basque Short Film 11

The Initiation and Development of the Kimuak Program
    Context and Creation 15

The Evolution of Genres:
    Narrative, Thematic, and Formal Styles in Kimuak   61

Most Important Filmmakers 97

Most Important Short Films 369

Final Words: Assessment and Challenges 403

Bibliography 409

Before the Prologue

Although it may perhaps be more sensible, and certainly less tedious, to sidestep both issues, I believe an introduction to a book examining a project to promote, disseminate, and distribute Basque short films must necessarily pose a pair of preliminary questions related to the words used to describe the subject of the book you have in your hands: "Basque" and "short film."

If we browse the film history books that have until quite recently dominated the shelves of our libraries, we will invariably notice that, primarily, what these often weighty (in every sense of the term) tomes present is not so much a history of cinema as a history of fiction cinema. In other words, these histories relegate various types of filmmaking to the background, addressed merely in footnotes or even appendices of varying degrees of relevance. Such is the case, if you will forgive the oversimplification, of so-called avant-garde cinema, but also of the "documentary" (the quotation marks are deliberate), and, of course, that undiscovered territory that the French call *"film de famille"* and that English- and Spanish-speakers refer to with the flagrant Gallicisms "amateur cinema" and *"cine amateur,"* respectively.

A similar fate has befallen the short film, the nature of which has been obscured by the constant repetition of at least two clichés that have informed critical approaches to this type of cinematic product for many years. It should really go without saying that the term "short film" refers not to a cinematic genre but merely to the length of a product that may be filled with any kind of content, provided its duration does not exceed one hour (for some time now the commonly accepted time limit).

The second cliché relates to the common idea that the short film is an almost ideal territory for novice filmmakers to show off their skills and take their first steps in the world of cinema. From this perspective, the short is seen as a mere space of transition, of preparation for greater (some would say more serious) endeavors.

Neither of these two assumptions can be maintained today, and not only because the arrival on the scene of new digital technologies and the growing range of opportunities for distribution of audiovisual creations have rendered the distinction between "short film" and "feature film" quite irrelevant.

If we take an unprejudiced view of the evolution of cinema in our times, we will be compelled to recognize the coexistence of two parallel and apparently contradictory phenomena: on the one hand, it is clear that the duration of films is tending toward expansion, in what in many cases is nothing more than a narrative metastasis that undermines the capacity to get to the point that distinguished several generations of filmmakers; on the other, we can also note that, directly associated with the existence of an increasingly "expanded" cinema, the question of shorter durations has taken on new meaning. Films created for museums and similar exhibition spaces (and there is an increasing number of filmmakers trying out this avenue for their productions) are characterized by much shorter durations than those of the classical feature film, in a phenomenon that is generally accompanied by a notable thinning down of the narrative structures of the works in question.

In short, in view of all the above we could argue for a critical reappraisal of the short film, based on its intrinsic flexibility and the ease with which it can be integrated into new exhibition contexts. Moreover, the short should no longer be viewed as the work of a director incapable of securing the funding necessary to put together a feature-length film. The significance of the short film today lies precisely in the fact that its duration is increasingly becoming an aesthetic parameter to deal with consciously, rather than a constraint imposed by budgetary limitations. Some of the greatest filmmakers today (I am thinking, to name but a few examples, of Jean-Marie Straub, Kaurismaki, and Chantal Akerman) have always rejected the notion of a qualitative distinction between the short and the feature film; a film is as long as it has to be.

More complex (and also much more controversial) is the other of our two key terms: "Basque." As in the case of the term "short film," we could ignore its implications and turn directly to the films that we decided, without excessive deliberation, to include under its umbrella (it should be noted, incidentally, that the criteria applied in this collection to assign films to this category were quite straightforward and functional). However, there would be nothing amiss in pausing for a moment to consider the relationship that exists between short films characterized as

"Basque" and other political levels in any analysis of their sociocultural context. Even if it is only because, whether we like it or not, they are created and in many cases funded by political structures operating below the national level (in the Spanish case we are referring here to the subnational regions that the Constitution of 1978 refers to as "Autonomous Communities"), which may (although not necessarily) be seen to raise a question of constant debate: is "Basque cinema" a subcategory of "Spanish cinema," or is it a challenge to the supposed classification that identifies any film produced within a given nation as a product of that nation beyond any further qualification? From this perspective, the set of works grouped under the umbrella of the Kimuak project offers extraordinarily valuable material to explore this question, if one should so desire.

As if that were not enough, the issue is further complicated (despite the considerable weakening of European self-esteem provoked by the institutional crisis and the general crisis in confidence) to the extent that all states (and the respective stateless countries existing within some of them) involved in the dream of building a single Europe are compelled to question themselves in relation to whether such a Europe exists and, if so, what the characteristics would be that would be adopted by a culture (and the cinema produced by that culture) that could be classified as "European."

Obviously, this is neither the place nor the time to answer these questions, and it is clear that this debate could be evaded with reference to a formula that some filmmakers have adopted when speaking of their work, which is less frivolous than it might seem in an era characterized by the desire to go to great lengths to highlight identity distinctions: the idea that beyond regional or national definitions, filmmakers inhabit a territory that, for the sake of brevity, we may term the "land of cinema," whose boundaries and regions are defined not by conventional delimitations but by a community of aesthetic attitudes that are at once diverse and shared. Viewed this way, none of the infrastructural questions associated with the facilities that governments make available to filmmakers to pursue their projects tell us a thing about the stylistic outcome of each film. In other words, an affiliation with a particular government reflects nothing more than an administrative issue, and sheds no light on the actual qualities of the films.

In sum, the "short film" is not a long film cut down, nor is it a crutch for filmmakers in training. It is, above all, a *distance* and an *impulse*. And it is here that its aesthetic validity comes into play. And if we turn to the question of what we are talking about when we speak of "Basque cinema," perhaps the most sensible approach would be, as is taken in the book you are about to read, to set out the administrative conditions underlying the films presented and, on that basis, scrutinize the many and varied ways in which each audiovisual piece articulates its artistic intention. Because, errors and omissions excepted, the idea that an aesthetic quality could be defined as "national" is highly dubious. It would therefore be best for our intention to be, as a political leader not very often quoted these days once remarked, to "let a hundred flowers bloom, let a hundred schools of thought contend."

Santos Zunzunegui

Introduction

Fifteen Years of Basque Short Film

The diffusion and promotion program of the Basque short film Kimuak celebrated its fifteenth edition in 2012. The first buds[1] that started to germinate in 1998 have grown significantly. This is a good occasion to critically assess the quality of the buds that the program spread over five continents, and to see whether they grew and developed into healthy, strong plants.

Kimuak is a public initiative sponsored by the Department of Culture of the Basque Government. Many other autonomous communities in the Spanish state later copied its concept and functioning. The program is managed by the Basque Film Archive Filmoteca Vasca/Euskadiko Filomtegia through the leadership of Txema Muñoz. His work, as he himself highlights, is based on three basic pillars: the *promotion* of short films and filmmakers; the *diffusion* of short films both at state and international level; and the *distribution* of short films throughout the world in order to reach the previous objectives.

The program receives annual subsidy from the Basque Government,[2] which is the only source of funding that sustains it. Given the public character of program's sources, there are certain questions that the program managers consider of primary importance when it comes to the execution of objectives. First, the philosophy of Kimuak is entirely based on the concept of service. Its objective is to offer comprehensive service to its direct beneficiaries (short filmmakers and producers), as well as its indirect ones (festivals, and potential buyers, or exhibitors).

Second and as a consequence, the program cannot be oriented toward profit. All income from the distribution of the select works is channeled back to their legitimate owners, the producers and directors.

---

1 The meaning of the word kimuak is "sprouts," "buds."
2 The figure increased gradually with the success and necessities of the program; in 2017 it rose to 127,000 euros.

Third, the vocation to service is based on a principle of equality. Since it is a publicly financed program, the continuity of Kimuak is not subjected to results. The works that get selected are treated equally, independent of whether they have greater or lesser success at film festivals. Although the short films and their respective trajectories end up having certain differences, Kimuak does not establish distinctions, and offers exactly the same opportunities for every film. They also apply this criterion of equality to festivals and exhibitors who ask for the catalog; Kimuak aims to attend all demands, whether they come from a prestigious international competition, or from the culture hall of a local small town.

Finally, the public origin the funds that sustain the program require an absolutely transparent management removed from any kind of profit speculation. Above all, it is required that the program optimizes resources with a single aim: the maximum national and international diffusion of select Basque short films.

These are the identity markers that Kimuak has developed and strengthened throughout its fifteen editions, which is a long trajectory for a project whose beginnings were not withtout complications. This will be precisely our point of departure: a review of the circumstances that surrounded the program's birth, and the major milestones that have marked its evolution and development. In this sense, we will particularly emphasize the presence of short films at state and international festivals through the number of selections (to a competition or in the information section), and the awards they received.[3]

There are several reasons why we emphasize this point. First, because festivals are Kimuak's most important channel. The short film has disappeared from commercial movie theaters; television is not especially interested in featuring these types of formats;[4] the DVD is in crisis and, except for a few initiatives, it was never a channel of diffusion for short filmmakers. And while nowadays

---

3   The data presented cover the period until June 2014, and were provided by the program itself.
4   With the exception of TVE (with spaces like Versión Española), Canal Plus, or the channels of the autonomous communities (even if these latter ones sometimes play movies at inconvenient hours, and are generally tied by agreements with corresponding departments of culture).

there exist portals like filmin or filmotech, which allow the download and prepaid viewing of certain short films, the potential of the Internet for audiovisual distribution is not entirely exploited yet, and it is difficult to quantify the real scope of diffusion. Festivals are, therefore, the most likely places to feature and watch short films. Here we must note that Kimuak only relates to the non-commercial rights of films, and does not keep any records of sales to distributors and television. This question goes beyond the scope of our research.

The ultimate objective of the program, as we pointed out, is that the short films that constitute the catalog receive the widest diffusion possible, and the number of selections in festivals is a great way to assess their achievements. Awards recognize the quality of films, and are the only indexes to calibrate their reception. Box office results or specialized criticism are lacking for short films, and the movie industry only cares for them when they achieve something exceptional such as nomination to the Hollywood Academy Awards. Given the difficulty of selling short films to television or other distributors, and the drop of revenue from renting copies for other types of projections, awards have become practically the only way to recover the investment put into short film making. This is of major relevance, because only the amortization of costs and the procurement of benefits may propel the creation of films. Similarly, the formation of a stable and productive context (a question that we will also address in the first part of the book) allows that the short film not only becomes a cultural, but also an industrial product.

In any case, we believe that it is the films themselves and their creators who have the leading role in the program and, therefore, constitute the main focus of our study. Through the revision of the functioning and the evolution of the Kimuak program, the following pages will focus on the content and form of the films collected across its fifteen editions (between 1998 and 2012) from the perspective of film analysis. We will first provide a general picture of the generic, thematic, narrative, and formal styles that characterize the hundred plus short films of Kimuak. Later, we will focus on the analysis of the most significant films. When it comes to the configuration of the corpus of works that will be subject of this study, we start with the creators themselves. The criterion was not left for chance. Of the complete list of filmmakers who have participated in Kimuak, some names are recurrent as they are associated with titles of greater interest from a cinematographic point of view, or have a more prolific trajectory at festivals. There are titles that demonstrate a constancy of narrative and formal style in the work of their authors. In light of these arguments, we have selected those filmmakers who have two or more distinguished titles in Kimuak. We present their work in the program through the textual analysis of each of their films, accompanied by a personal interview with the director. We finish the book with the analysis of certain pieces that stay on the margins of the above criteria, but deserve attention due to their quality and repercussion.

Before starting our work, however, we wish to express our acknowledgment of the contribution by persons and institutions that made this book possible. First of all, of course, we would like to thank the Basque Film Archive Filmoteca Vasca/Euskadiko Filmategia, and above all the team responsible for Kimuak: Txema Muñoz, Esther Cabero and Amaia Revuelta, who have solicitously responded to our petitions, questions and necessities, offering their knowledge and views during the elaboration of the text.

Many thanks to Raúl Pérez as well, who collaborated in the transcription of the interviews. Most importantly, we are grateful to those who have generously shared their time with us to meet and talk: Koldo Almandoz, Asier Altuna, Telmo Esnal, Luiso Berdejo, Borja Cobeaga, Jon Garaño, Jose Mari Goenaga, Tinieblas González, David González Rudiez, Igor Legarreta, Isabel Herguera, Ione Hernández, Nahikari Ipiña, Izibene Oñederra, Emilio Pérez, José Luis Rebordinos, Koldo Serra, Oskar Santos, Begoña Vicario, Nacho Vigalondo and Haritz Zubillaga.

1

The Initiation and Development of the Kimuak Program

Context and Creation

The Kimuak program was born, unsurprisingly, in the late 1990s, a moment when the Spanish short film in general was undergoing an unexpected boom, which culminated in the 1997 Oscar nomination of *Esposados* (Linked) directed by Juan Carlos Fresnadillo. One of the great changes that this period affected was

> The shift from a model of production with great deficiencies in the area of technical and human resources agglutinating a small group of enthusiasts around a project who in most cases had almost no preparation ... to the paradigm of the second part of the decade, which presented a system of production that was rather more structured, with teams that had enormous economic solvency.[5]

The Basque Autonomous Community, a region that has a long cinematographic tradition especially in documentary and experimental type films, was not far from this tendency. The measures that supported the production and distribution of short films were during this decade

---

[5] Velázquez and Ramírez, Una década prodigiosa, 39. In their exhaustive study, the authors identify the factors linked to the production and exhibition that made such progress possible in the second part of the decade: the creation of several cinematographic schools (championed by the ESCAC in Barcelona, or the ECAM in Madrid), and university programs in Audiovisual Communication that elevated the level and professionalism of technicians; the increase in sales of short films to television channels, which was to a great degree fomented by the apparition of thematic channels dedicated exclusively to cinema in digital forums, and programs like Piezas and La noche + corta in Canal Plus, or Versión española and Metrópolis in TVE; the continuous proliferation of specific festivals in the past years; and the emergence of the Internet as a new channel of promotion and distribution.

relevant and fruitful. The public association Euskalmedia was created in 1990 as a complement to the subsidies granted by the autonomous administration for the production of short films. This organization was dependent on the Basque Government's Department of Culture, and its objective was to serve as coproducer of short films that were considered important during its operation until 1995.

In the 1980s, Euskadi was already the quarry of some of the most interesting filmmakers such as Enrique Urbizu, Julio Medem, Juanma Bajo Ulloa or Álex de la Iglesia.[6] The new climate that created a favorable atmosphere for filmmaking served as fertilizer, and the harvest of short films in the Basque Country would be plentiful in the following decade both in quality and quantity.[7] Proof of this is the Goya Award for Best Animation Short Film that Bego Vicario won for his work titled *Pregunta por mí* (Ask for Me, 1996); the award given to *Por un infante difunto* (Due to a Dead Prince, Tinieblas González, 1998) at the Semaine de la Critique de Cannes; or the programming of *Razielen itzulera* (The Return of Raziel, Koldo Almandoz, 1997) in the Zabaltegi selection of the Donostia-San Sebastián International Film Festival.

Encouraged by this thriving panorama, Amaia Rodríguez, director of Cultural Creation and Diffusion of the Basque Government, and José Luis Rebordinos, representative of the Cinema Unit of the Municipal Patronage of Culture of the Donostia-San Sebastián municipality (Donostia Kultura), had several meetings during the year 1997. From these encounters, a definitive conclusion emerged: "The nonrefundable subsidies granted for the production of short films helped their creation, but did not guarantee their distribution."[8] The creation of films required such economic effort that producers rarely had enough money left to invest in their distribution. The meager international presence and repercussion of Basque short films did not reflect the notable quality that some of them possessed. Therefore, both institutions concluded that "all citizens had the right, if they wanted, to see all short films produced

---

6   We may emphasize Patas en la cabeza (1985) and Las seis en punta (1987) by Julio Medem, Akixo (1988) and El reino de Víctor (1989) by Juanma Bajo Ulloa, Mamá (1988) by Pablo Berger, and Mirindas asesinas (1990) by Álex de la Iglesia.
7   According to the data provided by Velázquez and Ramírez between 1990 and 1999 the Basque Autonomous Community was, with a total of forty-four registered titles in the ICAA, the third ranked center of short film production in Spain after Madrid and Catalonia.
8   Angulo, Rebordinos, and Santamarina, Breve historia del cortometraje vasco, 172.

in the Basque Autonomous Community. The Basque Government had the responsibility to create ways that allowed the exercise of this right."[9]

José Luis Rebordinos worked out the details, inspired by two previous experiences in France and New Zealand (Unifrance and New Zealand Film Commission), which he knew well through the San Sebastian Horror and Fantasy Film Festival organized by the patronage. The Department of Culture looked at the proposal favorably, and in 1998 Kimuak was born with the firm intention to foment the promotion, diffusion, and distribution of Basque short films.

Initially, Kimuak consisted of two catalogs. The first collected all the short films that were presented at the annual application period. It was enough for a producer to fulfill two requirements for the registration of their short film in this catalog: that they provide for use a copy of the film in 16 or 35mm, and that the tape be produced partly or entirely in the Basque Autonomous Community, and/or its director is resident of the same. In turn, the Department of Culture created a folder with information about each short film (including a synopsis, artistic and technical index, a photograph, and commentary about the film), sent these folders to various cinematographic program makers of the Community (municipalities, culture halls, film clubs, etc., which could rent the copies for a fixed price of ten thousand pesetas plus tax), and showed all short films in, at least, the three capitals of the Basque Autonomous Community.

The second catalog, also called the "international catalog," had greater ambitions. A jury of short film experts selected pieces that, based on their quality and characteristics, had a chance of successful international diffusion. The corresponding files of this catalog included a VHS tape with the films subtitled in English and Spanish (if it was a film originally in Basque), a booklet of two transparencies for each short film, and information about them in Basque, Spanish, and English. The Basque Government was responsible for sending these promotional files to the greatest possible number of international festivals and television merchants, as well as providing English subtitles for at least one copy in 35mm for those short films that were selected for international competitions.

---

9   Ibid.

The Evolution of the Program

The first two years of the project were difficult. The Department of Culture was responsible for its management, but did not designate anyone in particular to take care of the necessary tasks. The first catalog consisted of nineteen short films, and the second of ten:[10]

- *Luis Soto* (Luis Soto, directed by Irene Arzuaga, produced by Meltxor Villarrubia and Román Rey - Solo Spot Producciones, 1995).
- *Por un infante difunto* (Due to a Dead Prince, directed by Tinieblas González, produced by Tinieblas González - Tinieblas Films, 1998).
- *Pregunta por mí* (Ask for Me, directed by Begoña Vicario, produced by Begoña Vicario, 1996).
- *Razielen itzulera* (The Return of Raziel, directed by Koldo Almandoz, produced by Marian Fernández Pascal - Medusa Kuttuna Filmeak, 1997).
- *Tortolika eta Tronbon* (Tortolika & Tronbon, directed by Joxean Muñoz and Txabi Basterretxea, produced by Fernando San José - Ikuskin E.M., 1998).
- *Txotx* (Txotx, directed by Asier Altuna and Telmo Esnal, produced by José María Lara - Alokatu, 1997).
- *La vaca* (The Cow, directed by Gorka Esteban, produced by José María Lara - Alokatu, 1997).
- *El viento africano* (The African Wind, directed by Merche Álvarez, produced by José María Lara - Alokatu, 1998).

The results were scarce. In fact, a great many of the four hundred edited films did not even have any distribution. Nevertheless, some of the titles such as *Por un infante difunto*, and *Txotx* earned some recognition, and the festivals and televisions that received the catalog valued the initiative quite positively. So much so that, the following year, the Basque

---

[10] Since it was the first edition, they made an exception and accepted works that were produced in years prior to the year of the application period.

Government decided to launch a public tender and delegate program management to a company unaffiliated with the Department of Culture.

Eighteen short films were presented for the 1999 edition, of which eight were featured in the second catalog:

- *40 ezetz* (40 Against, directed by Asier Altuna and Telmo Esnal, produced by José María Lara - Alokatu S.L., 1999).
- *Amor de madre* (Mother's Love, directed by Koldo Serra and Gorka Vázquez, produced by Raquel Perea - Sebastopoleko titiriteroak S.L., 1998).
- *Haragia* (Human Flesh, directed by Begoña Vicario, produced by Begoña Vicario, 1999).
- *Muerto de amor* (Dead for Love, directed by Ramón Barea, produced by José María Lara, 1997).[11]
- *The Raven* (The Raven, directed by Tinieblas González, produced by Tinieblas González - Tinieblas Films, 1999).
- *Réquiem* (Requiem, Óscar Currás and Iñigo Royo, produced by Enrique Santiago - Sarobe Film School, 1998).
- *Sarabe* (Sarabe, directed by Beatriz de la Vega, produced by Beatriz de la Vega P.C., 1999).
- *El trabajo* (The Job, directed by Igor Legarreta and Emilio Pérez, produced by Carlos Juárez, Raquel Perea - Sebastopoleko titiriteroak S.L., 1999).

In spite of the favorable reception of short films like *El trabajo*, *Amor de madre* and *The Raven* (included in the Official Section of the Donostia-San Sebastián International Film Festival, and selected in 180 competitions), the idea of externalizing the program's management did not prove satisfactory. The program seemed to be destined to end, but Donostia Kultura did not want to let an idea in which it firmly believed die. Convinced that negative outcomes were due to matters of

---

11   Although it was a short film from 1997, it was selected by Kimuak two years later after it competed at the Critic's Week of the Cannes Festival. This was the last edition where they admitted works produced in the previous years. From this moment on, the program only accepted films that were made during the year of submission.

management and not the relevance of the program itself, Rebordinos proposed to Ricardo Bilbao, who had replaced Amaia Rodríguez in the Department of Culture, that the Patronage should provisionally take charge of the project.

Donostia Kultura contracted the services of Ane Segurado to take charge of Kimuak, and her work between September 2000 and November 2001 was a turning point in the development of the initiative. In 2001, Ana Arizaga replaced Segurado until 2002, when Txema Muñoz took charge of the program.

This period was key for the survival and eventual consolidation of Kimuak. With Ane Segurado's leadership, the four hundred folders of the 2000 international catalog were all distributed, especially in state festivals but also in some international ones from which they otherwise would have been absent. This was greatly facilitated by a network of connections that Donostia Kultura had in Spain as well as abroad (Cannes, Sitges, Gijón, Clermont Ferrand, etc.). They started to send the catalog systematically to festivals, televisions, and buyers. This resulted in the considerable increase in number of selections and awards that the short films of the second catalog won. Although the most important titles of this edition were *Jardines deshabitados* (Uninhabited Gardens, directed by Pablo Malo, produced by Pablo Malo P.C.) and *Torre* (Tower, directed by Oskar Santos, produced by Norberto Ramos del Val, Oskar Santos - Norberfilms), the international catalog consisted of four more short films among a total of sixteen presented:

- *Hauspo soinua* (The Sound of Bellows, directed by Inaz Fernández, produced by Carlos Juárez - Ikusmen S.L., 2000).
- *Hilarri* (Tombstone, directed by Manu Gómez, produced by Aitor Mantxola S.L., 2000).
- *Hyde & Jekill* (Hyde & Jekill, directed by Sara Mazkiaran, produced by Yolanda Mazkiaran - Errotari Produce, 2000).
- *Inventario* (Inventory, directed by Óscar Currás and Iñigo Royo, produced by Rober Ors, Miriam P. Montroig - Grup Cinema-Art, 2000).

The 2001 edition may still be considered a little irregular in terms of results. Of the eleven films presented, six were selected for the second catalog:

- *Aizea, City of the Wind* (Aizea, City of the Wind, directed by Ione Hernández, produced by Ralf Weinfurtner, Ione Hernández - Ione Hernández Films/Aizea Film, 2001).
- *Hombre sin hombre* (Man Without Man, directed by Michel Gaztambide, produced by Roberto Cibrián, Michel Gaztambide, Mireia Lluch - Cibrián, Gaztambide y Lluch P.C., 2001).
- *El método* (The Method, directed by Haritz Zubillaga and José Antonio Pérez, produced by Carlos Juárez P.C., 2001).
- *Primera persona* (The First Person, directed by Gorka Merchán, produced by Unai Ibarbia - Orio Produkzioak S.A./U-Bit S.L., 2002).
- *La primera vez* (The First Time, directed by Borja Cobeaga, produced by Oihana Olea, Julio Díez - Altube Filmeak/Allmura Films, 2001).
- *…ya no puede caminar* (…Can't Walk Anymore, directed by Luiso Berdejo, produced by Koldo Zuazua, Mónica Blas - Koldo Zuazua P.C., 2001).

From that year on, they started to systematize the records refereed for participation in state and international festivals (competitions or new sections), as well as the awards the films received.[12] The yearly tables included in this book provide data about the trajectory of short films until June 2014; they are in any case provisional given that the exhibition of short films does not end with the yearly catalog. Some of them continue to participate in competitions and even win awards years afterward.

---

12 We only have isolated data from the first three editions. Nor does Kimuak have information about the commercial life of short films, given that the management of these rights does not belong with the program's tasks. For this reason, the participation and awards received at festivals (main realm of exhibition and of the vital development of short films) serve as a barometer to measure the diffusion and repercussion of each piece.

The 2001 data reveal that *La primera vez* (nominated for the Goya Award for Best Fiction Short Film), and *... ya no puede caminar* were the landmarks of an edition which first showed clear and hopeful signs of Kimuak's progress.

KIMUAK 2001

SHORT FILM	FEST. Total	FEST. SPAIN	FEST. Europe	FEST. Other	AWARDS
Aizea, ciudad del viento. Ione Hernández	25	17	4	4	3
Hombre sin hombre. Michel Gaztambide	25	16	7	2	2
El método. Haritz Zubillaga, José A. Pérez	18	12	4	2	2
Primera persona. Gorka Merchant	17	7	6	4	0
La primera vez. Borja Cobeaga	92	42	26	24	33
... ya no puede caminar. Luiso Berdejo	97	47	31	19	33
TOTAL	274	141	78	55	73

Table 1.1

After his incorporation in management in February 2002, Txema Muñoz consolidated and extended the program's network of contacts with state, and especially international festivals. For the first time, they edited six hundred folders, and once again the number of short films presented for Kimuak increased, now to a total of sixteen. Six films were selected:

- *Belarra* (Grass, directed by Koldo Almandoz, produced by Marian Fernández Pascal, Iñigo Martínez - MK Filmeak/Napartheid, 2002).
- *Dortoka uhartea* (Turtle Island, directed by Maru Solores, produced by Carlos Juárez, Marc Daniel Dichant - Sebastopoleko titiriteroak S.L./Deutsche Film und Fernsehakademie Berlin, 2002).
- *La pescadilla que se muerde la cola* (The Fish That Bites Its Tail, directed by Txema Matías, produced by Ramón Orlando, David Cuesta, Txema Matías Ramón Orlando P.C., 2002).
- *Tercero B* (Third Floor, B, directed by Jose Mari Goenaga, produced by Xabier Berzosa - Moriarti Produkzioak, 2002).
- *Terminal* (Terminus, directed by Aitzol Aramaio, produced by Aitzol Aramaio, Pako Ruiz - Aitzol Aramaio/Sonora Estudios, 2002).
- *Topeka* (Topeka, directed by Asier Altuna, produced by Asier Altuna, Xanti Ezkurra - Alokatu S.L., 2002).

Participation at festivals practically doubled in comparison with the previous year, and the number of selections at international competitions (especially European) considerably increased. Although the most popular short films were *Terminal*, *Tercero B* and *Topeka*, it is important to highlight that *Belarra* was selected for the Semaine de la Critique de Cannes.

The intensive work that the program produced first got its reward in 2003, which was an important year for Kimuak's take off. It was the beginning of its authentic international recognition. In February, *Topeka* became part of a small selection of Spanish short films which, promoted by a group of Valencian and Madrid-based professionals with Piluca Baquero and Carlos Gil's leadership, was presented at the fair of the Clermont-Ferrand International Short Film Festival in France. This is the most important short film forum of the world.

KIMUAK 2002

SHORT FILM	FEST. Total	FEST. SPAIN	FEST. Europe	FEST. Other	AWARDS
Belarra. Koldo Almandoz	54	18	21	15	10
Dortoka uhartea. Maru Solores	53	17	26	10	8
La pescadilla que se muerde la cola. Txema Matías	18	7	7	4	0
Tercero B. Jose Mari Goenaga	128	71	31	26	45
Terminal. Aitzol Aramaio	65	32	23	10	18
Topeka. Asier Altuna	125	51	43	31	18
TOTAL	443	196	151	96	99

Table 1.2

In September they published the 2003 catalog, which was an authentic success for Kimuak owing to, principally, the title *7:35 de la mañana* (7:35 in the Morning). Encouraged by the great results of the previous year, the program increased the number of edited folders to one thousand. VHS tapes and transparencies were replaced by DVD and CD. Also, they started to provide French subtitles for the films. Only ten short films were presented, and six were chosen to constitute the catalog:

- *7:35 de la mañana* (7:35 in the Morning, directed by Nacho Vigalondo, produced by Eduardo Carneros, Javier Ibarretxe - Ibarretxe & Co., 2003).
- *Ecosistema* (Ecosystem, directed by Tinieblas González, produced by Joseba Vázquez, Tinieblas González - Tinieblas Films, 2003).
- *Expreso nocturno* (Night Express, directed by Imanol Ortiz López, produced by Imanol Ortiz López, Manu Gómez Álvarez-La rana verde, 2003).

- *El tren de la bruja* (The Spook House, directed by Koldo Serra, produced by Álvaro Alonso, Antonio Lobo - Jaleo Films in collaboration with Arsénico P.C., 2003).
- *Lepokoa* (The Scarf, directed by Safy Nebbou, produced by Laurence Darthos, Laurence Diaz, Safy Nebbou, Iñaki Gómez - Tara Films/Les films du Zephyr/Irusoin, 2003).
- *Las Superamigas contra el Profesor Vinilo* (Superfriends Meet Professor Vinyl, directed by Domingo González, produced by Pedro Ruigómez Momeñe, 2003).

If the outcomes of 2002 were great, those of 2003 were excellent, reaching more than eight hundred selections at festivals, almost double of the previous year.

KIMUAK 2003

SHORT FILM	FEST. Total	FEST. SPAIN	FEST. Europe	FEST. Other	AWARDS
7:35 de la mañana. Nacho Vigalondo	270	105	106	59	77
Ecosistema. Tinieblas González	93	51	28	14	7
Expreso nocturno. Imanol Ortiz López	107	57	29	21	6
Lepokoa. Safy Nebbou	66	23	28	15	12
Las Superamigas… Domingo González	113	67	32	14	10
El tren de la bruja. Koldo Serra	153	78	43	32	21
TOTAL	802	381	266	155	133

Table 1.3

Besides its fruitful presence at state and international competitions, *7:35 de la mañana* won important awards, among them the Festival of Gijón, the Youth Award in the prestigious Clermont Ferrand International Short Film Festival, and two nominations to the Academy Awards and the European Film Awards. The success of Vigalondo's film opened the doors to the much desired international market, thus far avoided due to the program's unwillingness to pay entry fees required by some US competitions.[13] Many festivals all over the world started to be interested in the program, and asked for the catalog, which positively influenced the trajectory of the rest of the short films. In fact, *7:35 de la mañana* is not the only title that stood out that year. It is also worth mentioning the Méliès d'or that the European Fantastic Film Festivals Federation awarded to *El tren de la bruja* in Amsterdam, directed by Koldo Serra with a script written by Vigalondo himself.

The results of 2003 were difficult to surpass, and indeed the expectations that they generated were not immediately met. Although in 2004 as many as twenty-four short films were presented, only six were selected:

- *El aire que respiro* (The Air That I Breathe, directed by Sara Bilbatúa, produced by Sara Bilbatúa - Tanami Producciones, 2004).
- *Amuak* (Fish Hooks, directed by Koldo Almandoz, produced by Marian Fernández Pascal. MK Filmak/ Napartheid, 2004).
- *Ana y Manuel* (Ana and Manuel, directed by Manuel Calvo, produced by Roberto Butragueño, Alicia Rodríguez, Koldo Zuazua - Elamedia/Encanta Films/Koldo Zuazua P.C., 2004).
- *El despropósito* (The Hurlyburly, directed by Zoe Berriatúa, produced by Zoe Berriatúa P.C./Koldo Zuazua P.C., 2004).
- *Dos encuentros* (Two Encounters, directed by Alan Griffin, produced by Carlos Juárez, Esteban Ibarretxe, Javier

---

13 After the success of 7:35 de la mañana, some North American festivals permitted other Kimuak short films to participate without having to pay the entry fee. The fee does not guarantee that the film is selected.

Ibarretxe, Eduardo Carneros, Juanma Díaz Avendaño Karbo Vantas/Elemental Films/Basque Films, 2004).
- *El soñador* (The Dreamer, directed by Oskar Santos, produced by Carmen Rico - Himenóptero S.L., 2004).

Responding to the demand provoked by the previous catalog, the program created 1,200 copies. However, while the results surpassed those of 2002 and some titles such as *El soñador* are noteworthy, the success of this edition did not approximate that of the year before.

KIMUAK 2004

SHORT FILM	FEST. Total	FEST. SPAIN	FEST. Europe	FEST. Other	AWARDS
El aire que respiro. Sara Bilbatua	48	21	9	18	2
Amuak. Koldo Almandoz	77	39	24	14	7
Ana y Manuel. Manuel Calvo	128	77	23	28	16
El despropósito. Zoe Berriatúa	42	29	8	5	4
Dos encuentros. Alan Griffin	75	38	19	18	11
El soñador. Oskar Santos	141	81	35	25	64
TOTAL	511	285	118	108	104

Table 1.4

Nevertheless, 2004 was an important year in the history of Kimuak. It participated for the first time at the Cinema Jove International Film Festival fair in Valencia, which was the only state platform of this nature related to the world of short films.[14] With 1,300 edited folders, the program started to soar spectacularly in 2005, and it reached the greatest results of its history. This was the year of Kimuak's international consecration. Seven titles, selected from eighteen, completed the most successful catalog until this point:

- *Choque* (Crash, directed by Nacho Vigalondo, produced by Carlos Juárez, Galder Gaztelu Urrutia - Basque Films/ Arsénico P.C., 2005).
- Éramos pocos (One Too Many, directed by Borja Cobeaga, produced by Oihana Olea - Altube Filmeak, 2005).
- *La gallina ciega* (Blindman's Bluff, directed by Isabel Herguera, produced by Isabel Herguera, 2005).
- *El gran Zambini* (The Great Zambini, directed by Igor Legarreta and Emilio Pérez, produced by Igor Legarreta, Emilio Pérez, Carlos Juárez, Raquel Perea - Aprieta fuerte/ User T38/El pollito cowboy y Conbarba/Ahí Está, 2005).
- *La guerra* (The War, directed by Luiso Berdejo and Jorge C. Dorado, produced by Koldo Zuazua, Mónica Blas - Common Films & Koldo Zuazua P.C., 2005).
- *Los ojos de Alicia* (Alicia's Eyes, directed by Ugo Sanz, produced by Ugo Sanz and M.C. Rodero, 2005).
- *Sintonía* (Syntony, directed by Jose Mari Goenaga, produced by Aitor Arregi - Moriarti Produkzioak, 2005).

The number of selections at festivals was almost double of 2003. All the short films went beyond a hundred participations, and Éramos pocos, *Sintonía* and *El gran Zambini* even surpassed two hundred. The first two had an unusual harvest of awards that was only comparable to that of *7:35 de la mañana*, and Borja Cobeaga's film was also nominated to the Hollywood Academy Awards.

It is also important to mention *La Guerra*, nominated to the Goya Award of Best Short Fiction Film, and *La gallina ciega*, which competed at the Annecy Festival (the most prestigious animation festival), and

---

14 Although the festival was active in 2018, the market disappeared in 2009.

was also a candidate for the Goya Award. For the first time, the two short films delegated by the Spanish state to the Clermont-Ferrand belonged to Kimuak: **Éramos pocos** and *Choque*.

KIMUAK 2005

SHORT FILM	FEST. Total	FEST. SPAIN	FEST. Europe	FEST. Other	AWARDS
Choque. Nacho Vigalondo	170	75	49	46	8
Éramos pocos. Borja Cobeaga	275	130	73	72	80
La gallina ciega. Isabel Herguera	163	44	77	42	22
El gran Zambini. Igor Legarreta, Emilio Pérez	211	87	70	54	54
La guerra. Luiso Berdejo, Jorge C. Dorado	185	84	48	53	48
Los ojos de Alicia. Ugo Sanz	135	57	41	37	23
Sintonía. Jose Mari Goenaga	240	110	73	57	88
TOTAL	1.379	587	431	361	323

Table 1.5

Besides its great results, 2005 was a decisive year because it produced several landmarks in the trajectory of the program. In February that year, Kimuak participated for the first time at the Clermont-Ferrand fair with its own stand within the project "Spanish presence at the Clermont-Ferrand," promoted by the aforementioned Piluca Baquero and Carlos Gil.[15]

In March, the management of the program went from Donostia Kultura to the Basque Film Archives Filmoteca Vasca/Euskadiko

---

15 After 2009, Kimuak dissociated from Spain and, similarly to the Council of Andalusia, had its own stand and representation.

Filmategia at the request of Joxean Arbelaiz (the Basque Government's Director of Diffusion), although Txema Muñoz continued to direct it. It was a logical transfer of responsibilities, given that Donostia Kultura was a municipal institution, while Kimuak was a nationwide program. In addition, modern technical developments required continuous updates to exhibition formats that varied from celluloid, and the film archive's infrastructure notably facilitated those operations.

The last great change that happened in 2014 was the disappearance of the first catalog. The introduction of digital technologies in the cinematographic industry, as well as the success of the program itself had catapulted the production of short films in the Basque Country. The number of pieces presented exceeded the possibilities of Kimuak, and the proper management of a catalog in limited demand became impossible. In fact, the eighteen short films presented at the 2005 round went to forty-two in 2006. Kimuak, which had been created for international diffusion, could not allow that the volume of work that the maintenance of both catalogs meant should jeopardize the proper management of the international selection. The boom of the program in 2005 also caused many international festivals to directly get in touch with Kimuak to ask for folders, a dynamic that greatly extended the network of relationships established until then by Txema Muñoz, and a dynamic that continued as of 2018. In order to cope with this notably increased amount of work, Amaia Revuelta joined Kimuak in 2006 to complete certain tasks related with the management of registrations and material preparation. She was in charge of state festivals until 2010, when she left the Film Archives to join the Cinema Unit of Donostia Kultura.

Aware that the successes of the previous year were unrepeatable, the objective of the 2006 program was to at least keep the standards high. Seven works were selected for a catalog that increased its print run to 1.500 copies:

- *Cirugía* (Surgery, directed by Alberto González, produced by Nahikari Ipiña - Querido Antonio/Arsénico P.C., 2006).
- *For(r)est in the des(s)ert* (For(r)est in the des(s)ert, directed by Luiso Berdejo, produced by Laura Berdejo, Luiso Berdejo - Hermanos Berdejo, 2006).
- *Juego* (Game, directed by Ione Hernández, produced by Ione Hernández and Alicia Produce, 2006).

- *Máquina* (Machine, directed by Gabe Ibáñez, produced by Igor Legarreta, Emilio Pérez, Gabe Ibáñez, Raúl Bernabé - Aprieta fuerte/Tapadera/User T38, 2006).
- *Midori* (Midori, directed by Koldo Almandoz, produced by Koldo Almandoz, Marian Fernández Pascal, Angel Aldarondo - MK Filmak/Kosmikar Studio, 2006).
- *El relevo* (The Relief, directed by David González, produced by David González Rudiez/Cinetika S.L., 2006).
- *Sarean* (In the Net, directed by Asier Altuna, produced by José María Lara - Alokatu S.L., 2006).

All of the short films, with the exception of two, exceeded a hundred festival participations. *Cirugía* and *Máquina* became the works with greatest resonance. Gabe Ibáñez's *Máquina* was selected at the Clermont-Ferrand Festival, where it won the Special Jury Award at the Labo competition.

KIMUAK 2006

SHORT FILM	FEST. Total	FEST. SPAIN	FEST. Europe	FEST. Other	AWARDS
Cirugía. Alberto González	188	92	62	34	22
For(r)est in the des(s)ert. Luiso Berdejo	111	51	36	24	13
Juego. Ione Hernández	81	34	30	17	11
Máquina. Gabe Ibáñez	196	61	88	47	41
Midori. Koldo Almandoz	30	13	13	4	3
El relevo. David González	120	62	39	19	14
Sarean. Asier Altuna	107	42	39	26	8
TOTAL	833	355	307	171	112

Table 1.6

Although it did not reach the heights of the 2005 results, the 2006 numbers allowed for an optimistic vision of the future. These high expectations were again met in 2007, the year Kimuak reached ten years of age; a veritable achievement for a pioneering initiative that emerged modestly, and whose continuation was debatable at one point.

Eight were selected of the forty-three short films presented which, as had happened with the 2005 catalog, surpassed a thousand festival participations. Among others, there was the selection of the animated film *Hezurbeltzak, una fosa común* (Hezurbeltzak, a Common Grave), directed by Izibene Oñederra, at the Clermont-Ferrand Festival. The almost two hundred selections of *Taxi?* (Taxi?) and *Traumalogía* (Traumalogy) also stand out, as well as the sixty-eight awards given to the latter, and the thirty-three given to *Las horas muertas* (Killing Time).

These were the 2007 titles, and their results:

- *Columba palumbus (Uso basatia)* (Wild Dove, directed by Koldo Almandoz, produced by Koldo Almandoz, Marian Fernández Pascal, Angel Aldarondo - MK Filmak/Kosmikar Studio, 2007).
- *Decir adiós* (Saying Goodbye, directed by Víctor Iriarte, produced by Víctor Iriarte, Margarita Olaso - Caja con cosas dentro/Vio, 2007).
- *Hezurbeltzak, una fosa común* (Hezurbeltzak, a Common Grave, directed by Izibene Oñederra, produced by Pello Gutiérrez - T(arte)an, 2007).
- *Las horas muertas* (Killing Time, directed by Haritz Zubillaga, produced by Carlos Juárez, Galder Gaztelu - Urrutia, Haritz Zubillaga - Basque Films, 2007).
- *Limoncello* (Limoncello, directed by Jorge Dorado, Luiso Berdejo and Borja Cobeaga, produced by Koldo Zuazua, Mónica Blas, Manuel Calvo, Yolanda González, Borja Crespo, Borja Cobeaga, Nahikari Ipiña, Koldo Serra, Nacho Vigalondo - Koldo Zuazua P.C./Encanta Films/Common Films/Arsénico Producciones, 2007).

- *No es una buena idea* (Not a Good Idea, directed by Ugo Sanz, produced by Carlos Taboada, Álex Sampayo - Producciones Ciudadano Frame, 2007).
- *Taxi?* (Taxi?, directed by Telmo Esnal, produced by Asier Altuna, Marian Fernández Pascal - Aupa Films, 2007).
- *Traumalogía* (Traumalogy, directed by Daniel Sánchez Arévalo, produced by Koldo Zuazua, Mónica Blas - Koldo Zuazua P.C./Common Films, 2007).

KIMUAK 2007

SHORT FILM	FEST. Total	FEST. SPAIN	FEST. Europe	FEST. Other	AWARDS
Columba Palumbus. Koldo Almandoz	112	47	43	22	9
Decir adiós. Víctor Iriarte	35	10	14	11	4
Hezurbeltzak. Izibene Oñederra	150	50	66	34	16
Las horas muertas. Haritz Zubillaga	139	56	56	27	33
Limoncello. J. Dorado, L. Berdejo, B. Cobeaga	121	66	30	25	19
No es una buena idea. Ugo Sanz	87	20	38	29	9
Taxi?. Telmo Esnal	199	92	63	44	17
Traumalogía. Daniel Sánchez Arévalo	180	94	60	26	68
TOTAL	1.023	435	370	218	175

Table 1.7

Kimuak celebrated its tenth anniversary in a very special way. Thanks to a donation from the Ministry of Culture and the Spanish Film Archives, they made a metal box with a DVD that contained the twelve best short films of the 1998–2006 catalogs. They trusted seventy-eight professionals from all over the world with the selection, which was presented at Zinebi (International Short and Documentary Film Festival Bilbao).[16] Among others, they were representatives of prestigious festivals; from all communities with a promotional program of short films; and from institutions like the Basque Film Archive Filmoteca Vasca/Euskadiko Filmategia, Spanish Film Archive, CGAI - Centro Galego de Artes da Imaxe, the Cervantes Institute, the program *Versión Española*, Canal +, and so on. The films selected were the following:

- *7:35 de la mañana* (7:35 in the Morning, Nacho Vigalondo, 2003).
- *Éramos pocos* (One Too Many, Borja Cobeaga, 2005).
- *La guerra* (The War, Luiso Berdejo, Jorge C. Dorado, 2005).
- *La primera vez* (The First Time, Borja Cobeaga, 2001).
- *Topeka* (Topeka, Asier Altuna, 2002).
- *Máquina* (Machine, Gabe Ibáñez, 2006).
- *El tren de la bruja* (The Spook House, Koldo Serra, 2003).
- *Sintonía* (Syntony, Jose Mari Goenaga, 2005).
- *... ya no puede caminar* (… Can't Walk Anymore, Luiso Berdejo, 2001).
- *Tercero B* (Third Floor, B, Jose Mari Goenaga, 2002).
- *For(r)est in the des(s)ert* (For(r)est in the des(s)ert, Luiso Berdejo, 2006).
- *Belarra* (Grass, Koldo Almandoz, 2002).

This box was distributed among diverse festivals and institutions. Given that there existed 35mm copies of all titles subtitled in English, the collection was programmed at numerous competitions and events.

---

16 Like Clermont-Ferrand, Cannes, Locarno, Teheran, Toronto, Venetia, Rotterdam, Río de Janeiro, Sao Paulo, Sidney, Uppsala, Donostia-San Sebastián, Gijón, Alcalá de Henares, Sitges, Huesca, Albacete, Zaragoza, Granada, etc.

A year later in March 2008, they presented another box that contained ten DVDs with all the catalogs created between 1998 and 2007, subtitled in English and French, and accompanied by a short script that had basic information about each one of the short films. Similarly to the commemorative box created the year before, this edition propelled the promotional work and external image of the program even further. It further strengthened the Kimuak heritage, given that it allowed the recovery of some short films that did not enjoy great diffusion in the first years of the program, and which in some cases had not even been released on DVD.

Since 2007, the results of the works disseminated by Kimuak have been stable, and consolidated the firm trajectory of the program. This is evidenced by the fact that the 1,500 files released in the 2008 edition were sold out before the catalog's tour was over. In 2008 the number of short films presented grew again. Eight were selected out of fifty-four:

- *Asämara* (Asämara, directed by Jon Garaño and Raúl López, produced by Jose Mari Goenaga - Fundación Haurralde/Moriarti Produkzioak, 2008).
- *Autorretrato* (Self-Portrait, directed by Javi Alonso and Raúl López, produced by Javi Alonso - Producciones La Burla, 2008).
- *Berbaoc* (Berbaoc, directed by Arteleku animation workshop coordinated by Vuk Jevremovic and Xabier Erkizia, produced by Arteleku/Gipuzkoako Foru Aldundia, 2008).
- *Cotton Candy* (Cotton Candy, directed by Aritz Moreno, produced by Sancho Rodríguez, Yolanda Ruiz de Larramendi, Javier Agirre, Jon Barco - Pok Produkzioak S.L., 2008).
- *On the line* (On the Line, directed by Jon Garaño, produced by Asier Acha, Jose Mari Goenaga - Moriarti Produkzioak, 2008).
- *El tiempo prestado* (Lent Time, directed by David González, produced by David González Rudiez, 2008).
- *Tras los visillos* (Behind the Curtains, directed by Gregorio Muro and Raúl López, produced by Gregorio Muro, Joxan Ruiz Miner - Comunicación Línea Uno TV, 2008).

- *Yo solo miro* (I Only Watch, directed by Gorka Cornejo, produced by Koldo Zuazua, Mónica Blas, Gervasio Iglesias - Koldo Zuazua P.C./Common Films/La Zanfoña Producciones, 2008).

As in 2005 and 2007, the short films that the catalog featured participated in more than a thousand festivals. They included subtitles in Italian and German, and for the first and last time, two directors had two films in the same collection: Jon Garaño with *On the Line* and *Asämara,* and Raúl López as codirector of three short films, *Asämara, Autorretrato* and *Tras los visillos.* It is important to highlight the spectacular trajectory of the two documentaries directed by Garaño (especially the fake documentary *On the Line*), a circumstance that has special relevance given that this genre has been absent from the program since its beginnings.

Besides, in 2009 a process that had started to take shape in the previous editions was definitely confirmed: the decrease in percentage of selections at state festivals, and an increase of the same at international ones.

KIMUAK 2008

SHORT FILM	FEST. Total	FEST. SPAIN	FEST. Europe	FEST. Other	AWARDS
Asämara. Jon Garaño, Raúl López	157	46	60	51	24
Autorretrato. Javi Alonso, Raúl López	77	21	29	27	4
Berbaoc. Vuk Jevremovic, Xabier Erkizia	132	45	48	39	6
Cotton Candy. Aritz Moreno	146	55	51	40	25
On the line. Jon Garaño	201	106	60	35	62
El tiempo prestado. David González	111	49	37	25	18
Tras los visillos. Gregorio Muro, Raúl López	152	67	51	34	22
Yo sólo miro. Gorka Cornejo	91	42	30	19	15
TOTAL	1.067	431	366	270	176

Table 1.8

In view of the year before, in 2009 they created two thousand folders for a catalog that once again attracted a great number of candidates: sixty-three. This rise was to a great degree due to one of the main novelties that Kimuak incorporated in this edition: yielding to the pressure of new technologies and the growing digitalization of the audiovisual industry, the program decided to remove the requirement of presenting a 35mm copy of the short films.

Kimuak distributed the following eight titles in 2009:

- *Cinco recuerdos* (5 Memories, directed by Oriana Alcaine and Alejandra Márquez, produced by Enrique Flores, Lisl Gutiérrez - Emigre Film/Televisa, 2009).
- *Ahate pasa* (Duck Crossing, directed by Koldo Almandoz, produced by Marian Fernández Pascal - MK Filmak/Kosmikar Studio, 2009).
- *Amona Putz!* (The Inflatable Granma!, directed by Telmo Esnal, produced by Asier Altuna, Marian Fernández Pascal - Txintxua Films, 2009).
- *Dirty Martini* (Dirty Martini, directed by Iban del Campo, produced by Iban del Campo - Limbusfilmak, 2009).
- Él nunca lo haría (He'd Never Do That, directed by Anartz Zuazua, produced by Koldo Zuazua, Mónica Blas - Common Films/Koldo Zuazua P.C., 2009).
- *Los que lloran solos* (Those Who Cry Alone, directed by David González Rudiez, produced by David González Rudiez, 2009).
- *Marisa* (Marisa, directed by Nacho Vigalondo, produced by Nahikari Ipiña, Borja Crespo - Arsénico P.C./Notodofilmfest, 2009).
- *La presa* (The Dam, directed by Jorge Rivero, produced by Emilio Pérez, Jorge Rivero, Pablo Domínguez - Aprieta fuerte/Jorge Rivero P.C./User T38, 2009).

The data corroborate the well-being of the program with regards to its numbers (about a thousand selections at festivals and more than one hundred awards, with at least four awarded films in some twenty competitions). The aforementioned tendency of international diffusion exceeding state diffusion continued this year. For the first time, state festival participation dropped under 40 percent, which was surpassed by participation in European competitions. Selections at competitions in the rest of the world exceeded 25 percent.

KIMUAK 2009

SHORT FILM	FEST. Total	FEST. SPAIN	FEST. Europe	FEST. Other	AWARDS
5 recuerdos. Oriana Alcaine, Alejandra Márquez	156	44	68	44	28
Ahate pasa. Koldo Almandoz	153	46	61	46	25
Amona Putz!. Telmo Esnal	191	67	73	51	20
Dirty Martini. Iban del Campo	78	27	31	20	7
Él nunca lo haría. Anartz Zuazua	164	66	59	39	28
Los que lloran solos. David González	55	22	17	16	1
Marisa. Nacho Vigalondo	124	56	34	34	9
La presa. Jorge Rivero	68	26	26	16	6
TOTAL	989	354	369	266	124

Table 1.9

The 2010 catalog, which maintained a circulation of two thousand copies, was the first one to contain nine short films, one more than the two previous years. Overall seventy-six pieces were presented. The titles are the following:

- *Ámár* (Ámár, directed by Isabel Herguera, produced by Isabel Herguera, 2010).
- *Artalde* (Flock, directed by Asier Altuna, produced by Marian Fernández Pascal - Txintxua Films, 2010).

- *Daisy Cutter (La cortadora de margaritas)* (Daisy Cutter, directed by Enrique García and Rubén Salazar, produced by Enrique García and Rubén Salazar - Silverspace, 2010).

- *Exhibition 19* (Exhibition 19, directed by Alaitz Arenzana and María Ibarretxe, produced by Marianna Dobkowska - Artists In Residence Laboratory/Centrum Sztuki Wspolczesnej/Zamek Ujazdowski Warszawa, 2010).

- *La gran carrera* (The Great Race, directed by Kote Camacho, produced by Marian Fernández Pascal - Txintxua Films, 2010).

- *Everything's Allright* (Everything's Allright, directed by Miguel Ángel Jiménez, produced by Luis de Oza, Koldo Zuazua, Miguel Ángel Jiménez, Gorka Gómez Andreu, Imanol Gómez de Segura, Luis Moya, Zurab Masgalashvili - Kinoskopik Film Produktion/Cinetech Ltd., 2010).

- *Un novio de mierda (*A Shitty Boyfriend, directed by Borja Cobeaga, produced by Borja Cobeaga, Nahikari Ipiña, Marta Galante - Arsénico P.C./Notodofilmfest, 2010).

- *Ondar ahoak* (Mouths of Sand, directed by Angel Aldarondo, produced by Angel Aldarondo - Kosmikar Studio, 2010).

- *El premio* (The Award, directed by León Siminiani, produced by Koldo Zuazua, Daniel Sánchez Arévalo, León Siminiani - Common Films/Tinnitus/Kowalski Films, 2010).

This was an eclectic selection in a sense that it contained bold narrative elements that bordered on experimentation. After the absence of animation in the previous edition, we find three works of this genre: Ámár, *Daisy Cutter* and *Ondar ahoak*.

That year's harvest was excellent: more than 1,200 participations at festivals, and more than two hundred awards. These were the best results earned by any Kimuak collection after the unsurpassable successes of the 2005 edition. And while the 2010 selection contained more short films than the previous editions, even so, the weight of the awards was concentrated in four or five titles. Although some works of veteran

Kimuak directors like *Ámár* by Isabel Herguera and *Artalde* by Asier Altuna had great runs, there were two debuting pieces in the collection that no doubt excelled with more than two hundred selections and sixty awards each. They were the animated short film *Daisy Cutter* by Enrique García and Rubén Salazar, and *La gran Carrera* by Kote Camacho, which competed in Clermont-Ferrand and was finalist at the European Film Awards.

KIMUAK 2010

SHORT FILM	FEST. Total	FEST. SPAIN	FEST. Europe	FEST. Other	AWARDS
Ámár. Isabel Herguera	202	53	89	60	29
Artalde. Asier Altuna	154	53	63	38	33
Daisy Cutter. Enrique García, Rubén Salazar	257	91	95	71	63
Exhibition 19. Alaitz Arenzana, María Ibarretxe	38	10	16	12	3
La gran carrera. Kote Camacho	227	82	102	43	71
Khorosho (Todo bien). Miguel Ángel Jiménez	47	12	19	16	5
Un novio de mierda. Borja Cobeaga	142	70	41	31	8
Ondar ahoak. Angel Aldarondo	78	27	32	19	7
El premio. León Siminiani	115	60	31	24	19
TOTAL	1.260	458	488	314	238

Table 1.10

In light of the great reception of the previous catalog, the 2011 selection also included nine short films. Among them were works of fiction, animation (*Zeinek gehiago iraun* [Who Lasts Longer]) and documentary (*Coptos* [Copts]), a diversity that had been proper to the 2008 edition. These were the selected works:

- *Bucle* (Loop, directed by Aritz Moreno, produced by Aritz Moreno, 2011).
- *La calma* (Calm, directed by David González, produced by Fernando Díez - Bitart, 2011).
- *La casa del lago* (House on the Lake, directed by Galder Gaztelu Urrutia, produced by Carlos Juárez, Mónica Ausín, Mario Suances - Basque Films/Peccata Minuta, 2011).
- *Coptos* (Copts, directed by Álvaro Sau, produced by Álvaro Sau, 2011).
- *Lagun mina* (Close Friend, directed by Jose Mari Goenaga, produced by Lander Camarero, Jon Garaño, Aritz Lazkano - Moriarti Produkzioak/Pressure Filmak, 2011).
- *La media pena* (Half As Bad, directed by Sergio Barrejón, produced by Iker Ganuza - Lamia Producciones, 2011).
- *Muy cerca* (Nearby, directed by Iván Caso, produced by Koldo Zuazua, Iván Caso - Kowalski Films, 2011).
- *She's Lost Control* (She's Lost Control, directed by Haritz Zubillaga, produced by Jon D. Domínguez, Álex Montoya - Morituri, 2011).
- *Zeinek gehiago iraun* (Who Lasts Longer, directed by Gregorio Muro, produced by Gregorio Muro, 2011).

Among the nine titles *Zeinek gehiago iraun* stands out especially, which was the second Gregorio Muro short film that Kimuak selected. Besides its respectable trajectory with regards to selections and awards, the film was a candidate for the Goya Award for Best Animation in 2012.

KIMUAK 2011

SHORT FILM	FEST. Total	FEST. SPAIN	FEST. Europe	FEST. Other	AWARDS
Bucle. Aritz Moreno	164	70	65	29	14
La calma. David González	39	8	19	12	1
La casa del lago. Galder Gaztelu-Urrutia	86	41	33	12	10
Coptos. Álvaro Sau	39	10	15	14	0
Lagun mina. Jose Mari Goenaga	115	59	34	22	14
La media pena. Sergio Barrejón	132	41	60	30	30
Muy cerca. Iván Caso	43	16	17	10	5
She's Lost Control. Haritz Zubillaga	101	45	36	20	19
Zeinek gehiago iraun. Gregorio Muro	174	55	77	42	41
TOTAL	892	345	356	191	134

Table 1.11

The year 2011 was important in the history of Kimuak for various reasons. First, Amaia Revuelta, who was responsible for state festivals, left in order to work for the Cinema Unit of Donostia Kultura, and Esther Cabero joined the program. Since then, she has closely collaborated with Txema Muñoz on the direction of Kimuak. Second, the institutional changes that occurred that year were noteworthy. On the one hand, the retirement of Peio Aldazabal in August 2009 and Mikel Arregi in December 2010 was followed by the appointment of Joxean Fernández as director of the Basque Film Archives Filmoteca Vasca/Euskadiko Filmategia. Fernández knew the program well, given that he featured various short films of Kimuak in the festival that he had directed before, the Rencontres du Cinéma Espagnol de Nantes (France). Besides, he had been part of the selection committee on two occasions. On the other hand, in April 2011 they established a cooperative agreement by which the Etxepare Institute took over the financing of Kimuak, which was until then managed by the Basque Government's Department of Culture.

With these rejuvenating currents that further consolidated the strength and continuity of the program, Kimuak celebrated its fifteenth birthday in 2012 with the presentation of a new cast of seven short films, among which once again featured fiction, documentary (*Casa vacía* [Empty House]), and animation (*Beerbug* and *Bajo la almohada* [Under the Pillow]), and brought together old acquantences of the program (like Koldo Almandoz or Isabel Herguera) with new blood. These are the titles that constituted the 2012 Kimuak catalog.

- *Agua!* (Water!, directed by Mikel Rueda, produced by Eduardo Barinaga, Mikel Rueda, 2012).
- *Bajo la almohada* (Under the Pillow, directed by Isabel Herguera, produced by Isabel Herguera, 2012).
- *Beerbug* (Beerbug, directed by Ander Mendia, produced by Katue Studio, 2012).
- *Casa vacía* (Empty House, directed by Jesús M. Palacio, produced by Jesús M. Palacio, 2012).
- *Deus et machina* (Deus et machina, directed by Koldo Almandoz, produced by Marian Fernández Pascal - Txintxua Films, 2012).
- *Monsters Do Not Exist* (Monsters Do Not Exist, directed by Paul Urkijo Alijo, produced by Andrés Torres, Christian Gálvez, Paul Urkijo Alijo - Protect/47Ronin, 2012).
- *Voice Over* (Voice Over, directed by Martín Rosete, produced by Sebastián Álvarez, Koldo Zuazua, The Rosete Brothers, Manuel Calvo, Luiso Berdejo, Gabriel Omania - Kamel/Volcano Films/Kowalski Films/Encanta Films, 2012).

The 2012 data certify the stability of the program: almost a million selections; participation at international festivals are double of participation at state level; and more than 170 awards. The short film *Voice over* by Martín Rosete is the absolute star of the catalog with an extraordinary trajectory that culminated in the nomination for Goya in 2013, and winning the Méliès d'or award for best European short film of the genre. Moreover, the great results of two debuting directors in the Kimuak program is also noteworthy, with works outside of the terrain of fiction: the animated *Beerbug*, and the fake documentary *Monsters Do Not Exist*.

KIMUAK 2012

SHORT FILM	FEST. Total	FEST. SPAIN	FEST. Europe	FEST. Other	AWARDS
Agua! Mikel Rueda	62	26	22	14	4
Bajo la almohada. Isabel Herguera	143	29	61	53	10
Beerbug. Ander Mendia	186	64	68	54	22
Casa vacía. Jesús Mª Palacios	23	6	8	9	0
Deus et machina. Koldo Almandoz	69	25	30	14	6
Monsters Do Not Exist Paul Urkijo	141	59	47	35	31
Voice Over. Martín Rosete	292	110	89	93	98
TOTAL	916	319	325	272	171

Table 1.12

The Operation of the Program

The yearly trajectory of the Kimuak program starts in March with the opening of the call to which Basque short filmmakers submit their work. As in 2009 they eliminated the requirement of submitting a 35mm copy.[17] The only indispensable requirement for a film to be part of the collection is that its director was born or had residence in the Autonomous Basque Community, or that the company that produced the film is based in there. Those directors who were born in the Basque Autonomous Community but are currently not residents of it are required to have lived five continuous years in the Basque Country, or ten years on and off. Furthermore, if the short film is the result of a coproduction between a Basque company and another or others which are not from the Basque Country, it is required that the Basque producer is owner of at least half of the production, or that it is the owner of the majority of the production (with a minimum of 35 percent) in case of more than three production companies. Since 2009, it is also required that the short film presented does not form part of another, similar program of another autonomous community.

The call for submissions closes in July, when an independent jury decides which short films would constitute the catalog. The committee consists of five professionals from the audiovisual industry, and it varies from year to year, but it is always made up of members of the Basque Film Archive Filmoteca Vasca-Euskadiko Filmategia, Donostia Kultura, and the Donostia-San Sebastián International Film Festival, as well as other recognized professionals, normally representatives of renowned film festivals. Throughout the years, the number of selected items has oscillated between six and nine, according to the characteristic features and volume of annual production. The criterion that the committee observes always has to be the quality of the work (technical quality), and its suitability for participating in the program. This implies that they prioritize works that are easy to understand beyond the borders of our country, and which have the potential to reach considerable international diffusion.[18] They announce the decisions, and in case there

---

17   This is a recommendation given that some festivals still want this format for their projections, but the fact of not having it does not exclude a short filmmaker from submitting their work to Kimuak.
18   Although there are no established quotas with regards to genres, program managers and selection committee members noticed that the inclusion of documentaries and animation in the catalog widened the spectrum of diffusion, allowing for

are no appeals, they start the process of the preparation of materials. The Kimuak folders consist of a DVD that contains all the short films selected with English, French, Italian, and German subtitles. When a film is made in Basque, they also provide Spanish subtitles, and if it is made in a language that is neither Basque nor Spanish, they provide subtitles in both languages. The DVD is accompanied by a CD that contains the promotional material that may be of interest for festivals that feature short films when they prepare their program: synopsis, bio filmographies of directors, technical and artistic record, lists of dialogues, photos of the film and the filmmakers, and so on. Together with the CD, they include a printed sheet of information for each short film in Basque, Spanish and English.

The short films are presented at the Donostia-San Sebastián International Film Festival at a session behind closed doors, with the participation of the short filmmakers and their teams, as well as a few invited guests from Zinemaldia (fundamentally, representatives of other competitions and potential buyers). The showings cannot be public, given that some festivals in which Kimuak is especially interested, such as the ones in Sitges or Gijón, require that the films presented for competition had not debuted elsewhere before.

Days later, they present the catalog to the media, and they start the work of distribution. The program carries out a more or less massive delivery of folders to different competitions with which Txema Muñoz has established contacts throughout the years. Kimuak pays special attention to festivals of great prominence such as Clermont-Ferrand, Gijón, Sitges, San Sebastian Horror and Fantasy Film Festival, Zinebi, Dresde (Germany), Interfilm (Germany), Aspen (United States), and so forth The festivals that require the payment of an entry fee for registration (majorly in case of North American festivals, although it is becoming increasingly widespread elsewhere) remain outside of the scope of Kimuak first of all for financial reasons, and given that public moneys finance the program. Second, the program managers believe that the filmmakers contribute enough to the organization of festivals by giving them the right to exhibit their work. Kimuak normally asks for a fee waiver, but not all competitions grant it. In these cases, Kimuak does not participate.

---

participation in specialized festivals in those areas. Documentaries had been absent from the Kimuak catalogs until the 2008 edition, but animation had a more or less continuous presence since its beginnings, with special impact in the 2010 catalog.

The program creates its own distribution strategy by selecting the festivals that it considers most interesting for the selected works of each year, and tries to make sure that the first step of each short film is a renowned film festival. Nevertheless, if a competition asks for a folder, Kimuak sends it. One of the main features of the program's identity is precisely that it listens to all petitions without distinction, from the most prestigious film festival of the world to the culture hall of a small village that wants to feature short films on its program. In the same manner, when a filmmaker wants his or her film to be sent to a specific festival, television or distributor, all they need to do is tell Kimuak, which will act accordingly.

In general, the program wants its folders to arrive to the greatest number of festivals possible, whether they are more prestigious, or closer. This is why Kimuak does not participate in some very important festivals like Berlin, Cannes, Venecia, Valladolid, or Locarno. These competitions have the condition that the works presented may not have been internationally featured. The first one of these festivals in Berlin takes place in February, which means that the films that want to participate must be put on hold from September on, with the aggravating possibility that the film may not be selected for the festival. In any case, the last word about the distribution strategies of the films always rests with the producer. When a festival selects one of the short films, it gets in touch with Kimuak, and the program communicates it to the director and the producer. Kimuak also takes care of the delivery of the film in the projection format required by the festival: 35mm copy, a videotape or digital formats uploaded to an Internet server. All the producers have to do is submit a master copy or celluloid copies, given that the program undertakes the elaboration of the necessary material, the costs of delivery, and the first subtitling of the 35mm copy in English or French.

Therefore, Kimuak takes care of gathering information about festivals, managing the registration of selected films, and sending the final copy for projection. This work saves a considerable amount of money, effort, and time for producers and directors. The only terrain where Kimuak does not intervene is the potential participation of the director at the festival, which is managed directly between the filmmaker and the festival organizers. If the film receives an award, the producer or director receives the entire amount of money.

Although the rights of commercial exploitation stay with the producers, Kimuak also does the work of unpaid mediation. The program provides copies for the institutions or associations that request it for projection upon payment of the rights of exhibition (the rate changes depending on the format used). Afterward, it invoices the managers these projections, and sends a report to the producers so that they give them a check charging Kimuak for the given amount. It also provides the folder for television channels and other possible buyers either through direct delivery or through fairs and festivals. When any of these entities shows interest in a short film, the program liaises between the two parties (producer and company), without in any way intervening in the transaction.

Thus, Kimuak takes care of the management of the non-commercial rights of the films. All economic benefit that the short film may bring for example by selling exhibition rights to television channels and international distributors, or by renting copies for exhibitions, or by receiving awards at festivals, remain in the hands of producers. Thus, as owners of the commercial as well as non-commercial rights of the short films, it is the producers who have the last word about the trajectory of the work. Kimuak always consults them before making a decision in case of conflict between festivals.

The Industrial and Artistic Fabric of the Basque Short Film in Kimuak

During the fifteen editions of Kimuak between 1998 and 2012, it globally disseminated and promoted 109 Basque short films directed by a total number of seventy-eight filmmakers.[19] As we already mentioned when we described the operations of the program, quality is the criterion that drives the selection of the pieces, without any consideration for language or gender quotas. Therefore, although the majority of selected short films are in Spanish, a not insignificant amount of films are

---

19 We should add the animation workshop Arteleku coordinated by Isabel Herguera, Vuk Jevremovic, and Xabier Erkizia, person in charge of Berbaoc (2008). It is also important to mention that some of these seventy-eight filmmakers directed their work in partnerships, as is the case of Joxean Muñoz and Txabi Basterretxea (Tortolika eta Tronbon), Igor Legarreta and Emilio Pérez (El trabajo) and El Gran Zambini), Iñigo Royo and Óscar Currás (Réquiem and Inventario), Alaitz Arenzana and María Ibarretxe (Exhibition 19), Enrique García and Rubén Salazar (Daisy Cutter), Oriana Alcaine and Alejandra Márquez (Cinco recuerdos), Asier Altuna and Telmo Esnal (Txotx and 40 ezetz) or José Antonio Pérez and Haritz Zubillaga (El método), although Altuna, Esnal and Zubiaga also made films by themselves. The three Kimuak works of Raúl López are signed together with Jon Garaño (Asämara), Javi Alonso (Autorretrato) and Gregorio Muro (Tras los visillos).

produced in other languages: sixteen short films partially or entirely in Basque (and six without dialogues but with title credits in Basque),[20] seven in English (and another two with credits in English), one that combines Cambodian and English, two in French, and one in Fula and Creole—Russian, Polish and Italian.

At the same time, in line with the global cinematographic pattern, the scarcity of women filmmakers in Kimuak is ostensible. In fact, in the 2003, 2008, and 2011 editions, they did not select any short films directed by a woman.[21] Of the seventy-eight directors, only fourteen are women, and among them only four have works in more than one catalog: Ione Hernández, Bego Vicario, Isabel Herguera and Izibene Oñederra (with a segment of the choral work *Berbaoc*). Curiously, the latter three are specialized in animation and visual arts.[22] Although the apparition of documentary in Kimuak was tardy (2008), none of the short films of this genre selected until now has been directed by a woman, in spite of the fact that Ione Hernández and Merche Álvarez have ventured into the terrain of the documentary in their feature films *Uno por ciento, esquizofrenia* (Hernández, 2007), *El cielo gira* (The Sky Turns, Álvarez, 2004) and *Mercado de futuros* (Futures Market, Álvarez, 2011). These data with regards to the participants of Kimuak are the first sign that over the years, an increasingly creative and productive structure evolved around the Basque short film.

The labor and repercussion of the program surely affected this tendency in a positive way. It is not for nothing that the short film production in the Basque Country started to soar exponentially since Kimuak started in 1998. In that first edition, nineteen films were presented; in 2010, this number was 76. It is obvious that digital technologies have democratized access to cinematographic creation, and there are more and more options for professional training in the audiovisual sector. Nevertheless, distribution continues to be one of the most expensive and difficult aspects (in terms of time and money) of the process of production and exploitation of any audiovisual product. The help that Kimuak offers in this difficult terrain achieved that both filmmakers and producers embark with greater security on the creation of short films. The director and producer Jose Mari Goenaga considers that "Kimuak

---

20 The fact of writing the credits in one language or another normally indicates that the script of the short film was originally written in that language.
21 Four of them worked in partnership: Oriana Alcaine and Alejandra Márquez (Cinco recuerdos) and Alaitz Arenzana and María Ibarretxe (Exhibition 19).
22 The other woman directors have chosen fiction.

serves as a revitalizing agent in the world of short films in the Basque Country. It has without a doubt resulted in that people make a greater effort so that they are selected in the catalog. Many times, films are produced with the Kimuak submission dates on mind." In fact, after the emergence of the 2005 catalog, the number of films presented for admission went from eighteen to forty-two. It could be treated as a coincidence, but the direct relationship between the emergence and success of Kimuak, and the rise in the production of short films in the Basque Country seems to be more than probable. There are many producers whose participation in Kimuak has been recurrent over the years, but the case of Koldo Almandoz is especially noteworthy. This San Sebastián-based filmmaker considers that the short film offers the ideal environment for experimentation, and the right measure to produce the type of stories in which he is interested. We could say that he is one of those exceptional cases of the pure short filmmaker who does not wish to move on to feature films; nor does he wish to use his short films as a channel or medium toward other ends. This philosophy, and the consequent care that characterizes his works are reflected by his long trajectory in the program, which has selected seven of his short films since the first edition (*Razielen itzulera*, 1998) until the latest one (*Deus et machina*, 2012).

Although they do not yet reach Almandoz's figures, other filmmakers also have more than one short films in Kimuak. Asier Altuna, for example, has five (one by himself, and two with Telmo Esnal), before the four of Borja Cobeaga, Luiso Berdejo, David González, and Esnal himself (two with Altuna). There are six directors with three titles: Tinieblas González, Haritz Zubillaga, Nacho Vigalondo, Isabel Herguera, Jose Mari Goenaga and Raúl López (together with Jon Garaño, Javi Alonso and Gregorio Muro, respectively), and fourteen with two titles: Bego Vicario, Koldo Serra, Igor Legarreta and Emilio Pérez, Iñigo Royo and Óscar Currás, Oskar Santos, Ione Hernández, Ugo Sanz, Izibene Oñederra, Jorge C. Dorado (one with Luiso Berdejo), Aritz Moreno, Gregorio Muro and Jon Garaño.

These data with regards to the participants of Kimuak are the first sign that over the years, an increasingly creative and productive structure evolved around the Basque short film. The labor and repercussion of the program surely affected this tendency in a positive way. It is not for nothing that the short film production in the Basque Country has soared exponentially since Kimuak started in 1998. In that first edition, 19 films were presented; in 2010, this number was 76. It is obvious that digital technologies have democratized access to cinematographic creation, and there are more and more options for professional training in the audiovisual sector. Nevertheless, distribution continues to be one of the most expensive and difficult aspects (in terms of time and money) of the process of production and exploitation of any audiovisual product. The help that Kimuak offers in this difficult terrain achieved that both filmmakers and producers embark with greater security on the creation of short films. The director and producer Jose Mari Goenaga considers that "Kimuak serves as a revitalizing agent in the world of short films in the Basque Country. It has without a doubt resulted in that people make a greater effort so that they are selected in the catalogue. Many times, films are produced with the Kimuak submission dates on mind." In fact, after the 2005 catalogue, the number of films presented for admission went from 18 to 42. It could be treated as a coincidence, but the direct relationship between the emergence and success of Kimuak, and the rise in the production of short films in the Basque Country seems to be more than probable.

A progressive increase of technical quality accompanies this growth in the volume of production. According to the director Haritz Zubillaga, on this too the program has had an impact: "The fact that your short films are selected in many festivals, and that they accumulate quite a considerable audience drive you, and increase your level of requirements for the next piece of work." After the almost amateur character of some titles that inaugurated the project, the formal quality of the selected works kept improving until it reached the professional level that the tapes of the catalog have represented for a few years now. This is owing to, as previously mentioned, the existence of a network of first-rate technicians and professionals, a modest *industrial* and artistic fabric around the production of short films in the Basque Country. It includes spheres and disciplines that have a role in cinematographic creation, contributing to the formation of collaborative networks, and even work teams that are practically stable.

The principle support of this structure is no doubt that of production. It is habitual that short filmmakers produce and finance their own work due to circumstances: either because they can't find a professional producer to support their endeavor, or because they prefer to have total freedom when they develop their ideas. In case of Kimuak, filmmakers financed a total number of 49 of the 109 short films selected until 2012.

They assumed all responsibility alone, or with the collaboration of other companies and producers.[23]

Nevertheless, there were a few tendencies in the past years that deserve to be mentioned. The first one of them is the work of some filmmakers who produced short films that they did not direct. This is the case of Emilio Pérez who, through the company Aprieta fuerte produced *Máquina* (Gabe Ibáñez, 2006) and *La presa* (Jorge Rivero, 2009); Asier Altuna, producer of short films without his co-filmmaker Telmo Esnal (*Taxi?*, 2007 and *Amona Putz!*, 2009); Angel Aldarondo, co-producer through the Kosmikar Studio of two titles by Koldo Almandoz (*Midori*, 2006 and *Columba Palumbus - Uso basatia*, 2007); Galder Gaztelu-Urrutia, a member of Basque Films, with which he co-produced *Choque* (Nacho Vigalondo, 2005) and *Las horas muertas* (Haritz Zubillaga, 2007); or Luiso Berdejo who, besides writing the script, participated in the production of *Voice over* (Martín Rosete, 2012). This tendency spread over to other realms: the prolific director of photography Javier Agirre served as one of the executive producers of *Cotton Candy* (Aritz Moreno, 2008); another photographer, Jon D. Domínguez, created his own producer company under the name Morituri, with which he produced *She's Lost Control* (Haritz Zubillaga, 2011).

The second and most important tendency is the emergence of companies that specialize in the production of short films. This is in fact nothing new, given that the continuous presence, for example, of José María Lara as producer of as many as five titles in the first two editions of the program is proof of the interest that traditionally some Basque producers had in the cinematographic short form.[24] Others like that of Oihana Olea (Altube Filmeak), Raquel Perea (Sebastopoleko

---

23   There are sixteen filmmakers who figure as only producers of all or some of the short films they have in Kimuak: Tinieblas González, Bego Vicario, Beatriz de la Vega, Pablo Malo, Sara Bilbatúa, Isabel Herguera, David González Rudiez, Javi Alonso, Iban del Campo, Angel Aldarondo, Gregorio Muro, Aritz Moreno, Álvaro Sau, Jesús M. Palacio, Enrique García, and Rubén Salazar. Another twenty-five feature as coproducers: Michel Gaztambide, Ione Hernández, Oskar Santos, Koldo Almandoz, Asier Altuna, Txema Matías, Aitzol Aramaio, Zoe Berriatúa, Imanol Ortiz López, Safy Nebbou, Alberto González, Ugo Sanz, Igor Legarreta and Emilio Pérez, Gabe Ibáñez, Jorge Rivero, Luiso Berdejo, Víctor Iriarte, Haritz Zubillaga, Miguel Ángel Jiménez, Iván Caso, León Siminiani, Mikel Rueda, Martín Rosete, and Paul Urkijo Alijo.
24   In the 1998 catalog Lara had three short films, Txotx (Asier Altuna and Telmo Esnal), La vaca (Gorka Esteban) and El viento africano (Merche Álvarez), and in the 1999 catalog they had two, 40 ezetz (Asier Altuna and Telmo Esnal) and Muerto de amor (Ramón Barea). Its name returned once again in 2006 as the producer of Sarean (Asier Altuna).

titiriteroak), Eduardo Carneros or Javier Ibarretxe also have a couple of short films collected in different catalogs.[25] Nevertheless, it is particularly interesting that in the last few years stable brands have emerged that are more identified with the production of short films than feature films (although they do not exclude them). They work intensively in this terrain in search of certain continuity. Jara Yáñez defines these specialized producers as:

> "Those who do not emerge with the help of a single project and then disappear; rather, they operate through a certain politics of production and entrepreneurial objectives that, at one place or another, with lesser or greater consequence, consider the short film as their target product in the long run. . . . In all of them, and it is here that a qualitative jump has been produced over the years, they keep searching for a greater degree of professionalism in both the media and mechanisms of production, and the aesthetic and formal results. For this purpose, they start managing industrialized designs of production, in which they look at the possible income of a short film as something to be invested in the beginning of the next one. It's a model of stable production that nourishes itself precisely through continuity."[26]

There are five names in Kimuak who, to more or less degree and in different ways, have this profile: Marian Fernández Pascal, Carlos Juárez, Arsénico P. C., Moriarti Produkzioak and Koldo Zuazua. Marian Fernández produced eleven short films selected by Kimuak, first through MK Filmak and later Txintxua Films (together with Asier Altuna). Her professional identity revolves around experimentation: productions that are not too big and give voice to riskier narratives, and match the particular poetic, metaphorical, or surrealist universes of directors with whom she usually works, such as Koldo Almadoz, Asier Altuna, and

---

25 Altube Filmeak produced two of Borja Cobeaga's pieces, La primera vez and Éramos pocos; Perea worked on the production of the two works of Igor Legarreta and Emilio Pérez (El trabajo and El gran Zambini), as well as on Amor de madre by Koldo Serra; and Eduardo Carneros and Javier Ibarretxe produced 7:35 de la mañana (Nacho Vigalondo) and Dos encuentros (Alan Griffin), this last one together with Carlos Juárez.
26 Yáñez, ed., *La medida de los tiempos*, 172–73.

Telmo Esnal. She is also the producer of *La gran carrera* (directed by Kote Camacho) on the basis of an original idea by Altuna.

Carlos Juárez (presently member of Basque Films together with Galder Gaztelu-Urrutia) is another of those names that have recurred over the fifteen years of the program. He promoted the short films of diverse authors and genres, either in collaboration with other directors, or alone. He had nine short films between 1999 and 2011: *El trabajo* (Igor Legarreta and Emilio Pérez, produced together with Raquel Perea), *Hauspo soinua* (Inaz Fernández), *El método* (Haritz Zubillaga and José Antonio Pérez) *Dortoka uhartea* (Maru Solores, German co-production), *Dos encuentros* (Alan Griffin, produced with the Ibarretxe brothers and Eduardo Carneros), *Choque* (Nacho Vigalondo, produced with Galder Gaztelu-Urrutia), *El gran Zambini* (with Raquel Perea and the directors Igor Legarreta and Emilio Pérez), *Las horas muertas* (with Galder Gaztelu-Urrutia and the director Haritz Zubillaga) and *La casa del lago* (directed by Galder Gaztelu-Urrutia and produced with Mónica Ausín and Mario Suances).

Arsénico P.C. and Moriarti Produkzioak follow a similar pattern, as both were founded by groups of short filmmakers who wanted to launch, almost exclusively, their own projects. Nahikari Ipiña, Borja Crespo, Koldo Serra, Borja Cobeaga and Nacho Vigalondo formed the first one in 2001. It is Nahikari Ipiña who usually leads the production in this company, which fundamentally focuses on starting up the ideas of its directors. They are however also coproducers of *Cirugía*, a short film that belongs to the 2006 catalog, directed by Alberto González; as well as other titles not selected by the program like *Pornografía* by Haritz Zubillaga (2003), *El encargado* (The One in Charge) by Sergio Barrejón (2008) or *Avant pétalos grillados* by César Velasco Broca (2006). They all belong to a circle of friends of the members.

Moriarti Produkzioak also started its trajectory in 2001 at the initiative of Jose Mari Goenaga, Jon Garaño, Aitor Arregi, Asier Acha, Xabier Berzosa and Jorge Gil Munárriz. Until now, its operations have been characterized by producing works directed by its members Goenaga and Garaño[27] in different areas and genres: short or feature film of fiction, documentaries, and works for theater or television. One of their habitual practices is that neither Goenaga nor Garaño really

---

27 Alone or in collaboration with other directors, it is not for nothing that Asämara, for example, is signed by Garaño and Raúl López, or the feature film documentary Lucio by Goenaga and Aitor Arregi.

lead the productions under their names. In general, some other member of the company takes charge of the production work.

Finally, there is the trajectory of Koldo Zuazua, a producer from Donostia-San Sebastián who is based in Madrid as he left for ECAM. He is the person who best embodies the specificities indicated by Jara Yáñez with regards to specialized producers. Together with Mónica Blas, Zuazua created the production company Common Films[28] to start with work solicited by external companies. Thanks to the profit margin of their advertising and video art activities, they produced a good number of short films with a clear industrial objective: that the income that each piece generates would serve for the production of the next one. With this objective Zuazua, the producer who most titles has in Kimuak (twelve), always prioritized careful and very professional production that guarantees the greatest possibility for distribution. He traversed through all kinds of genres (from romantic comedy to family drama), and alternated between projects with new directors. For example, he worked with Luiso Berdejo (for whom he produced three of his Kimuak short films), Manuel Calvo, Anartz Zuazua, Gorka Cornejo, and Iván Caso, as well as with more experienced and renown directors: Daniel Sánchez Arévalo, León Siminiani, Martín Rosete or Miguel Ángel Jiménez.

Before closing the section about the circumstances that surround the production of Kimuak short films, we should briefly mention the coproductions that have been present since the beginnings of the program. In the international realm, there have been six co-productions with other European and American countries: *Dortoka uhartea* (Maru Solores, 2002) with Germany, *Lepokoa* (Safy Nebbou, 2003) with France, *Exhibition 19* (Alaitz Arenzana and María Ibarretxe, 2010) with Poland, *Khorosho* (Miguel Ángel Jiménez, 2010) with Russia, *Decir adiós* (Víctor Iriarte, 2007) with Uruguay and *Cinco recuerdos* (Oriana Alcaine and Alejandra Márquez, 2009) with Mexico.

The collaborations of Spanish companies in the production of some Kimuak short films is more habitual[29] to which we have to add the important economic participation of other autonomous communities by

---

28   Although he also undertook productions by himself under his own brand, Koldo Zuazua P.C.
29   The Madrid-based User T38, for example, served as member of Aprieta fuerte in the production of *El Gran Zambini* (Igor Legarreta and Emilio Pérez, 2005), *Máquina* (Gabe Ibáñez, 2006), and *La presa* (Jorge Rivero, 2009); *El soñador* (Oskar Santos, 2004) was produced by the Madrid-based Himenóptero S.L., *El tren de la bruja* (Koldo Serra, Andalusian Jaleo Films, 2003) *No es una buena idea* (Ugo Sanz, the Gallician Ciudadano Frame, 2007), etc.

way of subsidies. The following works, for example, relied on financing from the Community of Madrid: *Las Superamigas y el Profesor Vinilo* (Domingo González, 2003), *Ana y Manuel* (Manuel Calvo, 2004), *El despropósito* (Zoe Berriatua, 2004), *Dos encuentros* (Alan Griffin, 2004), *La gallina ciega* (Isabel Herguera, 2005), *Limoncello* (Jorge C. Dorado, Luiso Berdejo and Borja Cobeaga, 2007), *Traumalogía* (Daniel Sánchez Arévalo, 2007), *Yo solo miro* (Gorka Cornejo, 2008) or *Él nunca lo haría* (Anartz Zuazua, 2009). Similarly, the Council of Castilla-La Mancha has participated in *Juego* (Ione Hernández, 2006), the Principality of Asturias in *La presa* (Jorge Rivero, 2009), and the Council of Andalusia in *Yo solo miro* (co-produced by Koldo Zuazua, Mónica Blas and the Andalusian company La Zanfoña) and *Voice over* (Martín Rosete, 2012), to which we should add the financial support of the Almería City Council, the Government of the Canary Islands, and the Tenerife Film Commission). Although traditionally short films have functioned as a testing ground for directors, and for technicians from other disciplines as well, the quality of the works selected by the program reveals the presence of teams that consist of real professionals behind the cameras. They are technicians and artists who trained themselves and matured with short films and who, in spite of participating in feature film productions sometimes, continue to have a more or less continuous commitment to the world of short films. They are very often in direct relation with concrete filmmakers or creative groups; a question that is not irrelevant, considering that short film making is still not professional, and its production (almost) never results in economic compensation.

In the area of cinematography, which is one of the closest areas to direction, names like Gaizka Bourgeaud stand out, who worked in eight short films;[30] David Tudela, in six;[31] Jon D. Domínguez in five (among them the three that Nacho Vigalondo has in Kimuak).[32] Besides doing the title credits of many Basque short films, Eduardo Elosegi has been cameraman in a good part of the animation works in Kimuak from the first catalog with *Tortolika eta Tronbon* (Joxean Muñoz and Txabi Basterretxea) and *Pregunta por mí* (Bego Vicario) until the last one with

---

30 *El trabajo* (Igor Legarreta and Emilio Pérez, 1999), *Hauspo soinua* (Inaz Fernández, 2000), *Hyde y Jekill* (Sara Mazkiaran, 2000), *Torre* (Oskar Santos, 2000), *Sarean* (Asier Altuna, 2006), *Taxi?* (Telmo Esnal, 2007), *Amona Putz!* (Telmo Esnal, 2009) and *Artalde* (Asier Altuna, 2010).
31 Three by Luiso Berdejo (... ya no puede camina, La guerra and Dio vi benedica a tutti), El despropósito (by Zoe Berriatúa, 2004), El gran Zambini (by Igor Legarreta and Emilio Pérez, 2005), and Juego (by Ione Hernández, 2006).
32 The other two are She's Lost Control (Haritz Zubillaga) and La media pena (Sergio Barrejón), both from 2011.

Bajo la almohada, which was preceded by two other works by Isabel Herguera, and the choral work from Arteleku, *Berbaoc*.

The extensive career of Javier Agirre stands out in an exceptional way: he is a cameraman who has photographed the greatest number of short films in Kimuak, and whose presence in some title or another has been constant since 2002. Agirre displayed his versatility in works as diverse as *On the Line*, which has a documentary texture; *Asämara*, based on the lyrical beauty of its images; or the surrealist *Cotton Candy*. He is the first person to suggest the existence of the aforementioned stable work teams given that, in spite of signing the photography of thirteen short films collected in Kimuak, in reality he collaborated with only four directors. He established an enduring relationship with Aritz Moreno (*Cotton Candy*, *Bucle*), Koldo Almandoz (*Amuak*, *Ahate pasa*, *Deus et machina*), David González Rudiez (*El relevo*, *El tiempo prestado*, *La calma*), and the creative group formed around Moriarti Produkzioak (*Tercero B*, *Asämara*, *On the line*, *Autorretrato*[33]). Something similar happens with music composers. Aránzazu Calleja, for example, composed in great part the sound track of those filmmakers who emerged from the first year cohort of the Audiovisual Communication program at the University of the Basque Country (UPV/EHU). His are the agreeable melodies of Borja Cobeaga's traditionalist comedies (*La primera* vez, Éramos pocos[34], *Río Puerco*), as well as the disturbing accords that enrich the atmospheres of Haritz Zubillaga's thrillers (*El método*, *Las horas muertas*, *She's Lost Control*).

In a completely different tone, the unclassifiable compositions based on emotion and experimentation that Xabier Erkizia proposes accompany all the animations that emerge around the creative art workshop Arteleku:[35] the three titles by Isabel Herguera *La gallina ciega*, **Ámár** and *Bajo la almohada*; *Hezurbeltzak, una fosa común* by Izibene Oñederra, and the collective short film *Berbaoc*.

Fernando Velázquez is the composer who has created the greatest number of soundtracks throughout the fifteen editions of Kimuak: nine. He is one of the most relevant names of the program in the area of music

---

[33] Raúl López, one of the directors of this short film, codirects with Garaño Asämara, and serves as film editor of almost all the short films and feature films produced by Moriarti.

[34] Besides, he also composed the sound track of La media pena, which was part of the 2011 catalog and was directed by Sergio Barrejón, coscriptwriter of Éramos pocos.

[35] In fact, Erkizia appears as responsible not only for the music but also the sound of these works.

because, the same way as many directors, he too grew up with Kimuak until he earned important reputation in the Spanish cinematographic industry. He started during the first years of the catalog with *Hauspo soinua* by Inaz Fernández, and the short films of Koldo Serra (*Amor de madre*, *El tren de la bruja*), Igor Legarreta and Emilio Pérez (*El trabajo*, *El gran Zambini*), Oskar Santos (*Torre*, *El soñador*) and Nacho Vigalondo (*7:35 de la mañana*). These were stories where the music, sometimes terrifying and other times romantic, revealed the influence of Bernard Herrmann, Danny Elfman or John Williams, and acquired an essential weight in the narrative. Thanks to these experiences, he shifted to feature films in the past years with titles like *El orfanato* (The Orphanage, Juan Antonio Bayona, 2007, for which he was nominated for Goya and the European Film Awards), *Los ojos de Julia*, (Julia's Eyes, Guillem Morales, 2010) or *Lope* (Andrucha Waddington, 2010). Nevertheless, he did not abandon the short film: he composed the music of *La casa del lago*, a violent thriller without dialogues directed by Galder Gaztelu-Urrutia, selected in the 2011 catalog.

Velázquez's trajectory is the opposite of Pascal Gaigne: an acclaimed composer who in the '90s was charged with the music of films like *El sol del membrillo* (Dream of Light, Víctor Erice, 1992), or *Flores de otro mundo* (Flowers form Another World, Icíar Bollaín, 1999). Without ever abandoning feature films, he developed an interesting trajectory in the world of short films. In this terrain and as far as Kimuak is concerned,[36] he composed music for almost all short films produced by Moriarti. He also authored the melancholy soundtrack of *Lepokoa* by Safy Nebbou, and that of *Traumalogía*, following the line of collaboration that links him to Daniel Sánchez Arévalo since their first short films, and which was continued into in the latter's feature films.

Besides musicians, the work of technicians was doubtless indispensable for the creation of soundtracks, let it be direct recording, montage or post-production. In this area we must mention the constant presence of studios like Rec, Sonora Estudios or Sounders Creación Sonora. Professionals like Aurelio Martínez, Alazne Ameztoy, Álvaro López, José Luis Rubio, Iñaki Olaziregi, Iñaki Díez, Xanti Salvador, Javi Alonso, Roberto Fernández, Pablo Bueno, Pablo Sanz or Iñaki Alonso stand out with their work in this area.

---

36 He also worked in almost all projects, short or feature film, of Eduardo Chapero-Jackson.

The inventory of technicians and artists who have made the hundred plus Kimuak titles possible exceeds the pages of this study. We should however highlight artistic directors Menó Martín with eight short films,[37] and Vicent Díez with six.[38] All the aforementioned artists prove that, even in the absence of a solid and firm cinematographic industry in the Basque Autonomous Community, the short film does enjoy a creative, productive, technical, and artistic *fabric*, with a more or less stable quality.

---

37 The two by Jose Mari Goenaga, Tercero B and Sintonía; two by David González, El relevo (2006) and El tiempo prestado (2008); Amuak (by Koldo Almandoz, 2004); Sarean (by Asier Altuna, 2006); Cotton Candy (by Aritz Moreno, 2008) and On the line (by Jon Garaño, 2008).

38 ...ya no puede caminar (2001) and La guerra (by Luiso Berdejo, 2005), El soñador (Oskar Santos, 2004), Juego (Ione Hernández, 2006), Traumalogía (Daniel Sánchez Arévalo, 2007), and the choral short film Limoncello (2007).

2

The Evolution of Genres: Narrative, Thematic, and Formal Styles in Kimuak

A General Overview of Fifteen Years

Fiction takes up over 82 percent of the total of short film productions of Kimuak, and has been by far the dominant genre in the majority of the editions. Animation follows it at considerable distance with 10 percent of the total production. The least produced genre is the documentary, with almost 6 percent. Nevertheless, the tendency of the last years shows that there is considerable increase in both documentaries and animation films in the catalog of the program.

The case of the documentary is particularly noteworthy. It is a very recent phenomenon that, nevertheless, points at a tendency of greater presence and constancy. The first documentay appeared in the 2008 edition with two short films directed by Jon Garaño, *Asämara* and *On the Line*. The following year in 2009, there were three documentaries in the catalog: the biopic *Dirty Martini* by Iban del Campo, the fake documentary *Ahate pasa* by Koldo Almandoz, and *La presa* by Jorge Rivero. In 2011 only one documentary was selected, *Coptos* by Álvaro Sau, and in the 2012 edition there were two short films of the documentary genre: *Casa vacía* by José Luis Palacios, and *Monsters Do Not Exist* by Paul Urkijo. This tendency corresponds with the general global increase of documentary film production since the 1990s.

The media interest that controversial US documentaries by filmmakers like Michael Moore and his *Bowling for Columbine* (2002) and *Fahrenheit 9/11* (2004), or Morgan Spurlock's *Super Size Me* (2004) provoked worldwide contributed to the popularization of the documentary genre as a product of cinematographic consumption all over the world. In addition, new technologies have brought down production costs, and facilitated the completion of these projects. It is not a coincidence that in the past years, numerous feature film documentaries were produced in the Basque Country. Basque directors whose short films formed part of Kimuak directed some of them. This is the case of *Lucio* (2007) by Aitor Arregi and Jose Mari Goenaga, *Bertsolari* (2011) by Asier Altuna, or the television documentaries directed by Jon Garaño or Jose Mari Goenaga. For all these developments, it is probable that in the near future the documentary will be consolidated as a stable format in the catalog.

Animation has been present since the first editions: *Pregunta por mí*, (1998) and *Haragia*, (1999), both by Bego Vicario, and *Tortolika eta Tronbon* (1998) by Joxean Muñoz and Txabi Basterretxea are prime examples. Nevertheless, this genre has had a sporadic presence, which has been stabilizing since 2005. It has two clear tendencies: experimental animation that plays with form, and classic narrative. Within the experimental current, which has been dominant, there are more narrative projects, and others that are purely artistic. *Hezurbeltzak, una fosa común* (2007) by Izibene Oñederra, and *Berbaoc* (2008) form part of the more radical line.

In recent years, four new short films emerged: two of them, *Daisy Cutter* (2010) by Enrique García and Rubén Salazar, and *Zeinek gehiago iraun* (2011) by Gregorio Muro follow the trend of classic narrative. Meanwhile, the other two, *Ondar ahoak* (2010) by Angel Aldarondo, and *Bajo la almohada* (2012) by Isabel Herguera, are experimental animation films with narrative leaning.

But beyond all these questions, there is one that without a doubt is fundamental when it comes to tackling the evolution of short films in Kimuak: the transformation that global cinematographic productions have undergone for the past years. It is characteristic of today's image-focused society where, among other aspects, the hybridization of genres, forms and expression and languages impose themselves as a principal feature of contemporary creation. The film integrates to greater or lesser degree the characteristics of the video clip, the commercial, the video art, or video games. This transformation is materialized in such aspects as the concept of gender or filmic form, and implies, necessarily, giving new meaning to concepts whose significance has been stable until now.

During recent decades, fiction, documentary and animation have suffered a progressive devaluation in terms of their purity. The aesthetic, narrative and formal canons that defined each one of these categories lack value at present. There are no clear boundaries between them, and sometimes it is very difficult to ascribe a specific genre to an audiovisual product. Proofs of this tendency are, for example, the fine line that in many cases distinguish the documentary from fiction; fragments of animation present in documentaries and fiction films; and animation documentaries.

The result is a panorama of changing and ambiguous formats that is repeated especially, and indisputably, in the secondary categories. These include all the genres in which the three great areas are divided (fiction, animation, documentary). Therefore, in case of fiction films for example, secondary categories are, among others: drama, western, thriller, fantastic, and horror films. The hybridization of genres has been a natural tendency in fiction since the first years of cinema, and by today their occurrence has multiplied in an exponential manner. In case of documentary, the **expository, interactive, reflexive, observational, or poetic** modes are some examples of this second level. Finally, classic narration and the numerous modes that form a part of experimental animation offer a most varied panorama of what we call the secondary categories of animation.

This global current, whose influence has become more widespread in recent years, has swept through the short films of Kimuak. In this sense, the hybridization of genres between fiction, documentary and animation is minor, and starts to have a more obvious presence with the 2006 catalog, in which we find six very illustrative examples of this phenomenon: *Sarean* by Asier Altuna, is fiction with documentary appearances. *Midori* by Koldo Almandoz uses the documentary look and animation as narrative tools. *On the line* by Jon Garaño, and *Monsters Do Not Exist* by Paul Urkijo are documentaries that border, to some extent, on fiction. *Ondar ahoak* by Angel Aldarondo, or *Bajo la almohada* by Isabel Herguera are animation films that brush against the documentary. Nevertheless, hybridization is a dominant tendency in secondary categories of fiction, and has fewer occurrences in case of documentaries and animation films.

In spite of the fact that it is a Basque program, local themes occupy a marginal position limited to a group of short films, majorly fiction, which tackle the Basque sociocultural universe and its idiosyncrasies from four different viewpoints. The first one offers a traditionalist, bucolic vision focusing on local customs and manners in the Basque country. This group includes two short films of classic cut, which take place in a rural environment. Its *laws* condition the life of its main characters, two elderly who live by themselves. The two short films are *Hauspo soinua* by Inaz Fernández, and *Lepokoa* by Safy Nebbou. The second perspective changes the traditional vision of Basque idiosyncrasies in order to give space to horror, *Txotx* by Asier Altuna and Telmo Esnal, and thriller, *40 ezetz* by Telmo Esnal and Asier Altuna. The third angle is a poetic vision that introduces distorting elements in this universe in order to bring more profound questions to light with regards to Basque society. *Topeka*, *Sarean* and *Artalde* by Asier Altuna, and the experimental animation short film *Haragia* by Begoña Vicario belong to this category. And finally, there exists a nostalgic vision that focuses on recovering the idealized image of the past, as the documentary animation *Ondar ahoak* by Angel Aldarondo shows. Besides these four lines, in the rest of the short films where the Basque sociocultural reality appears it always occupies a secondary position, and frames the events: *Belarra* and *Amuak*, by Koldo Almandoz, or *Hilarri* by Manu Gómez, are clear examples.

Also, it remains extraordinary that, contrary to the tendencies of the 1980s, contemporary directors and visual artists are little interested in addressing the Basque political conflict in their work. In interviews with Txema Muñoz and José Luis Rebordinos, both indicate that this line is clearly secondary among the productions that are presented for the annual selection. In other words, political violence and conflict are not present in the works that remain excluded from the selection, either. To this we must add that the majority of the directors we interviewed for this book have taken a distance from this topic.

In fact, we must go back to the beginnings of Kimuak in 1997 to find a short film that discusses the conflict: *La vaca* by Gorka Esteban. In this family drama, a young ETA activist accidentally kills his sister in his first action. The author stresses the terrible consequences of the attack with the objective of rejecting violence. Nevertheless, there are two short films that treat this theme implicitly to more or less degree. *Topeka* by Asier Altuna is a metaphor of the lack of understanding in a society immersed in meaningless confrontations that lead to violence. *Haragia* by Bego Vicario tackles tortured bodies buried in common graves during the Civil War, and indirectly alludes to the ETA members Lasa and Zabala, who were assassinated by GAL.

As a consequence, it is clear that one of the distinctive features of Kimuak is the universality of its themes. Topics like the family, old age, personal situations, and childhood are dominant. With regards to this last theme, there is a group of short fiction films and animation, and even a documentary, that constitute sorts of childrens' tales. The protagonists of these narratives are normally very young children, mostly boys although there are also girls, who face extraordinary situations. Most of them are severe, and involve a rite of passage whose overcoming brings them either maturity or, in the opposite scenario, death.

The tone, the ending, and the *leçon de vie* that emerge from these stories depend on each situation. Thus, within this category there exists a stream of marvelous narratives that offer a positive and innocent vision and interpretation of life, as do, for example, *Aizea, City of the Wind* by Ione Hernández, *El gran Zambini* by Igor Legarreta and Emilio Pérez, the animation documentary *Bajo la almohada* by Isabel Herguera, and the three short films directed by Luiso Berdejo, *For(r)est in the Des(s)ert*, the segment of *Limoncello*, *Dio vi benedica a tutti*, or to a lesser extent, *. . . ya no puede caminar* . This latter one is more ambiguous, and projects an obscure shadow over the consequences of the innocence of boys and girls. Children may watch it without problems, which cannot be said of the other films that constitute the group. These are more obscure and dramatic stories, especially for the cruelty of the experiences that the main characters undergo. There is no positive outcome, nor reconciliation with the world. The fictional short films *La guerra* by Luiso Berdejo and Jorge C. Dorado, *Por un infante difunto* and *Ecosistema* by Tinieblas González; animations *Daisy Cutter* by Enrique García and Rubén Salazar, and *Zeinek gehiago iraun* by Gregorio Muro; or documentaries *Asämara* by Jon Garaño and Raúl López, and *Monsters Do Not Exist* by Paul Urkijo constitute this group, which is greater than the previous one. All of them are intended for adult audiences due to the stark nature and and varied interpretations that frame these children's tales.

Dortoka uhartea (2002) by Maru Solores, and *La pescadilla que se muerde la cola* by Txema Matías are two narratives whose main characters are children. They are, however, more conventional, which is why they don't form a part of the above categories. Themes of social issues remain a minority in Kimuak, however, surprisingly, they occupy a salient position within animation. The documentary rather focuses on personal or everyday situations instead of tackling social problems. In fiction, *Sarean* by Asier Altuna, *Dos encuentros* by Alan Griffin, *Amona Putz!* by Telmo Esnal, and Él nunca lo haría by Anartz Zuazua, are the only short films with a social vision. In fact, in the rest of the few works in which social issues dominate, they always do so discreetly, in the background.

Beyond thematic questions, one of the principle identities of Kimuak short films is the importance that all give to form. Fiction, documentary, and animation offer a creative panorama that is very rich and heterogeneous in their engagement of the formal and narrative systems through which the stories evolve. Fruit of fifteen years, this eclecticism makes it possible that the hybridization of audiovisual forms, which is inherent to contemporary productions, may coexist with other paradigms that situate themselves between the classic and the experimental. In the same way, the directors of fiction, animation, and documentary maintain very different positions with regards to their preferences or formal style. Many of them are eclectic and operate through more than one mode, whose choice always depends on the objectives that they pursue in each one of their short films. Others, in turn, choose a single mode whose conventions they repeat in all their works, and they become masters of that mode. The fact is that in both cases, the works explore the expressive possibilities that these modes offer. The result is a group of interesting contributions to the audiovisual panorama in fiction as well as documentary and animation.

The program's fifteen-year-long trajectory allows us to observe the evolution of genres, themes, narrative, and formal tendencies according to the three great categories in which they belong: fiction, documentary, and animation.

Fiction. Genres and Themes of Fiction

As we mentioned before, the majority of the Kimuak fiction short films are a result of a combination of different genres, although some short films do have *sensu stricto* genre. When it came to the classification of the cinematographic genre of the program's short films, they considered two criteria. On the one hand, the concept of pure genre, to which various short films subscribe; on the other hand, the meaning of the genre label in the context of contemporary hybridization.

The classic concept of genre refers to a group of situations, themes and icons that, through repetition, become laws or conventions that affect a corpus of films. The spectators recognize the features of genre, and enjoy the pleasure of observing how their laws are repeated and change. Obviously, genres are not stable; they evolve through time, and their conventions vary to the delight of the audience. Film directors and producers are aware of the advantages and inconveniences of cinematographic genres when it comes to launching a project. This implies, as Rick Altman argues, that genres have their own life cycles, which are likely to be redefined and even resuscitated.[39] What's more, he questions their purity on the basis of the mutations produced through the evolution of genres. From this point of view, genre-specific dynamics allow the insertion of contextual features proper to other genres, as a result of which it consolidates or renews itself without changing its initial label.

> With the development of each new genre, films go through a predictable pattern in which they are initially identified with two or more quite different categories before eventually stabilizing into the generic identity with which they are associated today.[40]

Nevertheless, there exists a substantial difference between the mixture of genres of the classic era, and contemporary hybridization in terms of degree and intensity. Today, the mixture of genres implies the integration of more than one genre in the same text, although the issue is more complex than it seems. Hybridization means incorporating languages and characteristics of other visual formats that make it possible to consume this product in various channels and media in ways that match the audience's new consumer practices. The classic concept of genre is no longer efficient and therefore, when it comes to classifying films, we must modify the meaning of this label. Rick Altman argues that when a current film defines itself under a generic denomination, this refers to the dominant genre in the hybrid; it does not mean that the film only bears this specific genre. Rather, the dominant genre's label is accompanied by others that signify the rest of the labels that occupy a

---

39 Altman, Film/Genre.
40 Ibid.,140.

secondary position in the hybridization. For this reason, cinematographic criticism takes the dominant label as a point of departure, and studies the consequences and contributions of hybridization of other genres in the film.

Returning to the issue that concerns us, the Kimuak catalog has numerous hybrid short films, and few examples of pure genre. Drama, comedy, horror, and fantasy are the genres that dominate in hybrid short films as much as in pure ones. By way of exception, we must emphasize that there exists only one western in the catalog, *Limoncello*, in which three short films interpret conventions in their own way. *A Good Man* by Jorge C. Dorado modifies classic patterns; *Río Puerco* by Borja Cobeaga directs them in a comic vein; and *Dio vi benedica a tutti* by Luiso Berdejo is a fantastic film in the iconography of the western. With regards to themes, children's tales and the problems of the elderly are some of the more recurrent tones. After these follow relationship problems, and then at a considerable distance teenage problems.

Drama

Family is one of the central issues in the Kimuak dramas. They constitute an extended argument that features radically opposing, negative, positive, or critical points of view with regards to questions like the relationship between family members, or the portrait of the institution. Elderly people and children gain special weight in the family portraits.

Tinieblas González voices the toughest opinion about family structures in his two short films *Por un infante difunto* and *Ecosistema*. The first one is a horror film whose main character is a boy who suffers the terrible consequences of living in a less than wholesome, marginalized family. The second one postulates a critical portrait of the family as transmitter of bestiary human impulses. Both have social connotations.

In *Belarra* and *Columba palumbus* by Koldo Almandoz, drama emerges suddenly and unexpectedly in an apparently normal context. In the first film, an accident interrupts family harmony tragically. The negligence of the parents results in the death of their child, a heavy burden they will have to carry for the rest of their lives. In turn, in *Columba palumbus* the spectator discovers that the protagonist, a young hunter, is in fact an assassin who kills himself after killing his wife and son.

Without a doubt, the crudest family drama of the catalog is *La guerra* by Luiso Berdejo and Jorge C. Dorado. This horror film is situated in the Second World War and it is filmed in French. It narrates the agonizing situation that a boy has to face in order to survive the last days of the German occupation of France. The armed conflict erupts in the everyday life of the main character, and quickly destroys his family, and the security of his previous life. In spite of all his efforts to go forward, the reality of the war imposes itself forcefully, and condemns the child to a slow and heartbreaking death. Differences aside, the war theme is repeated in *Khoroso* by Miguel Ángel Jiménez. In classic voice and in a different context, the film tackles the trauma that the two main characters experience after they spend their youth fighting on the front.

In a very different tone, *El gran Zambini* by Igor Legarreta and Emilio Pérez is a children's tale full of tenderness, where family love triumphs over social prejudice. The drama focuses on the difficult relationship between a midget father and his son. Thanks to the magic universe of the circus, however, the child recovers his admiration for his father. Through nostalgic tone and colorful aesthetics, Oriana Alcaine and Alejandra Márquez face the family drama of Alzheimer through tenderness in *Cinco recuerdos*: the fifth ingredient of a recipe becomes an excuse to focus on a grandmother's memory loss, and the love of her granddaughter. The rest of the family dramas are of a more classic or realist character, and tackle general situations with some social undertones. *No es una buena idea* by David González Rudiez narrates the isolation and abandon that an elderly man suffers once his family has taken control of his property. *Lepokoa* by Safy Nebbou, and *Hauspo soinua* by Inaz Fernández are family dramas of a similar vein. The first one shows the suffocating universe of a small village at the Basque coast, where a woman is expecting with great hope the visit of her son. But just as the inhabitants of the village suspect, he stands her up on Christmas Eve. In spite of the obvious, Teresa refuses to accept the painful truth. She is able to lie to other people, but it is more difficult to lie to herself. The short film is a heartbreaking portrait of a lonely woman. With an equally classic staging, in *Hauspo soinua* by Inaz Fernández the main character boy discovers his roots when he spends his vacations at the baserri (Basque farmhouse) with his grandfather.

We cannot ignore the importance of romantic dramas in Kimuak, either. *Hilarri* by Manu Gómez, and *The Raven* by Tinieblas González are two paradigms of romantic melancholy, although they treat it in different ways. Set in the Basque front of the Civil War, *Hilarri* shows the moment when the gazes of a nurse and a dying soldier meet in the field hospital. The reflection of the young woman is etched in the retina of the young man in the moment of his death. Paradoxically, however, it is her that will be marked for the rest of her life by the look that captivated her soul. This impossible and fleeting love is an irrational sentiment whose intensity will cause her to mourn the memory of an unknown soldier with whom she never exchanged a word. Based on the namesake poem by Edgar Allan Poe, *The Raven* is a romantic drama that recovers the decadent spirit of the North American writer. Death comes to the home of the poet in the shape of a majestic crow, and, tormented by the memory of his dead wife, the man opens the window for him. The dismal bird takes his soul. Although his spirit crosses over to the other side, the shadows keep him from meeting hers again.

El soñador by Oskar Santos takes the same theme in the vein of the fantastic, and with a less dramatic tone than the previously discussed films. The main character Don Diego de Robledo searches for a solution to placate the profound sadness that the death of his wife provoked. Dream becomes a treatment of escapism that allows him to live in a dreamlike and unreal world, where he is happy with the dead woman. Although at first it seems like we are witnessing two parallel universes, in the end both collide in a single field where it becomes difficult to discern between the real and the imaginary.

Terminal by Aitzol Aramaio, and *Juego* by Ione Hernández also feature stories of impossible love. In both, the circumstances of life win over the romantic hope of a relationship. Also, there are three short films that use a realist vein and classic staging to tell the deterioration of relationships. *Yo solo miro* by Gorka Cornejo relates the lack of communication bewteen a married couple whose life together is only sustained by the necessity of companionship, and the force of habit. *El premio* by León Siminiani is the chronicle of an announced death, that of the couple's relationship that ends the same night the woman wins an important award for her professional trajectory. *El relevo* by David González Rudiez shows the difficulties of a couple whose relationship is conditioned by the work of both, and the fact that they would like to have a family. The result is that their family life is reduced to twenty minutes daily, when they have sex in a mechanical manner. On the other hand, *Réquiem* by Óscar Currás and Iñigo Royo employs an innovative staging to show the pain that a breakup may cause. Seated by the table of a café with his back showing to the camera, the main character talks about the details of the end of his relationship, and the profound pain that he feels.

Hombre sin hombre by Michel Gaztambide, and *Tercero B* by Jose Mari Goenaga are more difficult to classify. The first film is a story of a friendship between two elderly men, which breaks down due to the emergence of a woman who is only interested in the wealth that one of the men inherits unexpectedly. This dangerous triangle finally explodes in an ending replete with violence and death. The loneliness of elderly people appears as a thematic background to the story. In the second film, drama and thriller mix in order to narrate the obscure relationship between a tyrannical mother and her daughter when a third person enters their life: an unscrupulous thief. The story reveals the twisted family life where both women live, and the madness that the sweet and sly appearance of the daughter hides. The possibility of having found real love in a man that she met on the beach drives her to kill her mother. But her wrath does not end there: when she discovers the real intentions of the thief, her amorous fantasy becomes poisoned, and prompts savage violence in its crudest state.

Marisa by Nacho Vigalondo is an impossible love story that is approached from a more philosophical and existential angle. The short film has an innovative staging, full of photography and shots of different women. It revolves around the inherent drama concerning the romantic ideal of the beloved woman, an intangible projection that the main character may never reach. The eternal search provokes only frustration and anxiety.

Although social drama constitutes a minor part of Kimuak, *Sarean* by Asier Altuna is no doubt the most forceful and socially committed among all of them. The bucolic images of *arrantzales* (Basque fishermen) who go out to fish—as if it was a documentary—subtly transform into a bleeding metaphor. The *arrantzales* thrust their hooks into the bodies of sub-Saharan immigrants caught in their nets, and the blood of the illegal migrants paints the deck red. The film serves as a point of departure to shed light on a global drama that is often forgotten or normalized. In fact, the Africans who work as fishermen on Basque ships, a work that locals shun due to its harshness, have been able to overcome impossible obstacles in order to come to our country. *Sarean* is a powerful reminder that there are many more who die each day as they attempt to do the same, and that we can't look the other way. Through more conventional treatment and classic staging, Alan Griffin's *Dos encuentros* rejects the terrible consequences of the forgotten conflicts of the African continent. Condemned to go forward amid the most absurd miseries, a family survives by selling military scrap metal, an activity that will cost the life of one of them.

The rest of the dramas that in some way address social issues always do so in an indirect way. *Por un infante difunto* and *Ecosistema* by Tinieblas González, or *Columba palumbus* by Koldo Almandoz are a clear example of this ambiguity. The latter film is a sideway glance at the terrible consequences of gender violence. Pablo Malo's *Jardines deshabitados* follows the same line but in a less dramatic tone, and so does Zoe Berriatúa's *El despropósito* by to a lesser extent. Both tackle teenage marginality that is expressed in a violent way in the first film, while the second one reflects the negative consequences of unhealthy habits during puberty. *Decir adiós* by Víctor Iriarte addresses adolescent issues from another point of view. He exposes the frustration of a young woman who desires to play the main character of a movie, and who is left only watching the shooting of the film from her motorbike. But without a doubt, *Agua!* by Mikel Rueda is the paradigmatic adolescent drama. The film's main characters are two youngsters who live in diametrically opposing families, but nevertheless share the same anxiety, impotence, and emptiness that both families provoke in the youngsters due to excessive control, or the lack of attention.

Before we finish, we must note six dramas that don't fit with any of the above categories. *Inventario* by Óscar Currás and Iñigo Royo is a philosophical drama, a sort of existentialist essay that reflects in nihilistic tone about remembrance and forgetting. *Amuak* by Koldo Almandoz represents the drama of a lonely *arrantzale* who is unable to find love. The necessity to feel loved drives him to buy the services of a prostitute that he tries to catch, but whom he kills by accident. *Midori*, also by Almandoz, is the drama of impending death narrated through the testimony of the murderer, a pederast condemned to prison for this crime. Ivan Caso's *Muy cerca* is a personal drama that implies the loss of reason as a consequence of a family trauma. The son and the daughter of the main character go missing, but she thinks the truth is elsewhere. And finally, Martín Rosete's *Voice Over* is a false drama, or rather, a drama with an unexpected happy end.

Bittersweet Comedy

The characteristic humor of most Kimuak comedies is bittersweet. They typically maintain a more obscure tone sprinkled with sad irony that treats human miseries without reservations. The greatest representatives of this kind of comedy are the directors Nacho Vigalondo and Borja Cobeaga, nominated for an Oscar for *7:35 de la mañana* and **Éramos pocos**, respectively. Although they did not win the coveted statue, both works received important international recognition. All of them praise the interest that the bittersweet comedy awakens among critics and the public.

In his short films *La primera vez* and Éramos pocos, Cobeaga reflects about the loneliness of old age, while in *Un novio de mierda* he tackles the irreconcilable differences between masculine and feminine thinking in a relationship. Nacho Vigalondo's cinema maintains the same tome in *7:35 de la mañana*, where the leading role's disturbed mind becomes visible in a plot that the director carries to the extreme end of grotesque. The young man in love executes an absurd and suicidal plan to declare his love to the woman of his dreams: he kidnaps the employees and patrons of a bar, and obliges them to act out a choreography whose lyrics express his sentiments. The staging radically inverts the conventions of classic Hollywood musicals, and transforms the bittersweet comedy into absurdity with a tragic end.

Él nunca lo haría by Anartz Zuazua is also a bittersweet comedy about the inhuman treatment elderly people suffer in our society. It offers a surrealist and ironic insight where grandparents occupy the spaces of dogs as family pets. *Amona Putz!* by Telmo Esnal is similar in tone and message.

Traumalogía by Daniel Sánchez Arévalo is an equally bittersweet film from a more realistic perspective. The human miseries and the obscure secrets of an apparently normal family emerge during the hospitalization of the father. *La media pena* by Sergio Barrejón revolves around another theme: the unlikely encounter between a high-level executive who is about to commit suicide, and an illegal immigrant woman who was fired from her job as cleaning woman from the company. The woman's fighting spirit eclipses the pathetic actions of the executive, who can't even kill himself with a minimum degree of integrity. And finally, *Muerto de amor* by Ramón Barea mixes bittersweet comedy with romantic tenderness.

Its likeable character provokes a smile on the spectator's face for his naive and charming character.

Other comedies contribute to the heterogeneity of Kimuak. The obscure ways of Telmo Esnal's *Taxi?* turn an absurd, almost surreal situation into a sort of black comedy. It is to this genre that *Luis Soto* by Irene Arzuaga, and *Expreso nocturno* by Imanol Ortiz López also belong, although they feature more conventional situations. As isolated and exceptional examples, we must also cite the romantic comedies *Ana y Manuel*, by Manuel Calvo, and *Sintonía* by Jose Mari Goenaga; the situation comedy *El viento africano* by Merche Álvarez, featured in the first edition; and the fantastic comedy *El aire que respiro* by Sara Bilbatúa. *Ana y Manuel* stands out because it distances itself diametrically from everything that has to do with drama. It exhibits a colorful and happy tone that strongly contrasts with the rest of the comedies. Calvo's objective in this film is to sing the praise of love above all other circumstances of life.

Horror Films

Although this is one of the most popular genres of the program, it appears in pure form on very few occasions. Hybridization dominates this genre. More precisely, some Kimuak short films situate themselves on the slippery frontier that separates the psychological terror from the thriller. *She's Lost Control* directed by Haritz Zubillaga, and *El trabajo* by Igor Legarreta and Emilio Pérez are clear examples of this tendency, within which we also see *Los ojos de Alicia* by Ugo Sanz. This latter film maintains some parallelisms with *El tren de la bruja* by Koldo Serra, and narrates the frightening kidnapping of a woman locked up in a white cell, recorded by a security camera. Her captor's voice-off keeps her in a state of constant terror, from which Alicia tries to escape. Haritz Zubillaga's short films *El método* and *Las horas muertas* belong to this current. In all of them, the figure of the lonely killer appears, who threatens people from a superior place. By way of exception, we must mention that thriller is in pure state only in Galder Gaztelu-Urrutia's *La casa del lago*, and in *Tras los visillos* by Gregorio Muro and Raúl López.

Horror merges with black comedy in two short films: *Txotx* by Asier Altuna and Telmo Esnal, and *Amor de madre* by Koldo Serra and Gorka Vázquez. The first film transforms the bucolic ritual universe of the *sagardotegi* (Basque cider house) into a horrific story where the owners of the establishment serve delicious chops of human meat to their guests. From a very different prism, *Amor de madre* is a pastiche that plays with the encounter of the great masters of the genre, while it ridicules their conventions.

La calma by David González Rudiez mixes terror with family drama. The hereditary and incurable mental illness that weighs over the members of a family is a curse that persecutes them and leads to their unavoidable death. At the beginning of the plot, the main character is shown as the only one who remains beyond this chain. However, the final scene reveals that madness has overcome him, and that his newborn son will also be victim of it. Tinieblas González's *Ecosistema* is a horror story that mixes fantastic elements and which, to a certain degree, has a thematic similarity with *La calma*. In this case, the curse that is transmitted from generation to generation is the violent and self-destructive character inherent to human beings. We must also highlight *Por un infante difunto*, also by González, which is a family drama that, as we observed above, bears features that are very characteristic of this genre.

Among the pure horror films we find *The Raven* by Tinieblas González, *Los que lloran solos* by David González Rudiez, and *Torre* by Oskar Santos. In this last one, however, the influence of psychological horror becomes clear. A block of apartments turns into a site of mysterious and violent deaths, among others the death of the leading role's wife. The ending reveals the supernatural and malign origins of the building: it is children who provoke this series of murders.

And finally, there is *Máquina* by Gabe Ibáñez, which is very difficult to categorize. It tells the horrific story of a woman, in whose vagina the aliens implant a grinder. It's a mixture of science fiction, horror film, and fantastic film. Something similar happens in *Autorretrato* by Javi Alonso and Raúl López, which positions itself on the border between detective movie, romantic drama, and fantastic film. Two women, the wife and the lover, are in deadly confrontation over the same man. The picture that the young maid is painting in her study becomes an element through which the dark side of the plot emerges.

Fantasy Film

The distancing of established reality, and its transformation into a parallel universe is the distinctive characteristic feature of this genre.

> Ultimately, the *fantastique* always uses Reality as a point of reference either to deform it and convert it into something else, a no man's land whose landscapes and inhabitant share features with our everyday existence, and at the same time they subvert it through certain elements that are foreign from it.[41]

In Kimuak, fantasy mixes with the marvelous in two romantic short films: *El soñador* by Oskar Santos, and *Aizea City of the Wind* by Ione Hernández. This latter film fits well within magical realism, which allows the irruption of supernatural elements without breaking the verisimilitude of the plot. The love of the couple triumphs over the curse that separates them, as it becomes clear in the final happy end. The children's tale *For(r)est in the Des(s)ert* by Luiso Berdejo uses the theme of extraterrestrial abduction to start a story of fraternal love. However, among all the works that belong in this epigraph, *Cotton Candy* by Aritz Moreno is the paradigm of fantasy in pure state. In comic tone, it tells the story of a man, for whom the simple gesture of putting on a sweater becomes a marvelous journey.

It becomes much more difficult to define other works where surrealism may get confused with the fantastic. This is the case of *Razielen itzulera* and *Deus et Machina* by Koldo Almandoz; *Sarean, Topeka* and *Artalde* by Asier Altuna; and *Hyde & Jekill* by Sara Mazkiaran. Besides, as it happens, these short films are also part of formal models such as poetic or experimental cinema.

Formal and Narrative Models in Fiction

Once we defined the panorama of the cinematographic genres in which the Kimuak films belong, our next objective is to describe the systems or models, as well as the narrative, formal and aesthetic tendencies that are manifested in the short films of the catalog.

---

41 Losilla, El cine de terror, 36.

Eclecticism is the dominant tone, which is why the models traditionally established by criticism coexist with paradigms and tendencies that have been generated in the cinematographic corpus of Kimuak. Thus, we may distinguish four formal systems or models indicated by critics:[42] classical cinema or Institutional Mode of Representation IMR; mannerist cinema, or divergence from the classical model; postmodern cinema; and experimental or narrative cinema. Poetic cinema emerges together with these four paradigms, and its characteristic features are reflected by a group of Kimuak short films that are closer to evocation than narration.

On the other hand, there exist two very clear tendencies that are manifest in all of these models (classical, mannerist, postmodern, experimental, or poetic): cinema without dialogue, and the pieces that are constructed on the basis of a narrator, or character's point of view.

Classical Cinema, or the Institutional System

Noël Burch[43] describes in detail the evolution and configuration of the distinctive modes of cinematographic representations. All of them rest on a narrative and formal logic that nourish their respective conventions. Burch distinguishes three paradigms: primitive cinema, the institutional mode of representation (IMR), and its alternatives. The IMR or classical cinema[44] consolidates itself as the dominant model, and it is a reference point from where mannerism and postmodern cinema depart.

---

42 The definition and characteristics of each one come from the reflections of experts who have analyzed these models, their logic and signs of identity, as well as their evolution throughout the history of cinema. The authors that have principally studied classical, mannerist cinema and the nonnarrative alternatives are:: Burch, El tragaluz del infinito; Bordwell and Thompson, Film Art; Aumont, Bergala, Marie, and Vernet, Aesthetics of Film; Burch, La Lucarne de l'infini. The bibliography that addresses the transformations of contemporary cinema and the concept of postmodern cinema include, among others, the following: Jullier, L´écran postmoderne; Buccheri, Sguardi sul postmoderno; Palacio and Zunzunegui, Historia general del cine; Calabrese, Neo-Baroque; Zunzunegui, "Lo viejo y lo nuevo: La reinvención de la tradición cinematográfica en el final del siglo XX," Letras Deusto 25, no. 66, ref. 12 (1995): 59–74.
43 Burch, La Lucarne de l'infini.
44 Classical cinema is a model of creation and production that was established during the golden age of the great Hollywood studios. Besides the references highlighted before, David Bordwell, Janet Staiger and Kristin Thompson wrote an in-depth study about this standardized formal and industrial system whose fundamentals survive and condition contemporary cinematographic production. This study explores the characteristic features that we mention here in general terms. Bordwell, Staiger, and Thompson, The Classical Hollywood Cinema.

The narrative premises of this model are influenced, among other things, by the nineteenth-century novel. The plots are therefore linear, and have the classic structure of exposition, climax, and resolution. Causality imposes itself as an element that launches the future of the events, and conditions the dynamics of people's action. Besides, there is a fixed outline of roles that is repeated ad infinitum, and cinematographic genres that assign the film into a determined category. Without a doubt however, the most relevant characteristic feature is that the stories are narrated from only one point of view. The director occupies a distant position with respect to the events, and limit themselves to show what happens in a detached way. This false position does not prevent them from being the ultimately responsible person of the narrative strategies that the plot hides. For their part, the spectators become witnesses, and cling to following the events that take place before their eyes. Often, the classic text relies on an omniscient narrator whose voice-over in third person focalizes the story, or narrating characters whose voice-off focalizes[45] the account.

The mise-en-scène, in turn, employs the transparent montage whose formal conventions produce the *illusion of reality*; that is, cinema becomes a window open to the world. The images and the sounds are articulated with the sole objective of giving body to the fiction by recreating spatial-temporal continuity. The laws of the raccord and of the axis impose themselves when it comes to giving volume to the habitable space where the events take place. The plot is constructed around the dialogues that tell the story. The ambient sound's function is to give verisimilitude to the inhabited space, and reproduce the sonorous depth of the image. Meanwhile, the music is used in a one off and emotive manner.

The institutional model is clearly the majority within the Kimuak catalog, although it is closely followed by mannerist cinema. The short films of Borja Cobeaga are an illustrative example of the classical model. The director distances himself from the events, and uses transparent montage in his bittersweet comedies. *La primera vez* and **Éramos pocos** display the masterful treatment of classical conventions in the strict sense of the word.

---

[45] Focalization is a narrative strategy directed at managing information. There are three different types of focalization. The first is called zero focalization, in which case the viewer knows more than the character, which results in suspense. The second is external focalization, in which the contrary happens: the spectator knows less than the character, which results in intrigue. And finally, in internal focalization, the viewer knows exactly the same as the main character, which results in any unexpected event provoking surprise.

Another illustrative example of the classic model is *A Good Man*, which is part of Jorge C. Dorado's *Limoncello*. It perfectly represents the tendency that pivots around the voice of the narrator. In fact, the voice-over of the omniscient narrator inscribes itself on a carefully crafted mise-en-scène that leaves nothing to chance. The images, accompanied by the soundtrack, show the evolution of the events as if they were happening in front of the spectator. In the same way, Aitzol Aramaio's *Terminal* fits with the tendency of short films without dialogue. Following the classical logic, the universal language of images and sounds constitute this film.

The Mannerist Cinema, or the Deviation of Classical Cinema

Mannerism goes beyond the frontiers of the institutional model. It implies the transgression of the limits imposed by the classical system, whose intention is to explore the narrative and formal possibilities of audiovisual language with two very specific objectives: to vindicate the film's character of constructed fiction, and to use this logic to tell stories by using the expressive resources of cinema in different ways. This formal and narrative attempt leads to virtuosity at times; nevertheless, it does not imply a total rupture with the basic tenets of the institutional mode of representation. It is for this reason that mannerist representation ends up integrating itself in an open and wide definition of classical cinema.

As opposed to the IMR, mannerism considers film as a constructed fiction that opposes transparent cinema, and goes on to show the traces of enunciation. In this new paradigm, the aseptic distance between the director and the text is broken in a radical way. Creative freedom turns the director into a sort of demiurge that manipulates at their whim the narrative and formal resources in order to give birth to new ways of telling stories. In this sense, and keeping the canonic scheme of exposition, climax, and resolution, the stories may change the temporal order and the frequency of the narrated facts and, above all, they may be approached from multiple points of view. Or, which is the same, to give free rein to the distinctive narrative strategies, and to the mode or focalization. These stories may count with more than one narrator or narrating person that expose, and at times counterpose their point of view with regards to the facts against the rest of the narrators or persons. The greater complexity of narrative structure has an influence in the distribution of roles, in the archetypes and the conventions of gender that are questioned, and even subverted to give place to new interpretations. Obviously, the role of the spectator changes in a substantial manner: it shifts from mere witness to coparticipant. In other words, it recovers the information that the text gives them in order to complete the meaning of the story.

All this necessarily implies a mise-en-scène in which they foster and develop the expressive possibilities of audiovisual resources. It doesn't matter if they expose the devices that construct the fiction; what is important is to enrich the stories. The mise-en-scène is characterized, among other features, by the fact that the depth of field, the movements of the camera, the lenses, the camera angles and the unusual compositions are used to take part in the presentation of facts. Moreover, the sound liberates itself from the limits that transparency imposed on it in order to establish important relations with the images.

The Kimuak catalog is full of illustrative examples of mannerist short films. In *Tercero B*, Jose Mari Goenaga plays with viewpoints, focalization, and the quantity of information that he gives the spectator throughout the story. The same event is shown from two opposing points of view: that of a naive woman, and that of a thief. The parallel montage juxtaposes first her point of view, and then his. While she thinks that the man is a gallant with romantic intentions, all he cares about is his plot to plan the robbery of the woman's house. The spectator is given information about the terrible murder of the victim's mother, and discovers that the woman is demented. The ending of the deadly struggle between the thief and the young woman remains hidden through the kitchen door. For his part, Nacho Vigalondo shows his mastery when it comes to managing the laws of mannerism in *7:35 de la mañana*, in which he radically inverts the codes of the classic Hollywood musical through an agile mise-en-scène with a soundtrack occupied by the out of tune litany of the persons sequestered in the bar.

The short films *La guerra* by Luiso Berdejo and Jorge C. Dorado, and *Voice Over* by Martín Rosete are also good examples of this model. In the first one, the voice-over of a female narrator that tells the story in French and in second person singular addresses the main character boy, and the spectator at the same time. This omniscient voice keeps giving him instructions so that he saves himself, but builds expectations that collapse in a moment, and hit harshly the spectator. The temporal leaps and the repetition of the same fact on three occasions throughout the narration are also characteristic of mannerism. In turn, *Voice Over* plays with focalization and the expectations that it generates in the spectator. It maintains certain parallels with *La guerra*—not for nothing was the script written by Luiso Berdejo—but the focus is different. The alternated montage launches three stories, whose main characters find themselves in an extremely serious situation between life and death. Again, the voice-over of the omniscient narrator, this time masculine, addresses the three persons in second person to show the anxiety that they experience as they become conscious that death will come in a few brief seconds. This way, the narrator underlines the time that they have left of their lives. But finally and by way of magic, the plot radically changes direction, and the three extreme experiences are compared with the emotion of the first kiss. This sublime instant acquires the same importance as the last minutes of the main character's' life.

Postmodern Cinema

The audiovisual era is the result of the past century evolution of western culture, whose central axis is the image. The visual bombardment that comes from television, cinema, commercials, videos, video games, and other audiovisual forms is incessant. Moreover, image is immersed in a process of constant innovation. It is no accident that technological development brings with it new forms and habits of visual consumption, which multiply the ubiquity of the image. There are many labels that have baptized this era: Omar Calabrese[46] refers to it as the "neo-Baroque" era, and Umberto Eco[47] talks about "supermannerism." But beyond nominal differences, what is fundamentally important is that all of them refer to the evolution of the taste and consumption of visual products in an iconocentric era where image substitutes reality. It becomes obvious that, after almost a hundred years and in this new context, cinema experienced a crisis[48] of narrative and formal exhaustion. Because of this, the logic of the postmodern model is based on provoking emotions rather than telling a story. The mise-en-scène is transformed into a visual game in which the spectator does enjoy the aesthetic pleasure, the recognition of forms and encounters; what brings most pleasure, however, is the possibility to penetrate a story and feel emotions. So much so that the narrative remains secondary for the benefit of the image. The inherent

---

46   Calabrese, Neo-Baroque.
47   Eco, Postscript to the Name of the Rose.
48   The transformations of cinema and the characteristics of the audiovisual era are described in detail in Palacio and Zunzunegui, Historia general del cine; and in Zunzunegui, "Lo viejo y lo nuevo," 59–74.

characteristics of this model may be organized largely around four elements. The first one is the hybridization of visual forms which, as we indicated before, is a frequent practice in contemporary cinema. The pastiche[49] or mixture of aesthetic and filmic referents, in turn, refers to the procedure by which the directors nourish themselves of tradition in order to create new products. In other words, they take borrowed images, expressive resources, persons, and even plots and themes of literature, painting, illustration, commercials or cinema, among other sources, to insert them in their work. There are no hierarchical criteria when it comes to citing; they seek stimuli that are able to surprise or attract an exhausted spectator.

Postmodern nostalgy[50] and visual preciosity are the third axis of this phenomenon, and have to do with the previous characteristic feature. In this case however, the search for beautiful images of the past is justified by the necessity to construct a plot where verisimilitude is not important. This explains that, for example, period films shy away from showing misery, illness, or poverty. At the end of the day, the objective of visual reference is to construct a beautiful and idealized image of the past. Preciosity is linked to this inquiry, although it is extended over all films that seek to seduce the spectator by presenting them a beautiful, habitable space. Finally, there are the devices that facilitate the penetration of the spectator in the diegesis: the visual or sonorous devices that channel the immersion of the spectator. They are numerous, although usually only the three most relevant and effective ones are cited, which normally appear combined: the digital image,[51] the areal camera, and the *bain sonore*.[52] The first one is linked to new technologies able to obtain an image of simulacra, a representation so hyperrealist that it is confused with reality. This is normally accompanied by an aerial camera that penetrates the inhabited space further by amplifying, if it is at all possible, the sensation of immersion in a new world. *Bain sonore* refers to the enveloping sound that accompanies the previous two, and carries the spectator away.

There exists a group of Kimuak short films that affiliate themselves with postmodern cinema. Its specifications have to do with the importance of form and narration, and the equilibrium between the two. Thus, at one extreme there are visual exercises in which narration has no importance.

---

49 Zunzunegui, "Lo viejo y lo nuevo," 64.
50 Jullier, L'ecran postmoderne, 21.
51 Buccheri, Sguardi sul postmoderno, 111.
52 Jullier, L'ecran postmoderne, 60.

At the other extreme, there are short films that use the characteristic features and expressive resources of postmodern cinema to tell stories. These latter ones maintain equilibrium between form and narration, and are labeled as postmodern only in part due to their formal dimension, always indicating the narrative value of their stories.

The paradigm of pure formal exercise is represented by *Las Superamigas contra el Profesor Vinilo* by Domingo González, and *Cotton Candy* by Aritz Moreno. In the first one the plot is insignificant; the prime objective is to fascinate the spectator. For this end, the filmic texture becomes a sort of visual spectacle full of special effects, peppered with references to popular culture like comics or cartoons. On the other hand, *Cotton Candy* is an everyday act that turns into a surrealist situation: a man who intends to take off his jersey remains caught in the effort.

In the same line but taking a prudent distance are situated other visual exercises that stand out for developing some of the characteristics of postmodern cinema. *Bucle* by Aritz Moreno also revolves around an everyday situation, the accidental death of its main character, and its formal structure is simpler, although it pursues visual effect. *El aire que respiro* by Sara Bilbatúa, and *Cinco recuerdos* by Oriana Alcaine and Alejandra Márquez construct a universe with nice visual effects and the insertion of cartoons to give life to one off situations. *La gran carrera* by Kote Camacho may be categorized as an exponent of postmodern nostalgia. The short film is about a competition in the hippodrome of Lasarte at the beginning of the century. It recovers the imagery of the epoch, and lends the text great beauty and charm. And finally, *Ecosistema* by Tinieblas González uses aerial camera to show the gazes of the animals that cross in this particular and destructive universe. Through them, the spectator penetrates in the space of the action.

The short films that have clear narrative courage mostly use formal hybridization as an expressive resource, and the juxtaposition or inclusion of television fragments, cartoon, illustrations, photography, or other formal elements. This is the distinctive character of *Razielen itzulera*, *Amuak* and *Midori* by Koldo Almandoz; *Máquina* by Gabe Ibáñez; *For(r)est in the Des(s)ert*, by Luiso Berdejo; or *Marisa* by Nacho Vigalondo. All of them have a strong narrative structure, and are full-fledged stories. For its part, *Amor de madre* by Koldo Serra and Gorka Vázquez is a comic pastiche whose main character has the obsession of assassinating her friends by inviting them for coffee.

Experimental Cinema

The point of departure that distinguishes this model from the rest is that it is not narrative. It is a form of artistic expression that in the more extreme cases comes very close to video art. In fact, it uses audiovisual resources to express ideas, dreams, and/or emotions. The mise-en-scène does not tell a story; rather, it prompts or stimulates the spectator to reflect about the meaning of the work that they are watching. With two only short films, this model is clearly a minority in Kimuak.

Hyde & Jekill by Sara Mazkiaran juxtaposes the mental delirium of the poet Leopoldo Panero, and *Exhibition 19* by Alaitz Arenzana and María Ibarretxe is the prototype of experimental cinema. Set in Warsaw and shot in Polish, its objective is to portray women who lack their own iconography in a world based on the expectations of creativity and professionalism. The mise-en-scène consists of the succession of slow tracking shots of working women, young people crawling on the floor, and crystal cubes that impede female liberty. The ambient sound accompanies the images since there are barely any words. The symbolic, therefore, substitutes the narrative.

Poetic Cinema

Asier Altuna's short films represent the paradigm of poetic cinema in Kimuak. They are all narrative: they tell a story where suddenly something inexplicable that is nevertheless accepted as natural happens. They are stories with a surrealist aura through which emerge poetic figures who hide a deeper message. Based on the literary short story *Ahari Topeka* by Joseba Sarrionandia, *Topeka* is a terrible metaphor of the destructive and contradictory spirit of Basque society. The dramatic force of the hyperbaton of *Sarean* alters for a moment what starts out as a calm day of a Basque coastal fishing vessel. The short film reminds us of the human drama that takes place every day at the European coasts, and from which we turn the other way. *Artalde* plays with the substitution of the attributes of the competitions of Basque sheepherders, the sheep and the field, for others: persons and the city. Driven by an unknown force, the sheepherders dominate the citizens. The short film emphasizes the capacity to manipulate the masses, and the lack of one's own criteria. Another example of poetic cinema is *Deus et Machina* by Koldo Almandoz, which is a beautiful metaphor through which the director pays homage to workers, because "it is them who in reality move the world each day."

Cinema Without Dialogues, and the Irruption of the Voice of the Narrator

These two tendencies are representative of a considerable group of short films that could belong to any of the models described until now. In the first one, words disappear, and the stories take shape through images and sounds. This tendency implies, in a certain way, a philosophical return to primitive cinema. Together with the image, the sound and the music acquire vital importance in these films, which seek to communicate by the use of a universal language. *Terminal* by Aitzol Aramaio or *El gran Zambini* by Igor Legarreta and Emilio Pérez are an illustrative example of this current.

On the other hand, there also exists a group of short films that choose to tell stories through the voice-over of an omniscient narrator, or through a person's voice-off, who offers their point of view about the events. It is important to highlight that in both cases, there is always only one point of view, as it is very difficult to alternate more than that in so short a format. *Hilarri* by Manu Gómez, *Ana y Manuel* by Manuel Calvo, or *El soñador* by Oskar Santos are an example of the short films in which the voice in *off* of the narrator dominates. Meanwhile, *La guerra* by Luiso Berdejo and Jorge C. Dorado, *Voice Over* by Martín Rosete, and *A Good Man* by Jorge Dorado have narration in voice-over.

Documentary Genres, Themes and Formal Models in Documentary

As we mentioned before, the documentary appears very late in the Kimuak catalog. *On the Line* by Jon Garaño is the first one in 2008. This is a curious fact, considering that during the 80s and 90s, the documentary and political or social cinema dominated the Basque cinematographic panorama. In line with this question, the project called Ikuska[53] stands out, whose name refers to a collection of twenty documentaries that were made in the Basque language between 1978 and 1984. They served as a reference point in the wasteland of the Basque cinema of the time. Besides, the duration of many of them is similar to that of a short film,

---

53 Beyond informing in Basque about what happened in the country, the Ikuska films aimed to establish the bases of a future Basque audiovisual industry, which at that moment counted with a considerable group of very notable technicians and creators. However, this second objective was not fulfilled. It remains interesting to highlight that, in spite of relying on high quality professionals in all audiovisual disciplines, the Basque audiovisual industry continues without real foundations. Kimuak is proof of this.

which means that their production was not necessarily linked to a feature film format. In this sense, the lack of documentaries in Kimuak is even stranger if we consider that the first edition of Zinebi International Festival of Documentary and Short Film of Bilbao took place in 1959. There existed and there exists an important window for the projection of this type of creations in their long as well as short versions.

The recovery of a new type of documentary short film during the past decade was fomented by a new era, and the interest that the genre awakened in the public. The proliferation of festivals dedicated to the topic contributed to this tendency, among which stands out the Human Rights Film Festival of Donostia-San Sebastián established in 2003. Now, we must add that there is no generational hand-off between the directors of Ikuska and those of the Kimuak documentaries. Socially committed cinema is a minority. It is paradoxical that none of the directors address the social and political issues of the country, or the violence of ETA. In fact, there are only two directors who assume social responsibility in this regard: Jon Garaño and Paul Urkijo. Their work, however, revolves around problems that take place in other parts of the world, and which are very far from the questions that intrigued the directors of the 80s.

The rest of the documentaries are homogenous with regards to their focus. In *La presa*, Jorge Rivero creates a nostalgic tale in which the memories of Joaquín Vaquero Turcios drive the story of the construction of a dam. Iban del Campo directs in *Dirty Martini* a biopic that relates the adventures of a burlesque star. In a different tone, *Coptos* by Álvaro Sau describes the life of a young Copt. And finally, in a diametrically opposite way from the films before, Koldo Almandoz plays with the canons of institutional documentary in order to create, with much irony, a fake documentary (mockumentary), inspired by an absurd topic.

Beyond their distances, the only common characteristic feature between Ikuska directors and those of Kimuak documentaries is that the latter ones guard the restless spirit of their predecessors with regards to narrative and formal innovation. All of them set out to approach the historical world in different ways, and they distance themselves from the dominant model of the documentary. In this sense, *Ahate pasa* by Koldo Almandoz, *On the Line* by Jon Garaño, and *Monsters Do Not Exist* by Paul Urkijo are three fake documentaries that question the expository[54] or institutional mode, the interactive and the observational,

---

54 In Representing Reality, Bill Nichols describes the characteristic features of the expository mode, which we briefly summarize here. As Nichols argues, the logic and

respectively. They take a critical distance from the paradigms that aim to recreate a real situation from a supposedly objective point of view. What these three systems have in common is constructing an argument that supports a discourse; what varied was the mode and logic from which each model approaches the historical world, and reconstructs it.

Ahate pasa by Almandoz subverts the conventions of the institutional paradigm. The mockumentary is an ironic parody of the classic mode that takes as a point of departure an absurd hypothesis, and tests its *truth-value*. In many films there is a shot in which a group of ducks crosses before the camera, which the director calls *Ahate pasa* or the passage of the ducks. Almandoz considers it crucial in the history of cinema: the most important producers on five continents contracted the family of geese that dedicates itself to this occupation, in order that they play this key moment that must be included in any self-respecting production of quality. In order to demonstrate this meaningless hypothesis, the film combines archival image, film fragments, photography, or cartoons with false testimonies—including, among others, those of the ducks—and with the voice-over of the omniscient narrator. With these devices of the institutional mode, the director constructs a powerful argumentation about this curious thesis. The ironic tone and the absurdity of the story reveal that it is a *joke*, which aims to prove that following the steps of the expository mode, it is possible to prove just about any hypothesis.

On their part, Jon Garaño and Paul Urkijo appropriate the characteristics of interactive documentary and observational documentary, respectively, to create two fake documentaries that are in fact stories of fiction. The choice of this road goes beyond the hybridization of genres or the questioning of informative and documentary formats: it is an issue of emotional effectiveness. Situating oneself on the fine line that separates the documentary from fiction allows one to work with fictitious material under the appearance of a represented reality, where there is

---

the mechanisms of the expository mode are the same as those that dominate the rest of the informative formats of the media. All of them are based on maintaining a distance with regards to the world that is presented, that is, a detached view that allows the reproduction of a fact or a topic of the real world through a series of devices that guarantee "objectivity." Thus, the narrator's voice-over gives coherence to the story in which the witnesses' points of view of the real world alternate on the one hand; on the other, contrasting data proves the veracity of the events that are told. Nevertheless, this mode of representing reality hides the construction of a discourse; an argument guided by voice-over, and based on clues that are strategically juxtaposed due to the montage. Its objective is to consolidate an "interested" interpretation that always carries within the ideological charge of what happens or happened in the real world. Nichols, Representing Reality, 34–38.

no room for chance. The director controls all aspects of the narration. This becomes impossible in case of the documentary, since its primary material is the real world and the persons that inhabit it. The outcome is uncontrollable, although it is true that all documentary is fiction. That is, all documentary searches, identifies and collects those elements of the historical world that it is interested in, with a view to construct an argumentation whose structure and whose narrative strategies are the same as those of pure fiction.

> Documentaries are fictions with plots, characters, situations, and events like any other. They offer introductory lacks, challenges, or dilemmas; they build heightened tensions and dramatically rising conflicts, and they terminate with resolution and closure. They do all this with reference to a "reality" that is a construct, the product of signifying systems, like the documentary film itself.[55]

Nevertheless, in both cases the text situates the viewer in a very different place than what they occupy when they watch fiction, because the documentary genre codifies the film as a representation of reality. This effect of verisimilitude achieves that the dramatic events have a greater emotional impact than what is produced by fiction. Similarly, the revelation of the ending of the story once again locates the viewer in another place: they learn that it is a story of fiction after all. In spite of being aware of the falseness of the plot, the viewer is able to reflect on the very real problem that underlies the story.

On the Line tells the story of voluntary border patrols and their families. They are working class United States patriots who believe in the official discourse against illegal immigration, without really considering the real dimensions of the problem. As the US Constitution grants him the right to do so, Adam takes his rifle and, as a good citizen, shoots at the enemy that attempts to invade his country: a Mexican woman and her baby. This fake documentary uses three devices. First, a newsreel that presents the immigrant woman, which keeps the detached distance and look proper to the expository mode. Next, it uses the conventions of interactive documentary[56] in order to focus on the main character and

---

55 Ibid., 107.
56 Ibid., 44–56.

his family. It follows him to his post where, finally, the development of the story reveals that in reality, the script is fiction. The interactive mode allows us to know the real main characters of the story, the voluntary border patrols and their families.

This documentary paradigm reveals the mediation of the journalist, and even that of the team, when it comes to telling what is taking place in the world. Showing their intervention guarantees honesty and verisimilitude about the representation of real events that are taking place. The spectator accompanies the team in its cover of the historical world. There are no tricks: everything is there to see. Besides, the presence of the camera allows that, depending on the case, the persons turn to it in an indirect manner. In this short film, the presence of the camera is clear but subtle, which allows for greater credibility of what is presented. In the same way, the decision to reveal this manipulation at the end corresponds to an emotional strategy. If the narrated events are a fictitious construction, the meaninglessness of the story comes from a real situation and from real persons. On the one hand, they are US patriots who act in concord with their ideas. On the other hand, they are Mexicans who risk their lives in search of a better future in the "land of opportunity." The photography of the credit titles shows the voluntary patrols in action and the coffins of those who fell when trying to cross the border.

In Paul Urkijo's *Monsters Do Not Exist*, fiction appropriates the documentary form to denounce the defenselessness of Thai boys and girls against foreign pedophiles. The Yeak is a monstrous creature of local mythology that terrorizes children, which Urkijo uses as a leitmotif in his story. In fact, its horrid image starts the film, and continues to burst throughout the film to remind us of the fear and anxiety of the main character. The child thinks that the Yeak stalks him, and fears that it will hurt him. The monster symbolizes the pedophile: a latent and real pest that preys on the children of Thailand. Urkijo subverts the canons of observational documentary by introducing two disturbing elements: the insertion of the obscure images of Yeak, and the main character's first person in voice-off. It is this latter device that is more transgressive of the two, because observational documentary explicitly prohibits its use. As Nichols describes it,[57] this mode locates the camera before the real world, and limits itself to showing what takes place there. It is about deleting all the elements that may reveal the mediation of the machine.

---

57 Ibid., 38–44.

The objective is to treat reality in a detached way, and that the viewer may be, just like the filmmaker, a mere witness to the facts.

The two new elements introduced in *Monsters Do Not Exist* modify the effects of the observational mode, because the Urkijo's objective is to reach a greater identification with the main character. The script focuses therefore on the child's worries, while the observational style brings harmony to the story. The children's fears are contrasted with a descriptive vision of everyday life. The director shows the everyday life of the child: the marketplace, the streets, the traffic, the school, that is, the big Thai city. This equilibrium breaks down abruptly in the ending of the story: a hand camera shows a group of policemen entering the home of a foreign professor who is just about to rape a boy. This television device reveals the constructed character of the fake documentary, and brings up the spectacularization of the real world, which the media often does.

In turn, *Asämara* by Jon Garaño and Raúl López is also a short film with a social message, although it positions itself differently than the ones before. It is about the everyday life of boys and girls in Ethiopia who, in spite of their young age, are obliged to work under awful conditions, or to survive in an inhuman way. Poetry runs through the montage in which the voice-over and even the words of the boys and the girls are eliminated. Their images, tough and beautiful at the same time, are supported by a sound track dominated by the echoes of nature. Through these sounds, the documentary is a forceful evocation of the African landscape.

Jorge Rivero's *La presa*, and Álvaro Sau's *Coptos* assume an intimate point of view. The first film is about nostalgia. It is homage to the workers that constructed the dam Salto de Salime in Asturias, which changed the life of the valley. The melancholy voice-off of the painter Joaquín Vaquero Turcios revives his memories of that era, while the images show the countryside of the environment that are repeated in the different seasons of the year. The beginning and the end of the documentary revolve around two very different tracking shots, and a very strong contrast is created between them. The first one is very fast: it takes the viewer to the dam, and situates them in the heart of the story. The second in, in turn, is very slow, and discovers the mural that Vaquero Turcios painted in the turbine hall of the dam. This allegorical image reveals the time and the effort that the painter and the workers of the dam took to finish their work. In a totally different vein, *Coptos* is an example of observational documentary carried to the extreme.

It verges on the experimental. It shows the lives and times of Copts through a young person of this religion. Nevertheless, the obsession to eliminate mediation results in that the text has no meaning at all. Even obscurity is absolute in the last images of the short film. There is no plot, only isolated looks.

Something similar happens with Jesús Mari Palacios's *Casa vacía*. In this experimental documentary of reflexive nature,[58] the images shot with a hand camera travel through the ruinous house in which Jorge Oteiza and Néstor Basterretxea lived. There are few static images: two fixed shots of the sculptures of both artists that we see at the beginning, and the photography in black and white of the building or the persons that inhabited it. The rest are careless images that are in movement; they are shots that neglect to the extreme even such basic aspects as framing. They are not meant to show from a classic point of view; they rather limit themselves to attesting to the fact the operator enters a place and records it. It becomes obvious that he highlights his presence to empty the text of meaning. His images are only a ghostly trace. The soundtrack alternates two types of sounds. On the one hand, raw sound—you can hear even the conversations that the operator has with other persons that are outside of the field of vision. On the other hand, the reflections in the voice-over that the sculptor from Orio recorded when he worked on his project *Acteón*; a failed initiative, like so many other that he made from the moment he lived in this place. These last reflections, together with the quotes of his work that are inserted periodically among the images, are the ones that construct meaning and fill the text with content. In them, Oteiza speaks of the nature of the documentary, of the plot, of cinema, of the void, while the ghostly trace traverses this uninhabited space.

The leap to the particular universe of the New York *burlesque* of Iban del Campo's *Dirty Martini* surprises the viewer. This biopic of twenty-four minutes of duration, which is somewhat unusual among the Kimuak short films, narrates the avatars of *Dirty Martini*, the star of the nightclubs. The documentary follows the principles of the interactive mode in order to recreate the underground atmosphere of this spectacle, and collects the testimonies of the main character in first person. Her, as well as the rest of the dancers and the spectacle itself verges on the

---

58 Nichols details the reflexive mode of documentary as a metalinguistic mode that questions the very nature of the documentary itself, its forms of expression, and its function. Nichols, Representing Reality,, 56–68.

bizarre. To this effect, the quality of the images seeks to highlight a grainy texture that imitates the appearance of domestic movies; this one changes from color to black and white unproblematically, and also relies of photography. Also, the title credits in black and white recover the advertisement iconography of nightclubs in the era. All this serves to fully enter in a marginal and extreme universe, in a grotesque spectacle. The documentary shows that, in spite of the fact that the body and the movements of its main representative should be diametrically opposed to the striptease dancers, the burlesque survives in the New York clubs in 2009.

Animation

There exist two tendencies in the animation cinema of Kimuak: the experimental current, and the narrative one. The first one is the majority, although in the past years the classical format has recovered some position. Ander Mendia's *Beerbug*, *Daisy Cutter* by Enrique García and Rubén Salazar, and *Zeinek gehiago iraun* by Gregorio Muro have thus reinforced the line of *Tortolika eta Tronbon* by Joxean Muñoz and Txabi Basterretxea.

Narrative Animation

This current is characterized by telling stories by following, in the majority of the cases, the classic narrative and formal parameters. In spite of the fact that the illustrations are always figurative, the technique and the graphic style that they use condition the mode of representing and perceiving the world and, inevitably, have a bearing on the narration. By definition, 3D implies a high level of faithfulness or iconicity when it comes to representing the depth and volume of forms. We mustn't forget that this technique became popular through the videogame, whose objective was to create a simulacrum or hyperrealist image that is very close to the world represented. This is combined with two other devices: the postmodern aerial camera and the *bain sonore* to intensify the immersion of the spectator in the space inhabited. *Beerbug* and *Daisy Cutter* are animations without dialogues that utilize the 3D technique. The first one is a story that mixes the fantastic and the comedy. Its objective is to entertain, while it showcases the technical virtuosity of its creator. In sum, it is a postmodern visual exercise, a trick.

Daisy Cutter is a children's drama about the consequences of war. Although it has minimal structure, the plot centers its focus on provoking emotions in the spectator. To achieve that, it relies on the possibilities that the technique affords. In this case, the postmodern form is not void of content. In fact, the BLU-82B, better known as daisy cutters, are high efficiency bombs that the United States uses in the conflicts in the Middle East, bombs that inspire the title of this film. The everyday life of Zaira, a ten-year-old Iraqi girl takes place under the allies' attacks on Baghdad. One of her friends dies, and the girl collects daisies to keep his memory, and to close herself into something beautiful among so much destruction. She deleafs the flowers with the hope that he, wherever he is, does not forget her. This naive gesture that illustrates the purity of the child's first love will cost her life.

Traditional cartoon animation offers greater liberty to its creator when it comes to representing the world. They are not obliged to do so in a mimetic way, and may choose in function of its graphic preferences. This affects that the diegetic universe, in general, tends to be more schematic. *Tortolika eta Tronbon* and *Zeinek gehiago iraun* present distinctive visual styles and in both, the word is the main thread of the story. The graphic style and the narrative line of the first one is part of commercial animation. During its ten minutes of duration, the short film narrates in a happy and jovial tone the adventures of the clowns of ETB1 (Basque Television Channel 1), Txirri, Mirri, and Txiribiton. On the other hand, the style of the cartoons *Zeinek gehiago iraun* resemble the illustration of children's story books. The persons are outlined around the colorful and simple landscape of the background that serves as a setting for this family drama.

Experimental Animation

Within this category, there are two very distinctive currents. The first one maintains the narration as main thread. This tendency is dominant and heterogeneous. Besides drawing, it uses techniques like sand animation or photography. We find seven short films under this category: Cirugía by Alberto González Vázquez, Pregunta por mí and Haragia by Begoña Vicario, La gallina ciega, Ámár and Bajo la almohada by Isabel Herguera, and Ondar ahoak by Angel Aldarondo.

The second one is a current that radically breaks with narration to embrace artistic expression in its pure state. In fact, the objective of these works is double: to provoke feelings, and to seek a genuine form of expression, that is, art for art. This latter trend of pure experimentation is a minority; among them we find short films by contemporary artists who situate themselves around Arteleku. In fact, *Hezurbeltzak, una fosa común* by Izibene Oñederra, and *Berbaoc* by José Belmonte, Izibene Oñederra, Mercedes Sánchez - Agustino, Gustavo Díaz, and Irati Fernández belong to this second tendency in which, besides animation, they use animation techniques in accordance with the artistic creation of our days.

Now, both experimental currents have a fundamental element in common: they come from a process of artistic creation that is very different from that of fictional or documentary narratives. The images and their evocative power are the motor of these works. The drawing, the photography or the illustration mark the evolution of the plot and not the other way around, as it happens in classic animation.

Alberto González Vázquez's *Cirugía* is an animation cartoon that revolves around the thinking of the main character. Its designs bear a clear influence of the comic, of graphic commercial, and of 1960s popular culture but, most of all, they resemble the visual style of Roy Lichtenstein. González Vázquez eliminates from his drawings the explosion of color and energy of pop art in pursuit of simpler illustrations against a black background. This allows the spectator to focus their view on the objects that change forms. Thus, the drawings are immersed in constant metamorphosis, whose function is to show the thoughts the protagonist expresses in voice-off and in first person. They are phrases that lack global meaning and are unconnected, just as much as the dreams or automatic thoughts that come to mind in an unexpected manner. Not for nothing, this is what happens to the young leading role while he has a drink with a friend.

Pregunta por mí and *Haragia* by Bego Vicario maintain the voice-off of the main characters as a narrative thread that gives meaning to the succession of beautiful and evocative images. The first one is a sand animation in which we learn about the terrifying testimony of a migrant woman who fears that they snatch her vital organs. In the second one, the photography is used as a base, although it is combined with home made films and hair-splitting camera movements to talk about those missing persons whose cadavers are buried in forgotten common graves.

They both denounce unfair situations that come from reality, that is, they have a background that is committed to social causes.

Isabel Herguera also shows, in her way, a preoccupation with social issues, although in her case the arguments focus more on the difficulties that sick people, or people with some kind of deficiency, suffer. Her works of fiction *La gallina ciega* and *Ámár* use the technique of animated drawing, and present a scheme in their forms that resembles those of children before they learn to represent the world mimetically. *La gallina ciega* relates in an optimistic tone the adventure of a blind man whose guide dog has run away, while *Ámár* goes into the world of schizophrenia and its strange visions. The creative work with documentary features *Bajo la almohada* is an animated collage based on the drawings of girls and boys with AIDS, and live in a hospital in Goa (India).

Ondar ahoak by Angel Aldarondo is also a kind of documentary that evokes the life of fishermen and their families in a nostalgic tone. The beautiful photography of the persons and of a world that no longer exists are presented in a harmonious way in an animation that, just like the ships, balance from one side to the other. The ox's eye marks the entrance of the furtive look into this lost and marvelous universe, which is accompanied by echoes of seagulls and the horns of ships.

With regards to the trend of animation of pure expression, we must note that it is linked to the world of creative art in the strict sense of the word, and it relies on two important influences. On the one hand, the Arteleku Animation Workshop that Isabel Herguera coordinates is a corollary to the most radical experimental animation short films in terms of form and content. On the other hand, there is the influence of Begoña Vicario as professor and forger of new art talents at the Faculty of Fine Arts at the University of the Basque Country (UPV/EHU). Both maintain a very close relationship with the new generations of creators. This is evidenced by the fact that *Hezurbeltzak, una fosa común* by Izibene Oñederra is developed in the animation classes of Vicario. The short film is a paradigm of this avant-garde trend. On its part, *Berbaoc* is a group work in which various visual creators participate (José Belmonte, Izibene Oñederra, Mercedes Sánchez-Agustino, Gustavo Díaz, and Irati Fernández) under the coordination of the Arteleku Animation Workshop. Each artist contributes a small creative fragment to the short film. The leitmotif of this *exquisite cadaver* is an unintelligible sonorous composition full of metallic echoes that Xabier Erkizia builds over an interview with another musician, Santiago Irigoien.

3

Most Important Filmmakers

The short films of Kimuak are available on www.kimuak.com

Koldo Almandoz (Donostia-San Sebastián, 1973)

It was the passion for photography, which his uncle inculcated in him, that awoke his interest in cinema. After earning a degree in Journalism with a specialization in Audiovisual Communication at the University of Navarre, he earned a post-graduate degree in cinematography at New York University. He loved the short film format, and the Basque language predominates in practically the totality of his cinematographic work. His creative restlessness is not limited to the realm of audiovisual fiction. Besides working as a journalist, advertising director and musician, he has been directing the cultural journal, *The Balde*, for more than ten years. Kimuak has elected seven of his short films: *Razielen itzulera* (1997), *Belarra* (2002)—selected by the Critics' Week at the Cannes Festival—, *Amuak* (2004), *Midori* (2006), *Columba Palumbus* (2007), *Ahate pasa* (2009), and *Deus et machina* (2012).

Filmography as Director

2013. *Zoologikoak dira poxpolo kaxak* (animation short film)
2013. *Extasis* (short film)
2012. *Deus et machina* (short film)
2011. *Mantis estroboscópica* (short film)
2011. *Trikuaren hiztegia* (short film)
2010. *Censored Love* (short film)
2010. *Arteria de luz* (short film)
2009. *Ahate pasa* (short film)

2008. *Larunbata* (documentary short film)
2008. *Karea* (documentary)
2008. *Aurrescue* (short film)
2007. *Columba Palumbus* (short film)
2006. *Midori* (short film)
2006. *Desio ehiztaria* (short film)
2006. *Pasaia egunero* (documentary short film)
2004. *Amuak* (short film)
2002. *Belarra* (short film)
2000. *A dar ba kar* (short film)
1998. *Habana 3* (documentary short film)
1997. *Mon petit, mon amour* (short film)
1997. *Razielen itzulera* (short film)

Narrative and aesthetic experimentation define the short films of Koldo Almandoz. Normally, he plays with narrative limits to create suspense and to enchant the spectator. They are hybrid, dramatic and suggestive works endowed with a poetic formal style. Although they are in Basque, silence is the language that dominates in his short films; he expresses feelings through images supported by an elaborate soundtrack.

New York, New York

New York had a crucial impact on Koldo Almandoz in the way he understood cinema. He discovered a different kind of cinema in the theaters of the Big Apple: unique films that palpitated to the sound of the *underground* heart of Jonas Mekas. Its echoes still resonate today in the more audacious short films of the Donostia-San Sebastián based director. The New York experience would become indelible, and also impregnated his first work. In fact, it is impossible to understand *Razielen itzulera* without considering its context. Not only because the city of New York is the absolute protagonist of the story, but also because the short film exudes through its pores the spirit of its independent cinema.

Influenced by the new cinematographic tendencies, Almandoz merges fiction and documentary in *Razielen itzulera*, and champions a generic crossbreeding that he will continue to perfect later. His Project matches to a great degree what Antonio Weinrichter[59] defines as the hybridization of genres:

> The hybridisation of fiction and documentary, which breaks the barrier that separated both practices within the film world. It is not a new phenomenon, but fusion had never reached these extremes: auteur fiction film strips away the dramatics and adopts strategies that can only be called documentary; the commercial documentary becomes contaminated with dramatics.

It is the author himself who reveals to us the mixture between fiction and reality that characterizes his first work: "It's a story about an angel; a documentary about a city. It is a documentary story."[60] From a formal point of view, indeed, *Razielen itzulera* looks like a documentary. It is the narrative character of the voice-off of the leading role—played by Almandoz himself—and the poetic tone, more dreamlike than referential, that confer the short film the necessary dramaturgy to consider it a work of fiction.

Shot in black and white, *Razielen itzulera* is divided into five episodes with titles that refer to Biblical passages, and links the sins listed in the Sacred Scriptures with behaviors in contemporary society. In the prologue of the short film, the voice-off of the angel Raziel reveals to us that God had sent him to Earth to help humans, who live defenseless and terrified since their expulsion from Paradise. Situated on a terrace roof, the camera gradually shows the tall buildings of New York City through a slow pan. In this very moment, Raziel errupts in the scene dressed in black, with a sad countenance. The close-up of the face of the angel reveals his affliction, and the soundtrack features melancholy music. The slow panoramic views of the city appear as a reflection of the subjective look of the main character. This general vision of New York anticipates, without a doubt, the five episodes—more meticulous and detailed—that make up the radiography of the city—the hopelessness of human beings.

---

59 Antonio Weinrichter, .Doc: Documentarism in the 21st century, Donostia/San Sebastián, International Film Festival Donostia/San Sebastián, 2010, 266–67.
60 Angulo, Rebordinos and Santamarina, Breve historia del cortometraje vasco, 176.

Katakunbak (Catacombs) is the title of the first episode. The images of the New York subway, recorded like subjective shots of a traveller, dominate this part. This subterranean world is a refuge for human beings. They hid underground at the beginning of times to flee from the hatred of their fellow men, but anger hasn't yet dissipated. The tragedy of the lack of communication, another human drama, is the basis of *Babel*. Signs written in different languages follow one another. The towers of the World Trade Center constitute the new Babel's Tower. The words of Raziel reveal that silence is the only language that humans understand. Unfortunately, no one wants to listen to it. The low angle shots that aspire toward the top of the towers that scrape the skype leave the impossibility of communication obvious. It reflects the unattainability of the goal.

Sex and money are the main themes of the next episodes. On the one hand, *Sodoma eta Gomorra* (Sodoma and Gomorra) penetrates the streets of sin. The images of the bright signs that announce the live spectacles of sex intersperse with fragments from pornographic films. The temptation of the flesh subjugates the will of human beings. *Merkatarien tenplua* (The Marketplace), in turn, offers a brutal treatment of the financial heart of New York City. The images of Wall Street—those omnipresent panels that inform about the value of shares—strongly contrast with the bitter reflections of the tormented angel, who concludes that money does not bring happiness, nor does it help achieve it.

The last chapter—*Paradisua* (Paradise)—however, breaks with the documentary aesthetics that prevails in the previous ones. In spite of the fact that the music continues to be the same, Almandoz gives the images a unique poetic aura. The beauty of nature stands out in all shots. The trees are reflected in the unpolluted waters of a lake, and the close-up of the face of an attractive young woman dominates the screen. Little after that the voice-off of the narrator makes an apology for dreams. The sky, the birds, the trees and their reflection in the water configure the landscape of Paradise. The girl, naked in a scene that resembles the fresco *The Creation of Adam* by Michelangelo, touches a tree branch with a finger, which symbolizes her communion with nature. But suddenly, the idyllic tone of the episode is broken. The face of the girl bursts again onto the screen. But this time it reflects sadness. Her smeared make-up reveals that she has been crying. It is then that the desolate angel confesses the truth: "Just like in the real world of humans, it is also cold in dreams."

After this serious statement, there is a fade to black. The short film, however, is not over. The screen stays dark for a few seconds so that the voice-off of Raziel reveals the reason behind his existential angst: "Man, just like God, always kills what they most love." The crying eyes of this Eve that after the Fall lost Paradise are substituted by the extreme close-up of the eyes of the angel Raziel, whose look has guided the passage across the big city. What his eyes have before him is not the serenity of Paradise but that he has returned to the beginnings, to this rooftop where he started his trip and where successive pans show once again the gray skyscrapers of New York City. There is no dream of Paradise. Finally, the heartbroken angel looks up. The last panning shot follows slowly his look; it abandons the buildings, and settles in a part of the sky. The white color then briefly illuminates the screen before the final fade to black consumes its light, before hopelessness should consume the dreams of human beings.

A Suggestive Narrative Exercise

Belarra, a short film with which Almandoz reaches one of the highest points of his cinematographic trajectory, is a suggestive exercise of narrative experimentation. Formally influenced by the Dogme 95 movement, [61] the film was shot with a digital home camera, and was later transferred to 35mm. The director narrates here an intense drama of suspense that goes in crescendo, taking the montage as its base.

Just like *Razielen itzulera*, the short film is divided in a series of episodes—seven chapters, precisely-. Nevertheless, the presentation is much more stimulating. It is clearly visible that Almandoz reached a greater level of maturity as director, and is able to enchant the spectator without relinquishing his concerns and reflections with regards to the cinematographic medium.

After a brief introduction—with some images that take us to a shower in full function—in which we are told about the authorship and production of the short film, the title of the work *Belarra* appears in black letters against a white background. Little after, a series of mostly

---

[61] Dogme 95 was an avant-garde film movement created and developed by Danish filmmakers Lars Von Trier and Thomas Vinterberg. Its objective was to purify contemporary cinema, and liberate it from the vices acquired from big productions. It produced a manifesto according to which the films must be shot in natural environments, with a hand camera, direct sound, and without artificial lights.

brief shots portrays the grass that the title refers to. The chapter finishes relatively soon with a shot of a shoe stepping on the grass. In spite of the fact that this first episode is very short, it establishes the patterns that will guide the short film. The grass is the nucleus of the plot, the element that forms the backbone of the other episodes. It doesn't seem natural. Its color has been manipulated, saturated, so that it acquires more relevance. And, together with it, the sound ambiance obtains a vital importance.

The second episode titled *Emakumea* (Woman) gives continuity to the scene of the shower that started at the beginning of the short film. We see the naked body of the young woman (Ainara Gurrutxaga) in a steamy bathroom mirror. She comes out of the shower, she dries and covers herself and her hair with white towels. This is nothing but the beginning of a long sequence shot. Later, the camera follows her around the home through a tracking shot, and halts before the half-open door of her room. The young woman gets dressed and goes out with a huge basket full of sheets to the drying rack. Once there, she puts the basket among the grass and looks in the distance. In the background, we can discern the figure of a man that is cutting the grass. The woman returns to her room, takes her son (Iker Pernas) in her arms, and seats him on top of a small basket, close to the drying rack.

The following episodes—*Saskiak* (Baskets), *Haurra* (Boy), and *Gizona* (Man)—are shorter, and foretell the tragedy that will loom over the characters. The child plays with the clothespins of the small basket. But when he gets bored, he leaves the area of the drying rack. His mother doesn't notice it. The father (Peru Almandoz), after exchanging cold looks with his wife, quenches his thirst and returns to work near the place where the child went.

The formal characteristics of the short film are practically the same in all episodes mentioned. As we indicated before, the influence of the movement *Dogme95* is notorious. Almandoz circles the hand camera; the turn is finished in a natural scene; and, besides, the ambient sound is not mixed separately from the images. There is no extradiegetic music.

Nevertheless, although the filmmaker adopts some of the rules of the *Dogme95* movement, he does not aim to make a dogme film. In fact, he manipulates the color of the tape in the montage phase. He accentuates the green color of the grass, and reduces the saturation of the colors of the rest of the elements and persons that make up the picture. This chromatic choice seeks to strengthen the importance that grass possesses in history, and leave the rest behind as secondary. It is not, nevertheless, the only articifical option that Almandoz takes in *Belarra*. The two last episodes, namely, are proof of it.

Maindireak (Bed Sheets) is like a show guided by the music of a silent film from the beginnings of the twentieth century. The young mother is looking for her son among the drying sheets, which move gently and slowly to the sound of accordion melody. Music appears for the first time in the short film, and it imposes itself over the ambient sound. The rhythm follows the compass of the music. The mother does not find her son, only a wooden doll that he had with him before he disappeared. Her face reflects worry. Only the grass has color, everything else is black and white.

The main objective of Almandoz consists in creating suspense through montage. And for that, he constantly plays with the duration of the shots. At the beginning, he dilates the duration of the action. The sequence shot of more than ten minutes with which the drama starts is, exactly, the starting point of this brilliant narrative exercise. But little by little, almost imperceptibly, the duration of the shots is progressively reduced. Thus, the last episode—*Sega* (Scythe)—presumes the culmination of the narrative experiment plotted by Almandoz. The final segment makes it clear without a doubt that, consciously or unconsciously, the director relied on one of Eisenstein's statements with regards to staging: "a lengthy crescendo produces a powerful emotional climax."[62]

In the episode that ends the short film, the images of the man, the woman, and the child interlock at headspinning speed. The man is cutting the grass, the child is lost in the brush, and the woman is seeking him desperately. Almandoz shows the three main characters in isolation, locked up in their respective worlds. The shots, following the logic we already described, are each time shorter. An important shot that shows the father in the background as threat and the child in the foreground, reveals the danger that threatens the child. The rhythm of the scene accelerates, and unease grows. The man who cuts the grass becomes the focus of the scene. Short shots of the face of the desperate woman and the lost child constantly interrupt his leading role. The soundtrack intensifies the suspense even more. The noise of the scythe that cuts the grass represents mortal threat. The sound effects—very similar to those of horror films—that accompany the first shots of the woman's face intensify the fear. The story ends with a shot of the scythe in the air. In spite of the fact that the credit titles close the scene, the sound of the scythe suggests a tragic end. In fact, moments before the tragedy, one can hear a female voice whisper that repeats the words *mendekua* ("vengeance"), and *sega* ("scythe"). It is the whisper of the grass that demands vengeance.

The *Arrantzale*, the Siren, and Loneliness

In spite of the fact that *Amuak* lacks the experimental tone that characterizes the previous short films of Almandoz, it is by no means a conventional piece of work. Its director, faithful to its profound artistic inquietudes, continues to explore the narrative possibilities that he considers fitting for the creation of his unusual plots. This time the story starts at the end, and his challenge lies in maintaining the interest of the spectator during the rest of the film.

---

62 Bordwell, The Cinema of Eisenstein, 120.

A suggestive pan, gentle like the music that accompanies it, shows us a naked couple on the bed of a room lit by a small lamp. The woman (Lucía Quintana) is lying on the bed; the man (Kandido Uranga), on the side of the bed. His hand caresses the thigh of the woman. It looks like a normal love scene. But, suddenly, a fish hook runs across the body of the woman. Slowly and delicately. From the pubic hair to the nipples.

A low-angle shot offers a general view of the scene. The man draws the fish hook toward the mouth of the woman, and moves the fishing line as if he was fishing squid. Then, through a beautiful detail shot, we can see how the fish hook gently knocks against the woman's lips. The woman, finally, yields. She opens her mouth and bites the fishhook. And then, a light panorama shows how the hand of the man takes the fishing line and forcefully pulls it. In the same moment, the music of Mikel Azpiroz brusquely finishes the scene, and the title of the film is announced: *Amuak*.

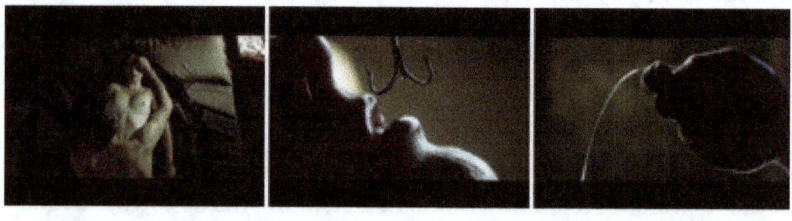

The bizarre and surprising scene with which Almandoz starts the short film reminds us of *Seom* (The Isle, Kim Ki-duk, 2000),[63] where fish hooks and passion fuse in a terrible story of *amour fou*. Starting at the end, nevertheless, always entails risk, especially when the beginning is so intense and disturbing. The danger, obviously, is that the rest of the film falls short of its promise. Nevertheless, Almandoz maintains intrigue right from the beginning; he stirs the curiosity of the viewer, who wants to know the story that hides such an atrocious ending.

In a certain way, the short film is a kind of flashback that gradually reveals the secrets that the first scene suggests. After this first impact, the director constructs a languid portrait of the leading character of the

---

63 Seom (2000), one of the darker but most suggestive jewels of the south-Korean director Kim Ki-duk shares many elements with Amuak. In it, there is a scene that bears a certain resemblance to Amuak—the girl fishes her lover with a rod, who swallows the hook—and could have served as an inspiration for Almandoz.

story. Just as his skill with the fishing line insinuated, he was an expert fisherman. He is a rough man. Silent and solitary.

Unexpectedly, Almandoz breaks the plot in order to insert a documentary section that presents different kinds of fish hooks, and indicates for what type of fish each one is used. It gives the sensation that this documentary insertion fractures the rhythm of the story, and does not contribute anything noteworthy. Nevertheless, this brief documentary becomes fundamental for the perfect understanding of the work. In fact, the last phrase of the voice-over of the documentary holds the key to the mystery:

> "Nevertheless, there exist other types of fish hooks. According to fishermen's legend, in order to catch sirens the only fish hook that worked were words. During long journeys the fishermen, in order to combat loneliness, went close to the edge of the boat and meowed, with the hope of catching a siren."

The legend narrated in the documentary insertion explains the strange behavior of the gloomy fisherman at the beginning of the short film: the reason why he meows during the night by the rail of his small boat. His strange behavior aims nothing but to mitigate the loneliness that torments his heart. It's a form of expressing the necessity of female companionship. After the documentary, he proves to be more pragmatic, and contracts the services of a prostitute.

Loneliness does not only affect the fisherman. The prostitute also suffers from it. She sleeps during the day, works during the night, and seems to have no social life. There is a scene that clearly shows her distress. In it, the prostitute stands before the mirror before going to the date with the main character. While she does her hair, she fixes her eyes on her image in the mirror. Almandoz fits in the same shot the body of the woman and her reflection until a camera movement goes around her figure and advances toward the mirror, cutting the corporal reference of the woman in order to focus only on her immaterial image. The duality in which the person is split, woman/prostitute, disappears and she finds herself facing her failure, before the unique face of loneliness. This forward movement of the camera also links the loneliness of both persons: in the shot that shows the man browsing the advertisments of prostitutes in the newspaper while having breakfast, the camera also moves forward until the frame of the door disappears which, just like the mirror of the prostitute, framed the figure of the fisherman. His eyes fill with tears. He breathes. A little later he leaves.

After reconstructing the hidden story after the horrifying opening scene, and dissecting the minds of its main characters, the text returns to the present, to the same room where the couple had been left. A soft panning shot repeats the same movement as that which started the film, except in the other direction, from the bed to the window. The two lovers are still naked. The fisherman, kneeling on the edge of the bed with his back to the camera; the prostitute, lying on the bed. Her eyes are still closed. It's an unequivocal sign that she was murdered. The suspicion becomes explicit. Loneliness returns, and the fisherman meows.

Almandoz breaks the chronological logic of the story, and reflects on loneliness and the search for love—the two principle axes of the short film—in a work of cyclical structure that reveals its ending. His ingenuity does not only consist in exploring the limits of narration by skillfully playing with staging but, above all, in the capacity he has to fill with suspense a bittersweet and personal reflection about loneliness.

Midori, Portrait of an Obsession

Chance had a determining role in the realization of *Midori*. During a visit to a Japanese temple, the director saw an adolescent in school uniform who walked with crutches. The girl had a special charm about her, and Almandoz decided to film her with a video camera that he borrowed from a friend. That's how the short film came about.

In the first moments of the recording, the camera makes its way through the crowd until it finds Midori.⁶⁴ Then the beautiful notes of *Clavier*-Übung by the German composer Johann Sebastian Bach start. Almandoz, with camera in hand, follows the steps of the adolescent constantly. He films her laborious walk through the innumerable staircases of the temple. The tracking shots are continuous and, occasionally, the director uses the breaks of the young Japanese student to create more aesthetic compositions.

Afraid of being discovered, Almandoz used the zoom of the videocamera to capture the face of the girl. Although he managed to snatch a shy smile, her face expresses melancholy in most of the images. The cause of this sadness can be, perhaps, the foot in bondage that the videocamera captures in extreme close-up.

Midori is not by herself on her walk in the temple. A friend of hers accompanies her every moment; she even carries her bag for her so that she can manage with her crutches. Nevertheless, the director isolates her

---

64 Midori's name is homage to Midori of the novel Tokyo Blues by Haruki Murakami, and to the comic Midori by Suehiro Maruo. Angulo, Rebordinos, and Santamarina, *Breve historia del cortometraje vasco*, 203.

from her most proximate environment. He makes her the only subject of his composition, and he thus confers on her a profound sensation of loneliness. Unexpectedly, the anonymous schoolgirl discovers the camera that is filming her, and looks at it fixedly. It is the end.

Almandoz converts this fragment extracted from reality into the nucleus of the short film. He constructs a fiction around this reality captured by his camera. His intention is nothing but to equip the documented images with a context in a story of fiction. This way, he starts the short film with an imprisoned man (Haritz Elizegi) in a kind of prison. While the subject colors some anime dolls with the crutches, his voice-off reveals to us that he is an entomologist, and he met Midori during a visit to a temple in Kyoto.

Although we are warned of the fatal destiny of the main character, after the aforementioned segment of fiction and the documentary segment that follows it, the director narrates what follows through the animation elaborated by Angel Aldarondo. In the canvas, the meeting takes place between the schoolgirl and the entomologist. A beetle flies off from the hand of the latter, which Midori observes attentively. A little later, from a panoramic position, we see how both go deep into the forest. The final panorama that accompanies the flight of the beetle shows Midori lying on the grass. She doesn't move, and her eyes remain closed. She is murdered.

Next, once the animation episode is over, the shadow of the bars that is projected over the body of the entomologist seems to certify all suspicions. Nevertheless, in the last scene of the short film, the animated Midori opens her eyes and smiles. It is an ambiguous ending, and seeks, to a great extent, to complicate the perception of the spectator, to confound the spectator. In spite of everything, the logic of the story remains the same. Midori's smile is nothing but the projection of the entomologist's fantasy, the portrait of his obsession.

Midori is probably the most irregular short film of Almandoz. The fiction of the entomologist, the documentary fragment and the animated chapter do not fit as they should, and the internal seam of the film remains uncovered. The objective of the director is, in the end, to create fiction on the basis of a piece of documentary, which is an ambition that is just as licit as it is suggestive. But unfortunately, the part of fiction becomes a pretext whose only purpose is to justify the three emotional minutes of the attractive documentary piece; this suggestive film fragment that, optimally developed, could have generated an interesting reflection on the dark side of our obsessions.

The Hunter's Morning

Columba Palumbus is a short, crude and ingenious piece of work. A disturbing atmosphere, which is partly achieved by the chromatic desaturation of images, impregnates the story right from the first frame. In fact, the birds that fly about the clouded sky are a premonition. Peru Almandoz, the director's brother, plays the obscure protagonist of the story: a taciturn hunter with evil intentions. The short film, in essence, is an original narrative experiment designed to create intrigue.

The story consists of two very differentiated parts. The first one of them starts when the main role gets out of his car, closes the door on the driver's side, keeps the shotgun in a case, and is ready to go hunting. In this scene, the hunter pushes the back door of the car, but it does not close. In spite of that, he leaves it open and he goes deep in the forest. There is something strange in his behavior, no doubt. But as the camera follows his steps, the suspicions go away.

Almandoz avoids cinematographic conventions, and opts for a continuous contrast of shots. The general shots—images that emphasize the insignificance of the hunter in the immensity of the forest—and the extreme close-ups—the steps of the protagonist in the mud, for example—are constantly mixed. This marked contrast of images aims to provoke a permanent state of anxiety in the spectator. In other words, they aim to keep the intrigue alive. In this work, the melody of the Cinematic Orchestra—especially a piece that is titled *Dawn*—fills a fundamental function.

The hunter's path ends when he catches sight of a small dovecot. He climbs the stairs until the hunter's stand several meters high and, once up there, he charges the shotgun. It is then that the director uses the montage to combine the images of the hunter and the doves. He plays with the alteration of shots with the intention to create false expectations in the spectator. A little later, one hears a shot. The hunter killed himself.

It is certainly the real turning point of the short film, and the point of departure for the second part of the film. This very moment, the time—haunted by the music of the Cinematic Orchestra whose melody goes backward—moves backward irredeemably: the clouds and the birds move back, the blood that stains the hunter's forehead disappears, the traces in the footprints of the forest disappear, the fallen leaves fly back onto the trees… And, finally, the camera arrives at the place where the hunter left his car. There a slow, vertically ascending panorama shows the massacre of the solitary hunter. The bleeding head of his wife—which blocked the door—and the lifeless body of his son.

The director could have chosen to show the horrible crime of the solitary hunter through a flashback. Nevertheless, instead of that, he opted for another, more attractive alternative from a formal point of view, with the firm intention to prolong the intrigue and surprise the spectator.

Columba Palumbus is not merely a brilliant narrative experiment destined to create intrigue: a reflection about gender violence is also implicit in its final outcome. It is a very delicate question and extremely complicated to adequately capture through fiction. Almandoz, in turn, reflects on this tough reality by focusing it in the aggressor. He is an apparently normal person who suddenly goes off and finishes with the life of his family. In the interpretation of the author, the condemnation of the facts is tacit. There is no justification, only perplexity before the irrational mechanisms that domestic violence generates

The Passage of Ducks

Ahate pasa is an original fake documentary, a subgenre that became very popular through *This is Spinal Tap*[65] (Rob Reiner, 1984), and which was inspired to a great degree by the first films of Peter Watkins.[66]

Removed from the dramatic tone that characterizes his previous short films, Almandoz uses the mockumentary to show his fine irony in *Ahate pasa*. In this work, he reflects about the shot that he calls the passage of ducks. Specifically, he refers to a shot where a group of ducks crosses the scene. The director argues that it is a constantly recurring image in the history of cinema, and aims to uncover its mystery in this ingenious work dominated by humor and curiosity.

The recourse to mockumentary is not something new in the heterogenous cinematographic trajectory of Almandoz. In a certain way, we may consider *Desio ehiztaria*[67] as a kind of rough draft of *Ahate pasa*: a precedent to consider. Not only because this is a mockumentary, but also because it has many elements in common with the latter: irony, intrigue, false characters, the use of archived material, and so on. Nevertheless, the structure of *Ahate pasa* is much more complex.

---

65 This is Spinal Tap (1984) is the first work of the North American director Rob Reiner. It is a fake documentary about the heavy metal group called Spinal Tap. Michael McKean, Christopher Guest, and Harry Shearer, who were scriptwriters with Reiner, played the members of the group.
66 The British filmmaker Peter Watkins (1935) was, together with Orson Welles, one of the great precursors of the fake documentary. His most well-known work is the medium-length science fiction film The War Game (1965); an Oscar winning fake documentary that narrates the story of a Soviet nuclear attack on England.
67 The short film Desio ehiztaria (2006) is a fake documentary about a man who hunts the wishes caught in the coins that people throw into public fountains. The work is in the project Iturriak by the artist Jon Mantzisidor.

The short film starts with a tracking shot. Through the front windshield of the car we may see how it circulates with difficulty on a country road. The car, finally, stops near a hut. And, in that very moment, a group of ducks passes in front of it. It is the presentation of the shot baptized as *the passage of ducks*, which will be repeated until the end. It is the curiosity around which the Almandoz's imaginative story revolves.

The subtitled quack of the main role duck of the documentary is the author's first wink of irony. Nevertheless, the narrator's voice-over tells us about the significant role that ducks have played in the history of cinema, which lends the story a certain verisimilitude. The illustrating images, a group of black and white photographs of important films, seems to verify his words. Shortly, Jean Louis Rebourdin, a film critic who expresses himself in French, ponders about the passage of ducks, while the images show the cited shot in a lot of films: *The Circus* (Charles Chaplin, 1928), *Days of Heaven* (Terrence Malick, 1978), *Chinatown* (Roman Polanski, 1974), *Crna macka, beli macor* (Black Cat, White Cat, Emir Kusturica, 1998), *Five* (Abbas Kiarostami, 2003), and so forth.

A little later, the voice of the narrator gives the floor over to the testimonies of some of the directors who made these films, such as Michael Winterbottom, Emir Kusturica, David Fincher, Roman Polanski, and Abbas Kiarostami. All of them praise the quality of the ducks as actors. Besides, the film unites the opinions of Tomás Sarasola, manager of the leading role duck, and the veterinary surgeon Jone Landaribar. Finally, the narrator recovers the thread of the plot to praise the acting talent of the ducks, and the technique of the passage of ducks.

With the exception of the subtitled quacks of the leading role duck—which could be considered as an artistic licence of the author—*Ahate pasa* follows all the conventions of documentary. But it's not a documentary but a fiction that wears the apparel of documentary. Thus, the black-and-white photography of the beginning has been tampered with; the declarations of the film directors are taken out of context and, to top it off, the characters are fake. Nagore Aranburu plays the veterinary surgeon; Peru Almandoz the manager of the actor duck, and Jesús Cuenca on his part plays the French critic Jean Louis Rebourdin—a fictitious name which Almandoz uses to pay tribute to José Luis Rebordinos, the director of the Donostia-San Sebastián International Film Festival.

Nevertheless, not everything is false in *Ahate pasa*. Although the approach and the development of the mockumentary may be absurd, its premise is very real. It is absolutely true that since the most remote beginnings of cinema until today, film directors all over the world have included in their movies a shot where a group of ducks emerges in the scene. The enormous work of research that the director has done—which is the most outstanding and amazing part of the short film—attests to that. It is this unquestionable reality, precisely, which incites the curiosity of the viewer, and captures them in the plot of the director. Once again, suspense defines the short film. But, just as with the most captivating mysteries, in this one there is no answer either. It doesn't matter. Because what mattered was the road traveled. Almandoz summarizes it perfectly with the last phrases of the voice-over of the narrator: "The absence of a logical explanation disturbs us. But it is, in the end, part of the magic of cinema, which continues to hypnotize us with these small details."

The Proletarian Wrath of God

In *Deus et machina*, the camera follows a man (Ramón Agirre) in the darkness. Only the sound of his steps breaks the silence. The long tracking shot that starts the film shows that he goes toward light. He enters a factory. A clock shows the time: 6.23. He climbs some metal stairs and enters an office. He leaves a letter on a table. He goes down the stairs and goes toward his locker. He changes clothes. Another clock shows the hour. Six thirty. Time to clock in.

The black-and-white images seem to reflect the workday of a factory man. But when he turns on the first machine—a contraption that looks like a film projector—the warm color of a beautiful sunrise breaks the black and white of the industrial routine. A mistake nevertheless interrupts it. Nervous, the man turns on the machine again and the images of the sunrise appear again. It is not accidental. With it, the author means to emphasize the fact that the sunrise is nothing but a projection.

Next, iconic and sonorous analogies are established between nature and the machines that the worker uses. Each machine has its correspondence with nature. There are projections in colors of waves, birds, and the rain ... images that connect through visual raccord with the scenes of the industrial elements. And, suddenly, three executives burst into the scene (Anartz Zuazua, Iker Bereziartua, and Koldo Almandoz). They walk up to the worker, and the encounter is rather cold. There is no greeting, no empathy. After the interruption, the analogies continue: palm trees blowing in the wind, clouds sitting on a mountain, on a great city, and rays that foreshadow a storm. Nature seems to be subordinated to the work that the worker executes daily. The humble worker is the representation of God: an all-powerful being that sets the world in motion.

Just as he would do in *Columba Palumbus*, Almandoz continuously uses the contrast of wide and short scenes to generate inquietude in the viewer. Nevertheless, this time, given that the short film is shot in black-and-white, the backgrounds of the short scenes appear blurred in order that they don't get crowded. Nevertheless, the effect is similar, and the uncertainty to understand the real activity of the main character and the identity of these strange men lasts all through the film. There are, besides, scenes that intensify this suspense. One of the most significant ones is the low angle shot in which the three executives observe with a sullen face from the heights of their office as the worker welds a piece.

In spite of high tension, the work is not exempt from intensely lyrical scenes. It is not for nothing that the breakfast scene is one of the most poetic and tender ones in Almandoz's ouvre. In that scene, the veteran worker offers the crumbs of his sandwich to the swallows that nest in the factory. The swallows and their nest, although they get embedded in the gray world of the factory, are shown in color. In the end, the natural world created by the worker's divinity end up sneaking in the monochromatic factory in which he works. The image very much resembles the metaphor of *Pleasantville* (Gary Ross, 1998). But if in Gary Ross's movie the colors that invade the black-and-white world of Pleasantville symbolize the triumph of passion and of personal liberty, in *Deus et machina* the same colors symbolize hope; hope that becomes manifest in the main character's smile.

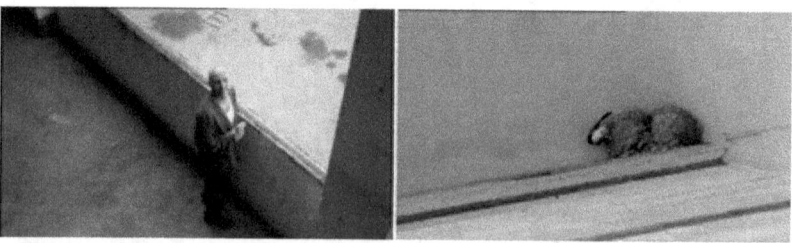

Latent hope does not influence the surprise ending. The worker goes up to the office occupied by the executives, and tells them angrily that he is leaving the factory. The superiority of the worker is obvious. Not only because of his tone, but because he occupies a superior position with regards to the executives; they remain seated and silent during the whole scene. Once the worker leaves the office, the boss, very annoyed, utters some surrealist words: "Damn it! With this situation, and he goes into early retirement. Son of a bitch!" Later, the worker hangs his work uniform and closes his locker for the last time. In this moment, the fade to black gives way to title credits. But the short film is not yet over. We hear Mozart's *Dies Irae* of the *Réquiem*. This piece was not chosen accidentally, but rather intentionally. The worker's wrath, God's wrath, which was contained during the whole story, now explodes in all its intensity during the title credits. It is the divine finger itself that puts end to the music once the credits are finished, pushing a button. *Deus et machina* is, in essence, an homage to the worker: an offering to the worker who sets the world in motion, and can no longer contain his wrath before unjustice.

Interview

How did you first get involved with the world of cinema?

I don't know, well, somehow organically. The truth is that I didn't start having a great passion for it when I was a child. I went trekking a lot to the mountains with my uncle. He liked photography a lot, and he transmitted his enthusiasm to me. In fact, I started to study photography and, before making films, I published photographs and even presented my work in several competitions. From then on, the evolution was natural. I started to study Audiovisual Communication at the University of Navarre, and as it happened, at that time there were young professors there who liked cinema. Some liked documentaries, others preferred fiction. Even our theology profesor liked cinema . . . Once I finished my degree, I became seriously interested in this world. It was then that I moved to New York and studied a cinema course. This experience was fundamental in my career.

You have always showed your inclination toward short films. Do you still refuse to make feature films?

It's not that I have anything against feature films. It is like when they ask me if the short film is a genre in itself, or only a bridge toward feature film. It is both, and neither. The short film fits better the way I am; it's not that I try to vindicate it against feature film. For me, the short film allows me to work the way I like. It offers me the necessary freedom to reflect on the ideas that I want to share. Many times, it would be impossible to put the things that occur to me in a feature film. They just couldn't be done. Besides, making short films allows me to work with people that I like. Enjoyment of the work is fundamental. I do not share the philosophy that one has to suffer when making films. At the same time, I really like watching feature films. But, because of impatience or the lack of money, I don't feel capable of setting up a company and working on it for three or four years until I can direct a film. It does not satisfy me. I have no intention of shooting a film for the mere sake of building my resume. It would be very gratifying to see people go to the theaters and watch my movies, but I am much more excited when one of my short films travels for two years in the world and I, as much as I can, live its trajectory first hand.

What's your model of making short films?

A free, very free format, which allows me to take risks. I am attracted to those short films where there is an original search or project, let it be for its script, for the way of presenting it, or for the aesthetic point of view. In the end, I like short films that contribute something, that surprise you, that seek risks, and are provocative. Among the possibilities of a short film, there are normally more than one that fits these characteristics.

Which are your principle artistic references?

My artistic references vary a lot. I don't like video games, for example. There was a time when I liked Nikita Mikhalkov. A few years ago, I was very much interested in Asian cinema, but then *Dogme* appeared, and called my attention. Later, I discovered Italian comedy. When I was younger, I had some qualms about a certain type of Spanish comedy, but now I go and watch a movie by Borja Cobeaga, and I enjoy it a lot.

I am very eclectic. I do not only consume films, but also all types of audiovisual material. I also read quite a bit; especially thrillers.

These preferences have some kind of influence on your artistic perception?

Yes, in a way. The sources of my work are diverse. I am more and more interested in audiovisual materials: cinema, video, video making ... With the passage of time, they are less and less distinguishable. Hybridization dominates. Concepts, aesthetics, genres mix ... I agree with the position of Michel Gondry or Chris Cunningham. It is the world that we aim at. I am very impatient and I have a lack of restraint; a necessity to act. I have a lot of ideas, and I want to realize them. I look at it like the photographer that takes photos and later uses them for this or that purpose.

All your short films are shot in Basque.

Not all of them were shot in Basque. Some of them are shot entirely in Basque. Others are shot in Basque and Spanish; and there are those that were shot without voice ... I do not shoot films in Basque for some militant reason. For me, it is something natural. Although I use both Basque and Spanish on a daily basis, I make the majority of my work in Basque. I went to an *ikastola* (Basque school), and I am used to working in Basque. Kaurismäki shoots his films in Finnish—I shoot them in Basque. But sometimes I have some mini projects that I like to shoot in French.

What are the principle problems that thwart the Basque short film, and what solutions would you propose to improve the situation?

There are very good short films out there. Proof of them is the Oscar-nominated pieces of Nacho Vigalondo and Borja Cobeaga. Nevertheless, I have a weakness for Luiso Berdejo's short films. There are also many interesting artists in the world of animation, people like Isabel Herguera and Izibene Oñederra. Then there are Asier Altuna and Telmo Esnal, directors who have their own outlook on things, and who constantly evolve. All this generation, which is probably mine, has taken risks and tried different things. However, younger people do not take risks. They repeat contents and forms, established patterns of success.

There are few young people who approach the format and provoke us, or who laugh at us older people and do new things. There is too much embourgeoisement, and little punch.

What role does the Internet play in the world of short film?

I am not a great fan of the Internet. I have neither Facebook, nor Twitter. The Internet can be, in a certain way, an alternative channel of distribution with a lot of limitations; a small window with bad quality ... I don't like watching short films on the Internet. There are people, even festivals, that post your work on the web. I don't want that a short film, whose sound and photography I worked on a lot, to be watched on a Youtube window. On the other hand, it is a very contemporary form of moving audiovisual material. I don't like it, but it is undeniably comfortable.

In *Razielen itzulera*, your first work, fiction and documentary merge. Hybridization is something characteristic in your cinema?

I think so. I have always been attracted by hybridization. It was one of those things that I discovered in New York. There, I saw different movies from what I was accustomed to. It was a kind of cinema that I knew nothing about. I was very much interested in those films, and started to want to apply some things in what I was doing. I also saw the work of Joaquim Jordà ... In the end, this mixture appears to me supremely interesting, a challenge. It is as if it was a game, and I am very much interested in this aspect of filmmaking.

Belarra, which was chosen for the Critic's Week of the Cannes Film Festival, was a turning point in your career.

A little after finishing *Belarra*, Rebordinos called me, and told me that it was selected for the Critic's Week of Cannes. I didn't even know what it was. They received thousands of short films that year, and mine was one of the ten selected ones. One of those surpirising turns that life gives you. Yes, it was a turning point, for if I hadn't gone to Cannes, my path would have been completely different. It had long been in my head, but it took time to make it because, in principle, it wasn't going to be a film. I wanted to create suspense through montage. Not with music or images of action, but with images of little action.

Intrigue is essential in *Belarra*, but its importance is not something isolated. Is suspense substantial for your cinema?

In one way or another, all films have to have an element of suspense, and they don't need to be a thriller. There must be something that keeps the viewers' interest to watch the films. For example, in *Ahate pasa* you hear something of the passage of ducks, and you ask, what is this? In *Amuak*, in turn, the challenge was to start it with the end. The suspense consists in discovering why all this happens. I always want my films to have an element of suspense.

In *Amuak*, narrative structure is broken, the story starts at the end, and has a cyclical structure.

It is something I like doing. It does not come from theoretical knowledge, nor from a necessity to be at the forefront. It is what I enjoy doing. There are times when the outcome is an introduction-climax-resolution kind of story, but what really attracts me is how to tell it. That is, before drawing the stories, I usually think a lot about them; I give it a lot of thought. The montage is, without a doubt, one of the phases that I most enjoy, because I go back to rewriting the film. In *Amuak* it was nice to put all cards on the table, and see if I managed to keep the suspense of the film.

The strategy is similar in *Columba Palumbus*.

It's a very simple film, elaborated with few pieces. Nevertheless, there are some elements, like the door that does not close, that I had thought out before. Besides, the film has very general and very short scenes. I was searching for these elements of suspense, of anxiety. I wanted to show the contrast of scenes because I thought it could work. It is the story of three persons who in the immensity of nature are nothing, but on the other hand, it is a very tough story.

Sound and music are very important in your short films, especially in *Columba Palumbus*.

As far as the sound is concerned, I am normally a minimalist. I like the sound to remain very natural. I don't like forcing sounds that have no meaning on the screen. At the level of music, I hadn't planned to give the film music, but Angel Aldarondo knew the song *Dawn* by the Cinematic Orchestra. It's a melody that goes backward. It was a music that adapted perfectly to the story and, finally, I changed my mind. For me, it is essential that the music does not unbalance the whole. This is my rule. I think that in this sense, we see more and more abuse. The music and the sound effects anticipate too much the trajectory of the film; there are soundtracks that *eat* the film. I particularly like the films of the Coen brothers. It seems like everything goes in contrary directions in their films; awful things happen, but with the music of comedy.

Silence is omnipresent in your short films. The characters barely speak.

It is the cinema that I'm interested in. I like that there's a story, but I prefer even more that the story is suggested. Orality does not suggest, it explains. The voice-off is something minimal that gives you a handle to hold on to. I love the films of Lynch and Kaurismäki. I also like *Ghost Dog* (Jim Jarmusch, 1999). In all these cases, the most important things are expressed through glances and images. Each spectator reads the film in a very personal way. I prefer that your viewing of the film is not exactly the same as that of the person sitting next to you, I like it when the spectator actively participates. My short films inspire very different interpretations.

There are people who consider that *Midori* is very ambiguous. It is not clear what you want to express.

In the film, the voice-over narrates a story, but it doesn't really tell us what happened. My idea was to tell a very *funny* love story. We may observe that society has punished the subject, but he lives it like a love story. He is completely obsessed with the little girl; he remembers her, he draws her, he talks to her. From his point of view, he didn't do anything wrong. This is why the final smile of Midori comes to say: "it's all right." In reality, it's not all right. Nevertheless, cinema must suggest, show things in an uncontaminated way. If I had included at the end a passage that refers to the number of women murdered by men, or the number of girls who are raped daily, with the UNESCO logo, I would make a different film. I would criticize something. I didn't want to criticize, but it is implied that I didn't want to defend something, either. I wanted to show the possibility that someone may take notice of another person, and become obsessed with him or her. I followed three minutes of this girl, but someone else may have fallen in love with her.

Does the fact that you are a cartoon author have to do with the role animation plays in your cinema?

I do not think much about what I do, but I know that I like it. I have liked cartoons since I was a child, my relationship with drawing and the sequence of drawing, which is in the end cinema. I like it. Before shooting my films I first draw them, because it helps me a lot to imagine, to decide, to choose a script, and to cut it into pieces. If I draw it, I see it.

How did the idea of *Ahate pasa* emerge?

I was watching *Un long dimanche de fiançailles* (A Very Long Engagement, Jean-Pierre Jeunet, 2004) in the movie theater. I watched the scene where the postman comes, and some ducks cross the screen. I thought that I had just seen the same recently in *Así en el cielo como en la tierra* (On Earth as It Is in Heaven, José Luis Cuerda, 1995). Then, I came to the conclusion that the world is full of the passage of ducks. In fact, the scene where a group of ducks cross the screen appears in many films. That's how the idea came. Nevertheless, it took me time to figure out what I would do with this discovery.

In the past years, the mockumentary has gained a lot of prominence. *Ahate pasa*, no doubt, follows this line. What is your idea of the mockumentary?

I share the view that all documentaries are false. I am interested in the theme of fictioning reality, or converting some fiction into reality. What I continue to like about *Ahate pasa* is that, although its presentation is absurd, it is based on something real. In *Frankenstein* (James Whale, 1931) there appears a group of ducks and also there is one in the television series *The Wire*. The explanation is, or may be, false; but what I show is real. In spite of being fiction, the movie *Rosetta* (Jean-Pierre and Luc Dardenne, 1999) is more real than many, supposedly objective documentaries. There are people who, with all certainty, suffer the terrible social conditions that the main character undergoes. This hybridization seems interesting to me because it proves that the borders between fiction and reality are not so lucid. To believe something, we need real image;

but for a long time now, real image is completely manipulable. The day must come when we recognize that real image is not a proof of veracity.

At the end of *Deus et machina*, there is explicit homage to the worker. Did the economic crisis have some kind of influence on the social criticism of the short film?

Not exactly the crisis as such. The film was not made during the crisis, but much before. The seeds of this short film were planted some twenty years ago. The factory that appears in the film was established by my grandfather, and my two uncles also worked there. I also I worked there during a summer. There were images, rhythms, sounds . . . the factory was a veritable landscape that interested me tremendously, with potentially doing something with it. I always had the intention to shoot a film there. I didn't know what until the idea of making a film about these small gods emerged, who go to the factory every morning and set the world in motion.

In spite of everything, the economic crisis seems to be present. At least latently.

For me, it is an apocalyptic film. God said, "Damn it!" This is what I think many times when I see in the news that in Greece people kill themselves because of the crisis. People shouldn't kill themselves. They should go into the parliaments and liquidate them. In the movie, God is fed up. If I was God, I would create the world for them again. Like I said before, with this short film I wanted to pay homage to the people who every day set the world in motion. These people who, in a way, are all of us. I was never positioned against cinema committed to social causes. There is socially critical cinema that I like a lot. What I am against is cheating, bland, corny, and lying cinema. In any case, I don't find it social criticism.

Why does the film finish with the fragment *Dies Irae* of Mozart's *Réquiem*?

I wanted to make a film about the Apocalypse with a naturalist tone with regards to the sound, and a balanced rhythm. And, when it comes to the end, I wanted it to show *Deus et machina* in enormous print on an eight-meter screen, and *Dies Irae* playing. I wanted that all the drama, all the tension that an Apocalypse has would erupt at the end. This is a little bit the way I imagine things happen. Not only the Apocalypse... In most cases, the movies do not faithfully reflect the death of a beloved person. We witness an hour and a half drama, silence ... and reality is not like that. Reality is much more normal. When such misfortunes happen, every one suffers them inside, but we all continue to do our everyday things. Because life goes on. In this film, where God becomes tired and takes early retirement, I wanted the tone to be a normal tone. In turn, yes, I wanted to shoot the final credits that way. I wanted it to serve as a reminder of what has been seen: Apocalypse.

Some of your short films are recorded with digital technology.

It democratizes the medium, but not talent. For the mere fact of using digital cameras, not all of us have the talent of a Berdejo, Vigalondo, or Altuna. I normally use digital technology. I am a very cheap director, because I like to be that way. I normally work with small teams, if that this gives me a lot of freedom when it comes to shooting the film. I lose patience when one has to prepare three hours before shooting a scene; I am a person of action. I am not very reflective and I think that digital cinema fits the way I am. *Columba Palumbus*, *Midori*, *Ahate pasa* ... they too are shot in digital, but I do not mean to promote it. Each project has its own characteristic features. There's *Amuak* and *Deus et machina*, for example, which I recorded in 35mm.

In your short films you prefer to work with nonprofessional actors. Why?

For modesty, really. My short works are not major montages, and the stories are not typically ones that an actor would like to play in to further their career. It is not their fault, it's mine. I am sure many of them would be happy to work with me. In fact, my experience with professional actors has always been very good. The problem is that I have no clue how to direct actors, and I am intimidated. For example, in *Columba Palumbus*, which was shot in a day and a half, I hesitated to tell someone to come with me, and with my tripod to Aralar, because they could have thought: "This guy is not making a movie ... " If I involve someone in a project, I want to compensate them in a certain way for their work. Which is why when it comes to smaller projects, I try to do them myself.

Your brother Peru is a main character of some of your work—*Belarra, Desio ehiztaria, Columba Palumbus* . . . and has an important role in *Ahate pasa.*

The case of Peru has to do with what I just said. In *Belarra,* I relied on Ainara Gurrutxaga because I needed an actress with weight. But I also needed a man, and he was at hand. In *Columba Palumbus,* three fourths of the same. Who am I going to order to climb up on a shaky dovecot in Aralar? My brother of course, because I can yell at him! Besides, I don't do films with a lot of dialogue. Peru does not have great acting quality, but he is my brother and I have the advantage that I can treat him like those "fascist" directors treat their actors.

How do you envision your cinematographic future?

I don't have great expectations. For me, short films allow me to travel, but they are ephemeral. An astonishing number of short films are shot each day. Right now, in China there are probably thousands of people shooting. Perhaps some day I will make a feature film, but it doesn't seem to me something extraordinary. Culture has excessive prestige; we think that everyone that works with culture has a seal of glamor.

Asier Altuna (Bergara, 1969)

Altuna was trained at the Andoain Cinema and Video School, and worked as electrician for directors like Ricardo Franco (*Después de tantos años,* 1994), La Cuadrilla (*Justino, un asesino de la tercera edad* [Justino], 1994; *Matías, juez de línea,* 1995; and *Atilano presidente* [Atilano for President], 1998), Daniel Calparsoro (*Salto al vacío* [Jump Into the Void], 1995; and *A ciegas* [Blinded], 1997) and Emilio Martínez Lázaro (*Carreteras secundarias* [Backroads], 1997). In television, he was scriptwriter of the program *Sorginen Laratza,* and director of the series *Brinkola,* both for ETB. In 1997, he wrote and directed his first short film with Telmo Esnal, *Txotx,* which was followed in 1999 by *40 ezetz,* both featured in Kimuak. Together, they went on to do feature films, starting with *Aupa Etxebeste!* (2005). He directed another three short films by himself that were selected by Kimuak (*Topeka, Sarean,* and *Artalde*), and the documentary *Bertsolari*. He is also producer of his short film *Topeka* (2002), of the two titles by Telmo Esnal *Taxi?* (2007) and *Amona Putz!* (2009), and of the *La gran carrera* by Kote Camacho (belonging to the 2010 Kimuak edition), the latter three with Marian Fernández Pascal, with whom he founded the production company Txintxua Films.

Filmography as Director

2013. *Zęla trovkę* (documentary short film)
2011. *Bertsolari* (feature length documentary)
2010. *Artalde* (short film)
2006. *Sarean* (short film)
2005. *Aupa Etxebeste!* (feature film)
2002. *Topeka* (short film)
1999. *40 ezetz* (short film)
1997. *Txotx* (short film)

Telmo Esnal (Zarautz, 1966)

After his training at the Andoain Cinema and Video School, he worked as assistant to such filmmakers as Icíar Bollaín (*Hola, ¿estás sola?* [Hi, Are You Alone?], 1995) and *Flores de otro mundo* [Flowers from Another World], 1999), Enrique Urbizu (*Cachito*, 1996), La Cuadrilla (*Justino, un asesino de la tercera edad*, 1994; *Matías, juez de línea*, 1995; and *Atilano presidente*, 1998) or Álex de la Iglesia (*La comunidad* [Common Wealth], 2000; and *Crimen ferpecto* [Ferpect Crime], 2004). He has four short films in Kimuak: two as single author, *Taxi?* (2007) and *Amona Putz!* (2009), and another two written and directed together with Asier Altuna, *Txotx* (1997) and *40 ezetz* (1999). He also codirected with him the 2005 feature film *Aupa Etxebeste!*, winner of the Youth Award of the Donostia-San Sebastián International Film Festival. This movie earned them the nomination for the Goya Award in the category of Best New Director. His last work until now has been the fiction feature film *Urte berri on, amona!* (Happy New Year, Grandma!, 2011*)*, directed only by him but cowritten with Altuna.

Filmography as Director

2012. *Hamaiketakoa* (short film)
2011. *Urte berri on, amona!* (feature film)
2009. *Amona Putz!* (short film)
2007. *Taxi?* (short film)
2005. *Aupa Etxebeste!* (feature film)
1999. *40 ezetz* (short film)
1997. *Txotx* (short film)

Black Humor with a Basque Label

Txotx and *40 ezetz*, written and directed in Basque by Asier Altuna and Telmo Esnal, are the result of the same narrative and formal strategy. They depart from typically Basque atmospheres and situations normally presented from a traditionalist and bucolic point of view, turn them around, and go deep into the more obscure aspects not only of this apparently idyllic society that lives in communion with the rural world, but also into human nature in general. Although the basic premise is the same, in *Txotx* there is an evident inclination to the genre of horror due to the sinister aspect of the cinematography of José Luis Moreno, and the setting that strengthens suspense. Meanwhile, *40 ezetz* clearly pursues intrigue rather than fearful effects. In both cases however, and this has become the directors' brand, there is an undeniable trace of black humor in both films.

The main characters of *Txotx* are members of the Azkune family lead by the patriarch Juan Mari (Pako Sagarzazu), and owners of an old and shady cider tavern that offers the best meat in the neighborhood. No one knows the identity of their suppliers.[68] One night, a group of friends, who are already drunk from their previous bar crawl, enters the restaurant. From this moment on, Joxe (Kandido Uranga), older son of Juan Mari and heir of the family business, starts to stealthily move around the cider bar, watching someone with furtive and sinister interest. A few emphatic and directed camera movements show without a doubt the object of his interest: the young Xolomo,[69] a corpulate man whom Joxe observes secretly through the walls like a voyeur spies on his victim.

---

68 Txotx is the noise of the cider cask when opened, and a sign that one can start drinking.
69 This word means "tenderloin" or "pork loin" in Basque; in this case it refers to the

In effect, the plump young man will become victim to the man's macabre caprices. When the young man goes out to urinate, Joxe leaves him unconscious by giving him a blow on the head. The next shots alternate his efforts to move the heavy body of the man to the basement through unstable shots, hand camera, the path of Juan Mari who, aware of his son's perverse intentions, searches for him in the dark and labyrinthic alleys of the old country house. The sound of the txalaparta marks the rhythm in crescendo of a montage increasingly accelerated, whose tension reaches its climax when Joxe confronts his father, and manages to shut himself with the boy in the pantry.

Father and son talk from both sides of the door, and it is then that we start understanding the secret of the splendid raw material that the Azkune serve: for generations, they resorted to the flesh of solitary clients to make up for the shortage of provisions. On this occasion, however, there is no necessity; Joxe kidnapped Xolomo because he wants him for himself, which goes against the norms of the family.

After the discussion between father and son, there is no way back, and the short film turns toward the conventions of mob films. Fearing that his son would ruin the business, and realizing that Xolomo's friends already noticed his absence, Juan Mari takes a shotgun. His wife (Arantxa Izeta) is worried, and asks him what he plans to do. When Juan Mari tells her about the situation, her answer, not without a certain humor, is surprising as she refers to her own son: "You can't kill Joxe. What will become of the cider tavern then?"

Her words clearly reveal the principles by which the Azkune family lives. They are also brilliantly summarized in the sentence of the younger son Iñigo (Anartz Zuazua), significantly stressed by the noise of Juan Mari's handgun magazine: "business is business." The mother wanted Iñigo to study and take him from the country house, while Joxe takes care of the family business. The young man, however, prefers to help his father by replacing his brother in the line of succession, for he has violated the norms of the clan. His placement in the foreground of the composition with the parents in the background reflects his new status in the family, a nuclear element in Basque society and culture, which both directors will satirize again with corrosive acidity in their feature film *Aupa Etxebeste!*

---

bodily corpulence of the young man who was given this nickname.

Once again, the txalaparta accompanies the violent alternating montage that combines the ritual of Joxe (in the purest style of slasher films) on the point of turning Xolomo into chops, with the providential arrival of Juan Mari and Iñigo. When they liberate the victim, who was so drunk on cider that he didn't notice anything, the young Iñigo assumes the role of Michael Corleone in *The Godfather Part II* (Francis Ford Coppola, 1974), and takes the responsibility of eliminating the traitor brother for the sake of the family business. The disturbing tracking shot that, starting from Xolomo's car, envelops this house of horror, with the threatening outlines of Juan Mari and his wife at the entrance, is tainted with ironic humor as the drunken party make their way home, singing, and utterly unaware of the misfortune that they just escaped.

40 ezetz shares a strong resemblance with its predecesor *Txotx* both in narrative and formal terms, although this time it is in the world of bets around oxen competitions that the directors' dark humor surfaces. Xegundo (Kandido Uranga) takes up a loan of an enormous amount of money to bet on Garai and Moron, Joxe Mari's (Pako Sagarzazu) oxen, which never lost a competition. This afternoon, nevertheless, the animals don't win, and all the money goes into the hands of a stranger (Isidoro Fernández). Xegundo's friend Antton (Jose Ramon Soroiz) suspects that something strange happened, and follows the stranger to Joxe Mari's country house, where he discovers a couple of oxen that are exactly the same, and eavesdrops the conversation of two men about a trick. Antton tells Xegundo what he has seen, who shows up furious in Jose Mari's country house demanding explanations with a scythe in hand. Joxe Mari offers him money in return that in the village no one discovers what he has done: Garai and Moron were getting old, and he didn't want to see them lose, so he had them cloned, although the new couple still needed some training to become like the original ones. Suddenly, the stranger emerges in the stable with the bet money, a moment that Joxe Mari exploits to give Xegundo a hit on the head and leave him unconscious. Joxe Mari tries to get away from the man, but in that moment, Antton appears, and drags along at gunpoint a man who looks exactly like the stranger. The stranger takes the shotgun, but Xegundo, who in the meantime came around, leads the oxen, and they trample over the man. His twin brother takes him home, and Xegundo stays there with the suitcase of the bets, ready to fulfill the promise he made to Joxe Mari, and make sure that no one in the village would learn about the foul play.

40 ezetz exploits the same tricks as *Txotx*: the semi-documentary overtone of some of the scenes that aim to describe atmosphere; the efficient acting of the two actors Pako Sagarzazu and Kandido Uranga to produce an atavistic presence; the powerful and comic effect of strangeness produced by the incorporation of a modern element like cloning in such an ancient activity, so governed by tradition, as oxen competitions; or the use of the hand camera and the sound of the txalaparta in the moments of high tension.[70]

Nevertheless, the narrative is not as perfect as it is in the case of *Txotx*. Although it is important to highlight a certain humoristic component in the acting of Jose Ramon Soroiz and Ane Gabarain, the intrigue and the plot end up too complex. The turns and surprises accumulate in the last five minutes of the short film with a rush that also affects the mise-en-scène. All in all, the characteristic irony of Altuna and Esnal remain intact in the final sentence, where Xegundo justifies the fact that he keeps the money of the village by saying that he promised to Joxe Mari that no one would discover his dirty tricks, and "the dead's wishes have to be respected." The same dark humor emerges behind Joxe Mari's decision to get rid of Xegundo, and take him to the cider tavern of the Azkune family—a funny metalinguistic wink to *Txotx* that, in the mouth of Sagarzazu himself, reflects the fictional universe created by these two directors driven by a healthy dose of maliciousness.

Animals and People

In the three short films that Asier Altuna did by himself, he recovers some of the ingredients proper to the titles he shares with Telmo Asnal, although he uses much less humor than those works had. If something distinguishes the creative brand of Altuna, it is the minimalism and the visual potential of images strongly rooted in the Basque culture and imagery, and they are not exempt from a certain poetic value. The director eliminates the dialogues, and fully essentializes the narration to transmit, always from a critical perspective, brief but powerful metaphors about society, humans, and their behaviors. This is a narrative and stylistic tendency that reaches its ultimate height in *Topeka*, an unusual piece of three-and-a-half minutes based Joseba Sarrionandia's short story titled *Ahari Topeka*.

Altuna uses an eminently Basque tradition, the ram fight, to speak in a metaphorical way about the duality between human beings and animals in a sick, violent, and intolerant society where its members aim to destroy one another, or simply destroy themselves. The structure is divided into three visually and sonorously differentiated parts. Descriptive

---

[70] Like the scene in which the choleric Xegundo goes to Joxe Mari's farmhouse.

images that approximate ethnographic documentary dominate the beginning.[71] However, they offer unique perspectives for a film of such characteristics, such as the shots taken from below at the height of the animals, or the shot taken from above the square with a camera hanging from the top of the trees.

This pattern is broken by a brief shot of a man who suddenly hits the person next to him with his head. The natural sound of the fiesta is substituted by the sound of the tambourine and the xtalaparta, two instruments of percussion that, through their beat, intensify the moment of hitting. The shots are shorter, the camera becomes unstable, and the montage is accelerated. Altuna shows this way how humans have occupied the primitive place of animals, and they do not only charge at the people next to them, but also hit their head against a stone wall that they could never destroy when they can't find another person that they could attack.

The next and last step in this game of inversions is the humanization of the surprised animals as they see what takes place around them. The camera adopts the perspective of one of the desoriented rams, and from its internal observation, chaotically captures the nonsensical spectacle that takes place before its eyes. As far as the sound is concerned, the internal hearing of the animals dominates the scene: the dulled and confused humming that comes to the ram's ears becomes the only element of the soundtrack. The ram bleats as he looks directly into the camera now situated at his height, and decides finally to escape from the premises where these mad people closed him. The camera parts from the animal, and rises to show in a great general shot the space where he seeks refuge: the mountains, the only clean and calm place uncontaminated by sick humanity, whose amplitude emphasized by the ascending movement of the camera receives and protects the ram.

The proposed duality between the animal behavior of human beings, and the human attitude of the animal is epitomized in the sculpture image of an anthropomorphic ram by Ricardo Hernández. It was suggested in a fragmented way at the beginning of the short film, but now we can see it in its entirety from a frontal perspective.

Without denying the universal message of the short film, it is almost inevitable to interpret these images as a metaphorical

---

71 These types of images also appear in Txotx and 40 ezetz to show the ambience of the cider bar and the oxen competitions.

treatment of the Basque Country. For this reason, it is particularly curious and ironic that, as José Luis Rebordinos aptly observes, the short film opens with an overprint that reads "Aurrera doan herria," "a nation progressing, a nation on track."[72] It is a slogan borrowed from the Basque government at the time, whose Department of Culture sponsored part of the short film.

The next short film of Altuna, *Sarean*, follows the same narrative formula, and appeals once again to the concept of animalization to criticize a social blemish, this time racism and the rejection of immigrants. The piece, which lasts four minutes and has no dialogues, unites two recognizable scenes for the Basque society: tuna fishing in the Basque Country, and the arrival each year of dozens of African dinghies to the European coast.

The film starts again with semidocumentary images of a fishing boat that leaves the port to fish. The song "Boga boga,"[73] solemnly played by

---

72 Angulo, Rebordinos, and Santamarina, Breve historia del cortometraje vasco, 190.
73 Basque traditional song paying homage to fishermen and their work.

a choral group, gives a certain romanticism to these bucolic images so characteristic of Basque iconography. The *arrantzales* (fishermen) throw in the nets and sweep the sea like they always do, and a few shots focus on the execution of what seems to be a daily routine. As it is, when they pull up the nets, none of the fishermen seem to be surprised by the kind of catch they have: a group of sub-Saharan Africans that struggle to liberate themselves from the trap where they are caught. When the fishermen have difficulty lifting their bodies on board, they resort to the help of hooks. Then they throw the men on the deck, and clean their blood with water coming from a hose.

The visual force of this brutal metaphor, which equates illegal immigrants to tuna caught in the nets of the first world, is based not only on the violence of oscillating close-ups that show without further ado how the hooks cut through the men's flesh, but also in the maintenance of the documentary tone that reigns right from the beginning in order to recreate with utter crudeness what for these workers seems like a simple mechanical activity. At the end, the song "Itsasoa laino dago" substitutes the epic "Boga, boga." The melancholy that emanates from its lyrics introduces a sad note in contrast with the calm images of the impassive *arrantzales*, who go home after finishing their work. At the exit of the port, a front view shows the ship's nose sailing across the sea; on the way back, the camera shows the rear of the vessel as it returns to the pier. And though the sound indicates that the hungry flock of birds that fly above are seagulls, it remains impossible to shake off the image of a circle of vultures stalking the macabre content of their cargo.

Artalde is the last show of the patricular poetic universe of Altuna. It is a short film dedicated to the sheepherders of Oxanguren, which reflects about the gregariousness of urban society where humans, alone and disoriented, may lose their autonomy and their critical capacity as they are captured by the call of a leader whose authority they don't even question.

The countryside, the rural environment is once again presented as a pure space far away from the vices of the city. In the first images the camera moves forward in a subjective shot through green vegetation accompanied by the sound of a herd of sheep, and a sheepherder. Right after the title, however, the scene switches to black and white, and moves to the streets of Bilbao. The jingling of the bells is replaced by the dull sound of traffic. There, a man (Paco Sagarzazu) seems to be lost in the middle of the great city. The context shows his disconcertedness by situating him in the middle of a blurred crowd, and by showing the reflection of a glass (probably a shop window), in which the figure of the man melts with the rest of the passersby who walk around him.

In fact, he is a sheepherder who does not know very well where to go. He finally decides to stand on a step nearby, and use the umbrella that he carries hanging on his back as a stick. The close-up of his face isolates him from the confusion that seemed to devour him, and gives him confidence to do what he knows: call his sheep. In the urban jungle, nevertheless, there are only people, and at first no one seems to pay attention to him. Finally, a young woman stops before him, and other passersby imitate her example, conforming into a kind of herd. When he has congregated a good number of animals/humans, the pastor looks in close-up at the group, and invites them to follow him with his particular call. In fact, it is a look directed into the camera, situated in the place of the herd and thus also the viewer, whom he converts into just another animal of the eccentric group, and to whom he extends the invitation.

The man, who seemed to be lost before, now moves around confidently in the streets of this unknown city followed by his sheep, and recruiting new ones on the way. The chaotic images of the beginning, which stressed the noisy disorder of a crowd that seemed to move without accord, contrast now with the general shots of the perfectly organized and compact herd walking behind their leader. Before, he was the only focused element in the frame, while the surrounding shapeless and diffuse crowd scattered around him. Once the herd is formed, however, the more extensive and open compositions show the collective focused through its leader. This strengthens the cohesion of the group, which advances in the same direction and with a clear objective: the only spot inhabited by trees that stands out for its green color in the midst of the gray environment of the city, and whose vision coincides with the re-apparition of the cowbells in the soundtrack.

The procession stops when at an intersection of two streets they run into another sheepherder who is leading his own herd. A front shot locates the two pastors in front of each other in the position of a duel. Facing competition, the sheepherders are overtaken by avarice, and try to snatch the followers of the other by calling the other's "sheep," each one with their own voice. The herds break up, and anarchy breaks out again as the figures move out of focus in different directions,[74] and some factious sheep even try to find their own way to call their companions

---

74 Images that recall *Topeka*.

and convert into new and opportunistic leaders. In the middle of the confusion, the *irrintzi*[75] of a woman resolves the injsutice by achieving that everyone disperses definitely. The sheepherder stays again by himself in the setting, the sounds of the herd are turned off, and the camera, elevated beyond him, shows in a desolate general shot the loneliness of his failure. He is unable to lead these urbanites, gregarious and uncritical like sheep, to a place where the world is not black and white.

Everyday Surrealism

If Altuna took *Txotx* and *40 ezetz* as the premise to explore the gloomiest side of the human race on the basis of certain traditional elements of Basque society, what Esnal expresses of the universe created together with his colleague is, above all, the particular humor that characterized their first short films.

Just like the stories of Altuna, *Taxi?* and *Amona Putz!* are too based on everyday and identifiable social situations. Their aesthetics, however, is not rooted in a typical Basque imagery, and is embedded in more general scenes and coordinates. Both films develop a simple and brief idea narrated in a clear and efficient way. Their main value is humor, transmitted to a great deal through the play of the actors. In case of *Txotx* and *40 ezetz*, this humor is surrealist rather than dark, which allows the scriptwriter and the director to apply their usual strategy of inversion or comic deformation of an everyday matter, which, on occasion, deserves to be criticized.

Taxi? presents a funny anecdote of five minutes, in which the filmmaker puts a man (Luis Tosar) in a repetitive loop, and submits him to a sort of nightmare from which it seems to be impossible to escape. The man leaves a building while he talks on the phone with his mother, and waves for a taxi. It appears out of the blue, and stops brusquely in front of him with an exaggerated sound effect that is more proper to a cartoon. This indicates that we are not in a realistic fictional universe.

From this moment, the short film is focused on the interchange of questions and answers instead of a conversation between the client and the strange taxi driver (Arturo Valls). Instead of starting small talk

---

[75] Loud, strident, and prolonged yell assicated with sheepherding, which is now used as a yell of happiness. It is possible that in the Middle Ages it was used to intimidate the enemy before a battle.

whether the passenger likes it or not, as it often happens, the taxi driver aims to establish the coordinates of the conversation according to the preferences of the client. A trip with conversation, or without? In favor, or against? With insults, or without? Sports, society, politics? National or international politics? Peace process or real estate corruption? The questions of the impassive driver continue, and the passenger responds to each one of them. He is each time more impatient to start the real conversation. A new phone call interrupts the questions, and when the passenger hangs up, and finally decides that they would talk about the the national soccer league, with insults, and more particularly about the Deportivo de A Coruña team, the taxi driver announces that they arrived. The man doesn't seem to have realized it, and with the car already stopping, he becomes excited as he recalls the great moments of his team. The undaunted driver, however, asks him to pay, and invites him to get out of the car.

From the moment the man gets in the car, Esnal's camera remains in front of the front windshield of the vehicle. It avoids the classic conversation staging of the shot/counter shot in order to capture the absurd simulation of dialogue in a single sequence shot that centers all attention on the actors' play. It is precisely in this moment when the nightmare begins for the protagonist.

The passenger gets out of the car. As at the beginning, he is speaking with his mother on the phone, and recognizes that the car left him at the same place where he got in. He automatically raises his hand, and a taxi stops immediately before him in the same way as before. The scene, accompanied by some sudden and disturbing musical notes, seems to turn toward suspense, while the man stealthily approaches the car in a slow and fearful subjective tracking shot. In the window he sees a woman (Marta Etura), who invites him to get in the car, and after a moment of hesitation, the man gets in. The same ritual is repeated: the passenger tells the driver again the street address, and the camera situates itself once again on the windshield of the vehicle, capturing the two persons in the same frame. The angle of the shot, however, is different, which makes us hopeful that there would be some change in the trajectory. That's at least what the unsuspecting passenger hopes, and when the driver asks him the fateful question "With or without conversation?" he refuses it as this way the spiral would surely break. But it is impossible. The nightmarish loop starts again, and through the next question of the taxi driver ("I play some music for you, or you prefer the radio?"), the story abruptly cuts off without giving the man the possibility to escape.

Amona Putz! is the name of a curious invention designed to make life easier for desperate parents who cannot control their sons through the usual channels: a blowup doll which, far from the usual function that is normally attributed to these items, sometimes turns into an energetic, multipurpose grandma capable of taking care of, and entertaining for hours, the most indominable little ones.

The short film starts with a married couple (Egoitz Lasa and Nagore Aranburu) preparing the car to go on a camping vacation. Esnal keeps the camera in one constant but gentle movement during a minute-and-a-half of sequence shot, in which we see the father putting all kinds of items in the trunk of the car. Meanwhile, the mother goes back and forth, putting the children in the car. The filmmaker avoids the cut or the ellipsis to show in all its dimensions the torment that the progenitors suffer due to the inexhaustible activities of their children.

The next scenes occur in the same manner. One of the little ones obliges his father to stop and get out of the car in the middle of a traffic jam because he has to pee. When they arrive at the campground and the father tries to put up the tent, the children sabotage him by hitting him with a ball, or sprinkling water in his face. All the operations of the family occur in real time and in general shots that aim to illustrate how the patience of this father, until now stoically enduring the ordeal without saying a word, is slowly pushed to the limit.

Far from exploding, however, the man gets a mysterious box out of the trunk, which contains an undefined inflatable object. He starts inflating it, and a succession of detailed shots of rubber hands and legs go on to form, little by little, the body of what the box hides: a grandma who, as she is completely inflated, takes up a human form. The grandma (Kontxu Odriozola) takes the children, and the parents seem to finally have some rest. That's what the peaceful tracking shot approaching the couple shows, placidly seated at the entrance of their tent in the night's silence, gloomier than ever, in contrast with the continuous murmur of the children's voice accompanying the previous scenes.

But when they least expect it, someone breaks the ephemeral state of peace. It is no other than the grandma herself, who after putting the children into bed, turns to her "son" and daughter-in-law in search of a little chit-chat. An uncontrollable torrent of words start coming out of her mouth, a verbal bombardement that is as unbearable as the screaming of the children, which the scene emphasizes by offering increasingly closed shots of the face of the woman as the rhythm of her talk accelerates. The sound of her voice is also distorted, adopting a kind of reverberation that alludes to the auditory saturation of the couple, no longer capable of discerning what the woman says.

Ready to liberate themselves from her, the father opens the doll's deflate valve. The doll starts flying around as the air leaves it. It finally drops in the trunk of the car. The camera moves closer, and shows as the door of the trunk falls on the leg of the grandma, and tears up the rubber. When the next morning the father once again gets the doll to inflate it and thus relieve themselves from the harrassment of their offsprings, he discovers the hole. He tries to fix it by tying a knot at the end of the leg, but as he inflates it the air pressure makes the artificial grandma explode before the stupefied look of the children accusing him of killing her.

In the surrealist world of Esnal, however, everything has a solution. It is enough to throw the broken grandma in the trash, and buy a new box of *The Inflatable Granma!* This will offer the stressed parents a grandma that is exactly the same as before at a modest price. It is a gentle social satire of the abuse that many parents, overwhelmed by the rhythm of life, do to their own parents when they charge them with the caretaking of their children, and discard them when they become a nuisance.

Interview: Asier Altuna and Telmo Esnal

You have made two short stories and a feature film. In similar cases, one of the directors takes charge of the writing of the script, and the other attends to the direction of actors and the team. Do you have such an established division of labor?

Telmo Esnal: We are like a couple! We started together because we happened to meet. One day Asier Altuna said to me: why don't we make a short film? Well yes, why not? When we work together, we do not split up the work. We do everything together.

Asier Altuna: It is a matter of going into the filming after having worked and discussed a lot; after having defined everything very well. And thus, you arrive to the filming to enjoy it, because directing in a partnership is more enjoyable. You are more relaxed because you think that the other by your side has a very clear idea of everything.

Telmo Esnal: The process is less painful, because shooting a film is always so long . . . it is like an eternal job. A lot of time passes from the moment the idea emerges, and you write it until you get the money to make it. But waiting does not end there. After that comes the phase before the shooting, then postproduction . . .

There is a common feature in *Txotx* and *40 ezetz*. It is based on themes, images, situations that are very significant for the Basque way of life and culture, and the films turn them around. They reflect the most obscure or sinister side of human nature.

In that time, what kind of image did Basque culture have? Folklore. They were selling a kind of country where everything was nice, we drank cider, and we danced under the trees at the feet of the Pyrenees . . . We try to bring a little humor into this. It was nice to reflect on this world, because it was true that it existed—now not that much, because there are fewer and fewer obscure cider taverns—but this postcard image was always portrayed on the calendars of Caja Laboral and of the Basque Government. And we turned it around because we are very much into laughing at ourselves. We enjoyed it a lot, we had no idea how the people would receive it, but they understood it and they liked it. It was a path that we started with *Txotx*, and continued with *40 ezetz*.

In *Txotx* you play with the conventions of the genre of horror films: the treatment of the photography, the scenes of Kandido Uranga spying on the victim . . .

Asier Altuna: At that time, I liked the short films of Álex de la Iglesia, which were very dark. There was no other way of understanding cinema then.

Telmo Esnal: It's that I think that I keep doing the same thing . . .

Because of the way the family is portrayed—conservation of the family business at the expense of its members—it seems to be reminscient of mob films.

Telmo Esnal: Of course, but not necessarily of the mob; what happens is that the family is very important here in the Basque Country, like it is in Italy or Spain. The family is essential in all Catholic cultures.

Asier Altuna: This reference is repeated in *Aupa Etxebeste!* and in *Brinkola*. The series that we are making for ETB does revolve around the real mafia; the organization of the village was carried out in a maffioso way. And in *Urte berri on, amona!* there are the family and the relatives, who are not from the family, and never will be.

Isn't the ending of *40 ezetz* a little bit hurried?

Telmo Esnal: We didn't know how to end it. We wrote fourteen versions, and we couldn't find an ending but we had to shoot, and the final joke occurred to us: "*hildakoek ere errespetua merezi ditek*," the dead also deserve respect.

Asier Altuna: We were aware on the day of shooting that we didn't have the ending resolved, but we already had eighteen minutes of length, and it had to stop. I watched the short film and I liked it, but it is not perfect. It was a short film that was born from *Txotx*, it was a kind of task we owed to ourselves. Although it is a partly failed short film, we learned a lot from it.

In *Txotx* as well as in *40 ezetz* you use the txalaparta to generate tension, and it has a lot of importance in the montage.

Telmo Esnal: It's a good instrument to give the story some tension.

Asier Altuna: And besides, the music was related to folklore. In *Txotx* and *40 ezetz*, it was all very Basque, Basque speaking, like a postcard. The *txalaparta* was part of this postcard.

Why did *Txotx* have so much success outside of the Basque Country with so many local stereotypes?

Telmo Esnal: Mostly because of the genre and form of telling the story. Besides, although it looks like the story is very local, it has a universal character. When you tell something so local, you may think we are very different from the rest of the world, but the basic needs of human beings are the same everywhere. It also has to do with the moment when it was filmed. The short films that they made back then had no genre, and it had success because there was a need to do something different.

Asier Altuna: It had genre, but it was camouflaged. It looked like it would be a very typical portrait of the depths of the Basque Country, and some people were very much surprised.

There is suspense in the eyes of the actors.

Telmo Esnal: There is suspense in *Txotx* and in *40 ezetz*. I always liked the movies of Hitchcock. When I was studying cinema, he was the director I was most interested in. I don't like overly elaborated tension, but yes, in the film there should be tension, a previous planning to create moments of suspense. Everything is very much planned in *Txotx*, nothing is left to chance. In *40 ezetz*, for example, on the contrary; we tried to do something different, and everything is less deliberate.

Interview: Asier Altuna

With the works you did by yourself, you have followed the direction of *Txotx* and *40 ezetz* in the sense that you start out with typically Basque themes and images, turn them around, and show their backside. You have fully essentialized this idea, reducing the narrative to minimal expression, and proposing metaphors in the place of stories.

I like narrating everything through images, and I always liked surrealism. The short film is a nice and accesible medium to tell my stories, and go far with very little. It is a real pleasure to shoot short films. If I find a good idea from which I can extract suggestive images, and tell something great in very little, I do that. And, in this process, I love using metaphors. While I'm shooting a film, the idea will gradually emerge, but I leave everything a bit open. I love to leave everything in the air, and let different interpretations emerge. It is very surprising and incredible to hear interpretations that people make.

In case of *Sarean*, it seems like this approach is a little more evident. *Topeka*, in turn, suggests a political interpretation.

The message in *Sarean* is very clear. It is also very clear to whom this message is directed. In *Sarean* they fish humans as if they were fish, and what this generates in the viewer is precisely what interests me. In *Topeka*, although the story comes from Joseba Sarrionandia, I don't see a political interpretation that clearly. The idea that's repeated in my short films—*Artalde*, *Topeka*, and *Sarean*—is the role change between humans and animals.

Sound has a lot of weight in your short films.

Sound is very important in my short films. It is partly essential for the process. Once I have the image, I always think of how to strenghen it with sound. In *Artalde*, for example, when the people go marching, I introduce the herd's sound, and the scene acquires more intensity. I must admit that when I make a short film, I think more of the image and the script than the sound. But in spite of this, I give a lot of importance to the sound.

In *Topeka*, there is a kind of turn when the camera becomes a subjective camera. It makes the ending look like an escape.

Everyone may interpret it in their own way. They are things that are repeated: nature, and the manipulation of nature by humans. The ram is in the middle of the human world, and goes where it needs to be, its natural environment. It aims to revindicate the animality of humans, and also the other way around: that animals also have a life.

In *Sarean*, you play with contrast. It looks like a traditionalist film, but at a certain point there is a turn. Some fishermen go out to fish, and suddenly, everything changes. Did you seek this confusion in the viewer?

Yes, effectively. *Boga, boga*, nice images, Pasaia ... all this, once again, for the same thing: to surprise, and that the impact may be tougher. Nevertheless, one must contextualize it. When we were shooting it, sub-Saharan youngsters arrived in dinghies at the Andalusian and Canarian coast every day. Everything was about turning it around. Also, the theme of humans and animals is also present. We normally fish tuna, and we consider it something normal, but when you see that the catch is a human being, it is brutal. I like to provoke and confuse. The extreme close-ups strenghten this sensation even more. I watch it now and it seems to me very tough, but that was precisely the purpose.

How did the idea of *Artalde* come about?

I don't know how ideas occur to me. I know how to make this call, because my father is a sheepherder. He calls the sheep that way, and I know how to do it because me too I worked as a sheepherder sometimes. It is homage to the sheepherders of the country house of Oxanguren.

Considering that the short film was shot in Bilbao, could it be a metaphor about the lack of communication?

More than a metaphor about the lack of communication, it is a critique of consumerism in a sense that we always follow someone who calls us. And, once again, the role change between humans and animals remains clear. Like in *Topeka*, when the citizens approach nature, color appears. The nice things are there.

You have created Txintxua Films with Marian Fernández.

The intention is to produce projects that are close. We are a very small production company, and we can't aspire for great projects, because that would necessitate a great infrastructure. We don't want to go big, because in these cases, failure is also of the same proportions. Nevertheless, I am more of a creator than a producer; Marian Fernández is the real producer, yes. If Telmo Esnal or Koldo Almandoz have some kind of a small project, we normally produce it. Mine too, of course. It can't really do more.

Interview: Telmo Esnal

After *Txotx* and *40 ezetz*, you have more clearly opted for humor than Altuna.

I wasn't going to do something similar to what Asier Altuna does. In any case, it can be that there was an effort to distance myself a bit, and do things differently. The humor of *Taxi?* is based on dialogue. It was a kind of comedy that I wanted to elaborate on carefully, and I wanted to do it with important actors. I remember that when I started, my friends told me that I had to do humor. And I responded that I never would do that. And then I ended up doing humor. But there is also a bitter taste. *Amona Putz!* is a joke, but for me it has a touch of sadness.

Did you write the script of *Taxi?* with Luis Tosar and Arturo Valls on mind?

I was thinking about Luis Tosar and Willy Toledo. I wanted to make a sequence shot of two men talking for a long while; to make a long shot and try to give it some humor. It was like an exercise, like a personal challenge. I tried to make the spectator laugh during the whole dialogue. Luis Tosar and I are very close friends. As it happened, he was shooting a film here with Arturo Valls, and we told him about it. In that moment, they could not shoot it because they finished the film and left. But in the end, they returned and we did it.

The treatment of color is special. It's not pure black and white.

I didn't want to shoot the short film in color. I thought that color could distract or bother the viewer. Nevertheless, it is true that it is not total black and white. There is a little color in it. I wanted to lower all the colors, because what I was interested in was dialogue. I wanted to see well the faces of those two. I tried to center the whole story on the conversation, and to imply Billy Wilder's black-and-white humor classics.

In *Amona Putz!* you depart from a very traditionalist and very recognizable situation to denounce something very current. Why did this theme interest you?

I spent many hours at the fronton with my son. I can't leave him with my mother or my wife's mother, because they don't live in my town. While I was watching my son play with his toys at the fronton, it occurred to me how we use grandparents when they are close. Frankly, I think that we exploit our parents a little bit. The story emerged on the basis of this idea. I wanted to pay a little homage to the grandparents who take care of our children, and to criticize the way we use them.

The humor is more naive in *Txotx*.

I wanted it to be like that on purpose. I wanted the characters to not speak a lot, for only the grandma to speak. For this reason, precisely, it is a short film with many gags.

How did the idea of relating the inflatable doll with the grandmother emerge?

When a person bothers us, the normal thing is to get rid of them. A way of doing it kindly is to desinflate it, and inflate it again. After all, you don't want to totally get rid of that person. You need him or her to fulfill their habitual function. In the time of *Txotx*, we would have killed the grandma ... but in this case I decided something subtler. That way one stays calmer in the conscience.

Interview: Asier Altuna and Telmo Esnal

Under the shadow of this humor or these metaphors, there is some social criticism that is not palpable in other Kimuak directors.

Asier Altuna: We are like that. We will not keep silent when we see an injustice.

Telmo Esnal: I am immersed in a society that I do not like very much, and when I make films I try to express my reflections. I don't like the direction our society is headed, and I criticize it. I do so in *Aupa Etxebeste!*, where there is criticism of pretensions, and thinking oneself superior than others. In *Amona Putz!* it is also obvious that there is social criticism. But I didn't want to make a pamphlet, either; I just sought to make us realize the way we are.

Asier Altuna: What I like about films is that, besides giving me pleasure, they also make me think.

Telmo Esnal: It is true that there is social critique in our short films. I like it when people enjoy themselves, but if the film also makes them think, it's even better. At the same time, I have no great expectations of changing the world.

Luiso Berdejo (Donostia-San Sebastián, 1975)

Berdejo made his first short film in video at the Larrotxene Culture House, in Donostia-San Sebastián, and decided to study cinema. His training started in 1997 at the Sarobe Film School. He moved to Madrid to continue his studies at the Cinematography and Audiovisual School of Madrid (ECAM). He left the school in 1998, but the friendships he made there were very important for his professional career. Together with Koldo Zuzazua, he presented the script of... *ya no puede caminar* (2001) at the San Sebastian Horror and Fantasy Film Festival. He won the project, he realized it, and Kimuak selected the short film. Later he met Jorge Dorado, with whom he codirected *La guerra* (2005), a short film selected by Kimuak. It was an important step in his trajectory due to the numerous awards it won at state and international level. More precisely, the Almería City Hall award allowed him to shoot *Dio vi benedica a tutti*, one of the three stories that constitute *Limoncello* (2007). This project, together with *For(r)est in the Des(s)ert* (2006) are the other two short films that have been included in the Kimuak selection. Berdejo's move to feature films came through a project selected at the Cannes Film Festival's L'Atelier, with which he traveled to the United States. There he met Peter Safran, who became his manager. Kimuak was fundamentally important for his entrance in the United States, as many professionals in Hollywood knew his short films due to the distribution work of the program. Finally, he was chosen to direct *The New Daughter* (2009) in the United States, a feature film starring Kevin Costner. Luiso Berdejo lives in Santa Monica, Los Angeles, and works in the US cinematographic industry, above all as a scriptwriter.

Filmography as Director

2013. *Violet* (feature film)

2009. *The New Daughter* (feature film)

2007. *Dio vi benedica a tutti* (segment of *Limoncello*)

2006. *For(r)est in the Des(s)ert* (short film)

2005. *La guerra* (short film codirected with Jorge C. Dorado)

2002. *Faraón* (segment of *Diminutos del calvario*)

2001. ... *ya no puede caminar* (short film)

The short films of this director are children's tales where suspense, magic, and innocence are key elements. In most of them, he makes use of an inherent resource of these types of fables: the voice-over of a heterodiegetic and omniscient narrator who narrates in various languages, French, English, and Italian, which reveals Berdejo's eclecticism. The director masterfully manages classic, mannerist, and postmodern staging.

Love What You Fear

. . . ya no puede caminar is the only one of the four short films in which Berdejo does rely on either the heterodiegetic, omniscient narrator, or the voice-over; it is also his only work shot in Spanish. This horror story revolves around the therapy that a father (Pepe Oliva) imposes on his son (Junio Valcerde) so that he overcomes his fear of insects and animals, and so that he is able to love them and live with them. Then, the process of healing becomes a game, and a way of understanding the world.

The point of departure of the story is the innocence of Pacheco, who understands his father's lesson verbatim, and behaves in the same way with Irene (Miriam Giovanelli) as with the rest of the beings that terrify him: he ties them, he locks them up, he catalogs them, he feeds them in the evening, and when he no longer feels fear, he would not separate from them. In the end, the boy's logic constitutes the axis of this children's tale, totally isolated from the world of adults. This way it maintains its original charm. At the beginning, the process of healing becomes a game that the classic mise-en-scène aims to reproduce by linking beautiful extreme close-ups, accompanied by a musical melody. The boy captures the animals, puts them in a bottle, carefully writes the labels, and organizes them on the shelves. When the sun goes down, he illuminates them with the light of his lantern; he feeds them, and wishes them good night.

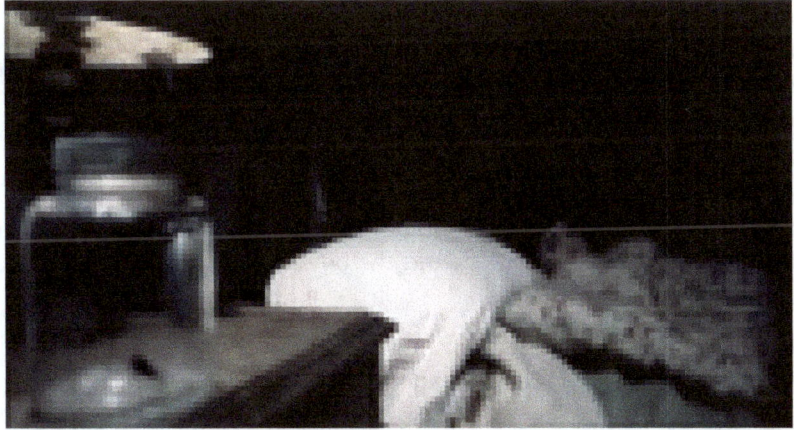

When it comes to creating a mysterious atmosphere around the forest where the events take place, the mise-en-scène recovers the classic imagery of the genre. As in Berdejo's other short films, the forest becomes another one of the characters that ends up seizing the soul of the boy. The obscure and ancestral side emerges from the combination of images of nature, generally fixed scenes of paused time, with a metallic sound that dominates over the rest of the murmurs. The image of the clouds that move before the mountains, the shots of the trees, or the clearing of the forest are an example of this device, of which a distrubing image also forms a part, and contradicts the laws of nature: the drop that flows up instead of down the thorny branch.

But without a doubt this strange metallic sound is above all synonymous with the fear of Pacheco. It accompanies the scenes of animals that the child fears, and also the image of Irene. During the first phase of the therapy, the echo makes it clear that the bug in the glass jar continues to terrorize the child who, in the background, tries to distance himself to the corner of the bed. Once he overcomes fear, the animals live with him and form part of the mysterious ancestral world to which he now belongs. The shots of the slugs in the bathtub or the centipede that runs on his hands testify to this.

A turning point arrives when the mother orders him out of the house, and obliges him to practice his hobby in a hut that he builds in the forest. From this point on, the game becomes a form of dominating the world that surrounds him. Through this innocent entertainment, the sinister spirit of the forest starts to consume Pacheco. His primitive instincts start to impose themselves over the the behaviors socially acquired at home. Therefore, the mother symbolizes the transmission of cultural values, and it's her who is in control at home. The father is more elemental and closer to the animal side of man. Thus, the home is the opposite of the forest. In fact, the images that describe nature with the sound that is appropriate of the environment, or where the house appears surrounded by clouds, continuously burst in during the short film to reveal this opposition, and the boy's path toward his obscure and savage side.

The transformation and the innocence of the main character explain that he is not aware of the terror he inflicts on Irene when he shuts her in the well, which is another typical element of children's stories. The last scene opens and closes by using the same expressive tool with which it metaphorically alludes to the full moon and indirectly, to its power as magic and terrorizing element that dominates nature. It is a nadir shot that shows how the light enters until it draws a circle or closes itself in the opposite direction. Following the healing ritual, Pacheco illuminates it with the torch; half naked and with water to the waist, Irene tries to stay alive. The metallic sound makes it clear that the child has not managed to overcome his fear. He says goodbye and closes the lid. Obscurity reigns, and one can hear the agonizing sob of the girl caught in the bottom of the well.

Wake Up. You Are Dead.

La guerra is a harrowing portrait of the state of terror, chaos, and dehumanization, where people have to survive in an armed conflict. The story takes place during the last days of the German occupation of France. The equilibrium of the rational and safe world where the main character (Pau Poch), a young boy lives, finds itself totally ruined in an instant. The Nazis kill his father (Roberto Arnaiz), and torture, rape, and murder his mother (Monsterrat Anfruna). Left alone and taking care of his newborn baby sister, he tries to save the life of both of them, and hides in the forest. An enemy soldier (Rolando Raimjanov) injured by the trap that the child had prepared is looking for them to kill them.

"*Deuxième personne du présent del indicatif du verbe être. Tu est. Oú? Dans un placard*". These are the first words that the voice-over (Julia Mattei) pronounces in French and in second person about the image in black. With them, the heterodiegetic narrator sentences the ending of the macabre game of hide-and-seek in which the main character has to participate. *La guerra* relies on elements of children's universe like hide-and-seek, and the prayer to the child Jesus, to invent them in a radical and dramatic manner in which innocence is annihilated by the destructive spirit of human beings that surfaces in all armed conflict. The rules of life do not count in this context, and as the fatal ending shows, they may change in any moment. It is war.

Like with other short films of Berdejo, these phrases have a double meaning directly related with the fate of the child. Literally, the sentence *tu est. Oú? Dans un placard* means to inform that the boy is hidden in a wardrobe. However, in French the pronounciation of *tu est* is very similar to the past participle of the verb *tuer*, to kill, *tué*, which means murdered, dead. The text hides a second possible meaning: "you are dead, where? In a cupboard." In fact, the film starts with the scene of the child in the wardrobe. This scene is repeated throughout the film, but this time it envisions the idea of a coffin, the form with which the final shot frames his body.

The staging starts the chronicle of an announced murder: the introduction implicitly carries the ending. The end of the story is not important, one can read it between the lines. For this reason, the narrator is interested in explaining how the events took place within a limited amount of time, five minues and thirty-four seconds, which coincides with the film's duration.

On the other hand, the use of the second person is rare in cinema. In this case it produces a kind of split that obeys a very clear narrative strategy. In spite of the fact that the child cannot hear her words, the voice-over is virtually directed at him to inform him in every second about the situation. It gives him instructions, and keeps the hope of his salvation alive. The boy acts of his own accord, which is why the voice-over is a tool that, on the one hand, accentuates the sensation of anguish—in part due to the monotonous rhythm of the narrator who acknowledges the events as a cold and calculating machine. On the other hand, it indirectly turns to the spectator to communicate to them the feelings of the child, which as omniscient narrator she knows.

This narrative split gives the false sensation that both the main character and the viewer have the same information. Nevertheless, the narrator knows the outcome from the very beginning, and together with the staging she continues to give clues. But they are impossible to decipher until the end. The scene of the wardrobe becomes a repetitive impasse on which expectations of salvation, which later become uncertain, are projected. No wonder; it is a false climax that delays the resolution of the story and contains tension, while it increases the emotional blow that the viewer receives with the unexpected and tragic final surprise. Logically, the viewer is able to recognize this double game and the clues that hide ambivalent interpretations only when the story ends. It is only then that the recurring scene of the wardrobe acquires a new meaning: that of reminding us time and time again that the child will die, he is condemned to die. There is no alternative.

The text has a complex structure of puzzle in which there are six fragments. Three correspond with the scene of the wardrobe, two with the flashbacks of the first part, and one with the final outcome. The mise-en-scène is articulated in the same way in all of them: an image in black separates each unity, and after a small pause that puts full stop to the previous unit, there emerges the voice-over of the next one to string together the events.

The story is temporally divided in two parts, the past and the present. In the first part, there are temporal leaps between the present—represented by the wardrobe scene—and the past. There are two consecutive flashbacks in which they narrate the antecedents of the drama, that is, the series of circumstances that lead the boy to close himself in the wardrobe. The first flashback tells us about the loss of his family, the escape with the baby into the forest, the trap, and the persecution of the injured soldier to the house. Meanwhile, the second one shows us the trick of the child who hides his little sister in the chimney, and seeks for refuge. It ends when the boy closes himself in the wardrobe to hide himself from the enemy. Thus, the second part of the film starts with the scene of the wardrobe in the present that marks the beginning toward the final resolution of the events. Or, what is the same, time and action move forward from this moment on.

Instead of structuring it, the mise-en-scène is based on narrative economy. It uses wide shots to emphasize the insignificance of humans threatened by a hostile environment. The death of the parents is presented with two brief fixed general shots. From this moment, the images of the chase are unstable, and present a light swing. Sometimes they show the action from the ground, other times from the height of the child, but they always refer to an areal look that observes the development of the game. In the same way the forest, which is a key element in Berdejo's cinema, embraces the ruined building where the boy tries to hide. All these images show the film grain, and its faded texture produces an aged character that reminds us of documentaries and newsreels of the epoch.

The reframing is a compositional criterion that dominates the shots of the house, and metaphorically alludes to the idea of a mortal trap. The ruined vault from which we can see bombers fly, the pointed arches, the threshold of the doors, or the marks of the windows create a sensation of anguish that weighs over the story. Besides, the trembling look of the camera covers all these rough tracks, and shows what the composition allows. The space that is denied visibility has greater intensity than the showed one. The soundtrack contributes to this considerably. The trembling images are accompanied by off sounds that come from the countryside, and which give greater emotional intensity to the voyeuristic effect that the filmic apparatus creates.

In the third and last scene of the wardrobe there is an exact repetition of the initial images and sentences, which also coincides with the climax. A ray of light filters in the hiding place from where the main character overhears the conversation of his pursuer (voice of Henrik Feldmann) speaking on the radio. The shot shades into dark. Nothing can be heard for a long while. The danger passes, and the child thinks of his little sister. The voice-over orders him to get out of the wardrobe. Nevertheless, fate plays a trick on him. He slips on the blood coming from the enemy soldier´s injury he had caused, and he breaks his spinal column. It is war. The child has suffered the most gratuitous, unfair, and disproportionate punishment. For this, the mis-en-scène uses extreme close-ups, something that is practically missing from the rest of the film, and thus emphasizes three symbolic elements of this tough *leçon de vie*: the puddle of blood, the inverted portrait of the child Jesus, and the shot of the child on the floor.

The puddle of blood represents the crime committed. The child becomes an adult, and loses his purity when he injures the enemy. On the other hand, they establish a mirror relationship between the nadir shot of the inverted image of the child Jesus, and the overhead shot of the main character who watches from the floor. This juxtaposition illustrates the unexpected and tragic turn of events. The reverse side of the story locates the viewer, suddenly, in the war, whose logic does not understand privilege. All people, independent of their moral disposition or comitted crimes, may have to pay the greatest price.

Also, the inverted image of the child Jesus refers to the total loss of innocence. Although the act of protecting himself from the soldier may be understandable in a war situation, the faith that the main character child has in an infant figure, in that of Jesus, is an obvious show of purity and ingenuity. A few minutes before, the main character said the children's prayer to Jesus in the wardrobe. This gave him strength to resist, but now the son of God abandons him. There is no place for either faith, or hope. The hosts that are spread around the boy on the floor summarize the total loss of the pillars that sustained his life at one moment (family, equilibrium, faith). Now all that is left for him is facing grim reality.

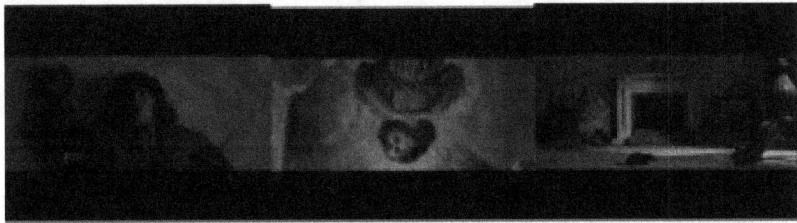

Obviously, the staging shows the radical change of circumstances, and makes use of the terrifying break of the spinal column to mark the death sentence. As the voice-over reminds us, from this moment on the rules of the game are different. Now the question is who will die first, him or his little sister devoured by rats—an eloquent insertion of a shot of the chimney shows the rodents prowling around. Then, a tracking shot rises and turns around the body of the child, and stops in an overhead shot, from where he seemes to be stretched out on the floor. The frame envelopes him as a kind of coffin that confirms the obscure prophecy of the beginning: *Tu est /tué*, you are dead.

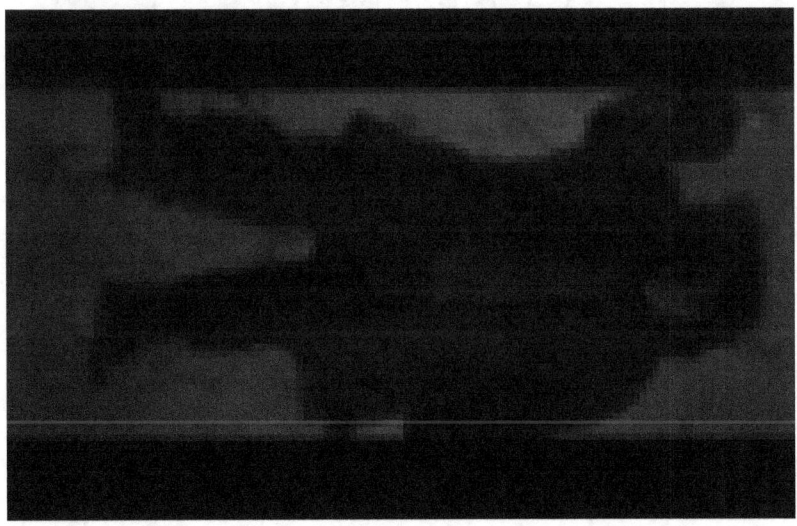

Beyond the Forest

The pun is a favourite tool of the director, and once again it appears in the title of this short film. *For(r)est in the des(s)ert* is a word play that contains the fundamental ideas of this story of brotherly love and science fiction. If we eliminate the letters in parenthesis as we read the title, we get "forest in the desert," which is a coded allusion to the two secret places where the brothers meet with the spacecraft. The forest, which is a fundamental element in Berdejo's cinema, is where Andy's mysterious disappearance takes place (Junio Valverde). It is also the place where Forrest turns to (voice of Alfonso Sánchez-Eguibar) to meet with the aliens. But if we take the title literally, it has another meaning, and it becomes somewhat ironic. It announces the final meeting as a "dessert," or ending of the narrative. This hypothesis gathers strength if we consider two inherent aspects of the story. In the first place, it is a children's story that aims to recover the innocence of the little ones. And in the second place, the secret codes and messages are a capital element in the magical universe of children. Thus, *dessert* may refer to the mysterious errand that Forrest asks Andy to bring to the spacecraft: a cream and caramel cake for him, which is his favorite dessert.

Like in tales, the voice-over of the heterodiegetic narrator (Paul B. Miller) is that of an adult who speaks in third person, and in English. His words explain the events approaching the naive point of view of Andy, a fifteen-year-old boy who embarks on a fantastic adventure to reunite with his brother Forrest, whom the aliens have abducted. The search is a game where the logic of the marvellous reigns.[76] Any everyday situation or element is likely to become something magical without losing any of its verisimilitude.

Nevertheless, we must emphasize that the lifestyle and the stereotypical situations of the US imagery represent normality. The shots of the town, of the flag, and the forest that appear in a circular way in the film are a good example of this happy Arcadia: just like the scenes *Golden Grahams* and *Da Frog* that reproduce the breakfast with cereals and the dissection class, respectively. In both cases, the mise-en-scène uses the high angle to show in detail the object of value, the cereals or the frog, in which one finds the message. In this children's play, the marvellous emerges from the ordinary.

---

76 Lenne, *Le cinéma "fantastique" et ses Mythologies*.

The structure of the narration is divided into units with titles: the prologue, *For(r)est in the des(s)ert*; the presentation, *Golden Grahams*; the climax, *The Frog*; the ending, *The Pickup*; and the epilogue, *The Reunion*. Nevertheless, the mise-en-scène radically distances itself from the classicism of the previous titles of Berdejo, and opts for miscellaneous audiovisual forms closer to postmodern cinema.

The animation, the photography, the drawings, the fragments of newsreels, and references to commercials make up the filmic texture. Except in case of animation or design, there is a manifest preoccupation with creating a washed-out effect of the film. Thus, the texture of the video remains clear in the shots that it borrowed from newsreels. With respect to the shot material, Berdejo makes use of tools that allow him to manipulate the appearance of the image, and distort its quality. This explains, for example, the over exposition in the shots of the town or the forest, the saturation of color in *Da Frog* or its absence in *Golden Grahams*, where by the way the tape shows the grain of the film. The commercial reminiscences of this scene are very eloquent in spite of the *dirtiness* of the film. There is no doubt that we find ourselves before a constructed text, whose quality brings forth the impulsivity of an amateur cameraman. Thanks to this intentional precipitation, the film obtains the freshness and agility that the story requires.

But above all, the collage reproduces the visual referents with which the main character grew up. The television, the commercial, the cartoons, and the rest of the visual sources form part of his personal baggage. With them and through them, he interprets and constructs the world that revolves around him. In summary, it is a way of approaching the childish world of Andy. The cartoons and the illustrations offer a beautiful example of the weight of the audiovisual imagery of children when it comes to understanding some events.

The animation of Luis Rojas is based on schematic illustrations that are very close to the style of children's drawing, and show the abduction exactly the way he imagines it. That is, on the basis of the way he saw it happen in movies, cartoons or comics of science fiction. But in fact, the film plays to deconstruct some preconcieved ideas and myths that derive from this imagery. Andy discovers that the extraterrestial kidnapping is produced in a natural way, without much paraphernalia. The staging uses a very simple tool with which Méliès played in the first years of cinema. It is the juxtaposition of two identical frames, with the exception that the second one misses the most important element, in this case the child. The same way and contrary to what many science fiction films would tell us, the aliens do not aim to sequester humans, but rather to save them from the destruction of the planet. A series of shots of catastrophies shown in the news are combined with the atmospheric soundtrack of *Alone Again, Naturally* by Gilver O´Sullivan, to evoke the loneliness that the boy feels without his brother. The image of a gigantic wave is frozen the moment before sweeping off a tiny man who is walking on the shore. This shot marks the turning point of the story, that is, the moment that Andy asks the extraterrestrials that they take him with Forrest.

Another of the aspects that recover the naive spirit of the main character is that he is in love. The drawings of James Jean are superimposed in a photographic slide show, and show his science teacher, Ika Masami, trying to fall asleep. This series of representations show the last and only memory that makes him hesitate the moment before leaving. He knows that he will never see her again. This brief impasse brings forth the childish innocence of the first love. In the ending, while Andy (Mcarthur Moser) and Forrest talk about the errand of the latter, an insignificant theme, the vessel approaches on the firmament. This final image refers to the imagery of the *Star Wars* saga (George Lucas).

Ma liberaci del male

Dio vi benedica a tutti by Luiso Berdejo, *Rio Puerco* by Borja Cobeaga, and *A Good Man* by Jorge Dorado, form part of *Limoncello*. The project was born as a consequence of an award that the Almería City Hall granted to Berdejo and Dorado for *The War*, and whose objective was to shoot a short western film. Each director has liberty when it comes to developing the story in their own way.

Dio vi benedica a tutti is a horror film that is developed under the aesthetic coordinates of western, in which some of Berdejo's constant themes are repeated: the children's story, the narration in voice-over, and the use of a foreign language, in this case Italian, to tell the story. Like in the rest of his works, the image in black embraces the first words of a heterodiegetic narrator, a boy whose voice-over invoques the divine protection for the protagonist couple. The image in black switches to a close-up in which, ironically, a cross falls. The mise-en-scène is classic, and limits itself to the embodiment of this strange adventure. On its part, the fact of using some characteristic features of fantastic cinema in a story that situates itself in the far west is nothing but a mere artiface to tell the story of a wonderful love.

Unlike the other children's tales of Berdejo, this is the first one where the hero is a woman. In fact, it is one of the few short films of the catalog where the leading role is female. Tiziana (Miriam Giovanelli) takes up this role and, except for the fact that it is not her that takes charge of killing, she acts like a man. Her beloved is gravely ill owing to a voodoo curse which has also turned her beloved Luigi (Eloi Yebra) into a complete fool.

Deciding that she wants to save them, the girl shows her courage by facing all kinds of tests. To start with, she resuscitates a dead man in a scene that mixes parody and gore film—an African sorcerer brings the barman to life, whose blood and sludge keeps spurting from all his body holes. Once she knows the identity of his killer, the young woman confronts him and, finally, she gets the map of the jewel box where the cursed dolls are kept. In all this time she directs the action, and Luigi obeys her and kills without much awareness of his actions. Under the spell, he repeats endlessly the love he feels for her.

In many children's tales, the kiss of a woman to an enchanted person, whose appearance is usually that of a disgusting animal, brings about his metamorphosis. The main character recovers his original human appearance. Generally, this kiss is the reward of the person's internal transformation, whose maldition is always synonymous with the punishment of a previois bad behavior. But on this occasion, the voodoo curse is only an excuse that serves to start off the action. What is really important is to recover the power of the kiss that symbolizes love for Luigi, and to a lesser degree, for the rest of her family. In summary, it is pure sentiment that has pushed Tiziana to confront the world in a ruthless and violent way. Thanks to the kiss, the story recovers the naive spirit of the children's tale.

Besides, the last kiss implies a sacrifice that she is aware of: the return to normality, and the corresponding reversal of roles. Tiziana loses her power over Luigi. He becomes the man of the house again, who continues to hide his emotions for her. Coinciding with this return to normalcy, the light of the sun acts as a magical element in the final scene. Besides witnessing a happy ending, it returns to the film the aesthetic coordinates of western by recovering the amplitude of the desert. Obscurity dominates throughout the film, facilitating the emergence of fantastic elements. Finally, the circular story closes itself in the same way it began: at the beginning, the couple digs out the barman under the stars, and in the ending, both dig out the jewel box under the rays of the sun.

Interview

How has Kimuak affected your professional trajectory?

Absolutely. I live in the United States, and my carreer developed here due to the short films that I made; thanks to them, I had the chance to shoot *The New Daughter*. If it hadn't been for Kimuak, my short films would not have had the diffusion they had, and I probably wouldn't be where I am right now. When I arrived in Los Angeles and started to show my short films, there were people who had already seen *La guerra* at international festivals thanks to the work that Kimuak had done for years. Borja Cobeaga was nominated for Oscar because Kimuak sent *Éramos pocos* to the Aspen International Festival in Colorado, and won an award there. The work of Kimuak has been fundamental for all of us.

The main characters of your short films are children. What does a child's character give you when it comes to telling a story?

Frankly, I don't know. In my short films there are also forests ... for me, a forest is very mysterious. I think that in a film there always should be suspense, even if it is a love story. No matter what story you tell, you don't have to know what will happen later. Maybe children bring me a new and unique way to see the world, which is always surprising. For me, a bicycle is a bicycle, but for a child, it is a whole universe. I like this fascination for the everyday, this innocent way of approaching things. There is a will to discover all, to see it for the first time. Besides, what you feel as a child is so real! *La guerra*, for example, would not have been the same with an adult.

Can we consider your short films as children's stories?

Yes, because one is about a story that the father tells his son, and how he interprets it. The other is a story about what is going on in the world, and how a child experiences it. The third one is a story about a boy who goes to another planet to search for his brother, and the last one is a short story of searching, love, and overcoming difficulties ... They are stories of children's adventures. Yes, they are fables. In all the stories that they read to us when we were little, there was a moment when the narrator said: "and he did as he said." For me, this is a brutal order. The first week I was here, a director told me: "we don't like to talk about things, we like to do them." I share this philosophy. My short films are children's stories about someone who flees from something, lives an adventure, and fights to get what they want. . . . *ya no puede caminar* is a short film about innocence. Deep down, it is like saying: "educate while you are on top, don't think that you become a leader, and that's it. You have to make a following of the case; the case lives with you, and it's your son." When I was little, one of my best friends, the painter Iñaki Arizmendi always said: "shall we do some adventure?" and we went off to seek adventures and live them. I think that when it comes to telling stories, this spirit of adventure that we forged with Iñaki has always imbued me.

Your short films have the flavor of fantastic, science fiction, and even horror films.

I don't think I have ever written a horror story. I like what diverges a little bit from the normal, perhaps because it is the way I have always considered life. Besides, I am very much connected with the supernatural, I find it quotidienne, it is not strange for me. I integrate it unconsciously and naturally in my stories. For me, falling in love with a girl you met at driving shool is just as normal as falling in love with a photo that you have found. I never think: "I will do something supernatural;" no, it is something that simply comes. I like to write for other people, because they ask me various things, and suddenly I surprise myself reading and documenting absurdities. But when I write my own things, there is always a supernatural touch to it, even if only a little, because it comes from me organically. I think what matters is to be honest with oneself, and keep doing what you like doing and what you would like to see, without trying to please other people.

How could we categorize . . . *ya no puede caminar?*

Although the film was presented at the Fantastic and Horror Film Week in Donostia-San Sebastián, I don't think that it is a horror film, even if it is terrifying. The project *La guerra* also won at the Horror Film Week in Donostia-San Sebastián. But neither *La guerra*, nor . . . *ya no puede caminar* properly fulfilled the clichés of the genre. . . . *ya no puede caminar* in fact speaks of human and family relationships, Basque matriarchy, where it's the mother who is in control, and how everything affects us when we are little. There is a little anecdote in . . . *ya no puede caminar*: when I was ten years old, I liked a girl from my school. I spent all my time fooling around there, and I always dreamt that she would one day show up where I was. Of course, this never happened, so when I made my first short film, I decided that she would show up. So, when the boy is taking the jars to the mountain hut, the girl that I waited so many years to come and find me suddenly shows up. I don't know how to categorize or classify it, frankly, but it is something that happens to me a lot with my scripts, so I usually tend to invent the genre for myself. I said that *For(r)est in the Des(s)ert* was a story of fraternal and extraterrestrial love, and the great Txemari Muñoz moved it into the Kimuak catalog that year.

In *...ya no puede caminar* Pacheco learns to relate with the world through the rules that his father teaches him.

More than rules, by following the advice of his father. If you make a story with children, their world is the home and the relationships that he establishes there. In *...ya no puede caminar* it is the mother and the father, no matter what kind of relationship you have with them. In *La guerra*, they were killed, but you still have your baby sister. In *For(r)est in the des(s)ert* you have your brother Andy, who tells you one thing and you, since you are older, don't want to pay attention to him. In *Dio vi benedica a tutti (Limoncello)* she fights to save her grandparents and her love... Truth is, yes. I promote marvellous figures such as the brothers, fraternal love, and grandparents. I vindicate the purity of family relationships, at least the way a child sees them.

In *La guerra*, the main character has to grow before the challenge he faces.

...ya no puede caminar is a story of innocence, in which closing the girl is a metaphor that means closing love. The child is afraid of love, and closes it to get used to it. *La guerra*, in turn, is cruder. With this title, I couldn't be indulgent. Each time I watch the film, I am appalled that the child should suffer so much. It seems gratuitous, but in the end you reconciliate with the short film, assume your anger, and say: "you couldn't tell this in any other way." It is the way it is because it has to be that way. You can't speak of war without a bad ending. It was also an exercise in anticinema. We made a list of everything they tell you you mustn't do, and with all those elements we tried to move the viewer: the camera didn't move—wide lenses, general shots—the voice-off—which speaks to you in second person as if you were the main character—it was scientific, and told you coldly what you saw. There was no music, and the climax is repeated twice... Our objective was to do everything badly and, in spite of it, to generate feelings. And I think we more than managed to do so.

You codirected this short film with Jorge Dorado. What was it like to work with him?

It is very simple. I gave him a story that I had written and he made some corrections. Then he gave me another story, and I made some corrections... it went like that until we got the script, and we decided to do it together. We plan to codirect a feature film some time, because we enjoyed a lot the work at *La guerra*. He gets to places where I can't, and I get to places where he can't. During the filming I was the script, and he was the video assistant, but in the end it didn't matter ... We didn't even have a clapperboard because we did not shoot with direct sound. And the order of sequences ... ? We had about twenty shots, and we knew them by heart ... We understood each other perfectly. Golden is like a brother to me.

What is your contribution to *La guerra*?

My contribution is more present in the script, and his in the formal character of the short film. Nevertheless, I wouldn't have written this story without him, and he wouldn't have shot it the way he did without me. We challenged each other mutually. I always incline more toward the script, and he leans toward shooting. For me, shooting is a process to get to the montage, and for him that is the more creative process. For me, writing is my life, and for him, it's a process to get to shooting. We did it all together, but it is true that I think of more things that a person or a voice-off can say, and he can see more angles and where to put the camera. I think that the most positive part of our collaboration is that together, we were more daring. This constant challenge allowed us to get to places where we couldn't have by ourselves.

Why did you use the second person indicative for the voice-over?

I really like instructions, norms, laws ... I like the fact that they exist. I find law and order intellectually exciting, although I do not necessarily think that they always have to be followed. I loved being in the head of this boy, who in reality is you, to whom they tell what happens and what he should do. We tried to do it as if it was a book of instructions, a bit like the credits of ... *ya no puede caminar*. Very cerebral, very cold. The original idea was that it should be a child who does the voice-off, who would talk to you as if you too were a child who is watching. But then we recorded the voice of reference with a French friend, and we listened to it so many times in the montage phase ... that we got fascinated. Besides, fate presented us a marvellous idea: the pronounciation of the second person of the present indicative of the verb to be in French, *tu est*, is similar to *tu*é, which means murdered, dead. It wasn't on purpose, but then we didn't want to change it. The short film starts by saying *tu* *est*. Koldo Zuazua, the producer, didn't like the idea that the film should be in French. As it is logical, he thinks more in terms of who will watch the film, and how people will understand it. I, however, think that short film is a kind of honesty. I think there is nothing more egoistic and pretentious than thinking about who will see what you are doing. The more personal your work, the more people it will reach, because it is honest. In the end, we managed to convince ZZ, we achieved that the short film should be in French because it takes place in France during the Second World War. Besides, the French language gives it a special atmosphere.

The staging is quite classic, and narrative economy dominates.

Imagine that you find a box with twenty photos of the Second World War, and you want to tell a story with them. How would you arrange them? The camera, although it always floats, only moves two times. First, when the child enters the house for the first time. And second, at the end, when the boy lies on the floor. In this moment, there is a host next to him because he has little Jesus everywhere; by his head, above . . . he knows about the prayer, but did not pay attention to it.

What are the references that appear in the short film?

Nothing directly that I could mention, besides World War Two documentaries in color. To achieve this texture, this blurred image, we used a technique in which the person, when he moves, leaves a halo that is not only behind, but before what will happen to him. If the person stays still, the colors are in their place. But if the person turns, or moves, there is something that moves before him, which accompanies him. They are three stills, the eights of a second, but it's there. This we did with David Tudela, the director of photography, after analyzing documentaries in color of the Second World War. When we found the place, we walked it a million times to decide where we should shoot each thing, and to get inspired ... Also, in the acknowledgements I included Richard Donner, because he gave me the idea of how to shoot the fall of the boy in the making of *The Omen* (Richard Donner, 1976). In this film, the scene in which Lee Remick falls is done against a wall. They reproduced the parquet in the wall, and she goes backward; if you put this very fast, it seems like she is falling and hitting herself very badly. When I saw it, I said to Golden: "we have to do this." He also wanted to add the name of Rossellini from *Germania, anno zero* (Germany, Year Zero, Roberto Rossellini, 1948). Since the time we knew that we would shoot among some ruins, I have watched this movie several times, and for him the story of the bombarded city was very inspirative. As a funny story, I'll tell you that one day when we were in Molinare, we saw a very good 3D that they made of some planes for another film, and we asked Koldo Zuazua: "What if we change this 3D and we make it very small, could you give us a plane in the distance?" Jorge Dorado was more ambitious, and he asked for three. In the end, we got what we wanted. The aircraft that appear are those from *Soldados de Salamina* (Soldiers of Salamina, David Trueba, 2003).

The staging of *For(r)est in the Des(s)ert* is very novel for its formal hybridization.

I don't think you should make a short film in order to show that you know how to do something well, but rather in order to learn. *For(r)est in the Des(s)ert* is a learning exercise which, frankly, I never believed would go outside of my house. I always make what I would like to watch. In this case, instead of fantasizing, I thought about the elements that I had within my reach: a fifteen-year-old child, an artist friend who paints pictures and always wanted to do animation, I have El Espinar—the forest of Segovia where I had shot ... *ya no puede caminar* —and I was going to go to the United States where I could shoot some scenes ... Therefore, with all these elements and with some others, I wrote the short film. I had no intention of being either avant-guard or cool; it was simply an experiment to learn to make different things. But then, the short film got a lot of recognition.

Dio vi benedica a tutti is a fantastic film with the aesthetic features of western.

It is a very dry short film. The rest of my short films are wet, which is an abstract concept that unconsciously helps the spectator. Desert movies are rather uncomfortable to watch, but if in turn the Indians cross the river, there is something internal that captures their attention, perhaps a family relationship related with the past in the placenta. I will not go into this although it is true that it exists. This short film is very much me, very fantastic, with people searching for dead bodies, speaking with them, it has this strange and bizarre humor at which sometimes only I and my friends laugh. The exact same story in a forest would have been totally Berdejo. What happens with this short film is that it is not my location, but it's my plot. It is a story that is completely mine in an environment that is totally not mine. As I have already commented, I take short films as learning processes and experimentation, and for me *Dio vi benedica a tuIti* became very interesting in this regard.

In the end, what is a short film for you?

It seems to me that it is an artistic expression in its own terms. I understand what it means to work for someone or the specific job that they hire you for; but when I sit down to create something for myself, I like to do whatever I feel like. I also paint. I think that making a film is just as creative and satisfactory as painting a picture. CREATE. For me, a short film is an exercise of freedom, a painting. Therefore, it has to be honest, personal, and it has to have some artistic boldness because if not, it seems to me that it lacks interest. For me, the short film is a tale. And since it is cheap, take risks! Don't try to copy something that you know (or think) that it functions. Make the short film that you yourself would like to see! *Un chien andalou* (Luis Buñuel, 1929) is a masterwork, one of the best films that have been ever made, and it's a short film. It is true that it was done with a lot of talent and a couple of balls as big as two rottening donkeys. I want to make more short films because there are stories that occur to me, and last ten minutes. I don't think it is a step toward something else; I think it's an end in itself.

Borja Cobeaga (Donostia-San Sebastián, 1977)

Cobeaga earned his degree in the first class of Audiovisual Communication at the University of the Basque Country (UPV/EHU), where he met his friend and also filmmaker Nacho Vigalondo. His first work in television was as direction assistant in the program *El submarino* of the Basque public television ETB. After that, he served as director of the program *Vaya Semanita*; as screenwriter of *Agitación + IVA*; as assistant director of *Made in China*, and carried out direction tasks in *Big Brother, Confianza ciega*, or *Territorio Champiñón*. In cinema, his collaboration in the script of the films *La máquina de bailar* (Dance Machine, Óscar Áibar, 2006) and *Amigos* . . . (Marcos Cabotá y Borja Manso, 2011) are noteworthy, as well as his direction of two feature films: *Pagafantas* (Friend Zone, 2009), for which he was nominated for the Goya Award for Best New Director, and *No controles* (Love Storming, 2010). Kimuak has selected four of his short films: *La primera vez* (2001), Éramos pocos (2005), the *Limoncello* episode titled *Rio Puerco* (2007), and *Un novio de mierda* (2010).

Filmography as Director

2013. *Democracia* (Democracy, short film)

2010. *No controles* (feature film)

2010. *Un novio de mierda* (short film)

2010. *Marco incomparable* (short film)

2009. *Pagafantas* (feature film)

2007. *Limoncello* (short film)

2005. **Éramos pocos** (short film)

2001. *La primera vez* (short film)

***Costumbrist* Portrait of Human Loneliness**

La primera vez and Éramos pocos are no doubt the most interesting short works of this filmmaker from Donostia-San Sebastián. They are two bittersweet comedies that elaborate on the observation of everyday details and types characteristic of *costumbrist* approaches. They have an aesthetic line that is closely connected with the comic sketch, and which has a generous presence in Spanish cinema. Both works perfectly adjust to the patterns that, according to Juan Antonio Ríos Carratalá, characterize the comic scetch in Spanish cinema.

> The interest in everyday and traditional atmospheres, the anonymous persons who become character types and become involved in simple everyday stories, humor—often combined with melodrama and tenderness—as an efficient form of

approaching a reality that is not always agreeable, and by definition is vulgar... But, above all, the interest in approaching a concrete, immediate and simple reality with a moderately critical attitude, and without transcendental eagerness, through a formula that allows an easy communication with the average viewer." [77]

La primera vez develops a small and unusual anecdote that Cobeaga, also author of the excellent script, envelops in fine humor and irony. The short film presents a completely anomalous situation that is nevertheless based on a practice surrounded by recognizable clichés: prostitution delivered to home. What is different here is that the client is not a man, but an elderly woman interpreted by a splendid Mariví Bilbao. After overcoming the initial surprise, both of the young gigoló contracted by Begoña (Aitor Beltrán) and the viewers themselves, the story will have another unexpected turn: the elderly woman is a virgin, and doesn't want to die without experiencing something that, according to everyone, is so marvellous.

The image that opens the short film, a general high angle view that features the small figure of the young man from the top of the stairs before a huge door, predicts with its almost expressionist composition (homage to one of the most emblematic frames of *Le Procès* [The Trial, 1962] by Orson Welles), the terror that the young man feels inside of the house. Once he enters this particular nightmare, the first part of the film centers on a conversation (or rather, a monologue by Begoña), which surprises and amuses with the absolute normalcy with which the inexperienced woman expresses herself before the embarrassed young man. The body language, verbosity and colloquial language of Mariví Bilbao, in clear contrast with the corporal stiffness of the young man, embody this character that the viewer cannot help but associate with the archetypal lady who lives next door. Begoña talks with absolute naturalness about the earwax that makes it difficult for her to hear, and explains the young man that she called the agency because she cannot find someone that would do her this favor in the old people's home. She then jokes about the (im)possibility of becoming pregnant: "What a blunder! Just imagine, with the age I have, and the many gossips that live here!".

---

[77] Ríos Carratalá, *Lo sainetesco en el cine español*, 16.

The essential weight of the dialogue is visually strengthened by an extremely simple mise-en-scène in the aesthetic code of the sitcom, which alternates a general shot of the situation with the classic formula of shot-countershot of both persons. The stillness of the staging confers on the scene an air of theatricality, to which the unity of time and space also contribute.

In effect, Cobeaga skillfully avoids any temporal ellipsis, and closes the possible escape of the terrified young man by confining him among the four walls of the elderly woman's bedroom. The young man nervously undresses in a very long general shot that seems to make time last forever, and gets in bed covering himself with the sheets up to the chin. In the meantime, in the background we can hear the carefree humming of the woman who is getting ready for the occasion in the next room. The erotic preparation of Begoña consist of supplying herself with a nightdress buttoned up until her neck, a knitted shawl, and a bag of hot water for her feet. The woman gets in bed and moves gently closer to him. The camera is positioned above as a witness-voyeur external to the action. From this omnipotent ubication, it completely diminishes the self-confidence of the young man, and renders the strange image even ridiculous.

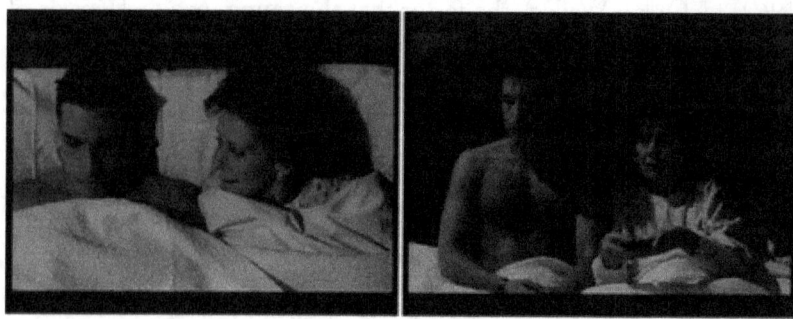

Before the intercourse, the young man turns off the light, and the screen becomes dark. Again, and without ellipsis, the black screen remains for ten seconds of suspense, when only the crackle of the sheets can be heard. Finally, the lights are turned on, and the young man accepts his incapacity to fulfill his task. Begoña is surprised, but assures him that she would wait, "and this I'm saying, because with this age of mine, I could kick the bucket any moment." The camera returns to its frontal position, and crudely and directly registers both of them seated in bed in front of the television. They lie next to each other without looking at each other in a long joint shot, which magisterially condenses the resigned frustration of the woman, and the confusion of the young man, lending the end of the short film a tender pathos.

Éramos pocos, once again written by Cobeaga himself this time together with Sergio Barrejón, follows the wake of its predecessor, and becomes a study of the most miserable face of humans. It is a portrait of the extreme to which man and women is able to go when they see themselves overcome by loneliness. When Joaquín's (Ramón Barea) wife abandons him and leaves him together with their son Fernando (Alejandro Tejería), he decides to get his mother-in-law Lourdes (Mariví Bilbao) out of the nursing home. From the moment of her arrival, the woman takes charge of cleaning the house, which by now is a pigsty, and prepares exquisite meals for the two slackers who do not lift a finger to help her. One day, however, during a phone conversation with his ex-wife, Joaquín discovers that the woman who lives with them is in fact not Lourdes; she is an elderly woman from the nursing home who was ready to become slave to these two egoistic idlers in order to escape her reclusion. Joaquín is at the point of confessing the truth to his son, Fernando, but when he sees the T-bone steaks the impostor has brought for lunch, he decides to let the sham continue.

In spite of the incredibilty of the unexpected final turn that dangerously borders on the improbable,[78] the bitter-sweet combination between the embarassing humor and the devastating drama provoques in the spectator a tender feeling of compassion for the characters.

The simple plot of Éramos pocos develops almost entirely in a domestic setting: the home of Joaquín and Fernando. The small details and gestures taken from the most everyday situations characterize these two persons that shamelessly embody the stereotype of the machista Spanish man who does not partake in the house work, and consider the female sex as no more than full-time housekeepers. Proof of this is the sequence in which father and son repeatedly attempt to squeeze a drop of coffee from the empty coffee pot, confused because the mother had

---

78   It is certainly difficult to imagine that neither the father, nor the son would recognize their mother-in-law and grandmother; that the woman would take refuge in the home of these two disoriented men, without knowing their intentions, without suspecting that neither of the two would notice the substitution; and that the residence personnel should authorize her exit without verifying her identity.

abandoned the home without making them breakfast; or the pathetic picture of the two sleeping on the sofa with the television on, and the living room spattered with bottles and empty potato chips bags.

After the arrival of the old woman at home, the narrative structure of the short film is weaved around a succession of shots that describe the cohabitation of the trio until the discovery of the fraud, and which emit a kind of humor that borders on cruelty. We refer to, for example, the gesture of Joaquín smelling and giving his approval of the sheets used by Fernando. Unable to find clean ones, he takes one from the mess on his bed to put them on the grandma's. The image of the men arguing as infantile vultures over the most delicious pieces of the first tortilla the grandma has made them; or the ruthless commentaries of the two men before the apparent stampede of the elderly woman after her first night in her new home. When Joaquín gets up from the sofa to urinate, and discovers that the bedroom of his mother-in-law (who left early to run errands) is empty, he bitterly laments: "we should have locked the door with the key," to which his son responds while he closes the fridge with a disappointed face: "*this one* hasn't left us anything either."

In contrast with the picturesqueness and the verbosity that normally characterize comedies that use *costumbrist* themes,[79] and which on occasion lean toward the coarsest variants of everyday language, Éramos pocos stands out for its laconic style. A verbal laconic style that seems to extend over photography, dominated by cold and naked that comes from the window, which plunges the characters in the shadows of a home where the chiaroscuro also reaches human behaviors.

The mise-en-scène is aesthetic, nevertheless, and Cobeaga's restrained realization overcomes the theatrical effect of *La primera vez*, and acquires here a more complete visual dimension. He uses general shots abundantly and jointly, in which the omnipresent corridors and doors that serve as markers of the domestic images presented. Only the formal construction of the last sequence escapes this pattern, and it is also the one that best condenses the bitter irony that comes off from the story. Joaquín, now aware of the lie, has to decide what to do with this impostor who has mastered to perfection the role of the maid that is expected of her. The false Lourdes and Fernando arrive from shopping, and Joaquín warns his son that he has something to tell him. Lourdes quickly goes in the kitchen, and leaves the two men on the threshold. Joaquín is on the point of telling Fernando the truth; however, the camera halts for a moment on the close-up of his profile of confused face, which from the doorpost looks inside the kitchen. Curious, Fernando urges him, and at this moment the image of the woman, blurred across the face of the boy, becomes clear before our eyes. "Lourdes," significantly caught by the diffuse contours of the two men in the foreground, shots toward Joaquín a look full of uncertainty, while she holds high a succulent steak, the only weapon of seduction to stay in this house that, even if it is a new prison, is still more agreeable than the decrepitude of the geriatric hospital.

The camera takes again for a second the shot of Joaquín, who is debating between ethics and necessity. Then it finally returns to the shot of father and son decisively entering the kitchen as if nothing had happened. A panoramic shot that covers the wall of the house hides the image of the now irrevocably reunited family from us, finishing it with the withdrawn camera, the representation of this strange incident. The sound, however, stays with Fernando's words in off, surprised why the butcher José Luis did not recognize grandma. And against a black

---

79 And in contradiction even with the feature films of Cobeaga himself, especially in No controles (2010), example of authentic verbal horror vacui.

background, Joaquín gives no importance to this detail, affirming that "José Luis is getting old, and he forgets things." It is an insuperable final irony that epitomizes the bittersweet reflection about human loneliness, and its consequences transmitted by the story.

Comedies on Order

The following two short films of Cobeaga, both made on order, aim to once again explore this *costumbrist* vein inspired by everyday events, although they do not reach the heights of his previous works. After the international success of Éramos pocos, Cobeaga shot *Rio Puerco*, a work that, together with pieces by Jorge C. Dorado (*A Good Man*) and Luiso Berdejo (*Dio vi benedica a tutti*), formed part of the choral short film *Limoncello* produced by Arsénico P.C., Common Films, Encanta Films, and Koldo Zuazua P.C., and promoted by the Almería International Festival of Short with the patronage of the Almería City Hall[80].

---

[80] After his Western Award for the best national production of the festival, they grant the director of the winning film a certain amount of money to finance the shooting in Almería of a short film of the western genre, which would be released in the following edition of the festival. As a result of this initiative, other titles of important Spanish filmmakers were produced, such as Peacemaker by Álex Pastor (2006) and

Although it is not as excellent as the previous works of its author, *Rio Puerco* is a segment of *Limoncello* that, from the very election of the title (in clear allusion to the three *Rios* by Howard Hawks and to *Rio Grande* by John Ford), it best employs the conventions of western, especially with regards to locations and characters. The authorities of a small town in the West (Álex Angulo, Gorka Otxoa, and Santiago Ugalde) tell to the sheriff, Mitch (Mauro Muñiz), that a telegram arrived at the saloon, and announced the visit of Governor Marshall. Worried about the image of the town, the three ask him to wash himself, given that he hadn't had contact with water for ten months. Mitch agrees, but only if he can sleep with Paulette (Marta Rubio), the manager of the saloon. At first, she resists functioning as a pawn in such an interchange, but then quickly falls into the man's arms. When the entire town congregates to receive the great notable, we discover that the telegram was nothing but a strategem by the woman to make Mitch take a bath. Aware that Mr. Marshall will never arrive, the couple drift back toward the bar, leaving the townsfolk and the orchestra waiting for the governor in vain.

Cobeaga moves away from the great feats of the heroes of the frontier, and once again submerges in a small, comical anecdote based on the most vulgar and routine elements of life in the West, in this case, the complicated issue of hygiene. Just like in **Éramos pocos**, the script aims to surprise with an unexpected final turn in which Paulette consults the hour of the arrival of the notable in a blank telegram. Nevertheless, just like it happened in the other short film, it seems to escape logic that the woman should have plotted such a conspiracy, when in the previous sequence we see her visibly excited by the confession that Mitch had gone ten months wearing the shirt she gave him as a present without taking it off.

In spite of the narrative simplicity of the piece, which sometimes verges on the category of a joke, the fine irony of its director stands out out in some moments of *Rio Puerco*. For example, in the wide shot that serves as background to the title, in which Cobeaga stretches the genre's conventions to the absurd when the sheriff gets on his horse at the exit of the police station to almost immediately get off it at the entrance of the saloon, which is situated just across the street. Or in the ending, there is an evident but nice wink at ¡*Bienvenido, Mister Marshall!* (Welcome Mr. Marshall!, Luis García Berlanga, 1952), which shows

---

The End by Eduardo Chapero-Jackson (2008).

the orchestra and the village people in their Sunday best waiting for a bigwig who will never arrive.

Un novio de mierda, produced by Notodofilmfest (online competition of compressed cinema), could pass for just another one of the many humoristic pieces that Cobeaga has directed during his time in television. Pablo (Ernesto Sevilla) goes up in the apartment of his ex-girlfriend Blanca (Bárbara Santa-Cruz) with the excuse of saying hello, although his real objective is to use her bathroom. She, knowing his revulsion of public bathrooms, reproaches him for his cheekiness. In order to get out of the embarrassing situation, he improvises an apology, and tells her that he came up to ask her to get back together again, which the girl accepts almost immediately.

Narratively structured as a sketch of somewhat more than three minutes, the short film benefits from the rhythm that results from a dynamic hand camera use, inspired by the semi-documentary aesthetics used by the sitcom *The Office* as a most paradigmatic example. Nevertheless, neither the mobility of the shots, with its sudden and abrupt zooms of reframing, nor the agile montage can mask the triviality of a plot that, in spite of having the characteristic features of the ironic humor of its author, falls short of his previous works.

Interview

In the majority of your comedies we can detect a bittersweet tone.

I remember that I gave the script of Éramos pocos to a friend and he told me that I could make a drama with it. This means that this bittersweet element is a point of departure. In effect, my films' points of departure could evolve into dramas or comedies. This is very evident in the feature film *Pagafantas*. As this bittersweet element is there at the beginning, it remains throughout the story. Because, in fact, you are telling a drama. The same happens with the comedies of Berlanga and Azcona. They are bittersweet comedies that, by the same token, could have evolved into a drama. I don't like comedy that is obvious. I like situational comedy; where the viewer laughs because they get to know the character. *La primera vez* and Éramos pocos don't provoke laughter in the first minutes, it will come little by little. Éramos pocos, like *Whisky* (Juan Pablo Rebella and Pablo Stoll, 2004), is a progressive comedy. The beginning does not have elements of comedy. The humor emerges when the characters find themselves caught in very unique situations.

How would you define the humor of your comedies?

It is a very serious humor. Very bitter. But there is also tenderness. Tenderness and pathos are a very real equation. I am not too interested in realism, although yes in verisimilitude. I always try to put myself in the situation of the characters that I imagine, and I live the writing process very much in the first person. My uncle, the cartoonist Juan Carlos Eguillor, used to tell me that every work should have a perfect mixture of cruelty and tenderness; elements that I like to work with very much. It is very cruel to put characters in very pathetic situations; but when they get to a certain moment, they inspire tenderness.

What are your main cinematographic inspirations?

They are very varied. You can be equally influenced by a video on Youtube, or a Tarkovski film, or even a small detail. Without going very far, Juancarlitros—one of the characters in the film *No controles*—was inspired by a video of a cat on Youtube. I grew up in a movie fan family—especially my mother—and classic American cinema is what influenced me most. The movies I most like are Howard Hawks's comedies. I wanted *La primera vez* to be a mixture between Hawks and Haneke. I aimed to fuse the dialogic rhythm of Hawks, with all those stomping dialogues, and the cruelty of Haneke. Nevertheless, possibly, the director I would most like to resemble is Alexander Payne. Almost all of his work inspires me: *Election* (1999), *About Schmidt* (2002) . . . I also like French comedy, from Louis de Funès to Francis Veber of *Le dîner de cons* (1998). My heros are very varied, crazy, and fiery.

There is a special sensibility with elderly people in your films. Why?

I was a little disillusioned, I was never happy with what I was doing, which is why I decided to apply the typical formula of writing about what you know. I lived in Bilbao with a seventy-year-old person, Agustina, the family cook all our lives. I come from a well-to-do family, and she by then no longer worked for us. She was part of the family; she nourished me! I found a lot of inspiration in her. Elderly people used to be very extreme persons with childish behaviors like jumping the line in supermarkets, but in turn, they were people with experience. These extremes seemed very good for comedy. In the end, contrast is the most important element of comedy (the annoying and the bland one; the fat and the thin one . . .). Since I decided to write about what I know, I started to do things that I most liked, I felt more identified, and I realized that the cliché was true. All the persons that Mariví Bilbao plays in my short films are inspired in Agustina. In conclusion, it's about taking a real situation, exaggerating it, and putting forth a question: And what if this happened to this character? For example, the question that we formed in Éramos pocos was this: What would happen if a father and a son were abandoned by the mother?

Mariví Bilbao is a fundamental actress for the short films of Kimuak.

I saw her in *La noche de autos* by Koldo Serra, who was just about to shoot *Amor de madre* with her. I liked her a lot. I saw her in Bilbao in the theater and in *Salto al vacío* (Jump Into the Void, Daniel Calparsoro, 1995). I thought that it would be incredible if such an energetic person spilled all this energy into sweetness. I got her address, sent her the script with my phone number, and she called me. When she started to play in the series *Aquí no hay quien viva*, they told her they had seen her in a short film where she played an elderly virgin. I was very happy to hear that. The fact that Mariví could earn fame and fortune thanks to acting in your work is the best that can happen to a short film director.

Something similar happens with Paco Sagarzazu

He is an actor that I would like to work with, I find him excellent. Like Txema Blasco.

The cinematography of Éramos pocos is faint and bluish. What did you mean to achieve with this mise-en-scène?

The idea has to do with the mixture of drama and comedy. In Éramos pocos I decided not to have a coherent plan in the mise-en-scène, and in some elements. On the one hand, I wanted the acting to be of a more comic terrain, and that the music is also something like a counterpoint. And, on the other hand, I took the decision that the photography and the entire staging would be related to the codes of drama. This marks a lot the tone of the film, certainly. It looked to me that the staging could be associated with another genre, and used as reference the photography of *L'emploi du temps* (Time Out, Laurent Cantet, 2001). Everything comes from this contrast.

In *La primera vez* the dialogue stands out, but in *Éramos pocos* the characters are rather laconic. This contrasts with the verbosity of costumbrist films.

I saw the movie *Whisky* when we were at the point of working on the sound in *Éramos pocos*, and I realized the many parallelisms that the mise-en-scène, the characters, the plot had... It influenced me a lot in the sound of the short film. During the shooting I realized that the dialogue was superfluous. I eliminated dialogues, and noticed that I said everything I wanted that way, and that it was sufficiently ambiguous. With regards to the montage, I aimed to achieve that within each scene, the rhythm would be very slow, but that the scenes would succeed very rapidly, at highest speed. *La primera vez* is more of a short film of dialogue, which could almost pass for a sketch.

In what way has the Oscar nomination benefited or harmed you?

At a more personal or mental level, yes it has had its dark sides. The impression that you arrived at the Oscar when you barely even started yet... I developed a certain obsession with not believeing it too much, and this lead to self-confidence issues. Besides, a week after the Oscars I shot *Rio Puerco*, the short film that I am least happy with. It was a tough blow psychologically. I started to think that the Oscar was tremendously accidental, that it happened to me, but it could have happened to any other person. It caused me insecurity. I was of low morale until the first script of *Pagafantas* came out. I had to accept that there wasn't going to come out a *Citizen Kane* (Orson Welles, 1941) the first time...

Nacho Vigalondo says that without the Oscar nomination, he would have never had the chance to make a feature film.

In my case it's not like that. *Pagafantas* was already underway when my nomination became public, there wouldn't have been differences with regards to the mechanics of production.

Do short films play an important role for making feature films?

It helps, but less than what people think. I think that in order for them to produce your first feature film, what they consider is the project that you have in your hands. The short film would imply 25 percent, and previous work another 25 percent. The short film is a guarantee for presentation; it shows that you are a person capable of writing scripts, and putting them on screen.

There are directors who make short films as a bridge to be able to make feature films. There are other directors, like Sánchez Arévalo, who combined the direction of feature films and short films. What is your way?

I continue to make short films. Between *Pagafantas* and *No controles*, I shot two short films; more than for the format, for professionalization. I would like to make a living from cinema, and for that, there is no other solution except making feature films. Nevertheless, the process is very long. After *Pagafantas*, I tried to continue making films, because I had ideas that could be turned into short films, and that is how I made *Marco Incomparable* and *Un novio de mierda*. They have nothing to do with the short films before, but they do have this spirit of immediacy that I miss from my time at television. I would not start a short film of the category of *Éramos pocos*, but I am always willing to, and I am amused a lot, by making short films. More than for experimentation, it's because the idea is there, and I feel like shooting it.

Rio Puerco and Un novio de mierda are commissioned works?

Rio Puerco comes from an award given to Koldo Zuazua, Luiso Berdejo, and Jorge C. Dorado with *La guerra* in Almería, which meant making a western the following year. They were not too thrilled about the idea but, since I like western so much, I convinced them, and we shot three short films grouped under the title *Limoncello*. *Rio Puerco*, my short film, was shot with the first draft, and wasn't sufficiently elaborated because it coincided with the Oscar nomination. But I was enthusiastic about the idea of shooting in Almería in widescreen format. The other short films, both Berdejo's and Dorado's are phenomenal. I feel a little guilty about insisting so much, and then not living up to the expectations of the circumstances. In case of *Un novio de mierda*, I had to make a short film as judge of Notodofilmfest, and I shot an idea that I had before. It is a hundred percent personal comedy, and digs into the comedy of the pathetic. Besides, I had the chance to give Ernesto Sevilla an opportunity; a splendid actor who moves around very well in these types of comedies.

In *Rio Puerco*, besides the western theme, there is a final turn.

In fact, it is pulling away from the manual when you don't know what to do. I was mistaken with the characterization of the sheriff, who should have been much filthier than he was. He looked just like anyone else; there was no contrast. And because the script was not well developed, the first idea was the turn, but I think it wasn't the type of story that needed a turn. I realized after the fact that in five minutes I couldn't do the ensemble film I aimed to make. It's ending is rushed, and a little disconcerting.

Un novio de mierda does have more of a touch of sketch.

Sometimes I miss sketches on television. It is something that contains this immediacy that the short film itself has. The quality of the film was given, because I had seen much comedy of a documentary type, and I felt like trying it. It is not a documentary, or a fake documentary, but it adopts this language. Besides, I had made a promotional piece of *Pagafantas*, which was like a false group therapy in which I had used this aesthetics and I aimed to work it a little more. Basically, it was about giving Ernesto Sevilla a somewhat longer role. In any case, I must confess that I was indeed experimenting with some elements.

How do you deal with the direction of actors?

I like to pick diverse and dispersed actors. I like this mixture. This has been present since *La primera vez*, and also in the feature films there exist this contrast: theater actors, humorists who work in television, actors who come from TV series ... I think that 80 percent of the work of actor direction is about the choice of the actors. Sometimes I write with a particular actor on mind, other times no, but the election is always very scrupulous. When it comes to facing the direction of actors, I feel very confident, and I like it to be an intellectual process; I am not at all sensory when I talk with the actors. The same way like in the script I intend to be very logical with what each character would do in each moment, and my behavior is the same in the dialogue with the actor. It is fundamental that they read the script from beginning to end, and transform the dialogues. From the perspective of dialogue, the script is never closed and this gives tranquility. It generates good atmosphere, and the actors feel comfortable. I direct in a very calculating way.

It is noteworthy that the profiles of supporting actors are very well elaborated.

They stand out, sometimes even too much. In *No controles* we overdid the carisma and importance we gave to Juancarlitros—Julián López—; who almost steals the show. As you can exaggerate with the crazier characters, I spare no expense when I portray secondary ones; so that there is a certain identification with the protagonists. If I made a main character with such extravagant features, it would be difficult for the viewer to identify with the story and follow it. Yes, there is clearly a strategy there. In the main characters there a more naturalist feature, which implies greater identification. When a crazy character occurs to me, I put them in a supporting role.

In your feature films the mixture between tenderness and cruelty continues to be potent.

Yes, this is how I like to work. It is a question of personal taste. In my comedies there always has to be poignancy and tenderness. It's the home brand. Like others like to shoot in black and white, I like this contrast between cruelty and tenderness.

Jon Garaño (Donostia-San Sebastián, 1974)

He earned his degree in Information Science at the University of the Basque Country (UPV/EHU), specializing in Journalism and Advertising in 1999. He studied film at the Sarobe Film School, the course 1999–2000, and later, between 2004 and 2005, at San Diego State University (SDSU), California. In 2001 he founded the production company Moriarti Produkzioak together with Jose Mari Goenaga, Aitor Arregi, Asier Acha, Xabier Berzosa, and Jorge Gil Munárriz. Since then, he has worked in many projects of the company, among which stand out the Basque language feature film *80 egunean* (For 80 Days, 2010), written and directed together with Jose Mari Goenaga; or the executive production of *Lucio* (2007), candidate for the Goya Awards the same year. Two of his documentary short films have been selected in the 2008 Kimuak catalog, *Asämara* and *On the Line*. The first one forms part of three documentaries that Moriarti made for the Guipuzcoan NGO Haurralde Fundazioa in Ethiopia. *On the Line* (2008) is a fake documentary about the volunteer border patrols who oversee the border between the United States and Mexico.

Filmography as Director

2011. *Urrezko eraztuna* (short film)

2011. *La casa del nazareno* (documentary)

2010. *80 egunean* (feature film)

2010. *Perurena* (documentary for TV)

2010. *El método Julio* (documentary)

2009. *Asämara* (documentary short film)

2008. *On the Line* (documentary short film)

2008. *FGM* (documentary short film)

2008. *Alamitou* (documentary short film)

2006. *Miramar Street* (short film)

2005. *The Dragon House* (documentary)

2004. *Bhutan's Secret* (documentary)

2003. *Sahara Marathon* (documentary)

2001. *Despedida* (short film)

Jon Garaño approaches audiovisual creation as an open space in which the frontier between formats and genres is not defined. The point of departure is to tell a story on the basis of real situations, be able to move the spectator for a while, and make them think about the themes presented. Form is at the service of this objective.

Walking on the Razor's Edge

On the Line is a fake documentary which revolves around the hybridization of three formats: the news program, the documentary, and the fiction. It relates the life of a volunteer border partol who oversees the Mexican-

American border in order to prevent the arrival of undocumented immigrants. The narrative and formal structure is divided into three consecutive units that correspond with three special audiovisual formats. The first two are a news program and a fragment of an interactive documentary, and the third one is fiction in its purest form. The function of the first two is to disguise the fictional character of the short film by using the audiovisual tools of formats linked to information. The third and only fragment reveals the trick, and aims to give credibility to the ending of the story, which could not be understood in the documentary or newsreel context.

Nevertheless, the strategy of masking remains rather ambiguous. On the one hand, the short film correctly uses the devices proper to news programs and the documentary, which is why, in principle, they guarantee the credibility of the narrated facts. But on the other hand, all the persons and the situations that emerge tend toward the excessive. They are portraits and contexts that are too close to the stereotype they present. Thus, on the one hand, Eugenia (Tania de la Cruz), the Mexican woman in the news, and on the other, Adam (Jeff Smallwood), his family, and his comrade Brian (Mikel Morris), in the documentary case, get too close to cliché. The shot of the patrol armed with a rifle, looking through his binocular with the American flag flying in the wind in the background is an illustrative example of this tendency to represent common images and places that are simply too perfect.

This game with correct codes becomes too ambivalent. The caricature profile of the characters, and the extreme situations of the story lead the spectator to question the real nature of the text, and finally, its verisimilitude. It becomes obvious that this representation cannot sustain itself for long. It is for this reason that the limit situation, toward which the story builds, suddenly and unexpectedly becomes a revelation. Coinciding with the ending, the spectator discovers that they are before a piece of fiction. Nothing of what has been narrated has to do with the historical world.

But in spite of Garaño's good work, the resolution of *On the Line* is not all that credible. This tour de force is by itself very complicated. In conclusion, we may affirm that the ending becomes little credible even in a fiction film, and could be considered as a thematic allegory.

The strategy of surprise only works for a short moment when the fatal outcome and the discovery of the fictional nature of the supposed documentary coincide, which is why the spectator does not have enough time to understand neither their new position, nor the abrupt ending of the story. Adam shoots the migrant woman without consideration, and with this act he crosses the border of morality and legality. His blindness leads him to kill her, and he tries to redeem his sin by adopting her son; a Mexican child who symbolizes all that he has been fighting against until then.

The short film departs from two real situations from the real world: that of the immigrants who cross the border, and that of the volunteer border patrols who defend them. Garaño proposes an extreme hypothesis about the encounter of these two realities. When it comes to representing each one of them, he chooses two devices that belong to the terrain of information with a double objective. On the one hand, to make evident the constructed and partial character of both the expository mode, and the interactive documentary. And on the other hand, to show that they can be used in an efficient way to narrate false events, but forcefully show the consequences of the collision between these two realities found in the real world. That way, the short film denounces the coldness with which the media treats the harsh reality of immigrants. This is an approach that immunizes the spectator, and comes from the expository mode. At the same time, it offers an interesting insight into the profile, lifestyle and values of the main characters, the border patrols, whom he endows with a human dimension.

Bill Nichols[81] affirms that the expository logic of the institutional format takes a distance with respect to the narrated events. The voice-over of the journalist constructs the story from the outside in order to guarantee, in theory, an aseptic and objective vision of the facts. The news presents the situation of the Mexican immigrants who try to cross the US border. Nowadays, many women undertake the dangerous trip; Eugenia is one of them. She speaks of her expectations while she holds her baby in her arms. The graphic effects of the news, and the music that accompanies the flashes and headlines turn the story into part of the daily spectatcle that the media offers. All this prevents the spectator from identifying with it, or with the immigrants who in this context are passive elements of the story.

In the same way, Nichols affirms that the interactive documentary distinguishes itself by trying to capture what happens in the real world with the greatest possible degree of verisimilitude. For this reason, he demonstrates the mediation of the device, and breaks the distance between the real world and the narrated one. In this case, the spectator accompanies the team of journalists who follow Adam on a workday as volunteer border patrol. They want to find out how he thinks, how he lives, and the reasons that motivate him to do what he does. The trembling and movements of the camera are intentional, its mission is to show the facts exactly the way the camera records them. They seek to leave the mediation uncovered when it comes to reproducing the story. Nevertheless, in this short film they minimize one of the characteristic features that distinguish the interactive documentary: the active participation of the journalist, or the technical team that participates in the shooting. In *On the Line*, the team does not clearly appear in the text; they are there, but they occupy the offscreen space. In fact, it is the main characters who reveal their presence when they turn to them as they talk. Adam suggests that they turn some music on in the car, or tells them that he will not use his rifle, and that his wife Jane (Yvette Filanc) tries to achieve that their smallest son loses his timidness and talks to them before the camera.

---

81 Nichols, Representing Reality.

An image in black separates the news program from the documentary, which starts with a shot of the US flag flying by the house on a sunny day. The piano melody composed by Pascal Gaigne accompanies these shots, on which the title of the short film is printed. Jane is preparing breakfast, and chats with the team about her children. It's a white, big working-class family. The woman is proud of her volunteer husband, and as a good wife, she brings Adam's lunch, and says goodbye to him with her baby in her arms. This mise-en-scène of the ideal family model of American society is opposed to Eugenia's figure. In fact, it is the inverse image of that of the immigrant. Eugenia is a single mother, and does not have the family structure that Jane has.

In the car, Adam chooses "You Are My Sunshine,"[82] a popular melody that forms part of the US patriotic imaginary, in order to enliven the trip. The conversation revolves around common places, he explains his motivations, how he does his job, affirms that he treats immigrants that he detains well, and that he uses the weapon as a deterrent. The montage alternates the images in motion of his declarations with the static shots of those of Brian. They both repeat the same ideas. When Adam arrives at the post, they tell him that a couple of Mexicans are crossing the border, and there is no trace of the police. He rushes to the place indicated, takes his rifle, and threatens the woman, who asks his mercy because she is carrying a child. For a second, Adam looks at the camera, and she takes advantage of the situation and tries to escape. He loses his temper, shoots, and kills her.

The fake documentary remains in the open from this moment on, and the expressive tools of fiction occupy its place in order to construct this drama with a kind of redemption that is not without ambiguity. Adam's anxiety is expressed through tools that betray that the character was constructed from fiction: the blurred focus of his face and a brusque zoom out show his expression of distress. He can neither talk nor shout. A sharp musical note covers his laments. Only the child's wailing can be heard from the distance. He takes him in his arms and takes him home.

The final sequence repeats some elements of the initial presentation, such as the musical melody, the desert environment, the immigrant woman's declarations, and the main character's home, in order to close

---

82 This is Louisiana's state song, that is, it is a kind of anthem that represents this state.

the drama. Besides, they imply the circularness of the plot. Eugenia's voice-off erupts over the images of the border spot, the musical melody and the sound of the wind. She recalls her expectations as Adam holds the child in front of the front door of his house. An inserted image brings in the shot of the news program, in which the woman talks about her desire to find a father for her son. She did it, even if it cost her life. Adam enters the house. A low-angle shot of the American flag flying against the gray sky gives the short film its final point. Without a doubt, one of the most interesting aspects of this short film is that the ending allows for two opposing interpretations.

On the one hand, this closure may be understood as redemption. After the death of Eugenia, Adam regrets his actions, and decides to take the baby with him in order to repair the damage he caused. The consequences of his actions, nevertheless, go further. He questions his principles, and takes notice of the other face of reality. Thus, the low-angle shot of the US flag symbolizes the union of all persons and all people under the same nation. This metaphor alludes to the origins of the country, where all its citizens arrived as immigrants in search of a better life.

On the contrary, this ending may be interpreted as a critique of double standards that US politics hides. Adam's guilt obliges him to take the child home with him. He made a mistake, and now he has to fix it. Nevertheless, he does not renounce his principles. The death of the immigrant woman was an accident. Eugenia is one more on the list of colateral damage caused by the defense of the United States from its enemies. In the near future, Adam would return to guard the border as every Saturday. Nothing has changed. As a compensation for the death of the mother, the government of the United States will take charge of offering a better future for the Mexican child. The low-angle shot of the flag symbolizes the obscure face of the land of opportunities, guarantor of peace and democracy in the world.

A Picture Is Worth a Thousand Words

Asämara is an experimental documentary that mixes some characteristics of the observational mode with a poetic discourse, whose objective is social criticism. The short film travels through a rural environment and a city to show the same reality: the harsh life conditions of Ethiopian girls and boys. In this country, there is no infancy. There is no future. Only present. Each day is a challenge, and one must work to eat. Life in the countryside is characterized by the physical hardness of its tasks. The boys fish, repair nets, or take care of the livestock, and the girls fetch water. On its part, the city represents the alienation of the human condition. It is a place where surviving is measured in astuteness, and cruelty isolates the weak. This is why the children of the street unite in order to create their own communities, and live in hollow holes in the ground, which look like tombs. The more fortunate ones make some small change by cleaning boots.

Following the inherent characteristics of the observational mode that Nichols[83] describes, words have been eliminated from this short film. There exists no extradiegetic narrator to lend cohesion to the story. One cannot hear the voice of those who have no voice, nor the opinions of the main characters. The camera limits itself to reproducing that which is happening. The montage reconstructs the real world by maintaining the spatial-temporal continuity of the scenes, and by excluding the narrator. In *Asämara*, the images turn into the axis of the story, and the ambient sound acquires great importance. Nevertheless, the experimental character of the short film allows it to skip a premise of the observational mode. The extradiegetic music is present in this work, although the echoes of the African landscape always impose themselves on it. Its function is emotive, and it highlights the poetic tone of the images.

The documentary is structured as a journey to the heart of misery, for which reason it juxtaposes a chain of situations in which each link is tougher than the one before. The emotional intensity of the realities represented goes in crescendo until it arrives to a final fragment where the montage shows all the faces of the children. It is true that the film repeats the same articulation when it comes to put in series each one of the situations that it presents during the story. Thus, after the presentation in a general shot, the montage focuses on showing the children working in the field, or surviving in the large city. The music disappears in the

---

83 Nichols, Representing Reality.

last shots of each fragment, and allows that the ambient sound invades the images. It is not about watching. It is about reflecting about what is shown. This effect remains especially eloquent during the scene of the water carriers. The music accompanies their steps to the fountain, and then disappears. The sound of the water and the detail shots of the tap and the bottles remind the spectator of the vital character of this task in Africa.

In this descent to hell, the traffic, the filth, and the frenetic sounds of the city mark a turning point with respect to the rural world. The shots of the cars that cross before the camera serve as a transition when it comes to showing the children of the big city. This image symbolizes childhood devoured by civilization. Precisely, cruelty reaches its maximum expression when the documentary halts at a naked adolescent who has lost his mind.

Life in a group emerges as a more humane alternative to survive in this jungle of asphalt. Proof of it is that the clan of street children integrates that which is different. The camera follows the boys to the holes in which they live, and shows them when they play football. One of them has a deformed foot, but this does not prevent him from participating in the game. The tough life conditions give greater intensity to these moments of happiness, and offer some kind of hope. Thus, the short film shows a positive aspect in the greatest mysery: solidarity and love to one's fellow human being, which children display with naturalness.

The ending of the short film is like a summary where all the main characters participate. It breaks the rule of the forbidden gaze[84] inherent

---

84 This norm refers to the fact that the witnesses who are situated in the real world can't look directly into the camera, because they thus break the distance with the spectator and the world that is represented. Besides, in the media, looking into the

to news texts, documentaries, and the dominant models of fiction. The shots of the girls and boys who have appeared in the story directly look into the camera. It is a deafening scream, a call for attention that transcends the limits of the screen. This rupture of the norm has as its objective to put a face on the victims of injustice that challenge the viewer.

Interview

On the Line focuses on a very central case, but its message is universal.

Yes, that's true. *On the Line* could have been set in Ceuta. Some local realities transcend their environment, and can be perfectly understood beyond their borders. In fact, we live very similar realities in the world. Here, in the United States, in France, or in Iran. Besides, if the films are about emotions, half the work is done already. Nevertheless, I don't think that when we sit down to make a work, we should think that it must be universal. But it is beyond doubt that it is present in our subconscious. In the end, you always have the intention that your work may be understood all over the world.

Although you have directed hybrid short films like *Urrezko eraztuna*, normally you work in the area of the documentary. What do you think of narrative modes?

First, we should define what a documentary is. It is not easy. But I do distinguish it from the report. A report, essentially, has an informative character. Its finality consists in offering information. I think that a documentary should be informative and emotional. Besides information, the documentary has to offer something more. In any case, the differences are not limited to the shot of the content; there are also formal differences. From a formal point of view, reports are very similar. The words structure the report in an expositive way. So much so that the images only illustrate what the text expresses. The documentary, on the other hand, offers the chance to reflect these realities in another way. It can also become expository, but through other cinematographic tools. On the other hand, the report possesses a very strong link with current affairs. The documentary does not have such a tight relation; it

---

camera is a symbol of power, of authority, which remains the privilege of journalists or presenters who, in theory, tell us what is happening in the world with rigor and objectivity.

should be contemplated in ten or twenty years without losing validity. The report, the expository mode predominates in television, where there are hardly any real documentaries. In any case, I like documentaries, but also reports.

In certain cases, the frontier between the documentary and the report is very diffuse.

I completely agree. It is the case of the documentaries of Errol Morris, for example. The estructure of his documentaries is very similar to that of reports, certainly. Although we can find amusement, normally his characters talk directly in the camera. In spite of everything, the documentaries of Morris achieve a transcendence that reports cannot reach. It does not limit itself solely to information, but offers something more.

What are the characteristic features of the short film *On the Line*?

In *On the Line* we must consider two things. On the one hand, the theme that it is about. And on the other hand, the form. The topic arose when I lived in San Diego. This US city is close to Tijuana. On the border. Every day there were news about illegal immigration into the United States, and it occurred to me that I should shoot something about this issue; to a great extent because there was a unique character who was very attractive to me. His name was Andrew Jiménez, and he was the leader of the volunteers who guard the border and prevent that illegal inmigrants enter. He was of Latino origin, and his attitude surprised me. I had the intention of shooting a documentary about it with a Colombian friend but, finally, the project didn't come through. Nevertheless, I recovered the topic for *On the Line*. With regards to the form, I must admit that I like playing with the forms of documentary and fiction. The short film, thus, is a fiction with documentary form. It's a fake documentary. Nevertheless, in spite of being a fiction, it documents a certain reality.

Gaining the spectator's credibility is essential for the message to be effective.

Although all the characters who appear in the short film are actors—even if not professionals—their testimonies are real. I collected testimonies that I compiled in the press, radio, and other documents to give veracity to the documentary. It was an arduous work of documentation. Behind all these words, there hides a tough reality. *On the Line* is a fake documentary; it is similar to *Forgotten Silver* (Peter Jackson and Costa Botes, 1995). My intention was to make the spectator believe from the beginning that they were watching a real story. To the extent that the short film advances, there are signs that betray its falseness. When the illegal immigrant appears, for example, to had been on television. Some viewers take notice of the falseness of the documentary in that exact moment. But the crucial scene is that of the shot. It is then that all the doubts about the verisimilitude of the documentary dissipate. My objective was to construct a verosimile story. And in a certain way I think I have achieved it.

The final outcome, this radical change of attitude of the main character, does it subtract certain credibility from the main character?

I tried to bring this situation to the personal realm. I wanted to know what I would have done in these circumstances. Probably, the most credible scenario would have been that the main character, after killing the illegal immigrant, escapes and leaves the child die in her arms. But, on the other hand, I thought that in such an extreme situation as this, one could also generate a very different attitude. Also, there was another thing that I wanted to transmit through this resolution of the story. Like us or any country that receives immigrants, Americans must recognize the importance immigrants bring; they have to realize that they are essential. They cannot but have to accept their arrival. And I wanted to reflect on this in a very subtle way. It is for this reason that we ended the story with a low angle shot of the US flag. I think that this shot has not been correctly interpreted. It was understood as a criticism. Possibly I erred in the form of expressing the message, but this is what I wanted to transmit. In short, that those who cross the border are now part of the country.

Through the images of the title credits you show the harsh reality.

Yes, effectively. They are real images of the situation that we show in the short film. By including these images at the end, I tried to reveal the harsh reality that exists through the fiction presented in *On the Line*. The short film is a re-creation, and the final images show the documentary character of the design. We cannot give the closing images the same importance as the fiction exposed before. Nevertheless, this ending implies a very clear reflection: the film is not real, but through it there exists a brutal reality. This photography proves just that. That which the short film relates should be understood metaphorically. There may be no immigrants who die of shots like this one, but people are dying. Because to the extent that the number of volunteers who watch over the border between the US and Mexico increases, the difficulties of immigrants to cross it become graver. They choose more dangerous spots to cross it, they get lost, they are hungry and thirsty . . . and as a consequence, many of them die in the attempt. This is exactly what some NGOs are condemning in the United States. Besides, the volunteers are armed. They say they don't use the arms. But if that is so, why do they carry them?

At a formal level, the camera moves a lot. Especially at the beginning of the short film.

There are certain conventions—documentaries are shot with a camera on the shoulder; they barely make use of montage; the persons speak to the camera, and so forth—which I use with the intention of diffusing my ideas. Even the shooting scene served me some of these conventions to underline the documentary character of the short film. After the shooting, the shots become more static, and everything changes. From this precise moment on, the more experienced viewer understands that they are watching a piece of fiction.

Asämara is a completely different documentary. It is experimental, has a poetic character, and fuses music and images in a balanced way. How would you define it?

In this case, I think that it is important to explain how the documentary emerged. It was commissioned by the NGO Haurralde Fundazioa. Its idea was to shoot a documentary about children who suffer difficulties in Ethiopia. The situation is terrible, and many of them are forced to work. It was a very tough topic, but it needed a different light. Thus, we decided to give the topic an original formal treatment, and we opted for a documentary with a poetic tone. It seemed interesting to us to treat such a harsh a reality through this style. Perhaps so that there is a great contrast.

What does formal experimentation contribute to the story?

I aimed to reflect a harsh and difficult reality in a different way. At the end of the day, I think this is the function of this documentary. Besides, the documentary has this bottleneck structure. At the beginning, it is very open. The children are at a lake, and the atmosphere does not seem very oppressive. Nevertheless, we already see some children working. A little later other children appear working with livestock, but still with a lot of air. Slowly, while the children are still immersed in a rural environment, the images start to have less air. Everything ends in the suffocating atmosphere of the city; in these tomb-shaped homes. This was precisely my intention; to maintain a certain formal preciosity, but to gradually harshening the images.

Is there a reason for intensifying the harshness in the part of the city?

It is important to show people the path that the children follow from the countryside to the city. The children, attracted by what they see on television, abandon the countryside and emigrate to Addis Ababa. They think that in the capital of this country they will find a great many opportunities. Nevertheless, they arrive at the city, and there is nothing but poverty. They scratch a living in the street or in the holes that seem holes in deplorable condition. My intention was to treat this terrible reality. The city, more than a dream, is a nightmare.

In spite of everything, there is a ray of hope in this severe world. Particularly, in the scenes where the children play soccer.

They are very young, but they got used to suffering. Although they are poor, they still maintain their dignity, and they don't want us to see them solely as miserable children. It is possible that soccer represents this spirit of rebelliousness before their destiny. The drama of the naked child who wanders about the streets of the city is something habitual in Ethiopia. Nevertheless, many try to live in such a dignified way as possible. It is this way of facing the harsh reality.

What do the children's looks transmit at the end of the documentary?

We spend the whole documentary watching them. And, in the end, they watch us. We haven't seen anything more than a postcard. A harsh but beautiful reality. But . . . what do they see in us? This is the crucial question. We see postcards. Landscapes and children. Nevertheless, at the shadow of these postcards there are also children who can watch like us. The children don't look into the camera intently, they look at the viewer. To remind us that, in the end, they too are human beings. What do they see? I have no answer for this question. It is possible that they reach out to our conscience.

It is laudable to reflect the messages through new formal channels. Nevertheless, this attitude may result in problems in the task of interpretation.

There exists this danger, and I am perfectly aware of it. But, on some occasion, one must make decisions and accept that, in all likelihood, your message will not arrive to everyone. Nevertheless, once this is accepted, the objective is that the message reaches the greatest possible number of people.

Why did you eliminate words from *Asämara?*

On the one hand, it is a formal option. And on the other, the children who are the main characters of the documentary are persons to whom words were denied. We found it interesting to reflect over this. They can't speak, but they can see us. They can challenge us.

Awards are important in the trajectory of a short film. Your works have won awards in festivals all over the world.

When you start a project, you never have awards on your mind. You want to express what you feel the best way you can. This is your only concern. Sometimes, your films arrive to the public and win awards. And many other times they don't. I honestly think that it is counterproductive to think about awards while you are making a film. Because if you do so, you would surely end up making a film without a soul. There are short films designed to win awards, and they even get what they want. Nevertheless, normally, it is clearly different when a short film is designed to win awards, and when it comes from the guts of its author.

Your two short films selected by Kimuak are documentaries of social criticism. Is this a coincidence or a declaration of intentions?

I think that reports should be objective. But documentaries, in turn, must be subjective. In a documentary, the author's point of view must emerge. In this sense, in the majority of documentaries there is almost always social criticism. Because, in the end, in each documentary the author reflects his or her thoughts. Their feelings. Consequently, the author has the moral obligation to appear critical before a reality that seems unjust. It is true therefore that in a great part of my short films, there exists criticism of social significance. But this is a reflection of the vision I have of the world. Each one of us makes the films they feel. I think that the character of short films is tightly related with the identity of its author. I think that what's most important is to shed light on your point of view. Reflect the things the way you see them. Without lecturing, of course. In sum, I show you this reality in this way, but this doesn't mean that it is that way. The only thing I say is that I see it this way. And, therefore, I make use of cinema or fiction to tell it from my point of view. In a certain way, the documentary reflects the vision of its director. It might not be the truth, but it is certainly my truth.

Jose Mari Goenaga (Ordizia, 1976)

Goenaga earned his degree in Business Administration and Management with specialization in Marketing at Deusto University (DU) in 1999. He spent part of his last semester at the Manchester Metropolitan University (MMU). He started his film studies at the Sarobe Film School, and completed his training with a course on cinematographic direction at the International School of Cinema and Television (EICTV) in San Antonio de los Baños, Cuba, in 2003. In 2001, he founded the production company Moriarti Produkzioak together with Jon Garaño,

Aitor Arregi, Asier Acha, Xabier Berzosa, and Jorge Gil Munárriz. From this moment on, his career developed prolifically, and he had tackled as diverse genres as fiction, documentary, and animation; the Basque language feature film *80 egunean* (For 80 Days, 2010) with Jon Garaño; and the documentary *Lucio* (2007) with Aitor Arregi, which was nominated for the Goya Awards in that same year. Two of his single authored works as screenwriter and director have been selected by Kimuak, *Tercero B* (2002) and *Sintonía* (2005), and he is the director and editor of a third *Lagun mina* (2011), whose script was written by Aitor Arregi. The rest of his filmography as director includes *Ayer te dejaré* (2002), and the documentary *Trabajando juntos* (2002), both in digital format. As member of Moriarti, he has been producer of the short film *Urrezko Eraztuna* (2011), of the documentary short films *Asämara* and *FGM*, and the television documentary *Perurena* (2010). He was also executive producer of *On the Line* (2008), and of the two television documentaries *Sahara Marathon* (2004) and *The Dragon House*. They are all audiovisual productions directed by Jon Garaño.

Filmography as Director

2011. *Lagun mina* (short film)

2010. *80 egunean* (feature film)

2007. *Lucio* (documentary feature film)

2005. *Sintonía* (short film)

2004. *Supertramps* (animation feature film)

2002. *Tercero B* (short film)

2000. *Compartiendo Glenda* (short film)

Goenaga's style is characterized by minimalist stories. He uses very concrete situations in which two or three characters participate, and of whom he constructs an exhaustive portrait with few details. The parallel editing or crosscutting is always present in his works, and he likes open-ended conclusions. He is an expert of cinema of pure genres as well as the hybridization of new formats.

Nothing Is What It Seems

The narrative structure of *Tercero B* is quite innovative in the Kimuak selection. It is the only short film that alternates various points of view, through which it plays with focalization and narrative strategies. It tells the story of a robbery and a murder which involves Irene (Blanca Portillo), the victim, the thief (Ramón Agirre), and Irene's authoritarian and sinister mother (Mariví Bilbao), who is stabbed to death. The parallel editing shows the points of view of the young woman and the thief: a woman goes to the beach by herself, there she sees a man who seems trustworthy, and asks him to watch over her things while she goes for a swim. By the time she comes back from the water, he had disappeared. Each one of the characters interprets this fact in a different way on the basis of their intentions, desires, and expectations.

The story develops through the collision of these points of view, which leads to the final situation where the thief and the victim meet at home. This last scene is presented from a neutral point of view: it does not favor either one of the two characters. With regards to this question, it must be emphasized that in spite of the alternation of the various points of views, the events succeed through external focalization, that is, they take place in front of the spectator. There is no narrator character to focalize their testimony, nor is there an omniscient narrator. The text keeps giving the viewer the information believed to be necessary in any moment, and it does so in function of the narrative strategy about what the story articulates. The first part plays with the element of surprise. Irene projects a romantic aura on her encounter, and the thief entertains the possibility that he can get some money out of the situation. Both of them run into an unpleasant surprise, which marks a change in the narrative strategy of the text. The final outcome remains open, and becomes marked by intrigue. The kitchen door closes, hiding the result of the deadly fight between the two main characters.

There is no doubt that this short film is an exercise that masterfully combines narrative structure and mis-en-scène. Generally, and owing to above all the duration and the format, the short film focuses on a single point of view, on a single event, or a single theme. Goenaga does not only alternate various points of view, but also goes unraveling unexpected aspects of the characters' lives, or the situations in which they live. The result is a richer and more complex narrative that reveals the hidden, harrowing, and miserable face of all three: of Irene, of the mother, and to a lesser degree, of the thief. Among all of them, however, stands out the delirious portrayal of the main character.

The text presents Irene as an innocent, kindhearted, and meek woman who has sacrificed her personal life to take care of her mother. The elderly woman is an authoritarian and dominant figure who takes advantage of the fact that her daughter depends on her economically, and restricts her liberty. The thief's call awakens the young woman's romantic fantasies, and develops expectations of a happy future with a man who can save her from her prison. This feminine portrait borders on the limits of normalcy, and evokes children's fairy tales in which the world is divided between princesses, witches, dragons, and heroes that save them. In spite of the opposition of his mother, Irene goes on the date, ignoring the fact that it was a strategy on part of the man to distance her from home, and to rob the house while she is away waiting for him.

The second part shows the thief's point of view, who discovers the real psychopathic nature of Irene. The man begins to search the house, and finds the sinister childhood room of Irene, where the pictures and the furniture are covered with a transparent plastic sheet. It is Irene's room, and portrays her trauma: she lives frozen in her childhood, lost under the authoritative presence of her mother. But he also finds the mother, who is dead. Irene did not hesitate to get rid of her in the most expeditive way. Now she has returned home, and only one of them will get out of the situation alive.

On her part, the mother is a woman who enjoys subduing her daughter. She lives anchored in the past, as the ID card shows that appears for a moment in the cafe, although her situation and quality of life have changed substantially. The house is practically in ruins, although it maintains a shadow of splendor and position of a gone by era. The woman controls her scarce fortune to keep her daughter next to her. Out of pure egoism, she did not allow her daughter to grow up, to confront real life, and now the mother pays the consequences. The masculine character is not excellent from start to finish, either. He is a middle-aged man without a penny to his name who spends his time robbing people, defenseless women, and the elderly as an insignificant petty thief. He will also pay the consequences of his miserable way of life.

Tercero B mixes the genre of family drama with thriller. It stands out above all for recovering the identificational features of this genre, and for subtly paying homage to Hitchcock. Just like the master, Goenaga plays with perspectives, and with the information he gives the viewer in order to go from surprise to intrigue. Besides, he takes some of his stylistic elements[85] when it comes to articulating the staging of the short film: Pascal Gaigne's music that introduces the film refers to Hichcock's melodies, and submerges the viewer in a mysterious atmosphere; the high angle shot that shows the moment Irene recognizes the trick, and which the British director used in the same way in his films; the play of lights and shadows that Hitchcock recovered from German expressionist cinema, and which he introduced in his filmography to create a disturbing atmosphere; and the theatrical sets of the living room where the murder takes place. It is a scene full of elements that refer to the cinema of the master of suspense, and whose function is to create the idea of a trap: the great mirror of the room, the arches, the red curtains and the baroque sofas are an ideal scene for this drama starred by a deranged mother and a frenetic daughter.

Nevertheless, without a doubt the most interesting reference with regards to the work of Hitchcock are the parallelisms established with his short film *Psycho* (1960). There exists a similarity between Irene and Norman Bates (Anthony Perkins), the main character of *Psycho*, but also between the split shadow of the mother of Norman, and the mother

---

85 François Truffaut conducted a long interview with Alfred Hitchcock, which features the emblematic style and characteristics referred here. See Truffaut, El cine según Hitchcock.

of Irene. A reasonable resemblance between the decorations of the homes where the events take place, and even the presence of the thief, a female thief in case of *Psycho*, which perturbs the familiar equilibrium and starts off the drama.

On the Air

Sintonía is a *rara avis* in Kimuak. It is one of the two romantic comedies of the catalog that lacks the bittersweet flavor that characterizes the majority of the comical short films of the program. Nevertheless, it has a particular feature: the parochial nuance with which Goenaga completes the profile of the universal archetype of the protagonist of this type of comedies. He (Joxean Bengoetxea) adds the features of the prototypical Basque man, timid and incapable of dealing with a woman face to face, to the rest of the characteristic features proper to the repertoire of romantic comedy: a man with few social skills for approaching a woman and who, from this position of insecurity, provokes a chain of misundertsandings and faux pas when he tries to do so. Nevertheless, there is another element that differentiates this type of masculine persona from others: his way of looking at the woman is subtle and delicate. He contemplates the details of the face and the back of the neck of the young woman. It is a clean look, it is neither lecherous nor aggressive; he shows a healthy interest to know the beautiful woman. In summary, the masculine persona is a man with interests that go beyond sexual attraction, which makes it especially attractive.

She (Tania de la Cruz) is a resolute South American young woman without problems of communication. Her behavior responds to the patterns of the feminine persona of this country. At the beginning she is elusive and irritated with the man, but in the end, by chance or not, she ends up yielding. Or at least this is what the outcome of the short film makes us believe.

The main theme of *Sintonía* is, as he affirms, to take risks before the possibilities that life offers us. But the fear of failure, of rejection, paralyzes our spontaneity. The film is sarcastic about the two levels of discourse that the main character presents: that of words, and that of facts. Also, *Sintonía* is a metaphor of the search for someone with whom one can "connect," or "tune in to." The soundtrack's role is to make visible this idea, when it shows the encounter of the two main characters. In the middle of the traffic jam on the highway, he sees that the girl in the car next to him has her scarf stuck outside the door. He tries to warn her, but she is absorbed in singing. Then he starts to tune in to radio channels, while a slow tracking shot approaches her; the music's lyrics match the girl's lips. Finally, he has found her.

It also remains obvious that the radio program is the main thread of the plot both with regards to stringing the events, and the development of the mise-en-scène. In this short film, the soundtrack gains greater importance than the images. The film plays with the sound montage to express the attitudes and feelings of the characters in this situation and, in general, the difficulties of communication that exist in contemporary society. From the beginning, the staging takes care of making visible the anonymity and the security that the radio offers to people when they publicly reveal their most intimate feelings.

María's (Vito Rogado) voice-off confesses against an image in black that she has fallen in love at first sight with a man that she barely knows. We see her back (Leire Orella), her voice through is talking with the radio presenter (Unai García) who, skeptical with regards to love at first sight, starts the music *You're the One* by Tracy Chapman from her 2002 album of the same name. The same one that the young woman sings, which alludes to the fact that she is unique and that he, finally, has found her. The title of the short film is in black. From this moment on, the soundtrack receives the harmonization of different radio channels that continue as a background over a tracking shot that, from a light high angle shot, takes us to the car of the main character.

The radio program takes a leading role in the relationship that is established between them. The story plays with the fact that she does not know that he is observing her, and that he hides his identity behind a false name, Manolo Ezeiza, which he borrowes from the sign on a minivan in the line. The impunity of the waves is key for him to try to approach her. When the radio presenter offers the opportunity to call, he takes advantage of it. His awkwardness becomes obvious. She realizes that the driver next to her car is the man from the radio, and she turns off the device. This gesture is equivalent to cutting the communication. At the beginning, she rejects him angrily, but her curiosity pushes her to tune in to the program again. The sincerity, and the raw but noble character of the man coincide with the lyrics of the music. Aware that life is presenting him an opportunity, he proposes to her to meet up at the next gas station.

Fortune intervenes in the last scene. The woman's car is on reserve fuel, and she has to stop regardless. Surprised to see that the car stops, and terrified before the impossibility of talking to her, the man shyly looks at the ground. She blurts out that she is there because she needs to fill up. Nevertheless, in the last shot the woman returns to start a conversation, and just like him, she decides to take risks.

A Non-Encounter

Lagun mina distances itself from the classic mise-en-scène of fiction in order to expose the cultural differences that exist between Ekaitz (Eriz Alberdi) and Román (Diego Santos), using the expressive tools of interactive documentary. This paradigm aims to reproduce the presented world by highlighting the mediation of the reproducing machine, and that of the human team that is behind the camera. Only through this mechanism does it obtain a veridical version of the represented facts. Following the interactive pattern, the text shows the tracks of the camera in a clear manner and by using easy tools, almost amateur ones, through those that activate a calculated realist strategy. There are four key elements that are insistently used: the use of a zoom that aims to correct the framing clumsily; the constant trembling of the device; the insertion of images over the voice-off of the testimonies; or the brusque change of focus that allows the highlighting of a person, and leave the other in the background without changing the scene. The mediation is very explicit, because the persons look into the camera, thus breaking the distance with regards to the viewer. Besides, in a given moment the voice-off of the journalist, which can be heard from behind the camera, asks something from Ekaitz, who answers with naturalness.

The crosscutting shows the two persons' points of view, and thus strings the story together. Both appear before the camera, and contribute their vision about the other, and their expectations about friendship that, supposedly, exists between them. Beyond the evident differences of the acting of both, the staging uses a tool that makes it clear from the first moment the impossibility of communication that exists between them. The short film uses two languages in an alternative manner and without any oral translation, Basque and Spanish. Besides, the text shows the disposition and necessity of the Colombian man to integrate in the world of his friend through the language. Román starts to learn Euskera, while Ekaitz does not make any effort to get closer to the Colombian. Everthing suggests that he has no intention to be his friend.

The story of friendship between the two starts when Ekaitz, a young Basque man and Román, a Colombian immigrant meet in a hostel. They spend a few but intensive days together, and they say goodbye as friends forever. The problem arises from the way each one of them interpret the value of their friendship from their cultural context. The distance remains clear in the first scene of the short film, Román enters naked in the room, while Ekaitz feels a little inhibited before him. The Colombian man frequently calls his friend, he tells him his intimate problems, and has a very open and positive attitude toward him and toward Basques. Ekaitz is a cold and distant person who needs a lot of time to trust someone. When Román visits him, he tries to get rid of him in a bad way. The Colombian takes notice of that. He says goodbye to Ekaitz making him think that he will take the night bus to return to Madrid. The mise-en-scène connects the shots of Román at the station during the night, leaving temporal leaps visible. This series puts an end to a brief encounter that the Colombian man ingeniously interpreted as a real friendship, when in fact it was a one-off and fleeting relationship.

The choice of the devices of the interactive documentary responds to the necessity to tackle a contemporary theme from a format that is more realist than fiction. For this, they use expressive tools that reproduce a real situation in the most naturalist way possible. Although in this short film, the point of departure is falsified. That is, it is not a real situation that may be known through this type of documentary look. It is a fictitious situation that is constructed by using these visual codes with the aim of achieveing the greatest degree of verisimilitude possible.

Arriving to this point, *Lagun mina* is also an exercise in a style that fits within the audiovisual hybridization that dominates the contemporary panorama. The border between formats (fiction, documentary, news program) or between genres (horror, comedy, fantastic film) ceased to exist approximately a decade ago. Hybridization has become a creative alternative to generate new formats that actualize old models, and which question the topics that have always interested the directors, critics and students of cinema. This short film once again proves that all audiovisual product is a constructed discourse; that there are no formats more truthful or authentic than others. Tackling a fiction through this mise-en-scène that shows the intervention of the director in the represented situation is a kind of return of the debate over realism. In this context, the documentary loses its original value, and becomes just another form of telling a story: a form that becomes more effective and innovative when it comes to presenting a fiction under another appearance.

Interview

In your short films, there are always two main characters around whom the story is centered. What is the reason behind that?

I couldn't explain that exactly. Considering the brevity of short films, I am interested in showing the moment in which the two persons enter into contact. I don't know why. I am not able to analyze it, but I recognize that this is something that is recurrent in my work. I always need to show the moment in which the relationship between two persons emerges. And, after that, its development. The same way, I try to achieve that the viewer does not get lost, that they can follow the events with interest. Maybe all is owing to the fact that I feel the necessity that in my stories everything should remain very clear.

Tercero B is a thriller that recovers the spirit of the classic movies of the genre; a film with clear references to Hitchcock's cinema.

It wasn't something conscious. Nevertheless, I grew up watching Hitchcock movies, and it is true that I like his way of telling a story. Many times, suspense is a language rather than a genre. A way of telling things. And in this sense, I feel comfortable applying these codes. In case of *Tercero B*, the influence of Hitchcock's works is very explicit. *Sintonía*, although it is a romantic comedy, is also narrated by keeping the codes of suspense. In the end, this generates a complicity between viewers and the main characters. A kind of identification.

Is your first work an homage to *Psycho*?

It could be an homage. But to say the truth, it wasn't anything deliberate. I realized it in the writing phase of the script. The origins of the story of *Tercero B* is an urban legend. In this urban legend, the woman who has trusted her belongings on an unknown person goes on a date with him to get her keys back, and after waiting for him outside and seeing that he doesn't come, she returns home and sees that it has been broken into. The story ended there. Later, I decided to develop it and add to it two perspectives. Thus, I did not write the script thinking about *Psycho*. But obviously it is one of my favorite films, and it must have had an influence. In fact, there are many shared elements. The game with the spectator, above all: at the beginning there is total identification with a character, then with another, and in the end, everything ends with a final turn.

How did you tackle the technical aspects of the film?

I didn't have much experience when I shot *Tercero B*. It was no doubt the first time I did something relevant in the world of short films. But I was much supported, and many decisions were taken by the production company Moriarti. Both in the technical aspects as well as the sound effects, Jon Garaño and Xabier Berzosa influenced me a lot. They advised me that I should give the story a more obscure tone. And what regards to the music, Bernard Herrmann was one of the names I told Pascal Gaigne to have on mind when it comes to the composition of the soundtrack.

In the first part, the spectator knows the same thing as the character. But in the second, although he has more information than the character, part of this information is false, and you play with it to create suspense. You project false expectations.

I like it that the spectator should get totally identified with a character, and then break this a little later. In *Tercero B*, I aimed to play with ellipsis, and leave to the spectator the task of filling the voids; projecting false expectations to malinterpret the events, so that the surprise is even greater. The intention was that the viewer thinks what would happen when the thief meets with the mother. I wanted the viewer to interpret that the old woman had fallen asleep. It is when the robber discovers her lifeless body that the spectator ties up all ends. It is then that the viewer realizes that something happened that they weren't told, and had been left out.

Although it is a thriller, the drama that develops around Irene is noteworthy; the character played by Blanca Portillo.

I had to achieve that the viewer identifies with Irene. I needed that the woman should have something that makes her vulnerable. It was a form of making the viewer feel pity for her. I was not much interested in portraying a person who is totally deranged; I wanted to achieve that the viewer was aware that the character has her motives for doing what she does. I am interested in the genre, but not the genre that simplifies the characters as much as possible. I prefer giving them a little dramatic touch. I suppose it is for this reason that I introduced this little story. It can be that, keeping the principal plot in mind, maybe it doesn't have that much weight, but it is important for me that it is there.

Your idea of suspense is certainly unique.

I am happy with suspense when it is a realist suspense. I like it when there is suspense in the films of directors who a priori are not considered directors of suspense. For example, I am fascinated by how Kieslowski sometimes treats suspense. He departs from very real situations, but he generates suspense in the form of articulating the story. In this sense, with the counterpoint that Irene's drama implies, I try to transfer the generic coordinates from their habitual universe into a more realist terrain.

In *Sintonía*, the radio program becomes the main thread of the story. Its listeners confess desires and feelings anonymously. Is this a way of talking about the lack of communication?

I am not a great friend of metaphors but, when I structured the script, I took the cars as metaphors for persons. And the persons who are inside are like our real selves. Even though we live surrounded by people, we have difficulty connecting, tuning in, with someone, and reach their interior. We see people talking on the radio and the phone, but we don't see anyone directly approaching another person. I wanted to show how two persons, in principle, isolated from each other, tune in to each other, and direct communication gets established between them. Also, there is a reflection on the incapacity that we sometimes have to open toward others or that others open toward us. This shyness ...

A specifically Basque shyness?

I didn't make this as something specifically cultural, but I have been repeatedly told that the person is very Basque. The truth is that, when I developed the story, I wanted it to have a universal character. What happens is that in the end you are Basque, you put your personality into this character in a certain way, and the result is that they tell you that it is very Basque. In any case, my intention was to make a universal reflection.

The mise-en-scène is very delicate. It shows details such as the detail shot of the woman caressing her nape.

I had the intention to give warmth to the sequence of the gas station; something that contrasts with the rest of the film. This, if we consider the photography—treatment of light, and so on—is very obvious. In sum, I was looking for something more carnal, something more physical. Until then, we saw everything through glasses. In fact, the characters appeared reframed in the windows of the cars. The gesture of the nape, on the other hand, wanted to show something physical. It was about giving the scene a warmth that the rest didn't have.

Warmth hides under the shyness of the couple.

I don't like characters who are too tough or cold. I always want them to have some tenderness. Life can be harsh in some things, but there is also a lot of tenderness, and I like that it should surface in persons. When I talked about the project, there were people who took it to a sexual terrain, but I preferred to keep it in a more naive terrain. I wanted to avoid entering in something more specifically sexual.

She becomes uncomfortable with him, his attitude looks invasive to her. Nevertheless, in the end, it is her who takes the initiative, who takes risks.

Her discomfort is related to the composition that she has made of Josean Bengoetxea's character. She responds to the prudent, or falsely prudent attitude that the masculine character shows. The guy throws the stone, but hides the hand. He calls the radio by phone, but then he remains silent; they ask him his name, and he gives a false one . . . In spite of everything I considered that, with face to the viewer, it was better that she would take the initiative. Because, after showing her his interest, he gives her total liberty to act. I thought that this was nicer than continuing to insist. He now sowed the ground. Now it depends on the girl, and she is free to decide what to do. The girl is in the end happy that she was running out of gas.

Chance is determining?

Totally. Nevertheless, the fact that she should stay without gas and need to stop at the gas station was simply a final turn. I wanted to isolate persons to make them enter in contact through the radio. And in the end, I wanted them to have an encounter. It was the beginning of something and the story ended there. Chance was the consequence of going along with the steps that the internal structure of the short film marked for us.

Lagun mina forms part of the project *What about Columbus* directed and produced by Lander Camarero, and is about how the same story is told in a different way depending on the characteristics of each culture. Could you tell us about this project, and about how this short film fits in that project?

What this short film contributes is a Basque perspective. In this case, the intention was that some of our cultural aspects should be present in the film. Specifically, Lander Camarero asked from us an adaptation of a fragment of *The Little Prince*—the part where the Little Prince meets with the fox. I proposed Aitor Arregi as screenwriter, and from the beginning we refused to make a literal adaptation of the story. In that fragment, the fox wanted the Little Prince to become his friend. It was noteworthy for us that the Little Prince and the fox did not consider their friendship on the same level; it gave the sensation that the fox showed more involvement. On this basis, it seemed interesting to us to show that every person has a different way of measuring friendship. And that, as a consequence, sometimes there are conflicts. In order to reflect about this question in the short film, Aitor Arregi recommended a personal experience that happens to many people. You go away, you meet someone, and you invite him or her to come and visit whenever they want. But when this becomes reality, you feel that you are invaded. Therefore, in *Lagun mina*, we aimed to investigate the reasons why in such situations we always feel very uncomfortable.

Is this a criticism of the way Basques are?

What we didn't want was portraying a friend who is a pain in the neck. In the first versions of the script, it seemed that it could turn into those typical movies about someone who is visited by a pain in the neck friend. We also wanted to give the story a cultural prism. Obviously, this implies self-criticism. We always accept positive things more easily, of course. We really like it when someone comes from abroad and tells us: "You Basques are closed at the beginning, but then you are very cool." Yes, this also exists. I don't doubt it. But there is also another aspect of ours that is more bitter. It was in the end about breaking with this myth that is so widespread among us, which says that it's difficult for a Basque to open up, but when he does so, it's for the rest of their lives.

If we make a comparison between the two main characters of the short film, does the portrayal of Ekaitz seem perhaps too cruel?

There was in the script of the short film a final gesture by Ekaitz that would redeem him, but it seemed to us that it could be interpreted as moralistic. And both Aitor and I wanted to avoid as much as possible the moral tone that *The Little Prince* has. We liked the fact that eliminating this last scene gave the story a cruder character. Nevertheless, it is true that with this tough ending that reveals Ekaitz's desire to get rid of Román, the viewer ends up identifying with the latter.

Does the fact that you are part of the production company Moriarti influence your cinema?

I wanted to highlight the importance of the group. Obviously, each one of the members of Moriarti have their own vision, and this remains very clear in the short films; given that the projects of long duration, with some exceptions, have been codirected. In this sense, I think that in the short films—the majority of which was directed by a single director—it shows better where each one of us is headed. Nevertheless, it is about short films in which everyone has had an opinion. It seems like only because I directed them, I invented everything that's in my short films, but it's not the case. In all my work the influence of my colleagues in Moriarti is very much present.

Is there a common denominator to the Moriarti brand?

It's a little too early to talk about it, but I think that the group, with the passage of time, continues to acquire a personality. I do have the impression that in our work we try to make sure that there is some tenderness in them. Maybe it is very tacky—he laughs—but we try to endow our characters with an affectionate side, and certain human warmth. Many times, this comes through a specific kind of humor. I don't think we are people who make comedy at all. In any case, we make an effort to imprint a very characteristic sense of humor on what we tell.

What is the difference between your cinema and that of Jon Garaño?

Garaño gives more importance to forms, without forgetting the substance, of course. Perhaps I pay more attention and focus to the script and to the characters. Garaño focuses more on realization itself, on its formal aspect. In *On the Line* or *Asämara*, for example, form is a very important and essential part of the short film. In *Sintonía, Tercero B...* form is important, but the content is fundamental. Garaño plays more with forms. There is a much clearer communication between the forms and what he relates in his short films. I think I have a more classic style than Garaño. In my short films, it is evident that the story takes precendece over the rest.

Tinieblas González (Ourense, 1972)

At the age of four, he moved to Llodio in the province of Alava with his family. He wrote short stories and poems inspired by late Gothic literature in an autodidactic and multifaceted way. His first domestic audiovisual work, *Tripas* (1989) is a pastiche of two hours elaborated on the basis of horror film fragments. He studied in the Basque Institute of New Careers in Bilbao, and it is there where he made the amateur documentary *A matanza do porco*. His three short films form a part of the Kimuak catalog. *Por un infante difunto* (1998) is his first work in 35mm and won, among others, the best short film at the XXXVII International Critic's Week of the Cannes Film Festival. The second, *The Raven* (1999), was inspired by the homonymous poem by Poe; and the last one, *Ecosistema* (2003) provides an obscure vision of the family. In 2002 he started the project of his first feature film *Raíces de sangre*, which he didn't finish. Shot in 2010, *ASD. Alma sin dueño* (Underground) was a great failure for the director. The production company Alma Ata obtained the rights of the film, and in order to get public subsidies, they launched it with another title *Sin Alma*, with an unauthorized montage. Tinieblas González lives and works in Los Angeles, United States.

Filmography as Director

2010. *ASD. Alma sin dueño* (feature film)
2003. *Ecosistema* (short film)
2002. *Raíces de sangre* (unfinished feature film)
1999. *The Raven* (short film)
1998. *Por un infante difunto* (short film)
1991. *A matanza do porco* (documentary)

Horror film and drama hybridize in his three short films in which the characters live locked up in claustrophobic universes, and without hope. The family as an alienating institution is one of his recurrent themes. His main characters, usually children, suffer the consequences of the lack of love, and the lack of family structure.

Once Upon a Time There Was a Boy Who Looked at the World through His Window

Por un infante difunto is a children's horror story with autobiographical color [86] and social critique. It narrates the anxious challenge that Julio (Jon Ander Ariz), a boy who lives in a dysfunctional family, find himself obliged to face. Because of it, his attitude to life will change radically. His family consists of an alcoholic and abusive father (Mikel Olabarria), and a submissive and timid mother (Esther Villar). Both project their frustrations on the child, who takes refuge in his room to watch the world from his window. It is the only place where he feels safe.

---

86 The director refers to his family in the final titles credits in the following words: "And most especially: to my Father, for being an alcoholic, and throwing me out from home. And for my Mother, for offering me 18 years of cohabitation with my father, for giving me a small part of the heritage and then throwing me out from home, so that she can live with another alcoholic."

Like in many children's tales, the mother sends him to run an errand, and the boy is confronted with the cruelty with which society punishes him for being poor. His wandering in the street starts with an image that announces the virtual death of the boy, that is, the loss of innocence. The composition of this shot stands out for its strange beauty. It is a general shot which, from a light high view offers an unusual view of the street: an iron pivot from which two iron chains hang on the side occupies the center of the image. A little lower and in the foreground, there is another one. In the background one can see the boy crossing the deserted street. This composition alludes to a sepulture from which one can observe from afar the figure of the boy walking alone. The sound of the wind and the ring of the bells of a nearby church break the silence, and seal the chronicle of an announced death. The loss of innocence is confronted by his encounter with the butcher. Julio pays the toll of poverty and marginalization, and his amputated hand is the visible symbol of the social stigma that will accompany him for the rest of his life.

The story is circular. It starts with the image of the boy showing his back to the viewer. The light inundates this image, whose careful composition evokes the protraits of the Romantic German painter Caspar David Friedrich (1774–1840), *Woman at a Window* (1822), but most of all *The Wanderer Above the Mist* (1818), which add an air of mystery

and loneliness to the boy. He presents himself as an ethereal being who seems to want to take hold of the external world with his hands. His look is clean and innocent. Nevertheless, this image is radically reversed in the ending, and makes the transformation visible: Julio passes into the adult world in a violent and unfair way, which is why he observes the world with different eyes, those of wrath. At home, he shoots a direct and inquisitive look at his parents, and he discovers that they too have suffered the mutilation. Furious, he forcefully clenches his fist while he scans the street from the window. The radical contrast between the two attitudes is also illustrated through the soundtrack. The sweet musical melody of the presentation is substituted by the intensive sound of the electric guitar.

It becomes obvious that Julio's look is the axis around which the mise-en-scène revolves. It is through that look that the short story projects the boy's point of view, and his change of attitude. Besides, it is the corollary that filters the looks of depreciation that he receives from the rest of the characters. People show themselves from a light low angle shot, which, besides justifying the height of the child, highlight his feelings of guilt and inferiority before the rest.

 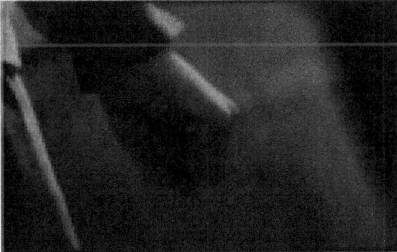

Shot in black and white, the illumination recovers the spirit of German expressionism at the hands of the director of photography, Unax Mendia. The shadows project themselves magistrally in all the spaces of the home, and show the idea of a prison. They also offer a miserable treatment of the parents. A beam of light emphasizes the extreme neglect of a slovenly man who sits in an armchair in front of the television, while the semi-darkness portrays the mother, whose face always appears partially covered by a shadow that shows the weight of her anguished existence. Within this tortuous logic, the look of the boy is combined with the expressionist illumination, the extreme angulations and the careful composition of the shots, which are used to make the environment that he inhabits visible.

The objective of the staging is to create a twisted image of the world. In this way, the obscure universe in which the action happens is situated on the fragile border between the real and the imaginary. The family drama becomes a horror story whose evolution is marked by a special effect, rudimentary and naive, which reveals the taste of the director for exhibiting the mechanisms of the film: a flash in black and white, which is accompanied by a loud crash. This tool results especially effective, for example, when it is combined with an exaggerated subjective zoom in, which illustrates the moment the mother discovers the empty plate in the fridge.

But without a doubt, the greatest degree of deformity is produced in the scene at the butcher's. Julio enters the shop, and finds there three housewives who look at him with depreciation, and amuse themselves by making comments about his family. The mise-en-scène uses shot devices that alternate the image in order to undress the three heartless harpies, and to get closer to the child's perspective. Thus, the lenses like the wide-angle lens deforms the proportions of their features, the lightly inclined frames betray the disequilibrium of the ladies, the illumination accentuates their ugliness, and the soundtrack reproduces the distorted echo of their voices.

Similarly, the butcher (Mikel Albisu) and his sinister establishment has a grotesque appearance. The characterization of the butcher reminds us of the main character of *Der letzte Mann* (The Last Laugh, Friedrich Wilhelm Murnau, 1924), the caretaker played by Emil Jannings. On his part, the butcher consciously evokes *Delicatessen* (Marc Caro and

Jean-Pierre Jeunet, 1991)[87]. The sum of this imagery contributes to the creation of a horrorific and sinister atmosphere. As a premonition, the shot locates Julio turning his back to the camera, and in front of the counter on which the butcher rests an immense knife. The boy stutters and tries to explain himself, but the butcher swings his weapon and cuts one of his fingers. From this moment on, the montage alternates the deformed images of the women's faces who smirk at him, and those of the butcher, who burns the child's finger while he tries to yell forcefully. Nevertheless, the shriek falls silent. The hysterical laughs and a celestial music impose themselves over the images. A tear falls over the face of the boy. As a climax to the scene, the butcher nails the mutilated finger and the mother's note on a plank that reads "On account."

Romantic Melancholy

Tinieblas González and Karra Elejalde wrote the script of this short film on the basis of the poem *The Raven* (1845) by Edgar Allan Poe. The adaptation keeps the same structure as the original. Divided into three acts that are separated through a fade to black, the staging of the short film alternates two ways of presenting the ode. On the one hand, the voice-off of Poe (Gary Piquer) in first person recites verses accompanied by suggestive images like, for example, the specter of the apparition of the deceased woman. On the other hand, the camera follows the theatrical acting of the main character, while he recites the verses of his conversation with the bird.

The writer closes himself in the room, which is converted into a mausoleum, to dedicate his existence to the memory of the deceased woman. The musical leitmotiv that evokes Leonor is associated with each of the apparitions of the image of the beloved woman, the picture, the flashback and the hallucinations that torture Poe. This musical composition is the work of Kike Suárez Alba, and stands out for its subtleness. On its part, the portrait of the beloved is one of the hallmarks of fantasic cinema[88] a ghostly surface through which the dead enter in the world of the living. It is thus that the sweet face of the picture leads to the luminous memory of Leonor (Savitri Ceballos) in life.

---

87 The reference is more thematic than iconographic. Delicatessen narrates the story of a butcher, a miserable usurer who, in spite of economic hardship, always manages to get by, because he nourishes himself from the flesh of his debtors.
88 Leutrat, Vida de fantasmas.

In effect, this portrayal dominates the room, whose Baroque decoration recovers the saturated red, and the iconography of the horror films of Hammer Films. Owing to the careful work of the setting of the artistic direction, and the chiaroscuro of Unax Mendia's photography, the spectator is carried back in time to the classic imagery of British cinema, with which the story gains a touch of authenticity. In the exterior decoration, in turn, a bluish tone glides over the snowed landscape that surrounds the mansion; it is a nearby forest where the woman is buried. The cemetery reproduces the suggestive imagery of *Monastery Graveyard in the Snow* (1818–1819) by Caspar David Friedrich, the Romantic German painter, whose disturbing atmosphere is transferred to the forest that surrounds the mansion. Death transforms the woods into a sinister place in which the branches of the trees reach toward the sky over a sea of snow.

Both inside the mansion and outside there is a strong contrast between lights and shadows, which respond to the necessity to highlight the looks of the main characters. That of Poe is full of profound melancholy, and is lost outside on the fields. Counter-posing this, Leonor sends a seductive invitation to her husband so that he passes over to the other world. It is a tracking look that is materialized in the breathtaking aerial camera that evokes the subjective vision of this tormented spirit. Decided upon meeting her beloved, she flies over the immense lonely landscape. Just like in the previous short film, the look of the persons is a key element in González's mise-en-scène.

The subjective look of the raven flies over the woods, and stops in front of the mansion to start the story. The staging uses two elements to present it: the constant movement of the camera, and the presence of numerous overhead shots, or high angle shots, which emphasize the point of view of the sinister animal. This look stays during the conversation between bird and writer, in which the low-angle shots lend them even more power, if it is at all possible. Although the high angle view is more effective than the movement as it gives the bird a majestic air, which is a characteristic feature of demonic creatures. Throughout the story, there are three high angle shots that have a specific importance. The first two are related with the entrance of the raven in the house, and the third one with the death of the main character. The first one emphasizes the line that separates two worlds, the frontier between the real and the imaginary, life and death. This limit corresponds with the image of the crack on the threshold of the door of the balcony. Poe opens it in response to the mysterious knocks that come from outside. The second high angle shot shows the gaze of the bird before it enters through the window. At this point we should remember that in the folklore and literature of horror, the fact of opening the door or window supposes an invitation for evil, who is outside of the house, to enter.

The third high angle shot receives the death of the poet, and comes accompanied by visual metamorphoses that allude to the union of the lovers in the other world. The gigantic shadow of the bird spreading his wings becomes a cross that, in its turn, becomes gusts of dust. One of them pierces the heart of Leonor, and soars over the writer; the bony hand of death emerges to snatch it. This image evokes the final scene of *Nosferatu, eine Symphonie des Grauens* (Nosferatu, F.W. Murnau, 1922), where the shadow of the hand of the vampire squeezes Ellen's heart (Gerta Schröder) to death. In this narrative poem, the visit of the majestic raven symbolizes the announcement that death comes to take the tormented widower with himself. At the beginning of the film, the raven sits on Elenor's gravestone, and in the end on that of Poe, thus closing the circle of his gloomy path.

The Big Fish Eat the Little Ones

The nihilist vision of the family that *Por un infante difunto* presents is repeated in *Ecosistema*. The home is a biotope in which the animals and the persons act driven by the law of the fittest. The story links a series of violent deaths that follow this principle, and equates people with animals. It is about the destructive instinct of human beings, who enjoy annihilating inferior beings. This impulse is irrepressible, and ends up imposing itself on the ethical and moral principles that arbitrate coexistence. In summary, the short film offers a devastating tableau of the family in which violence forms the backbone of the relationships.

Anny (Maite Pérez Danborenea), the girl, stamps her pet, the rabbit Bunny, to death. In the next room the parents argue behind the door. Unexpectedly and gratuitously, the father (Javier García Morán) gives a mortal hit to his daughter, and throws the cadaver into the garbage can. Afterward, without any consideration, he lies down beside the pregnant mother (Maite Martínez), who is knitting clothes for her baby. Both of them are watching a television documentary about the laws of nature. This succession of violent images reveals the hypothesis of the director: the family is a corrupt institution. It represents the germ of irrational, gratuitous, and instinctive violence that is reproduced ad eternum. This virus forms part of the primitive instinct that lives in human beings, and which equals them to animals. Their most basic impulses are present in everyday life, which is why the television symbolizes the container of this irrational violence, to which the media try to give an explanation. The images of military conflicts and the documentary on animals are equivalent; their diffusion contributes to the propagation of this intrinsic evil. The way things are, the home of this film is the battlefield in which all species, humans, animals and insects, confront one another to survive.

As opposed to *Por un infante difunto*, the short film is shot in color, which accentuates the presence of blood in the shots that show violent death. This choice reflects a clear influence of gore cinema that takes pleasure in attacking the spectator with this type of excessive imagery. The escathological detail shot of the rabbits brain spread on the floor, and of Anny's sneakers tainted with blood, offer a good example of the influence of gore.

As it happens in his other short films, the gaze once again becomes the backbone of the mise-en-scène. Nevertheless, in this case the number is greater, they are six, and the form of representing them is more heterogenous and experimental than on occasions before. The point of the view of the fly, the rabbit, and the spider are intertwined with the look of the doll and with the shots whose height is not what is normally used. Each one of them corresponds to a point of view, and channels part of the information. That is, it reveals the situation of the rest of the persons who inhabit the home, and the evolution of the fight that is established between them.

The look of the spider, the rabbit, the fly, and the doll are small narrative fragments in internal focalization that combine with the narrator's point of view in external focalization. While the first ones offer partial information, this last one is responsible for giving cohesion to the action. That is, the narrator limits himself to showing and connecting the events from the beginning to the end. Now, it stands out for the fact that it stops to underline an idea, the transmission of intrinsic violence, and for this it uses unusual camera positions. These give way to shots that negate the face of the main characters, and concentrate on showing other details. For example, the camera at the level of the floor that, among other things, shows the shoes covered with blood; or the shots of the parents in which the device is located before the sofa, at the height of the mother's hands to show her knitting on her pregnant belly.

The objective of all these visions is to create a polyhedral universe through which the home adopts a new appearance, that of the ecosystem. This is supported by the fact that the film lacks dialogues or voice-off, which is why the music and the soundtrack highlight the tension of this dangerous universe. For this reason, the subjective visions of the fly, the spider, and the rabbit are manipulated to materialize the physiological conditions of animal vision, always accompanied by a sound that distinguishes them.

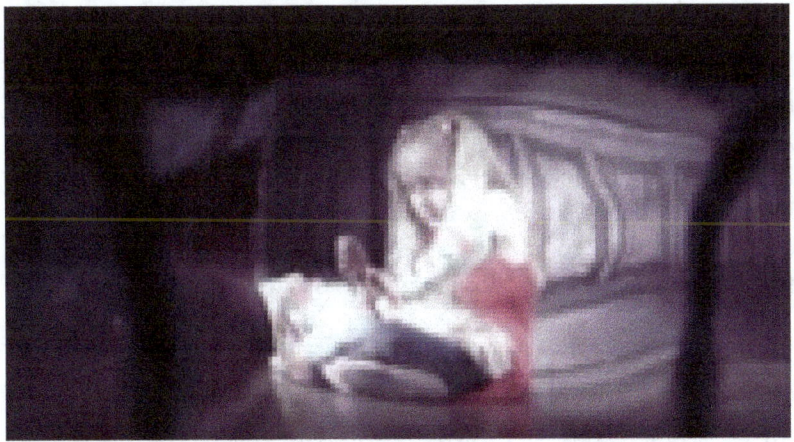

The front legs of the tarantula (Rage) come before the image filtered by sinuous waves, while we can hear the grunt of the insect. The rabbit identifies with the blurred image and the sound of a heavy body that drags on the floor. Finally, the look of the fly is the most complex because it holds an important role in the plot. It combines two expressive resources: on the one hand, the aerial camera that balances on the set in wide-angle lens, and offers a deformed vision of the world: and on the other hand, the buzz of its wings that overtakes the soundtrack, provoquing the *bain sonore*.[89] The result is a device that facilitates the spectator's immersion, and seeks to provoke *sensations* of anxiety or inquetude in them. Although without a doubt, the sinister look of the doll is the most disturbing of all, given that it presents the fly from the empty socket of one of its eyes,[90] the one Anny violently gouged out in a previous scene. For an instant, this perturbing subjective camera gives life to an inanimate and antropomorphic being, which it immediately converts into diabolical. Only the evil that inhabits the home is able to occupy the place of the toy.

Unlike the other short films, *Ecosistema* belongs with postmodern cinema, which is why it has as its objective to launch devices that are capable of creating a favorable atmosphere for the immersion of the viewer in the film. As Carlos Losilla argues, through these mechanisms, in "postmodern horror films a new relationship is established between the spectator and that which is filmed, which ends up characterizing the latter, no longer as a simple observer or accomplice, but as an active protagonist."[91]

Irony and citation are other characteristic features of postmodern cinema that are present in this work. Irony comes from the hand of the image of the pink stuffed toy rabbits on Amy's shoes, which is the last thing Bunny sees before dying. On the other hand, *Ecosistema* cites *Poltergeist* (Tobe Hooper, 1982), cowritten by Steven Spielberg, and inverts its meaning. In *Poltergeist*, Carol Anne is an innocent girl whom evil, which comes from the outside, tries to seize and take to the other world. Her parents desperately fight to save her and to recover family

---

89 Laurent Jullier argues that in postmodern cinema, the sound invades the image track and aims to recreate the depth of the space shown or, as it happens in this case, situate the viewer in the place of the fly, integrating the visual and sonorous dimension. Jullier, L´écran postmoderne.
90 The mutilation of the only eye of the doll by the girl evokes the branded eye of Un chien andalou (1929) by Luis Buñuel, and warns about the effects that the terrifying images of the story have on the viewer.
91 Losilla, El cine de terror, 162.

harmony. On the other hand Anny, the main character of *Ecosistema*, is a wicked person by nature, she carries this germ in her interior. She lives in a context of family and domestic violence, where love does not exist. The father is an abuser and an antifather who kills his daughter. The mother is a submissive figure who accepts the situation with normalcy.

Interview

What elements does horror cinema contribute to *Por un infante difunto*?

Por un infante difunto is not, exactly, a horror short film. Nevertheless, horror cinema no doubt influenced the construction of this strange and surrealist atmosphere. The film is, in reality, a drama of the fantastic genre. More than horror, it rather resembles the French line of cinema that championed in its days *Delicatessen* (Jean-Pierre Jeunet and Marc Caro, 1991), or surrealism, or even Luis Buñuel's films. Curiously, I don't think I have shot a horror short film yet.

The contrast between the crude reality that the short film reflects and its surrealist component is noteworthy.

This combination of drama and surrealism responds to what I wanted to say in that time. It was something that I had lived. A very tough atmosphere. Nightmares that you can almost dream in black and white, but at the same time, they make you feel much more indignant. In this sense, the fantastic genre offered me the opportunity to paint a portrait of things very much on the brink of reality. The scene at the butcher's shop perfectly reflects this spirit. In spite of being realist, *Por un infante difunto* also has a fantastic touch. It is a very strange mixture. It is a work that is very difficult to catalog. It came out like that and I don't know why.

At the beginning, Julio maintains his ingeniousness and takes refuge by the window to survive in a hostile environment. His encounter with the butcher supposes a turning point, and his attitude changes radically. What is the meaning of this scene?

The short film in fact has two types of interpretations. The first one of them is summarized by the title itself: the death of infancy. The crude reality obliges the children of the lower classes who live in difficult environments to grow up prematurely. It kills their childhood. And this is screwed. The place where you are born continues to be very important. Someone who was born in a hostile environment can also do great things. I don't deny that. But to a great degree, failure is determined by social origins. There is also a kind of revenge against my family. Because when you are young, you blame everyone. Nevertheless, they didn't have a much better life either. The second interpretation of the short film is a reflection on infancy. I think that children can't be treated as adults, nor can they be asked to do adult things. I remember that our parents sent us to the grocery store to buy on credit. We had to cross a dangerous highway and a truck ran my sister over. A parent should never send a nine-year-old to buy groceries on credit; they shouldn't even send them to buy groceries. They should take an effort to treat their children with the greatest dignity.

Why did you choose black and white?

There are two reasons that pushed me toward shooting a short film in black and white. The first one, and perhaps the most important one, was fear of the aesthetics of Spanish cinema. Whenever I saw a Spanish short film and then a French or a US film, I noticed that there was a great difference in quality. It always seemed to me that the Spanish short film was badly made. Over the years of my experience in cinema, I realized that everything depends on the quantity of money spent on lighting. Besides wanting to avoid the aesthetics of the Spanish short film, I also considered that the black and white would give more force to the short film, and could mitigate, in a way, the lack of quality at the level of color temperature.

What influenced you in this film?

I had seen a short film that I liked a lot. It was called *Txarriboda* (Manuel Lorenzo, 1994), and it had a very curious black and white that served as a reference for me. At the level of atmosphere, I had in mind a cartoon that I think *Cimoc* published. It was a rather horrifying cartoon, also in black and white, very run-down and dirty. And, of course, the surrealism of *Delicatessen* is present in the short film.

Ecosistema once again takes up the theme of gender and domestic violence, but it departs from a new point of view: violence is innate, impulsive. We are animals in the strict sense of the word, and we need to destroy the weaker ones.

The story of *Ecosistema* is written between *Por un infante difunto* and *The Raven*. It was a very complicated short story, and I wasn't sure how to tackle it; for this reason I postponed it. When I wrote the script, I had read some news of that era. There was one that impacted me very much. It was about a drunk father who, when he got home, he found his son crying, and he threw him out of the window. My family experience also had its reflection in the film. We function as animals, and we can't avoid it. But animals have an excuse. They only kill to eat, and nothing else. We however also do it out of rancor; because we hate our fellow beings. *Ecosistema* wants to say that within the big city, our own ecosystem exist; that it is as tough, or even tougher, than that of the savanna. It is a short film that mixes story and documentary, and maintains a thematic relationship with *Por un infante difunto*.

The portrayal of the family and the figures of the authoritarian father and the yielding mother, as well as the main character are more extreme than in the previous short film. The violence is also more explicit. Why?

In *Por un infante difunto* there are also violent images. For example, the scene in which they cut one off the fingers of the boy. But there is no doubt that *Ecosistema* is a very tough film; not for nothing, I meant to wake up the audience with it. The historical context of Spanish cinema also influenced a lot the tone of the short film. When we started to make films, Balagueró, Vigalondo, Serra and I, everything was very free in the world of short films. Nothing concrete was expected of short films. During the first years of the twenty-first century, however, the Spanish short film underwent great changes. Comedy and drama started to become more important, and they started to shoot short films with important actors. In the end, short films were nothing but small pieces of feature films. They became a mere excuse so that a producer contracts directors, and they can make a feature film. Given that situation, I found it timely to make a tough short story, a different and very experimental one.

The soundtrack is fundamental. Not only in *Ecosistema*, but also in all your work.

Cinema is an audiovisual genre; the soundtrack has as much importance as the image. For me, the soundtrack makes up 50 percent of the film. Many times nothing can be seen in the image. But then, the sound is added, and this achieves an unusual strength. In this sense, I think that Spanish short film has an outstanding debt with sound. *Ecosistema* has a lot of amplified sound in order to give the story a sensation of more dramatism. The exercise of the sound of *Ecosistema* consists, specifically, in magnifying the horror that one can suffer in the realm of a tale. The image is always very bucolic, very much like a fairy tale, until the tragedy occurs. Nevertheless, the sound keeps warning us that the story is not as idyllic as it seems; the sound of the fly's flight from the beginning is already an unpleasant sound. The image is bucolic, and the sound is very strident. This mixture seemed interesting to me as an exercise in *Ecosistema*.

The family as a castrating institution is a recurrent and personal theme, but it seems like it disappears from, or at least it is not the main axis in, the rest of your work.

More than anything, it disappears because the feature film is another format. I have a short film project titled *The Mirror*, and the topic has to do with abuse. I don't know why, but I feel more comfortable to treat these subjects in short films. Perhaps the reason is that I feel freer at the level of narrative. It is a different audience, very grateful, and they will watch the short films with an open mind. In case of feature films, in turn, things are very different. People pay their tickets, they have seen the trailer, and look for something very specific. You have a very tough and difficult audience with which you have to work at the level of the script, direction, and everything. In a short film I am very impulsive, and in a feature film I try to capture what I would like to see in the movie theater.

The cinematographic adaptation of the poem *The Raven* is a very personal challenge that comes from your passion for Poe. How did you start the project?

After releasing *Por un infante difunto*, I wanted to shoot a simple short film with very few characters. I was racking my brains because I couldn't find the right story, when Javier Moro, my roommate then, asked me why I didn't make a short film about the poem of Poe that I liked so much. That's how the project started. I hadn't won in Cannes yet, and my idea was to do something very simple and cheap; a man, a dark room, and a chair. It was rather going to be a filmic essay than a short film proper. But then, sure, came Cannes, I won various awards, and I spent all the money on *The Raven*. I wanted to do an adaptation of the poem. But Karra Elejalde challenged me. He told me: "I bet you don't have the balls to do the poem as it is?" And that is how I made it. By the way, all work took place at the level of aesthetics. It was not the usual short film, but something different, an experiment, a poem in cinema. I had the aesthetics very clear. I am very much a fan of Hammer, and I decided that *The Raven* had to be a Hammer film. In fact, Poe does not resemble Poe at all; rather, he looks like Vincent Price.

There was a certain controversy about *The Raven*.

The Raven had a design of excellent production, it was a short film that had a presence. I spent more than 19 million pesetas on it, and received a lot of criticism on part of some short filmmakers. They said that it was more like a feature film rather than a short film. Apparently, *The Raven* lacked the aesthetics of a short film. It was an accusation that did not at all correspond to reality. I had seen many short films at an endless number of festivals all over the world, and I knew that it was not the case. If a feature film cost 180 million pesetas and lasted ninety minutes, why couldn't I shoot a short film of twelve minutes with a budget of 19 million? In spite of the criticism, people started to become enthusiastic, and invest more money in their short films. Nevertheless, all of this disappeared. The design of production is fundamental in a short film, but in the past years it has been rather neglected. Without a doubt, the short film has lost efficiency with regards to the design of production. Depending on the story it tells, cinema can be poor. But there are films that need to offer a spectacle. Because at the end of the day, for me, cinema has always been about entertainment. I don't consider myself an artist, I consider myself a creator. A creator of ideas. I make films because I like entertaining. In fact, I think that cinema is first of all entertainment. And later, if a film stays in the annals of history, it may become a work of art. Nevertheless, it seems like in cinema, everyone is an artist. I rather dislike the word *artist*. Cinema is entertainment, and therefore, a short film can also be a superproduction. In this sense, the media is important. Making something "good, nice and cheap" is rather difficult.

The mise-en-scène recovers the imagery of American Gothic literature, and the spirit of the Hammer productions. Is this a work where the fantastic genre keeps its codes intact?

More than to the genre of the fantastic film, this work is loyal to the Hammer productions in terms of aesthetics, codes, and times. The camera is perhaps more modern, more American. In the short film, as it is palpable, we follow all the patterns of the Hammer productions that we could: the theatricality of acting, the setting, the spiderwebs, this special red color… It was very difficult for us to transmit the colors that the Hammer productions had. It was an old Eastmancolor, very strange. I saw the red colors of *Dracula* by Terence Fisher, and I felt incapable of reproducing them. In the end, following the advice of my director of photography—Unax Mendia—we studied Caravaggio, who became the main pictorial reference of the film. I think that there, yes, we tried to recover this potpourri, no longer of the fantastic genre, but the golden era of Hammer. This short film is my homage to Hammer … and to Poe, of course.

Is Caspar David Friedrich another of the pictorial references of the short film?

Effectively, all the exteriors are based on the paintings of Friedrich. We based ourselves, basically, on two painters. Caravaggio for indoors, and Friedrich for outdoors. In the exteriors, it is not only the photography that is inspired by Friedrich; we also designed a model by taking as reference *Cloister Cemetery in the Snow*. It is without a doubt one of my favorite paintings. In that painting, there is a half-ruined abbey; only a little more than the arch is left of it. And, in front of this abbey, there is a cemetery. In *ASD. Alma sin dueño* there is also a wink at Friedrich. I love his paintings.

You mentioned that you have a short film project. Will there be continuity in your trajectory as short filmmaker?

In any case, in a very one-off manner. By now I have sufficient means to make a feature film, and it would seem a little ugly of me to make another short film and compete with the younger generation. Like I mentioned before, it is true that I have a short film project. But it is something very experimental, and very complicated to shoot. More than a usable short film, it is a technical and narrative exercise. I don't think I would make short films again as a short filmmaker per se, although I will probably always feel more short filmmaker than feature filmmaker. Especially because of my rebellious spirit, and the desire to make new things.

Your complaint of producers has affected your career in Spain. How do you see the present and future of Spanish cinema?

I was already rather crucified before my public renounciation. If I, or other directors do not direct in Spain, it's because they don't like us. It is that simple. If I had to make *ASD. Alma sin dueño* with Alma Ata Producciones, it was because no other company wanted to produce it for me. Not because they didn't like the project... in fact, many producers were interested. The problem was Tinieblas. In the press conference that I offered, besides denouncing that Alma Ata had snatched my work from me, that they had altered it without my permission, and had released it with another title in order to collect the subsidy, I wanted to make it public what we all know in the world of cinema, but no one has ever dared say it: the fraud of subsidies in Spanish film making. In the year 2000, in the times of prosperity, they made eighty-seven films. From 2007 to 2012 they made on average 210 films a year, all subsidized. Each producer takes a million euros net for each film. Films that nobody wants to see. Robbery and pillaging has never been greater. I think that the film industry has to disappear in order to grow from zero again. Putting patches on it will not solve anything. The film industry has to terminate in order for the pillaging to end; so that they contract a director as a director, and not as an excuse to get more subsidies. This is the real cancer in Spanish cinema.

Do you have any intention to try yourself in the US movie industry?

I settled in Los Angeles not too long ago and, at this point, I want to know how the industry works. I am writing the script of a film, and I have a TV series of the fantastic genre that I will try to sell when the moment is right. I was sick of Madrid, and I came here to see what happens. The truth is that I like this. I don't think I will return to Madrid. If I return, I will go to Barcelona or back to the Basque Country. The problem that us directors have in the Basque Country is that we can't work. At the level of help and subsidies, they treat us well. But then there is no work for people like Bajo Ulloa, Serra, or me; because, normally, you work with the same small production companies all the time. If we went to Madrid or elsewhere, it is because of the lack of work. It's a pity. The Basque Country should not repeat the mistakes of Spain, and lose its talent. It would be advisable that it takes better care of the people in cinema so that they don't end up leaving.

David González Rudiez (Bilbao, 1980)

He started to study Fine Arts and Psychology, but he abandoned his studies for cinema. His formation took place in the Sarobe Film School (Urnieta), and he attended scriptwriting courses in the Larrotxene Cultural Center (Donostia-San Sebastián), where he also worked as a teacher for a year. From a very early age, he made audiovisual works that have been recognized at various festivals. Although he manages well in all genres, drama and horror stand out in his cinema. It is a cinema of static shots and dilated times, in which intrigue reigns. Kimuak selected *El relevo*, his first short film shot in 35mm. He also has another three short films in the catalog: *Lent Time*, *Los que lloran solos* and *La calma*.

Filmography as Director

2011. *La calma* (short film)
2010. *Carta a Julia* (short film)
2009. *Los que lloran solos* (short film)

2008. *El tiempo prestado* (short film)
2007. *Viernes* (short film)
2006. *El relevo* (short film)
2004. *El huésped* (short film)
2003. *Cecilia* (short film)
2002. *Parejitas* (short film)
2002. *Septiembre* (short film)

Existential Drama with a Varnish of Comedy

In *El relevo*, his most easygoing short film, David González narrates the ups and downs of a working-class couple with humor. Javi (Juanlu Escudero) is a cheerful man who works at night as a security guard. Cris (Miriam Martín), a strong-willed woman, is a cashier in a supermarket. Because of their work schedule, they only coincide for a few minutes during the day, a time that Cris invests exclusively in trying to get pregnant: a routine that seems to take a toll on the couple's passion. In spite of the fact that *El relevo* is imbued with humor, under the appearance of comedy there lies a deep existential drama: the shadow of disenchantment.

The initial moments of the film show Javi returning home. The close-ups of his face show fatigue; he yawns in the bus, and his eyes close because he is sleepy. Then we can see the night guard as he wearily climbs the interminable flight of stairs that lead to his house. Except for a brief ascending pan, all shots are static, and thus accentuate even more the sensation of fatigue that the male main character of the film feels. These first shots also serve to establish the context of the story. Javi and Cris live in an unassuming neighborhood.

Before entering the front door of the building where he lives, Javi throws away the cigarette he was smoking during the way home. The wooden stairs amplify the sound of his steps. The low angle shots of his slow walk, and the extreme close-up of his right hand leaning on the rail reveal the slowness and heaviness of his movements. His weariness, nevertheless, does not redeem him from his routine duty.

When Javi enters the apartment he shares with Cris, the mise-en-scène acquires more dynamism. The camera, through a tracking shot that follows him, accompanies the movements of the man from the hallway to the room in which the main part of the story will develop. In this precise moment, a conversation between the couple starts, which will last until the end of the short film.

Sexual activity determines the position of the camera during the rest of the short film. The low and high angle shots of the faces of the main characters come one after the other continuously, while the conversation reveals the abyss that separates Javi and Cris. Although the man tries to explain to her the existential fears that disturb him, the woman does not pay him any attention. She is only concerned that the sexual act may be consumed before her shift starts at the supermarket. The extreme close-ups of the clock on the wall constantly interrupt the scene as a kind of parody of action thrillers in which the hero fights against the clock.

This absurd situation in which sex and obscure reflections about death mix bring us back to the more classic comedies of Woody Allen. In fact, as Ramón Luque[92] argues in his book, sex and death are the most recurring obsessions in his cinema. But, unlike the genius from Manhattan, David González does not stuff his film with ingenious sentences. His humor comes from the unusual character of the situation, and the contrast between the two characters. Besides, the performances of the actors Juanlu Escudero and Miriam Martín accentuate the humor that the film exudes.

The overhead shot that shows the couple on the bed after the coitus reveals that, although they lie next to each other in bed, they are very

---

92 Luque, *En busca de Woody Allen*.

far from each other. Cris, caught in her obsession to get pregnant, has gravely hurt the sentimental ties that she shares with Javi. And he, as the continuous aerial shots reveal at the end, is at the mercy of his disastrous fate. In the last shot, the night guard lights up on a cigarette. It is not an act of rebelliousness against the prohibition of his partner; rather, it is a sign of resignation before life. This image, precisely, reveals the hidden drama under the veneer of comedy. Because, finally, the main character accepts the sad reality of his relationship, and the inevitability of death. It is the tragic resolution of the existential inquietude that the main character shares with the author himself.

Old Man in a Cage

González abandons humor, and penetrates the family drama with social relevance in *El tiempo prestado*, which is a lucid and bitter reflection that rejects the treatment that elderly family members suffer. The main character (José Ramón Argoitia), an elderly man who walks with crutches, is shut away in his son's house while he recovers from a hip surgery. His daughter-in-law (Miriam Martín) treats him coldly and, his grandson (Aitor Guisasola) with manifest disregard. The old man has become a nuisance for the family.

The formal dynamism so characteristic of *El relevo* completely disappears in *El tiempo prestado*. The shots are static, and there are no camera movements; it is the characters themselves who move within the composition. This austere formal style evokes in a certain way the Japanese master Yasujiro Ozu's cinema. In fact, Paul Schrader's comment about the transcendental style of the author of *Tokyo monogatari* (Tokyo Story, Yasujiro Ozu, 1953) could serve to describe the formal character of the short film:

> The camera, except in the rarest of instances, never moves; in the later films there are no pans, no dollies, no zooms. Ozu's only filmic punctuation mark is the cut, and it is not the fast cut for impact or the juxtaposing cut for metaphorical meaning, but the pacing cut which denotes a steady, rhythmic succession of events.[93]

---

93 Schrader, *Transcendental Style in film*, 22.

Nevertheless, unlike Ozu, the systematic repetition of the composition does not constitute in any way "a space of the return of the same" that would orient the film to an "aesthetic ascetism."[94] David González's intention is much more earthly. The director always locates the camera at the height of the main character, and constantly repeats the same compositions and shots—the shot in which the elderly man appears seated in the salon, for example—with the intention of showing the viewer what the elderly man feels. The idea that lies behind this formal strategy is to reach the most subjective experience possible without using the subjective camera.

If Wong Kar-Wai intentionally hid the faces of the spouses of the main characters in his story of impossible love in *In the Mood for Love* (Wong Kar-Wai, 2000), David González does the same with the family of the old man. The story centers on the old man himself. The camera is positioned at his height and, as a consequence, the figures of the daughter-in-law and the grandson appear fragmented. Nevertheless, the Basque director is not as categorical as the Chinese one; he nuances this stylistic tool in function of the attitude of the characters. Thus, when the daughter-in-law or the grandson gets to the old man's level, he shows their faces. It is neither an accidental, nor a formal caprice. The form and content are closely linked, and only when grandson and daughter-in-law pay attention to the old man are their faces shown. In the case of the son, in turn, David González affects a variation that takes us back to the opening sequence of *Vivre sa vie* (My Life to Live, Jean-Luc Godard, 1962).[95] The son, in spite of positioning himself at

---

94 Zunzunegui, *La mirada cercana*, 162.

95 In the film *Vivre sa vie* (Jean-Luc Godard, 1962), after the title credits, Nana—

the father's level, imposes his will over the old man. For this reason, we don't see his face during the conversation they have in the kitchen, only his back in the semi-darkness.

Anna Karina—and her husband Paul—André S. Labarthe—converse in the bar of a bistro, with their back to the camera. During the conversation, Godard chooses not to show the face of the couple. In the scene of the conversation between the old man and his son, however, we see the main character's face—which is even illuminated. But just like in the French director's film, González films the son with his back to the camera, in the semi-darkness, and avoids showing his face.

Similarly, sound is fundamental for *El tiempo prestado*. It perfectly adapts to the visual strategy that the director deploys in the short film above all in the scenes where he plays a lot with offscreen. Like for example in the scene where the old man gets up from the armchair, and talks with his grandson.

In any case, besides its formal attraction, the short film is full of the codes of the most classic thriller. In fact, the main character has many elements in common with the photojournalist that James Stewart plays in *Rear Window* (Alfred Hitchcock, 1954). The old man is also disabled, and cannot leave from home. But the similarities don't end there. Both carry out intense detective work, challenging the limits imposed by their enclosure.

The mysterious absence of his granddaughter Marta, and the paper boxes that are accumulated in the hallway of the house where he is imprisoned awaken the old man's suspicion. Besides, his daughter-in-law's lies add to the intensity of his mistrust. When he finally verifies that Marta's room is empty, and the paper boxes contain the things that he kept at home, his suspicions are confirmed. Marta is not away on vacation; she is occupying his apartment. It is then that he confronts his daughter-in-law and his son, and requires that they let him go home. However, he is captured.

The metaphor of the bird in the cage is a true reflection of his obscure fate. The old man, like the bird, is also captive in the house of his son and daughter-in-law. They took his books and belongings away, as well as his freedom. His daughter-in-law's last word confirms his death sentence: "The apartment has never been in your name. Besides, Marta needs it way more than you." His end, like that of the bird, is a matter of time. There's nothing left for the old man but to wait for his death.

Icy Horror Story

Los que lloran solos is a very personal work of David González who, besides directing it, also took charge of the photography, the montage, the script, and the production. It is a small and unique story of fantastic nature, shot with a lot of liberty, and with the inestimable performance of a small group of actors.

Enchanted houses, gloomy forests, and the obscure beings of the otherworld have always been favorite elements of the fantastic and horror genres. None of them are missing from *Los que lloran solos*. The director relates the story of a family in this film—father (Mikel Martín), son (Asier Vázquez), and daughter (Amancay Gaztañaga)—who live isolated in a country house, and take care of the sick grandmother (Mercedes Prada). She is an old woman who has supernatural powers, and can communicate with the dark side.

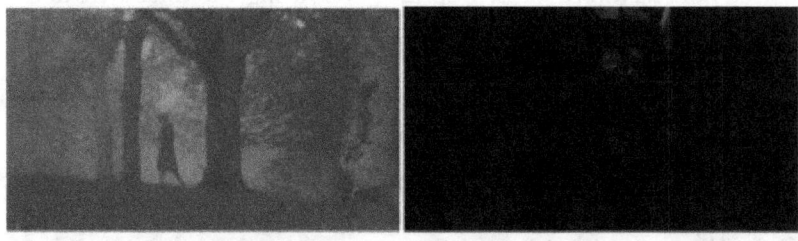

The house is cursed, because it is occupied by those who walk in the shadow: malign beings who come from the other side. Close to the house, there is an immense forest. It's mysterious, sunk in fog. It is just as threatening and dark as the cursed house itself. All members of the family seem to be condemned to death.

The short film, more than a horror film in general, is a disturbing horror story. In this sense, it resembles a lot *The Company of Wolves* (Neil Jordan, 1984), given that in *Los que lloran solos* there is also a grandmother who tells sinister tales, and a lush and dark forest. Nevertheless, in spite of the fact that David González's film perfectly fulfills practically all the characteristic features of a horror thriller, it disowns the conventions of the genre in its narrative development. The originality of his project lies in its experimental nature.

The voice-over of the narrator is the basis of the short film. The function of the images is limited to illustrate what the words expose. It is a film without dialogues, where the images do no more than sign and seal the spirit of the story. No doubt, the narration of the events is very peculiar, given that the author keeps interrupting it. Thus, at each two or three sentences, David González inserts a fade to black—the short film has no less than eighteen fades to black. It's a stylistic exercise that seems to be inspired by comic vignettes: a filmic puzzle that goes on acquiring meaning as its pieces are put together.

The viewer's sensation is that by segmenting the narration into small audiovisual vignettes, and prolonging the dead times of the transitions through the fades to black, the director aims to endow the short film with more intrigue by increasing its disturbing atmosphere. Besides, he completes this narrative strategy with the sound effects of Xanti Salvador, and the contrast between the foggy landscape and the twilight of the cursed house. Nevertheless, in spite of everything, the voice-over of the narrator strings the events—the disappearance of the father, the suicide of the daughter, and the murder of the grandmother at the hands of the son—in an overly hasty way, making the viewer's identification difficult. Also, the mise-en-scène manifests excessive coldness.

Nevertheless, the very long duration—twenty-two seconds—of the close-up of the son's face with which the short film ends, impregnates the story with ambiguity, and even suggests an unexpected argumentative turn that could well break with the supposed lineal character of the plot. The words of the narrator seem to blame the sick grandmother for the disappearance of the father and the suicide of the daughter. Consequently, in the last scene of the film the son takes revenge and kills the grandmother with the spade that he just used to bury his sister. But then why is the son's face highlighted with such insistence in the last shot? If we analyze the narrator's words attentively, we could also conclude that the grandmother invented the stories that she told her grandchildren about those who walk in the shadow. In fact, the father did not believe her at all. Thus, was it all a figment of the murderer's sick mind? This is what this last shot insinuates, which seems to question the mental integrity of the son.

Panic to Madness

Drama and suspense fuse under the wrapping of an obscure thriller in *La calma*, which is David González' most oppressive film. As opposed to *Los que lloran solos*, in spite of its singular narrative structure, *La calma* is a more conventional short film. Suspense advances by following classic channels, there is no formal experimentation, and the final reading of the story is crystal clear.

The short film starts with a mysterious scene in which a woman enters and leaves the different rooms of a narrow hallway, until she positions herself in front of the camera. Her intermittent breathing and the dread on her face reflect her anxiety and perturbation: the magnitude of the immense terror that overcomes her. Later, we realize that it is a flashforward that anticipates the suicide of the main character's sister.

Next, the main character (Mikel Martín) appears swimming in a swimming pool. His voice-off starts to reveal the past of his family; a secret shadow that seems to condition his present, and which he has not told about even to his wife (Irene Bau). A little later, through a series of flashbacks that continuously interrupt his everyday routine, he tells us that his grandmother went mad, and threatened the family.

The death of the sister, who suffered the same disease as the grandmother, evokes the memory of the father through a new series of flashbacks. His father, consumed by insomnia and headaches, locked himself in his room for two weeks. And, when he emerged, he attacked him and his sister. Madness is no doubt a hereditary disease in the family. It is precisely what he jealously guards.

David González connects form and content on the basis the reiterative character of the story. Both the grandma and the father suffer headaches and insomnia, lose their mind, and attack their family. But repetition does not only take place at the level of content and narrative. It is also reflected at a formal level. Thus, for example, both watch suspiciously behind the door the other members of the family, using the same point of view. The formal conception of the shot is practically the same.

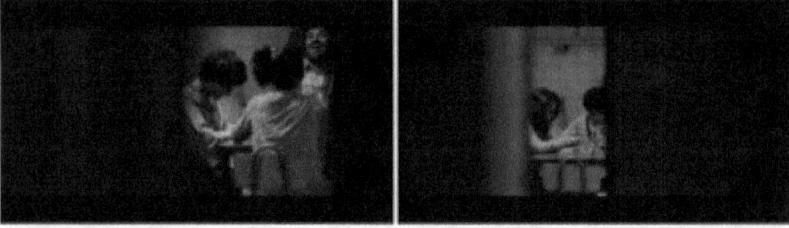

The determination that the main character has to hide his shady family past is strictly linked to the central theme of the short film: the fear of madness. As mentioned before, the main character's voice-off and the flashbacks reveal that the mental illness is hereditary in this family. But it is not the only thing that worries him. What really worries the main character is the fact that he is experiencing the same symptoms that have condemned his whole family to madness.

The director plays with the spectator by disseminating the signs of the terrible drama that devastates the main character throughout the short film. The continuous headaches that he suffers are very significant in this regard. Besides, it is clear that the insomnia he suffers not owing to the nervousness of being a first-time father. Like his own father, the main character also takes pills to fall asleep, to mitigate the effects of the cruel illness.

Nevertheless, all these signs do not by themselves reveal that the main character is victim of a hereditary mental illness until the final part of the story. Only when we get to contrast those signs with the information that the numerous flashbacks provide of the hidden past of the family, may we have our suspicions confirmed.

The fear of madness has been frequently expressed in cinema. *The Hours* (Stephen Daldry, 2002) is one of the movies that best reflect the pain of getting mentally ill in all its intensity.[96] The ending of *La calma* is not, however, as lyrical as the sensible drama of Stephen Daldry. After he covers the tragedy of the madness of the main character under the wrapping of a thriller of suspense, David González finishes the story with an ending proper to a horror film. The camera approaches the main character with a tracking shot that evokes the final scene of *Psycho*. The face of the main character, like that of Norman Bates, makes his madness explicit. However, there is no trace of badness in him. Only horror. The yelling and crying of his newborn son envision the drama that locks them up. More than a misfortune, the hereditary mental illness that the main character suffers is a curse that is perpetuated from generation to generation.

---

96   Little before she threw herself into the river, with the pockets of her coat full of stones, and drowning, Virginia Woolf recites the letter in which she explains her husband the reasons for her suicide. She confesses that she feels overcome by madness again, and she no longer feels strong enough to recover. She also recognizes that no one can have been happier than them until her terrible illness.

Interview

How has your cinema evolved since your short films in video format?

At the beginning, I tried to call attention. To shock. The short films of my beginnings had a more frenetic montage. I very much wanted them to be very impacting from the point of view of direction. With time, I have calmed down in this sense. The question of money has also been fundamental in this change. Before, I was alone with the camera. I had more margin of liberty. Now I have a lot of people around, and there's more money at stake. For this reason, it is important to polish everything, to try to achieve the same with fewer resources. This purge reached its zenith in *El tiempo prestado*, where there were practically no reverse shots. In this short film, it would have been impossible to make a more mobile mise-en-scène because, to begin with, the camera was very heavy. In sum, following the trends of the day, at the beginning I made montages of the Robert Rodríguez kind. And later, my style shifted toward more lyrical forms.

Is all short filmmakers' ultimate goal to make feature films?

When I started to make films, yes, this was my intention. I knew it very clearly. Then I went through a time when I thought that there weren't many opportunities, and it would be too much effort for the pleasures it brings. Recently, I seem to have changed in this regard, and I am trying to push forward for a feature film. Nevertheless, when I make a short film, what's most important is the short film itself. The rest does not matter. I choose short film for its own sake, without thinking whether it could serve me for a feature film.

What do you expect from the viewer?

I don't know. It also depends. For some time I made short films with the objective of provocation. *El relevo* has a provocative nature to a certain point. Probably in those times I was looking for humor. Until *El tiempo prestado*, I had worked more with the audience on mind; there was always a complicit humor with the audience. Then I started to think about doing something more singular, without thinking so much about the audience. *Los que lloran solos* was the limit. I wanted to do it, and I didn't care if people would like it or not. In fact, it worked very badly. In this sense, in the past years I have freed myself a lot from the pressure that satisfying the audience implies. Nevertheless, it is possible that soon I return to the fold.

What are your cinematographic influences?

There is in my work the influence of Aki Kaurismäki at a formal level from *El tiempo prestado* on. I refer to the static shots, the somewhat dilated times . . . The Swedish filmmaker Roy Andersson also has an aesthetics based on frontal shots and the rest. They are two of the directors that most influenced me lately. In turn, some years ago I liked Scorsese a lot, and I tried to make similar things. Ultimately, I make an effort to make relaxed cinema, but not necessarily boring one.

If we compare *El relevo*, your first short film in Kimuak with the other three, the differences are notable. The humor disappears, and the tone is more obscure.

It is true, and I am not sure if I simply followed my mood; I don't think so. With *El relevo* I intended to call attention by being as sincere as possible. I took it like a challenge, even economically, because I did it without asking for any subsidies. I asked for them afterward. It was a story that I liked, and I thought it could work very well. I made sure that it functions. In *El tiempo prestado* I decided to disregard humor a bit, and tried to do something more personal. It went very well, and I became enthusiastic about following this path.

Although *El relevo* seems like a comedy, in the end, it is a drama.

Before I said that it was a film of humor but, in fact, the background is very sad, given the situation in which the couple is. They seek to have a child, but it seems clear that they wouldn't be able to look after him or her. The story reveals the process that the main character lives when he confronts the tough reality. He realizes that he is worrying about things that he is not supposed to worry about; because they are the way they are, and there is no way back. In the end, he accepts that life is not as nice as he imagined. Without attempting to have a very profound or solemn tone, I wanted to tell with a touch of humor the story of these persons who are a little lost.

In *El tiempo prestado* one can perceive a high degree of maturity with respect to the previous short film. It is a solid work, dry, and very intricate.

Yes, the truth is that everything is simpler. But even when it is more simple, it becomes more effective. There are few movements, but they are well chosen. This is the sensation that it gives me. And we return a bit to the same thing before. When I made *El relevo* I said: "Shots with steady! This is cool." But then you watch it and you can't see it that much that it was shot with a steadycam. In *El tiempo prestado*, as there is not a single movement, I think that the mise-en-scène was better resolved, and we play more with the offscreen. From the point of view of production, this way of shooting was very useful, too. In any case, I couldn't have planned to shoot the story in another way even if I had wanted to, because it would have needed a lot of money. In this case, the resources that I had matched and what I wanted to say, and this benefitted the final result as well. It is a piece of work that I'm very happy with.

It is a very static film.

The scenes unfold as the main character moves. If he doesn't move, the camera remains immobile. And in the moments when it moves, there are more shots. For example, when he goes to the granddaughter's room, he opens the door, and then sits down again. Not everything is resolved in a single shot. I could have made the short film by merely chaining sequence shots, but it seemed more interesting to me to go beyond the rules a bit.

The rhythm of the film, the time, perfectly adapts to the story.

It is a story that couldn't be told in an agile way, because it was imprescindible that the passage of time gets noticeable. In fact, when I finished the first montage and we first released the short film, I regretted not having left a little more time between the shots. The truth is that I would have liked forcing the dead times a bit more; if I had added a few seconds more it would have worked better.

El tiempo prestado is a social drama that uses the codes of thriller. Why did you approach it from this perspective?

I liked the idea that the story should acquire the form of a small investigation of film noir. The main character, the detective, is disabled in a chair, and practically cannot move. This is precisely the story's point of view: someone who is investigating, to the best of his abilities, a series of tracks that are put before him during history.

Los que lloran solos is a short film that moves away a lot with respect to *El tiempo prestado* at a formal level.

In fact, there was nothing. There weren't any spotlights, nor a reflector, nothing. The day when there was fog, there was fog. I wanted to do something fast, simple, and very free. There was no excessive planning, and I think it shows. The short film has many weaknesses, and it's easy to attack it. The result was not what I expected, but I felt like shooting this story the way I did. What I have done moves away from everything. But as design, at least it's original.

The fades-to-black are constant, and very significant during the film.

It is a figure of style that seemed appropriate for the short film, but I didn't much think about its reason. Simply, I thought that it perfectly fitted the atmosphere of the story. It formed part of the design, but it wasn't something very conscious. After the intense filming of *El tiempo prestado*, where there was a lot of preproduction, I was on the point of undertaking a complicated project. Therefore, in this situation, I decided to take a breath and shoot *Los que lloran solos* with a reduced team. I had no great aspirations; I wanted to do something more freely. Nothing else.

What did you mean to transmit through the long final close-up of the boy?

Yes, there indeed is an intentionality, but it forms part of the project's lack of intentionality. It's a form of closing the somewhat ambiguous story in which they play with the fact whether this boy is all right in the head or no. The whole short film is a very particular artifact. It appeared with certain inertia, and not all its aspects are milimetrically designed. There was a lot of freedom and no responsibility from the economic point of view. Ultimately, it is a short film that is more instinctive than reflective.

The voice-over becomes fundamental in order to know the hidden aspects of the story. Why did you choose it, and deprive the characters from their words in the film?

This was also part of the design: "The story will be told. And the images will serve as support, but they will not be guiding principle." I recognize that the point of departure is a little anti-cinema and anti-everything. Nevertheless, considering the peculiar characteristics of the short film, I found it interesting to do it that way. The other way.

In *La calma*, although the dialogues are significant, you use the voice-off to explain the reasons why the main character is condemned to madness.

La calma is a more conventional project. Once again, we have a final close-up similar to *Los que lloran solos*. A long shot. Although in this case it is more elaborate. It is also more evident what it wants to say. That beginning of a storm that is coming... Let's say that it is like *Los que lloran solos*, except with more money.

Could we argue that suspense constitutes the nucleus of the short film?

It is possible. In *La calma* there are a series of clues that are offered to the spectator throughout the short film so that they can complete the puzzle. In any case, it is not difficult to guess the causes of the main character's inquietude. In *El tiempo prestado* the presence of suspense is also very evident. The old man is a kind of detective who keeps discovering clues and, besides, there is a girl that never appears. Everything is very mysterious. Nevertheless, there is nothing of this in *El relevo*, because it was about a story told in a very simple fashion so that it is understood well. I suppose that, after that I grew tired of making short films where two persons talk. And, in the end, I opted for the use of suspense with the intention of maintaining interest in the stories.

La calma is more complex production than usual.

I was thinking about doing something with more variety, more scenes ...One of the appeals that *La calma* had for me is that it allowed me to go to many places. It was interesting to me because in my former short films I barely had exteriors; I shot almost everything inside, because I was afraid that bad weather may ruin my projects. This is why my stories are so claustrophobic. Nevertheless, I must confess that I like films that take place inside, especially those of Polanski.

Some of your latest work belongs with the terrain of the fantastic.

That is true. Besides, I have a feature film project that goes along the same lines. The truth is that, as viewer, I am very interested in fantastic films and science fiction. And one way or another, preferences end up influencing what you do. Maybe I am more talented for doing tragicomedy, but lately I am attracted by the fantastic. I don't know if it is something one-off or no, but in these moments, I don't feel like shooting a comedy like *El relevo*.

Sound is essential in your short films.

Sound is very important. In fact, it is supremely important. If I know that I won't have good direct sound, I prefer that there is no dialogue. I can't stand sound that is badly made. *El tiempo prestado*, for example, had an almost horror atmosphere in some moment, and this, to a great degree, was a direct consequence of the sound. When the sound is not right, the entire work suffers it.

One way or another, death is very present in your work.

Yes, absolutely. There was a time when I felt sick even thinking about it. I suffered a crisis of anxiety because of it. And, consequently, I shot a short film that was titled *Tánatos*. Effectively, death is present in all my short films. I never made a short film where someone kills someone. In my latest ones there are people who die . . . but there are never any shots, nor explicit violence, nothing of that. Nevertheless, it is true that death is always present in my cinema. Not in the foreground, but yes in the background.

Do you seek a reflective cinema, or one of sensations?

I think that my cinema is halfway between one thing and the other; that there is as much reflection and feeling in my short films. *El tiempo prestado*, for example, unites both things. On the one hand, it is a story of sentiments. On the other hand, it is about a social issue that urges us to reflect about it. But sometimes reflection emerges in a natural way. When I wrote *El relevo*, I didn't seek to say anything transcendent. But in the end the story had an undertone. I think that the best works are the ones that fuse reflection and sentiments.

Isabel Herguera (Donostia-San Sebastián, 1961)

She earned her degree in Fine Arts at the University of the Basque Country (UPV/EHU) in 1985. The following year she completed a master's degree in the Kunstakademie, in Düsseldorf, Germany, with Nam June Paik. In 1990 she received a Fulbright scholarship to complete a master's degree in Animation at the California Institute of the Arts, CalArts, United States, which she finished in 1993. She worked in commercial animations studios in Los Angeles, and in 1994 she created her own, Loko Pictures, together with Satinder Singh with whom she collaborated as animator in *Balloo* (2003). She worked as teacher and director of animation workshops at the International School of Cinema and TV (EICTV) of San Antonio de los Baños (Cuba); in the National Institute of Design of Ahmedebad (India), CalArts, where she has regularly given classes since 2005; in the California Institute of the Arts (United States). Since 2007, she has coordinated the Arteleku Laboratory of Image in Movement in Donostia-San Sebastián. She has a wide experience in management, as between 2002 and 2001 she directed *Animac*, International Show of Animation Cinema of Catalonia. She is a very versatile visual artist who masters various techniques: the cutout animation that she applied in *Spain Loves You* (1988) and in *Los Muertitots (1994)*; painting on glass in *Safari* (1988) and in *Cante de ida y vuelta* (1989); the chalk on chalkboard in *El sueño de Iñigo* (1991); the sand *Baquine* (1992); the cartoons in **Ámár** (2010) and *La gallina ciega* (2005), which was nominated for best animation short film at the Goya Awards in 2006; and the animation of collage of cutout of children's drawings that compose *Bajo la almohada* (2012). These last three short films have formed a part of the Kimuak catalog.

Filmography as Director

2012. *Bajo la almohada* (animation short film)

2010. *Ámár* (animation short film)

2005. *La gallina ciega* (animation short film)

1994. *Los muertitos* (animation short film)

1991. *Baquine* (animation short film)

1991. *El sueño de Iñigo* (animation short film)

1989. *Cante de ida y vuelta* (animation short film)

1988. *Safari* (animation short film)

1987. *Spain Loves You* (animation short film)

Her visual style recovers the spirit of the schematic era of children's drawing. It is through this innocent imagery that she narrates profoundly human stories about blindness, madness or AIDS, and she does so as if they were a trip to another world.

I Spy with My Little Eye Something Beginning with . . .

The adventures of a blind man who loses his guide dog because of a capricious cat and its unpleasant owner are the main theme of *La gallina ciega*. This circular story develops like a game. A phone call establishes the beginning and the end of the narration. The blind man takes the phone that the man, in his fury, has thrown out of the window because its ringing did not allow him to enjoy the soccer match. With a lot of effort, the blind person enters in the building, finds the floor and the apartment, and returns the phone to him, but the unpleasant person throws him out of the house. In this moment the guide dog starts to chase the cat of the man, and abandons him to his fate. Luckily, the main character shows that he is not only able to live in darkness, but he also has got a magic wand, the television antenna that fell from his hands. Miraculously, an electronic discharge allows him to see for a second his dog through some glasses that show the image that the television emits. With it, he draws a new world for the animal, the same that the man and the cat are watching in their receptor device when, suddenly, the telephone rings.

The visual style of this experimental short film of cartoons is almost minimalist. It maintains the characteristic features of children's schematic mode,[97] which Rhoda Kellogg's study develops, but simplifies even more the elements, and reduces them to minimum expression. Besides the fade-to-black that alludes to the darkness in which the main character lives, she uses the blue and white as basic clolors. The persons are black forms in which straight angles dominate, with the exception of the cat that is curvaceous, and their silhouettes are marked by thick blue or white strokes. In concord with this minimalist tendency, the blind man's glasses, or the animals' expressive eyes are the only elements that distinguish them. The same logic is applied to other colors like the red and the yellow, which emerge occasionally to highlight a specific aspect. Thus, the red contour of the man who is watching the football game expresses the anger and wrath when he hears the phone ring. The yellow highlights the light of the stadium in which the cat and the dog enter. There is no voice-over or voice-off that should conduct the story, and the few dialogues of the personages are unintelligible. The soundtrack composed by Xabier Erkizia is a succession of rumors that come from the space that surrounds the blind man and which, on occasion, becomes an authentic bombardment of onomatopoeias. But it is not a baroque composition. It is as minimalist as the images. The function of the sounds is to guide character and help him find the way when he gets lost. It becomes evident that this disposition of visual elements and sounds has as their objective the construction of the world exactly the way the blind man perceives it.

From the point of view of the main character, the objects of the real world are the forms that are inferred through touch, and he is able to recognize their origin thanks to the trace, to the echo that their sound makes. But more than the sound in itself, what is interesting and new is the vibration that it creates in the objects and the way in which it is

---

[97] The children's schematic mode characterizes the phase when the children draw the world by following their own logic. Once they learn to master motor skills, and are able to elaborate scribbles, they extract the simplest forms of objects, and turn them into universal schemes with which they represent the world. This epoch is very rich, because in it, the children use their own language in which they prefer to communicate. In this sense, the schematic mode is very distant from the next phase, when the children are taught the techniques to reproduce in a naturalist way the world around them. Once they learn to copy the world, they lose the creative capacity to interpret it in their own way, with a different language. Kellogg, *Analyzing Children's Art*.

represented, the flickering of the silhouette, and the kinetic lines[98] that surround it. Thus, the image in black illustrates the moment in which the blind man is by himself and without help, the strokes of blue lines appear and disappear to the rhythm with which the main character touches the space and tries to feel his way. Also, the cinematic lines that accompany the barking of the dog appear and disappear in the darkness, indicating the place in which the animal is found; the same happens with the waves that alert the ring of the telephone.

Besides, the space where the events take place is represented by recovering two characteristic features of children's drawing: transparence, and the sum of points of view, or various perspectives. Both give priority to the narration, to the necessity of showing the events in a simple and elocuent manner, far from the laws of of mimetic representation. Owing to transparence, it is possible to show that which in theory is hidden through a wall or an element that impedes vision. Using this premise, it is possible to show the man watching television with his cat from the top of a building whose wall is an obstacle. The same happens

---

98   Kinetic lines are proper to the cartoon, although they are also used in animation. They are fine lines that appear with the characters or objects in order to express, generally, their movements. In case of this animation, they illustrate the vibration of the sound waves that a person or object produces.

with the elevator in which the blind man and his dog travel. A stroke of blue wraps them, and shows them ascending in the building. On the other hand, the sum of various perspectives to represent an object is a characteristic feature of children's scheme, which cubism recovered, and which in this work is present in the great images of cities. The streets are seen from above, but the cars were drawn from the side, just like the persons that we see inside the buildings, or the guard in the sentry box.

The Travel Notebook Hides a Treasure

This experimental animation short film narrates the story of Inés, a young artist who returns to the walled city to visit his friend Ámár, who is locked up in a mental hospital. Deep down, she hopes to find him somewhat recovered from the schizophrenia he suffers from. Nevertheless, the visit to the psychiatry confronts her brutally with reality: Ámár is another person, he lives in a parallel and deformed world, and he erased her from his memory. For this reason, in the story there is no re-encounter of the couple, only disillusionment. Downcast, the girl returns to the streets where they both spent hours contemplating the frenetic life of the city and, again, she starts drawing in her travel notebook. It contains the illustrations, the texts written by hand, the newspaper clippings, the photos, and the collages of a past time that the friends spent very happily.

The trip brings with it Inés's transformation, and the superation of a trauma that makes her recover her restless look on the streets and squares of the city. At her arrival, the veil of sadness converted them into dark, frozen landscapes. After the visit to the asylum, she once again watches with different eyes, and the strident color of India once again empowers her soul to help her heal her wounds.

The visual and narrative economy imposes itself as a creative criterion, which is why the voice-off assumes the function of guiding the viewer, and situating them in the beginning of the story. It is a narration with internal focalization, which reveals Inés's point of view in first person. It only appears at the beginning and at the end of this circular story. There is no doubt that this is the most classic animation of Herguera in what we mean by narrative structure; however, the visual work and the composition of the soundtrack situate it in the creative and experimental terrain.

With the exception of the flashback, the drawings loosely follow the same characteristic features throughout the short film. The graphic style is similar to the children's schematism. Simple forms, very recognizable silhouettes, transparence, and the sum of perspectives, to which we have to add the fact that the strokes of color are porous, and allow the viewer to make out the objects that are behind. This device gives a nice effect to the illustrations that show the way in which Inés contemplates the city when she is back. There is something that coats her look, and which prevents her from submerging in the landscape. The glasses of the windows or the porous strokes of the clouds allow us to make out the streets of the great city from the air, and it acquires a curious appearance thanks to the superimposing of perspectives. The cars and the cows that freely graze around are drawn sideways, and contrast with the palm trees of the roundabouts that are drawn from above, crushed against the ground. The sum of both allows a nice vision of the human ant's nest of the big city. Nevertheless, the use of color, and the articulation of the soundtrack are very different when it comes to illustrating the arrival of Inés to the city, the madness of Ámár, and the images of memory.

The exotic universe of the oriental metropolis becomes visible through muted tones and images, and a minimalist use of soundtrack, which show the profound sadness of Inés. Her return to the city in present time contrasts with the color and the animation of the images of the past. The black of the silhouettes harmonizes with the gray of the building and the blue of the arches of the old city. In fact, red and yellow are used in a one off way in order to highlight some feature, like for example, the ruby shirt of the main character, which distinguishes her from the crowd. Equally significant is the fact that the hustle and bustle of the city is produced by combining this type of animation with a minimalist articulation of the soundtrack, which gives priority to the voice-off. When the young woman returns to the station, the rattling of the train accompanies the human silhouettes crammed in wagons that flicker as they move. The cars, the motorbikes, or the bycicles that surround her pass at high speed. In spite of the strong presence of movement, Erkizia creates a sound that is not saturated with echoes and onomatopiaes of intensive city life. This articulation contsrasts with the colorist imagery and the liveliness of the sound of the flashback, which rerefs to the memory that the woman has of the city.

A horizontal tracking shot covers the static drawings of the square across various sheets that stuck together in Ámár's notebook. The color invades the illustrations; the intense red of the saris, the yellow of the cows, or the blue skin of the dancer highlight the intensity of the landscape. The style of these drawings distances itself from schematism without approaching the naturalist representation, and presents more elaborate forms of the animals, the persons, and the environment. The illustrations are accompanied by noisy sounds that give life to the images without harming the voice-off. In fact, the soundtrack is constructed in spacial depth; the intensity of sound corresponds with the location of the objects and gives volume to the drawings. Thus, for example, the sound of the drums that one can hear from afar becomes louder and louder as the row of musicians that approaches the foreground of the drawing appears in the image.

For the rest, schematism is also present in the episodes of madness, although with some differences than in the designs of the city. When the door of the subconscious opens, an explosion of sound and color happens, which alters the characteristics of the drawing.[99] The asylum is a sinister universe, opposed to the external world. In this world, Inés's melodious voice is the only intelligible sound, the only glimmer of reason. The nurse emits a muffled echo, and shares the same histrionic laughter as Ámár, when the accords of the saxophone announce the trip to paranoia. Red becomes a symbol of dementia, it is the color of Ámár's eyes, which see the world through the particular filter of his illness. The dark lines and their shadows reframe the main character in the cell of the asylum. She is caught in the spider's web of her friend's madness. Besides, this time the threatening silhouette of schizophrenia is present in the background of all images to make the bipolarism of the main character clear. He loves the girl who is going to celebrate his birthday, but the mental split makes him forget his feelings. While Inés sings "Happy Birthday," the silhouette turns into a seductive ballerina that drags Ámár to the dark side of his mind.

---

99 The combination of forms, lines, shades, and the strident use of color resemble expressionist painting. The distorsion's objective is to create an obscure and distrubing vision of the mental hospital, transforming the characteristic features of the drawing. That is, it breaks with the schematic line of the drawing; it transforms it to materialize a dismal reality.

Inés goes out of the room, and from this moment on, the second phase of the delirium starts. Crossing the door has a symbolic value in the short film. It establishes the phases of the main character's journey, the stations that he goes through until she finds her friend, and announces that this last gesture is a journey with no return. The young woman closes the door of the room of the asylum, and only Ámár and his world stays. She cannot communicate with him; her only comfort is to return to the station.

The articulation of schizophrenic visions implies giving free rein to the dissonant accords of the soundtrack that accompanies the lines or silhouettes against the black background. They are very schematic drawings, almost color stains that succeed one another at headspinning speed. It is a parade of coloristic images of the creatures that torment the main character's mind: Kali, goddess of creation and destruction who irrupts in the image with her seven arms, the serpent on which madness rides, the stairs and the elephant. All of them are the deformation of objects and themes that the sick man contemplated and drew with his friend in the past. They are recurrent themes that appear throughout Inés's trip. The serpent and the stairs symbolize the vertiginous ellipsis that gobbles Ámár's mind, and leads him to a new state; while the elephant acts like a main motif and pushes the young woman to draw again.

The travel notebook is a point of departure and a final point in the story. The collage of life, of the images of a moment that present themselves by using all types of material and visual resources. The objective is to capture the essence of the ordinary. For the main character, the travel notebook guards the moments of lucidity in Ámár's, and the memories of both.

Clinging to Life

The author selected, cut and composed the animation *Bajo la almohada*. It is a collage whose prime material are drawings of the twenty-seven HIV-positive boys and girls who live in the clinic Astro-Caritas in Tivim, Goa. Their testimonies and songs recorded with a tape recorder during the drawing sessions serve as a guiding principle of this children's story that is very close to documentary. The ambient sound designed by Erkizia lends energy to the children's voices, and the stories of their drawings. In fact, the main characters talk about their everyday lives in the hospital; they are aware of their illness, but they do not lose their innocence. Through their colourful illustrations and the voices that accompany them, they project a vital energy that achieves that the illness disappears for a few seconds, and turns them into boys and girls like any others. The disposition of elements replaces the documentary with a creative context, a collage of sentiments, thoughts, testimonies, and dreams of the children in the hospital. Contrary to a documentary, there are no filmic images that would show the face of the main characters; they show themselves through the portraits that they have drawn about themselves. There are no images of the place, or the persons who work there, either. Thre is no figurative visual reference of the presented world, only living illustrations of this space. Besides, at a narrative level the story juxtaposes poetic, fantastic and ludic fragments with the testimonies of the main characters. All of them show themselves through drawings.

The black-and-white photography of the beginning has the function of bringing the spectator to India. The roar of the Elephant imposes itself over black, and precedes the first image of the animal. The rest are black and white photos of the healthy children, which clash with the colored scribble that the hospital patients represent. Paradoxically, the external world seems not to have any life; its images are static and have no color. There is a strong contrast between the photography and their soundtrack, plagued with echoes that evoke the agitation of the country itself. In this short film the ambient sound is fundamental. It is very rich in onomatopoeic echoes, which are imprescindible when it comes to transmitting the vital energy of that which photographs and drawings lack so much. The voice-over of the narrator in first person presents the story, and disappears in order to give way to the children and the design.

The schematism of children's drawings is the dominant and common visual characteristic feature in the testimonies, the initial and final poetry, and the fantastic narrations of the children. Some of their most representative characteristic features are: the size and hierarchical collocation of objects to represent the place and importance that they have in the image—it's the case of the girl whose size is greater than that of the hospital; the simultaneity of various perspectives in the same object—as it happens with the palm trees or the buildings of the city that surround the squares and which we see drawn from a zenith angle; transparence—when for example the deep see creatures of the children who are inside a building can be seen without the wall or water surface hiding them; and finally, the repetition of patterns that appear time and time again throughout the drawing.

Nevertheless, there exist differences in the way of articulating the drawings of each fragment. The illustrations that accompany the testimonies and the poetry show in a rather graphic way the words of the children. The everyday chores of class, napping, and the nuns' work is shown through eloquent drawings. But in the case of the fantastic narrations of the children, the animation goes beyond adding the visual characteristics of children's schematism, and incorporates the way in which the children create stories while they draw. That is, the children's mode of imagining, telling and illustrating in this phase of their life. In her vast research on children's drawing, Rhoda Kellogg observed that children construct a mutant story that changes in form and content in function of the impulses of their imagination.[100] It is a story without closure, and without a causal relation. Its motor is the fantastic impulse that allows the changing of arguments without previous notice. Everything is possible and verosimile in this marvelous universe. This

---

100 Kellogg, *Analyzing Children's Art*.

is the narrative logic in the children's story *Bajo la almohada*. The story evolves on the basis of the narrator's impulse, in this case each one of the children who participate in this choral work, which is why the text keeps children's innocence in form as well as in organization. The scene in which the house transforms into a ship and drags the little girl, who is later rescued by a companion, is an illustrative example of the way children create stories while they draw during this phase of their lives.

Interview

The schematism of children's drawings is present in your works. What does it offer you?

It is a stylistic tool to tell the greatest possible number of things, in the possibly simplest way. One must be very schematic, and at the same time use strategies by which you can tell a story, without the necessity of having a word, in the shortest possible time. This is a stylistic option that I like. What you attempt is rid yourself of everything that is supposedly correct. When a child is a child and has no reference points, they draw and paint in a way that they later lose as they try to copy that which is supposedly good, and that which they think is correct. Everything is homogenized, and they lose this most personal language, and the potential that it may have for a more personal representation.

Is *La gallina ciega* a story about incommunication?

It's a work about interdependence. It suggests frustration and anger. It comes from Max Aub's *Crímenes ejemplares*. They are a series of events in which there is a criminal action, and many of them without reason. I remember a story in which a man left home every day, and met with a lottery vendor. One day he grew tired of seeing him and killed him. The blind man of *La gallina ciega* would be the lottery vendor, and the other would be the anonymous person who accumulates a series of frustrations, and ends up the way he does. In the end, through the relationship with the blind man, the other person rediscovers the world.

This short film has no voice-off. The story is told through the images and an elaborate soundtrack. What's the importance of each one of these elements?

Sound is fundamental. In *La gallina ciega* there is not even voice-off. Xabi Erkizia has a great sensibility to understand the sound as a fundamental, integrative part of the film, which is on a par with the image. He opens the windows of new possibilities, I see much more with him. The work process is very intuitive. In *La gallina ciega*, he made the sound after I had finished the image, and in the case of **Ámár** it was the other way around. I told him the story, I had a few sketches, and he, initially, gave me the sound and I made all the animation on the basis of the sound that he had given me. In **Ámár**, the sound also determines the emotion a lot, all that of which one doesn't speak. In the drawings of *La gallina ciega*, on the one hand, obscurity stands out, and the blind man and his world contrast with the other person, who is at home and who is red when he gets angry. With regards to darkness, the idea was that black would have much more presence from the point of view of the blind man, but little by little I saw that I had to give him a few details at the level of image. With respect to the rest, what I didn't want was too much color. I wanted to stay in the range of blues because they looked good with the black.

What is the point of departure of *Ámár*?

This story comes from journeys, from personal experiences and other people's experiences, from readings, and most of all from a trip to India in 2005, when I found many elements that can be seen, and worked on. It comes from the travel notebooks of which there was an exhibition. The story comes from two things that happen at the same time. The drawings happen at the same time as the writing; as you draw, you also write and send letters. Once you have the idea of what you want to say and how you want to say it, you organize them methodically. The most creative part is the development of the idea, until you can wrap it up and say, "this will be it." In fact, you could give it to someone so that they do it. The part of development is over.

The drawings are very schematic and simple, enough for the story to be easily understood. Why do you use the voice-off?

It was missing, I thought that without it couldn't be understood, and I wanted it to be more narrative. I had never done these types of things. It is a final decision, whether you want it to be understood, or want it more abstract and reach the viewer in another way. If you have voice, you are telling me what I have to understand, and not having voice can take you to other levels.

Nevertheless, the color and the soundtrack are articulated in a different way in function of what is narrated.

With the soundtrack one has to be very careful. It has to be on par with the image. Many times the soundtrack imposes the emotion with which you have to watch the film; an emotion that goes beyond the image. Because we had the narration in **Ámár**, it wasn't necessary to give so many clues with the sound. Inasmuch as color is purely an economic question, the more complexity there is in the color, the more expensive the digital composition.

Bajo la almohada was also born in India.

I was finishing **Ámár** there, in Goa, and I met a woman who worked in a clinic for HIV-positive children. We talked about painting a mural with the children. It was really liberating to be able to paint anything, and go with the flow. On that basis, I returned three more times. We dedicated two weeks to drawing about different themes, and the last week we painted a mural. In the end, in total there were two. The material of the development of the wall is the basis of the short film. Every day, we talked while we painted. I brought with me the recorder, and I recorded them a bit. They are children who, because of their situation, live in the clinic. Some got there at the age of nine, others lived there since they were born. The nuns teach them and, to a certain point, they allow them everything. They treat them with a lot of love, and there is not much discipline. The only really important discipline is that of medication. They cannot miss that. But at other levels, it was all fizzy. What was really difficult is concentrate with them on a topic, because they immediately jumped at other things. But at the same time, for me it was a very rich work, very delicious. And, above all, I tried to always maintain this freshness of the children. This innocence, and at the same time, this awareness that their life is what it is. As one of the children said at the end, he liked to watch movies of superheroes, but he knows that they aren't there to save him.

What is the theme that gives cohesion to all this material?

My works are very much linked to tracking shot, soon I found that this one was a journey around my room. I read Xavier de Maistre's book, who wrote during forty-two days how he was confined in his room, and it is a trip of meditation. It seemed to me that it was like a metaphor. These children do not leave the clinic for two reasons: for social rejection, and because they are so weak that, if they are not very rigorous in their diet and their regularity, they could die at any moment.

Is this a documentary, or a creative animation with documentary tone?

At the beginning it was a documentary. But it was very difficult to get the necessary concentration to develop the topic, which was a journey around my room, because the children went in all directions. And then I thought, let them go all over the place, this is what is marvelous. When I arranged everything, I found a poem of the book *Species of Spaces and Other Pieces*, by George Perec, "what is under the pillow?" It is also an idea that I extracted from this book; the children keep under their pillow those treasures with which they feel safe or comfortable. I asked a girl to tell me this question. Almost everything is edited documentary, and once it is edited, like a song or a poem, what is it that you need? And this *is* scripted.

It looks like the testimonies of the children have as their objective to give life to an innocent vision behind a tough reality?

Yes. That's what it was. The curious thing about this work is that it emerged in a very natural way. I made an effort to try to combine all the parts, and give it really the character that had voice. But the voice had been previously edited. What I first did was make the soundtrack, without what Xabier Erkizia did at the end. It is this almost musical voice of the children that gave character to everything. It is this character between half innocent, and half true. It is like music. Once you had the atmosphere, and you had the children's voices so present, came the animation. Sound was key to everything. For me this, in spite of the fact that it was text and it was voice, and that it was a voice with content, it was a soundtrack that told me about this character of children. It had everything. Sweetness, and at the same time reality; and, at the same time, musicality; and at the same time, tragedy; and at the same time, everything.

In this case, the children's drawings are the basis of the animation. How did the rest of the work develop, and how is it similar to other works?

What's incredible is that I didn't draw anything, but I did compose everything. This is why a palm tree comes from a boy's drawing, a figure comes from that of another; that is, the composition is the same. This is indeed personal. And, in this sense, it indeed is similar to my other animations. The end of **Ámar** with this city . . . , this is a composition. Here all the drawings belong to the children; the rest is Photoshop and after effects. And what's curious about all of this is that afterward, when I went to show it to the children, not the film, which they didn't see, but the animation, each one of them, and they were twenty, were able to recognize the little part they drew. They knew which smallest detail of the image was theirs.

What function do photographs have in this animation if they don't show the faces of the main characters of the story?

When I finished the animation work, and now I include the part of photographs, I realized that it was necessary to center it. It was necessary to put it into a format in which the viewer understands that this is a film of some normal and average children who live in a body, in a real cage, with a limited amount of time. A cage that is relatively fragile, and they are aware of it. Thus, I needed this part of the photography. I couldn't use the faces of the children of the hospital. And, in the end, I had these photos that I had taken in India during all those years. And I thought, this is the frame where they have to fit. And that is how I incorporated them at the end of everything. But I also think that they give another meaning to everything that the children say. It is something much more transcendent. The children of the beginning simply present India. And then the girl whose face is covered is a girl from the clinic;

and the children who are painting the mural, who are turning their back on us; or the hands of the children, they are also those of the children of the clinic. But I couldn't show them, because their caregivers were scared that their faces would be recognizable, and there was a social rejection of them. Because they can't go to normal schools, they can't do anything, nothing at all.

Ione Hernández (Donostia-San Sebastián, 1970)

She earned her degree in Information Science at the University of the Basque Country (UPV/EHU), with specialization in Journalism, in 1993. She continued her studies at the University Michel de Montaigne Bordeaux 3, in Bordeaux, France. She worked in Washington D.C., United States as a journalist. She won a scholarship from the Guggenheim Foundation to earn a master's degree in Cinematographic Direction in Los Angeles (United States). Her thesis, *Aizea, City of the Wind* (2001) and the short film *Juego* (2006) have been selected by Kimuak. She directed five short films in 35mm in the United States: *Kaleidoscope* (1995), *Sold* (1995), *I Don't Do Windows* (1996), *Ana* (1996), and *Stop for a While* (1997). She worked in the production department of the mini television series *From the Earth to the Moon* (Michael Grossman, 1998). After she returned, she participated with other eleven directors in the project *Diminutos del calvario* (2002) with the fragment *La novia*. She worked on the reality TV show *Gran Hermano* (Big Brother) at Telecinco. In the area of documentary, she conducted the additional interviews of *La pelota vasca: La piel contra la piedra* (The Basque Ball: Skin Against Stone, 2003), by Julio Medem, and in 2007 she directed the documentary *Uno por ciento, esquizofrenia*. Her last work, *El palacio de la luna* (2008), was selected by *Madrid en corto*, a program that is similar to Kimuak in the Community of Madrid.

Filmography as Director

2012. *JK5022 Una cadena de errores* (TV Movie documentary)
2008. *El palacio de la luna* (short film)
2007. *Uno por ciento, esquizofrenia* (documentary)
2006. *Juego* (short film)
2002. *La novia* (segment of *Los diminutos del calvario*)
2001. *Aizea, City of the Wind* (short film)
1997. *Stop for a While* (short film)
1996. *Ana* (short film)
1996. *I Don't Do Windows* (short film)
1995. *Sold* (short film)

Ione Hernández's creative process is born from emotions, and is purely visual. Sometimes these images come from a dream, a vision; other times they come from a piece of literature that moved her. All of those inspire stories that she wants to tell. Afterward, she writes them and directs them. Her works have an agile narrative, and above all a poetic imagery that lends them a sensibility and special charm.

Magical Realism

Aizea, City of the Wind is a marvelous story in which, as Gérard Lenne[101] confirms, the real is confounded with the imaginary without losing verisimilitude. The central theme is about the recompensation that those who do not lose hope gain, those who think that anything is possible: even the destruction of the old curse that governs the life of the people of this village called Aizea. According to an indigenous legend, no foreigner can live in this village where the train never stops. If someone breaks this norm, a strong wind carries them to a far-away place, and they lose memory. They will never be able to remember where Aizea is. They may never return.

---

101 Lenne, *Le cinéma "fantastique" et ses Mythologies*.

The life that they had there never existed. But there is no evil that lasts a hundred years. Confidence in true love is able to annul the spell, and make the foreigner return so that they can reunite with their families. We must note that the rhythm and the time of this short film are too slow, and they better fit a longer format. In fact, the film lasts twenty-four minutes. The tape's color tone is sepia, and the lights tend toward expressionism.

The narrative departs from the premise of magical realism, [102] which is materialized through the marvelous. The text presents a universe where the supernatural and fantastic elements mix with everyday existence in a natural way. Aizea is a mixed-race village, situated at some place of an immense and arid desert where the supernatural comes from native gods and from their reaction to the dominators. In this indefinite space, the idea of the limit goes beyond the line that separates the real from the imaginary, and translates into a symbol of the frontier par excellence.

One night in Aizea, Raúl (Dantes Sivilla) goes to the window where Aída (Laura Bayonas), his mother sleeps, to cover her with a blanket. The expressionist light of the mise-en-scène projects shadows on a setting where there is barely any furniture, and which reveals the poverty in which the family lives. The pointed arches frame the room, and the few sun rays that enter by the windows and the thresholds of the doors construct the metaphor home-prison, in which there is a forbidden room. The obscurity symbolizes the mourning for the absence of the beloved, and the weight of the double punishment that Aída and his son suffer: on the one hand, the loss of the father and husband; and on the other, the social marginalization for having transgressed the ancestral law. The voice-off of the main character imposes itself on these images as he talks about his long wait in first person. The narration of internal focus is accompanied by a sad melody that will appear and disappear on and off throughout the story. It is the musical leitmotiv of the melancholy heroic deed of the main character.

The myth of eternal return is related with the figure of Aida, and explains the stoicism and hope that envelope her sacrifice. Cyclical theories allowed the subject to confront suffering, because it wasn't

---

102 Magical realism is a label linked to a genre of Latin-American literature, which reaches its greatest splendor at the middle of the twentieth century, and whose principle exponents are Gabriel García Márquez, Julio Cortázar, and Mario Vargas Llosa. The feature that distinguishes magical realism is that its stories mix fantastic events with real facts in a verosimile way.

definitive, and had a solution; the unfortunate event responded to the necessities of destiny; and it didn't last forever, the situation could change; and through that change, it is possible to recover lost happiness. Aida hangs on to faith in change, which comes from the mysterious force that guides the passage of her husband.

This combination of elements associates Aída with the mythical figure of Penélope, a main character of Homer's *Odyssey*, an epic poem written in the eighth century before Christ. Her figure symbolizes the consecration of life to the eternal and loyal wait for the husband. In order to endure this burden, she knits and undoes a thousand times the tapestry, metaphorically alluding to the myth of the eternal return by Mircea Eliade.[103] The return of the husband is the aim of her existence. The parallelism between both women is clear, although the element that differentiates between them is the inactivity of Aída. She does not knit; the only thing she does is cleaning bottles to maintain herself. Even with her son her relationship is merely functional, she pays no attention to him. Her apathy isolates her even more from the world. It is a kind of dead natural beauty that crystalizes the sadness of the wait. But also, the symbol of internal exile to which Aizea is condemned; a cursed city frozen in time and space.

The sacrifice keeps her caught in an indefinite place, between the melancholy of memory and the weight of forgetting, which converge in the forbidden room. This is the sacred space of the home, closed with keys until its old habitant returns. Dressed in Assed's coat and ring, Raúl looks at himself in the mirror illuminated by a small lamp, and tries to occupy the place of the father, with little success. Just like Telemaco, the son of Penelope, tries to shield his mother from the men that approach her so that she keeps dedicating herself to the wait of the husband. Throughout the story, Aída enters the room on two occasions. The first time at the beginning of the story, when she discovers that her son broke the prohibition, and the second time when, bent by economic necessity, decides to rent out the room. On both occasions they introduce flashbacks that are articulated through a short cut, always accompanied by flute music. The forbidden bedroom is the space of memory. The luminous and colorful images of the past contrast with the obscurity that imposes itself on the present. The two flashbacks narrate the truncated wedding and the promise of future re-encounter, respectively.

---

103 Eliade, *The Myth of the Eternal Return*.

In the first one, the initial and final transitions are articulated like a theater curtain. The shot of Aída embracing the coat of her husband turns into an image of her face covered by a veil. She takes it off, and the action starts. In the end, a tracking shot out[104] distances from her body lying on the floor, and the church doors close behind her. The staging of the wedding recovers the poetic imagery of the floating brides of Marc Chagall to represent the irruption of the marvelous in the nuptial ceremony. The image of the small church, with the roof open to the sky and with grass growing at its floor, is the scene in which the wind grasps the man from the hands of the woman and takes her to a remote place. The veil, the Aztec chalice and the colorist fusion of the participants do the rest for the start of the Chagallian visual style of flying brides, imbued in a folkloric atmosphere of old traditions. Piano notes enriched the musical leitmotiv composed by Susan Hurley this time. It accompanies the ceremony, and disappears when the wind erupts into the church. The scene never shows the face of Assed because Aída doesn't remember it, although she knows that she loves it.

The second flashback is produced while the main character sleeps. It is more like a forgotten dream rather than a memory: an image that she guards to keep hope. This jump in the unconscious of Aída is represented through the ghostly superimposition of Ángela (Vira Montes), who approaches the young woman and whispers a secret in her ears: her son

---

104 This tracking shot out relates to the mise-en-scène of Elisabeta's death in *Bram Stoker's Dracula*, (Francis Ford Coppola, 1992). In both cases, the camera moves away from the woman's body lying in front of the altar, and the church building's doors serve as a curtain. The emotional force of the image rests in the fact of abandoning the female body. This ambiguous image between dream and death crystalizes the sinister beauty of feminine sacrifice.

will achieve that he returns. The woman disappears, and Aída wakes up confused in the church. On the other hand, the image of the bride lying before the altar refers to *beaux mort*,[105] a female model of late ninteenth century iconography symbolizing the sacrifice or immolation of the woman for loving a man. On this occasion, the promise that he will return wakes her up, and she hold on to life to wait for Assed.

The dark side emerges through the wind that surrounds the village, and just like the way it happens with the marvelous, its apparition takes place in a fluid and harmonious way. The wind aims to hinder the main character's return trip. Nevertheless, like in all fantastic stories, an unknown and magic force sets the events into motion. Assed (Edwin Bourgues) travels to Aizea guided by an old map in which there is no trace of the village. He doesn't know the reason for his trip, but he sees himself dragged into finding an answer in spite of the obstacles, the warnings, and the opposition of the locals whom he meets when he arrives at the village. It becomes obvious that when it comes to starting the return trip home, the short film adopts a canonical voyage of the fantastic genre, that of the journey to the unknown. The train scene, in which a passenger aims to dissuade him, and that of his arrival at the saloon where the locals react to him with hostility are inspired by the staging of a similar situation in *Nosferatu, eine Symphonie des Grauens* (Nosferatu, W. F. Murnau, 1922) and *Bram Stoker's Dracula* (Francis Ford Coppola, 1992). However, in this case the fantastic journey is mixed with the characteristic features of the western: the desert, the cultural mixture, the foreigner who arrives at the frontier town, and the inhabitants of the place who are against his settlement there.

On his part Raúl, the son, knows the story of his parents because Ángela, a star with which he talks every night, told him. The film shows him always turning his back to the viewer and in front of the window of his bedroom watching the world through a telescope. The composition resembles the portraits[106] of the Romantic German painter

---

[105] The theme of the beaux mort represents the sublimation of female sacrifice due to devotion or love for a man. The image of a beautiful corpse eroticized by death is a constant of late nineteenth-century painting and iconography, which appears cited in this short film. Not for nothing, as it crystallizes the beautiful dead nature, although in case of the main character it is rather a beautiful nature frozen by waiting. The image of Aída resembles that of Ofelia (1852) by the pre-Raphaelite painter John Everet Millais, or that of The Sleeping Princess (1896) by Frances MacDonald. Both are a representative example of a feminine model that produced turn-of-the-century sexophobia.
[106] The Wanderer above the Mist (1818), or Woman at a Window (1822) are some of the more representative ones. This type of composition creates adisturbing halo of

Caspar David Friedrich (1774, Greifswald–1840, Dresde) in a sense that his characters show their back to the viewer, and contemplate the landscape. This image symbolizes the hope of the return of the father. Just like Aída, the boy devotes his life to waiting for his father, although he maintains a very active attitude that, nevertheless, is little effective. For Raúl, the external world is a threat, and the window is a watchtower from which he defends his home. Ángela announces to him the return of Assed. Together with his friend Víctor (Andrew Aguayo), he watches the passage of the night train with the hope that one day it stops. The night that Assed comes, Raúl is unaware. When he meets with him at the market, he does not recongnize him, and rushes to prevent that he rents out the forbidden room. The curse annuls the revelatory effect that the mirror has in fantastic cinema[107] but, paradoxically, this incident will lead to the encounter of the family. Aída follows Raúl, who flees toward the station with the objective of apologizing to the stranger. When they arrive, the train has left. Assed did not get on. He approaches the woman and the child. First they do not recognize each other, but they look at each other fixedly, and the spell is broken. The family embraces. The superimposition of Ángela's silhouette walks toward the tunnel and turns into a star.

Letters from the Sky

Juego is a circular story whose principle themes are, once again, chance, memory, and forgetting. It has a minimalist[108] visual style that is very different from the previous short film. Ione Hernández takes inspiration from an anecdote that Luiso Berdejo told her about his childhood to write this story, in which she reflects about the belief in the weight of destiny, and the possibility of freeing oneself from it. Time acquires fundamental importance in the narration. On the one hand, it stops to emphasize the moments, expanding its duration with exquisite delicacy, which gives force to the melancholy tone of the story. On the other hand, it seems to be closely related with the journey in three different ways.

---

mystery around the main character, who is solitary and isolated, and they way he contemplates the world.
107 Jean Louis Leutrat affirms that the mirror is one of the blazons of fantastic cinema, and assumes the function of revealing the truth; however, it also establishes a door between the real and the imaginary universe. Leutrat, Vida de fantasmas.
108 In fact, there exists a certain parallelism in terms of topic and visual style with Julio Medem's Los amantes del círculo polar (Lovers of the Arctic Circle, 1998), and also with the personal universe of Isabel Coixet's filmography.

In the first place, the short film develops in function of the itinerary of the letter, and its duration is conditioned by the time the message takes to get to its addressee. In the second place, throughout the short film two trips are made in car, which form a part of this postal itinerary. And finally, in this story there are two temporal jumps to the past that recover the magic of the first children's love, and the ambivalence of play; paradoxically, Helena and Roberto are now a united matrimony. These two flashbacks are linked to the car trip or the irruption of the motorcycle of the postman.

The film highlights the moments that stuck in the memory of the characters forever, and which accompanies them throughout their lives. In particular, it recovers the indelible image of the first child love, the first time the child experiences this sentiment in an innocent and instinctive manner. It is a spontaneous love at first sight without complexes. This is the central axis of the story, embellished by the hopes Adrián deposits in a child's toy in which he believes. The case of his sister is proof of it. Nevertheless, the final outcome shows that predestination linked to this entertainment of childhood does not exist. His nephew covers his eyes, and over the black screen the voice of the child and Adrián's father mix to repeat the magic sentence of the game. The camera shows the main character smiling because he knows that life and love form part of a game in which chance may cause that the right person appears on the least expected day. In fact, the short film ends with Adrián's look, and plants the doubt whether the cycle repeats itself. It is circular story that returns to the past to start a new one.

Lying in bed, Laura (María Vallesteros) is writing a letter to Adrián (Daniel Grao), her former boyfiend, from London. A poetic flashback takes us back to the childhood of the main character (César de Juan) and his sister Helena (Elisa Drabben), who travel back home in a car with their parents. To entertain them, the father (Álex Pastor) proposes a children's game for them. The next boy or girl that they see will be their future husband or wife. Roberto approaches with his scooter and passes by the car. Helena protests angrily because she doesn't like the boy. Adrián's look meets with that of Laura, a girl who is older than him. The action returns to the present. The postman gives the missive over to Helena (Inge Martín San Juan), who decides to take it to her brother to the city. She starts reading it during the trip in the car with her husband Roberto (Paul Lousteau) and her son (Iván Martín). A new flashback shows Laura in her pilgrimage until she sends the letter. Finally, the married couple arrives at Adrián's house, who is visibly depressed and sorrowful for the amorous rupture. They give him the letter, and he goes away from home. He hesitates for a second, and forcefully throws it in the air. Then his nephew hugs him and proposes him the game.

The story starts with the narration that has internal focus on the main character. Laura's voice-off repeats in first person the words that she writes in her room in London. It is only the beginning of the letter. Her voice disappears, and only appears again when Helena starts reading the letter in the car. In this moment, their image walking in London until finding the mailbox accompanies the voice-off. In the rest of the story the events take place by themselves before the eyes of the viewer.

One of the characteristics that distinguish this story, linked to an itinerary, is that the staging creates a sensation of constant movement. This is achieved by the recurrent tracking shot and the discontinuity between fixed shots and movement. The shots of the main character in the streets of London are a good example of the effect of dynamism that temporal discontinuity provokes between various images. Both resources, the tracking shot and the discontinuity, combine with the two trips by car and create the sensation of the unstoppable advancing of events, whose rhythm and time change depending on the sensation that one wants to transmit in each moment. Besides, this text in movement makes the path of the guiding principle of the narration visible, that is, the itinerary of the letter from the sender to its addressee, and integrates the children's game that glides over the couple.

The sky is the cohesive element, and symbolizes the indefinite place where desires, the most intimate thoughts, and the memories of childhood are projected. At the beginning of the film, the camera flies and goes through the window of Laura's room; the title of the short film appears for a moment on the firmament. This shot unites with the tracking shot, in a light high angle shot, of little Adrián's subjective look, who contemplates the immense landscape where the clouds cover the sky. Javier Casado's melancholy piano melody accompanies his thoughts. In the final scene, the envelope that Adrián forcefully throws slowly crosses the firmament, and connects with a shot of Laura in London who, for an moment, looks up to the sky, and then looks at the ground and disappears. Damien Rice's[109] musical theme, *The Blower's Daughter*

---

[109] This musical theme is the leitmotiv of the film Closer (2004) by Mike Nichols.

starts with the throwing of the envelope. This transition reveals the definitive separation of the couple, and the end of the letter's journey.

In this short film, the majority of tracking shots and in particular the subjective one have a very slow time. Their function is to give value to pensive contemplations, or to the moment. This effect is particularly effective the moment when Adrián sees Laura for the first time. The shot of her is repeated in a more reduced size and to a lesser cadence, showing the decisive moment in which chance connects them.

Interview

Aizea and *Juego* are two short films that address the loss of love.

I always tell the same story. This story marked by drama is present in all my short films. Not only in *Aizea* and *Juego*, but also in *El palacio de la luna* and in *Inseparable de ti*. *Aizea* is the final work of the masters in cinematographic direction that I made in the United States. It is very innocent and its resolution is very American, I was too advised, and this is why it is so similar to a short film of school. My intention was to do something harsher. In the other works I had total liberty to do what I wanted. In *Juego*, concretely, destiny imposes itself, and you accept that everyone takes a path; life is more powerful than desires.

Melancholy and children are present in your work.

In the end, my short films always start with a woman who narrates—the mother of *El palacio de la luna*, the mother of *Aizea*, the girl who reads the letter in *Juego* ... All the stories start with a female voice-off who sounds like she is exhausted. There is a kind of surrender from a lost position, but it is not a total loss. And the children, yes, it is true that they appear.

Aizea is a story that has some parallelisms with magic realism. Did you try to embody this literary concept through an aesthetic construction?

At a formal level, I didn't plan to break with anything. *Aizea*, really, is the result of a dream. I imagined a girlfriend whose boyfriend left him. I saw him fly. Thus, I used magical realism to be able to justify this image. But, although I had never read anything about magical realism, I must have searched for something to find my way. In any case, I had no intention of appropriating anything. I wanted to tell the story of the dream that I had from a naive position. Therefore, in order for this dream to take life, I created all this world around it.

Does the poetic universe of *Aizea* allow the development of a poetics of the marvelous?

When I look for an aesthetically beautiful image it is to sublimate the tragedy or the pain, it helps as a support of something more tragic. By combining something tragic with something beautiful offers a new dimension when it comes to observing it. It is ultimately about searching marks where to express something difficult, and sublimate it.

The village is situated at a frontier. It refers to the western frontier, a place between the past and the present.

It doesn't exist. It's a non-place. It It is a symbolic place. Universal. I want to create my Obabas, the places where the characters live, I am not interested in the reference to reality. On the other hand, it is true that the village refers a bit to the western: the stranger, the masculine, the feminine, an arid horizon ... I also have a kind of uprooting. After spending seven years away, there is an attitude of not wanting to identify the space in *Aizea*. It is a very metaphorical story.

The beginning is very obscure, but when the flashback of the wedding appears, it contrasts with the previous one because it is very luminous. Is it something intentional?

Yes, of course. Everything is based on a woman who waits. It is a woman who is prey to her solitude. All my main characters are like that. There is no resignation, but disillusionment, yes. They are not losers of everything, but there is melancholy. There is an encouraging determination, but they are not fooling themselves, either. It is a mixture between the crude reality and the dream of desire. The luminosity at the wedding scene reflects the happiest day of the main character's life; for this reason it contrasts with the dark tone that predominates in the rest of the short film.

There are pictorial references. Chagall's *The Bride*, for example.

It is true. Marc Chagall's *The Bride* was one of the pictorial references. Besides, in the entire saloon scene, Goya and Murillo's painting is very much present. The references are not only pictorial. I also used as reference photos of Spanish women, dark ones, which denote loneliness and widowhood. With regards to the church without roof, we based ourselves on a photo of a Croatian church destroyed in the Balkan wars, published in the *New York Times*. On the other hand, I didn't want any primary colors; I wanted everything to be earth color, like aged.

Do you think that miscellany contributes something new to audiovisual creation?

The new is new because it goes through my filter, no matter what elements you use. If your filter is yours and it is real, of course it contributes. I don't know if it contributes something new to the audiovisual panorama, but it does help me at the level of creativity.

Juego is based on a story by Luiso Berdejo.

Yes, it's true. We are very good friends with Luiso Berdejo. One day he called me, and he told me a very nice anecdote. When he returned from vacations in London, he found the first woman he saw on the train very pretty and, then, he remembered a thing that his father told him when he was a child. It seems like that his father, once they returned from their holidays, told him that the first girl he would see would be his girlfriend. I liked this anecdote, and the principal idea of the short film came from it. I integrated this anecdote in my melancholy universe, and I gave it a certain poetic tone.

Juego also narrates a story of indifference, a nostalgic story, but it uses the indispensable minimum, it is more minimalist, subtler.

Everything is the result of developing your audiovisual language. It is the consequence of a long process in which I start to internalize the language of the short story. In spite of the fact that I do not yet have a concrete style, my universe is recognizable. I am starting to understand that it is not necessary to have so much weight to tell a story. The fear disappears, and I get more naked.

Nevertheless, your work continues to be very plastic.

It is the product of this evolution that I explained before. It is a process of finding your voice. And this has to come from within. Each time I am more convinced of this. I am profoundly visual, more visual than narrative. But, in *El palacio de la luna*, although the form is very important, I clearly opt for the story. I read this tale and I couldn't stop crying. It came to my soul, and I had the powerful necessity to tell it.

Where would *Juego* fit within the contemporary audiovisual tendencies?

When he saw *Juego*, the producer Alfonso Castilla told me that I was the new Isabel Coixet, but the truth is that no one called me to do the next one . . . I don't know. It is very difficult for me to identify with a concrete tendency. The best of short films is that they always appreciate the seal of the person who is behind it; because the direction of short films is very free. Although you collaborate with a team and there is a producer, it is very much your work.

How do you work the music and the sound in your work?

With regards to the music, I normally work with Javier Casado. I do not habitually come together with him, because the musical work that a short film requires is not that extensive. If I was directing a feature film, perhaps it would be fitting to work together more closely. We know each other well, and in the premontage there is already a register of tone, of rhythm. Normally I give him a few reference points so that he knows what I am looking for. I like the process very much. It consists of going, trying and feeling if it is all right or not. And soon, the music emerges. It is something magical. With David Mantecón, sound designer, there is also this connection. Even with the actors.

The music is not always original.

The last song of *Juego* is the same song with which *Closer* (Mike Nichols, 2004) starts and ends. I didn't know that this film started like that, and I didn't like it. Nevertheless, I no longer have a problem with this. In the credits of *El palacio de la luna*, for example, there is a song of *Marie-Antoinette* (Sofia Coppola, 2006). The truth is that we all pay attention to the soundtrack of other movies. But in your own work there is always a part where you have to be loyal to what you are telling with your images. If not, it doesn't integrate well. One must make this effort. Because if not, it shows.

How do you see the situation of women in the professional field?

We are a minority. There are very few female directors. Besides, it seems like men's stories generate more interest at the structural, thematic, and other levels. It is difficult to direct, whether you are a man or a woman. But for us women it is a bit more complicated. If you want to direct, become a mother, and find fulfillment in life, you must make great sacrifices because of the time it requires from you. In any case, I think they are things that go beyond the issue of gender.

Does the fact that you are a woman give you a distinctive look when it comes to working?

I am essentially a defender of good cinema. When you make a film, you express something very much from within. And if you are a woman, there will be an important part of this essence or this quality that will stay in your work. It is inevitable not to appreciate feminine elements in the work of a woman. Nevertheless, there are also men who have this feminine quality, and women who are very masculine. In artistic creation, as you have to connect rather more with your emotional side, it is difficult that the masculine side of a woman should hide the feminine. At the end of the day, creation takes place on the basis of emotions.

Igor Legarreta (Bilbao, 1973) and Emilio Pérez (Bilbao, 1974)

Both filmmakers earned their degrees at the University of the Basque Country (UPV/EHU) in the Audiovisual specialization of Fine Arts, and have collaborated in writing and directing scripts since 1994. *El trabajo* (1999), selected by Kimuak and awarded at the Locarno and Montpellier festivals, was their first 35mm short film after a few experiments in video like *El rincón del Salvador* (1994), *El hombre casto* (1996) and *Al, Ben & Gail* (1997). Kimuak has also selected *El gran Zambini* (2005), directed and produced by themselves through the company Aprieta fuerte, and with which they inaugurated the International Fantastic Film Festival of Catalonia (Sitges). Igor Legarreta cowrote the script of the television movie *Regreso a Moira* (Spectre, Mateo Gil, 2006), included in the series *Películas para no dormir* (Films to Keep You Awake). Emilio Pérez has combined the works of direction assistant (first as well as second) in advertising and in film, working on diverse feature films like *Dos rivales casi iguales* (Miguel Ángel Calvo Buttini, 2007), *Sangre de mayo* (José Luis Garci, 2008), *The Disciple* (Emilio Ruiz Barrachina, 2010), *Campamento Flippy* (Rafa Parbus, 2010), and *Camera obscura* (Maru Solores, 2011). Besides, both have participated in the production of *Máquina* (Gabe Ibáñez), included in the 2006 Kimuak catalog, and Emilio Pérez is coproducer of the documentary directed by Jorge Rivero *La presa* (2009), also present in Kimuak.

Filmography as Directors

2005. *El gran Zambini* (short film)

2003. *Lost* (short film)

2003. *Room 301* (short film)

2001. *La jaula* (short film)

1999. *El trabajo* (short film)

The most important characteristic feature of Legarreta's and Pérez's styles is no doubt their narrative and aesthetic solidity. Their two short films that have participated in Kimuak confirm, in spite of belonging to completely opposite generic registers, a great professionalness and ability in the use of narrative strategies, the direction of actors, and above else the knowledge of mise-en-scène.

Shadows of Madness

El trabajo features a stylized exploration of the psychological degradation that drives a man to madness, and finally to suicide. From its beginnings, the story follows the narrative conventions of film noir. Luis (Pepo Oliva), a hired killer, accepts the charge of watching a schoolteacher (Mariví Bilbao) until such time as he receives a phone call that will order him to finish her off. The man rents out a room in a hostel in front of the woman's house, and starts to photograph all her movements while he waits for the final order.

The voice-off of the character himself gives the details of his activities and thoughts while the images show time and time again his daily routine: waking up by himself in bed, the shower through the curtain, the walk on the street burned by the sun, the photographs of the victim's movements, the wait for the call seated before the television, the clock that shows the constant passage of time without the phone call, and so on.

The premise, characteristic feature of a more reflexive noir, and similar to the *The Conversation* (1974) by Francis Ford Coppola[110] goes on to acquire fantastic elements as time passes without anything happening in the life of Luis. Impatient and nervous because of the delay of the phone call, the man starts to suffer strange nightmares: he imagines that someone follows him in his attempt to assassinate the schoolteacher, and even that the cable of the telephone line has been deliberately cut. One day Luis starts to burn. Literally. He gets frightened and he thinks that it is owing to the terrible sun that enters through the windows, which is why he decides to close the house and work at night only. It is then when the "intrusion of a-normality into normality"[111] takes

---

[110] And even in a more conceptual and aesthetic sense, to another film removed from the noir genre, but exemplary in the representation of the gradual psychic disorder of a person reflected in the external world that surrounds him, to Barton Fink (Joel Coen, 1991).
[111] Lenne, Le cinéma "fantastique" et ses Mythologies, 61.

place, which is proper to the genre of the fantastic film. "In general, the fantastic ... is related with morbid states of conscience, which in phenomena like that of a nightmare or delirium, projects before itself the images of its anxieties and fears."[112] Effectively, the apparent threat of these strange and irrational dreams that interfere with the fixed daily routine of Luis are the result of his mind, and the incomprehensible burns that destroy his skin are nothing but physical marks of a gradual psychic deterioration, which the mise-en-scène reveals progressively. The excellent photography of Gaizka Bourgeaud becomes increasingly gloomier, as Luis tries to exterminate any crack of natural light inside the house, which is evidently a metaphor of his own mental evolution. And in these conditions of scarce depth of field, the variable focus, which moves from foreground to background, increases the sensation of claustrophobia provoked by the voluntary closure of the main character.

The shots that present the everyday routine of the killer (the shower, the wait in front of the television, the photographs, etc.) succeed in a repeated way showing, nevertheless, framings that are increasingly closed, which affects the asphyxiation of his reclusion. The rationality of the voice-off also disappears the moment that the man covers with insulating tape the last crack of light that enters through the window, and loosens the bulb, allowing the darkness to invade him completely. His last words are almost a confession of his physical and mental degradation: "I am sick. I am burning, and I don't know why."

In this moment, the repetitions that have been pushing Luis into a kind of loop end up becoming a violent spiral, and madness takes definite control of the narration. The schoolteacher appears to him like

---

112 Castex, Le conte fantastique en France de Nodier à Maupassant, 8.

a specter in his own house, and an emphatic sound montage takes over the soundtrack, recreating a new and deranged perceptive dimension inside of his head.

When finally the phone rings, the man, now prey to panic and intuiting what comes, smashes it violently against the floor. The montage accelerates to recover some of the images shown before: the photos of the victim hung on the wall, the shower, the walk on the street, the park ... But a terrible alteration has occurred in these familiar shots for the viewer: Luis has come to occupy the place of the old woman on the photographs taken during the surveillance (instantaneous ones that start to show signs of burning) and, on herpart, the woman has replaced him in some of his habitual scenarios.[113] Ultimately, the assassin has turned into his own victim.

The old woman is nothing but the macabre representation of the death that awaits him, and her hallucinated image as she puts her finger in the mouth in shape of a shotgun inevitably anticipates the outcome of the story. Sitting on the floor and howling in terror, Luis is cornered by a threatening tracking shot that swiftly approaches him. The montage suggests that the movement, which is accompanied by a disturbing, almost animalistic growl, corresponds to the schoolteacher's point of view: the man finds himself before death, which looms over him, and offers him a broken telephone that rings incessantly. The call that he impatiently waited to finish off the job has finally arrived, and Luis executes the order by firing a bullet in his mouth. The killer thought he had been following his next victim, and he wasn't exactly mistaken, given that by directly photographing death, it was hiding from him the real identity of the future cadaver, which is his. When Luis pulls the trigger, the crash of the denotation is replaced by the sound of the shutter release of the camera.[114]

The story, mediated by the voice-off of the main character, has constructed itself around his point of view in constant internal focalization. Always situated together with the main character, the viewer could not

---

113 This ending refers to in a way the story Ghosts collected in The New York Trilogy by Paul Auster. In it, a private detective is contracted to watch a man until with the passage of time he discovers that his victim is a projection of himself, and ends up killing his other.

114 In his last work, Camera Lucida: Reflections on Photography, Roland Barthes links photography with death as a register of that which will die. In cinema, the camera (photographic or cinematographic) has also been more than once related with the death theme, as evidenced by Peeping Tom (Michael Powell, 1960) or Arrebato (Iván Zulueta, 1978).

clearly discern what was real and what was not, either. They find themselves completely immersed in the delirious process of Luis's disintegration. The terrorific final tracking shot, nevertheless, associated with the old woman's point of view, situates the viewer in the place of the camera, separated finally from the main character, and accompanying for the first time the death that lurks around Luis. The spectators thus convert themselves, by the mediation of the mise-en-scène, into uncomfortable accomplices of this terrifying hallucination that vividly unfolds before the eyes of the main character, which the shot ends in the darkness of the final black screen.

A Marvelous Tale

Legarreta and Pérez completely leave behind the dismal and gloomy tone of their previous short film in *El gran Zambini*, a nice family drama full of tenderness, which traverses the courses of the marvelous tale.

The fantastic, present in *El trabajo*, is based on everyday reality, and metamorphoses it by introducing extraordinary or irrational elements. Also, "if the marvelous uses the impossible, it is to surprise: not to frighten or worry, but to please and fascinate."[115] This is what happens in *El gran Zambini*. Cowritten by both directors and David Abia, it is

---
115 Gérard Lenne, Le cinéma "fantastique" et ses Mythologies, 91.

the story of an impossible and magical challenge that serves to reunite a father and his son separated by social intolerance. At the same time, it conveys a brave lesson about respect for human beings.

Situated in the middle of a naked landscape, deserted, almost lunar, a rickety roulotte serves as home for a family that lives with the abandoned remains of an old circus. The son (Aníbal Tártalo) is ashamed of the father (Emilio Gavira) because he is a dwarf, and suffers the mockery of the other children. One day the father observes his son's fascination as he watches the images of a man stepping on the moon for the first time on television. He designs a plan to win his admiration.

According to Gérard Lenne, the enchanted-magical themes are nothing more than skillful and surprising means to obtain certain poetic effects.[116] Legarreta and Pérez offers us beautiful and studied framings accompanied by gentle camera movements in this film, which hits the tone of lyricism on more than one occasion. The directors reserve the last words in direct dialogue to the cruel jokes that the children throw at the dwarf, yielding the weight of the narration to the visual potency of the images. The difficult relations between the central characters are articulated through their expressive looks that rarely cross, but perfectly condense the emotions that live in each one of them: the son's shame, the father's pain, and the sadness of the mother (Esperanza de la Vega) divided between the two.

The distance between the son and the father is clear from the sequence that opens the film. The camera starts out from an abandoned canon, and moves until it captures the son sitting by the artifact. The man goes out of the roulotte to hang the clothes and directs his look at the son. He also looks in his father's direction, but the two persons never get to share shot. When the mother chases away the children who approached them to make fun of her husband, the camera returns to revolve around the canon in a movement that is identical to the one before, to show us this time that the little boy, ashamed, has hidden inside it to avoid having to watch the scene.

The following day the father waits for his son at the exit of the school, and notices that, in front of him, a little girl holding on to her mother's hand watches him fixedly. The man winks, provoking a timid smile from the little one. His own son, on the other hand, is incapable

---

116 Ibid., 95.

of showing any sign of love for his father. He hides in the bathroom until the rest of the students leave and when, worried by his absence, the father enters the school building and meets with his son standing on the top of the staircase. The boy, physically situated above the father briefly observes him with superiority, and then comes down lowering his look. When he reaches the last step, the composition positions them in front of each other, but with the boy still above the father. Both look at each other again directly, but the son walks past him without giving any explanation for his behavior.

The father doesn't tolerate his disrespect, and punishes him by not allowing him to have dinner. The mother however, who divides her love and understanding between them, finally takes him a sandwich to the canon, where the child once again hid from his father. The father observes the scene from the door of the mobile home, and understands that he must do something in order to recover the love of his son. In this very moment when his fabulous plan is born, we hear the emotive musical composition of Fernando Velázquez for the first time, announcing the eruption of magic into the story. The man lights a flashlight, and both the beam of the light and the zoom of the camera direct their look toward the old poster hanging on the wall. The camera runs through the details of the drawing on which, under a title that says "*The Great Zambini,*" we can see a man ball shooting out from the canon toward the moon. The camera softly closes the shot by highlighting the pensive look of the man. Then it shows us as he relocates and re-furbishes the canon that until then served as the hiding place of the embarrassed child. With exquisite subtleness and narrative economy, the filmmakers make us understand immediately the father's plan: resuscitate his old days in the circus, once again lighting the fuse of the marvelous scene where children's hopes and dreams become reality, and thus exchange the child's embarrassment with fascinated admiration, which this object has represented up to the moment.

After the boy spent the day spying from the window on the mysterious preparations of his father, an explosion suddenly illuminates the darkness of the night. The child goes into the street, and the sees the smoking canon. The camera approaches his eyes in high angle tracking shot, which is between surprised and scared, and the music ascends until the images show the object of his gaze: the moon. Although the viewer doesn't yet know, the long shot of the child observing the sky locates, for the first time, the father into an elevated position with respect to the son. The enormous moon (which inevitably refers to *E.T. The Extra-Terrestrial* [1982] by Steven Spielberg, another marvelous tale) is the destiny of the dwarf's impossible journey.

Next morning the father is not around. In the middle of the night we hear a whistle coming from outside, and a strong knock awakes the child. It is his father, covered with dust and dressed in the outfit of the human cannonball. The man leaves some things in the living room, which remain outside of the field, and leaves as he winks at the son, just as he did with the little girl in the school. It is a beautiful gesture of complicity that shows that for him, his height is not a problem that should make him feel ashamed.

For the second time during the story, father and son look at each other directly and tardily, although on this occasion it is the father who finds himself in a dominant position before the son sitting on the bed. When the door opens, the camera opens the shot to finally show the surprising gift of the father that explains his satisfaction: the US flag that Neil Armstrong planted in the moon's surface. With the sprout of dawn and already outside of the roulotte, the camera still continues to move back in slow tracking shot until the open hole in the smoking ground becomes visible, which bears witness of the sublime feat, worthy of a fairytale, carried out by this little great man.

This is exactly the message that fairy tales get across to the child in manifold forms: that a struggle against severe difficulties in life is unavoidable, is an intrinsic part of human existence; but that if one does not shy away, but steadfastly meets unexpected and often unjust hardships, one masters all obstacles and at the end emerges victorious.[117]

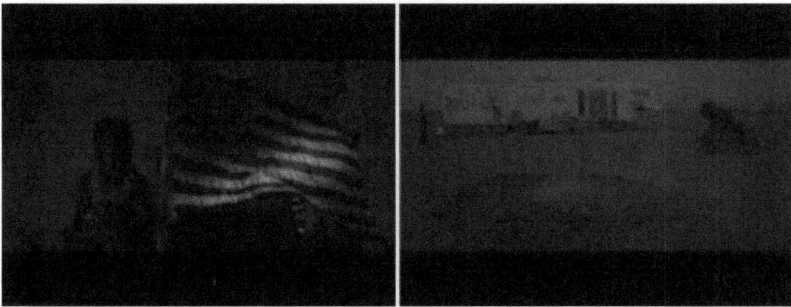

Interview

You direct your short films together. How do you manage this work together?

Emilio Pérez: The process is always more or less the same. We work on the script together, although it's true that Igor Legarreta has much more weight, because he is a better writer. In fact he habitually writes scripts for other people's projects. Once we have the script that we will shoot outlined, we decide in what terms we should tell the story, and how it will be visualized. It is, ultimately, about agreeing about this preliminary work so that once we get to the shoot, there is a single voice. There is no division of labor. We share the work of direction at all levels.

Achieving this previous consensus may entail difficulties.

Igor Legarreta: In the years that we have been working together we have fitted well together, we have supported each other, and we have been able to channel difficult situations. Besides, you have someone by

---

117 Bettelheim, *The Uses of Enchantment*, 8.

your side with whom you can contrast your opinion; it is possible to polish defects and improve the final product. Nevertheless, it is true that each one of us obstinately insists on our point of view. This, in the future, may of course lead to conflicts. If instead of enriching the project the creative debate becomes a war, it wouldn't make sense to continue working together.

El trabajo and *El gran Zambini* are different in register and in tone.

Emilio Pérez: The story of *El trabajo* is rather obscure and hermetic; a story that a lot of people do not understand. Possibly, a part of this hermetism was owing to the fact that we were just starting in the world of cinema. It is not a totally closed script either, but perhaps it has a lot to do with how we felt, and what we wanted to tell. *El gran Zambini*, in turn, is much more luminous. While *El trabajo* ends with a person killing himself, with an abrupt cut to black, *El gran Zambini* ends with the dawn of a new day. They are two completely opposing ideas, and perfectly define in what point each story is headed. *El gran Zambini* is a story that possesses a touch of sadness but, in the end, we can see some hope in the relationship between father and son.

Igor Legarreta: The two short films selected by Kimuak are very different in terms of register and tone. There is no doubt about that. *El trabajo* starts like a thriller and, as the story unfolds, it enters the terrain of the fantastic. It was 1998, and it was our first short film in 35mm. It is a brave idea in various ways, very hermetic. Besides, it was the university years, when things impact you more. In *El gran Zambini*, in change, these influences are much more screened.

How did you manage in *El trabajo* this transition from dark thriller to the fantastic genre?

Emilio Pérez: We were sure that *El trabajo* was going to have all the connotations and keys of a thriller; it is not for nothing that the main character is a detective who is charged with the search of a person. The fact that it should lead to terror was also in the initial script. Nevertheless, there are certain aspects, especially of the final part of the short film, which were defined very much a posteriori, in the montage. The process of the main character and his environment's decomposition was determined; all of this was filmed. We wanted to relate and resume what was happening to the person. It is for this reason that we chose such an abstract montage: frenetic and fantastic in many aspects.

The montage is excellent. The cinematography and the music intensify this sensation of anxiety that reigns in the film. It is difficult to envision the ending of the film.

Igor Legarreta: In *El trabajo* we drew all the shots. We worked with Gaizka Bourgeaud, director of photography, from shot to shot. And we handled the montage. We had just made a short film in video, *Al, Ben & Gail*, which won an award in the underground circuits. It was related in flashback, and had a very spectacular montage, which also influenced *El trabajo*. We wanted the story to be very sober in its development, that is should grow in tension, and that it flows into a very unexpected, intense, very dramatic ending. The montage was meant to shock, to startle.

Emilio Pérez: All of this was foreseen. We planned it thinking about it. Each time the character gets out of bed, we get closer and close even more on him, and we go evoking anxiety in the viewer. They are very basic and simple concepts, but they reach their objective. At the end of the short film, the character discovers himself in the photography panel, and realizes that he was pursuing himself. When he puts the rifle in his mouth, we do not hear a shot but a click of the camera, and you think: "the last photograph is now taken; it's over, the main character is dead." It is all very metaphorical, and perhaps it is not very clear what the objective of the film was, what it was that it wanted to tell. I like the story a lot, because behind the main character there is a husband, a woman, and a daughter. There is, ultimately, a life. But I am aware that everything is rather diluted by the dazzling montage, under such a dramatic mise-en-scène. It is, in part, our fault.

El trabajo resembles *The Conversation* (Francis Ford Coppola, 1974).

Emilio Pérez: Evidently, *The Conversation* is a major reference for short films, because the process of decomposition that Pepo Oliva suffers—Luis, the main character—is the same that Gene Hackman experiences in *The Conversation*. Also, *Angel Heart* (Alan Parker, 1987) is perhaps the clearest influence at the level of the script. The character of Mickey Rourke in *Angel Heart* is a detective whom a person charges with detecting another person. Curiously, he spends the film searching for himself, and when he finds himself, he dies. *El trabajo* could be a copy: there is a person who calls Luis so that he finds another person. The main character is going crazy because he thinks that he is searching for a person when, deep down, he is searching for himself. And the final explanation? It is Luis who appears on the photos. The coincidence is clear. *Angel Heart* had a lot to do with the story and the visual effects, and *Seven* (David Fincher, 1995) with the visual aspect.

Igor Legarreta: I would say that *JFK* (Oliver Stone, 1991) is very much present. But it is undeniable that it is a thriller with a fantastic turn, very much in the line of *Angel Heart*, as much as genre is concerned. It is a nihilistic thriller, a metaphor about suicide; it is the story of a man who is tired of living. We tell his suicide as if it was a search for himself. *El gran Zambini* came seven or eight years later, and it caught us in the mood of doing something more positive.

Both in *El trabajo* as in *El gran Zambini* the visual shot imposes itself before the dialogues.

Igor legarreta: In our first short films there were more classic conversations. It is something that was not premeditated; it came up naturally. The voice-off was very good for us in *El trabajo* to show the madness of the main character. In *El gran Zambini*, in turn, it was brave. We wanted to tell the story without dialogues, and that it doesn't end up very mannered, very affected. Now for me it is a little challenge to film with dialogues, to direct them, to refine them, and that they acquire rhythm.

Music also acquires great importance.

Igor Legarreta: I think that we could have contained the music a bit more. The short film is divided between two parts. The first one doesn't have music, and it is more sober and static. The father realizes that his son rejects him, and he takes notice of the conflict that exists. A little later the father punishes the son. He closes him in his room. The parents have dinner by themselves, thoughtful and pensive, until the mother enters the son's room, and finds that he is not there. The father looks out of the other door and, outside, sees that the mother puts a sandwich inside of the canon where the child hides. The father closes the door, he stays in the son's room, and notices the man-bullet on the poster; he understands the dimension of the problem. The music enters to take us all to the second part, where the conflict will be resolved. It sweeps us emotionally together with the main character. In the end, the son recovers the admiration for his father, and understands that he can be a great man.

Emilio Pérez: Visually, the short film is magical, and the great work of Fernando Velázquez with the soundtrack has a lot to do with this. No doubt, the music acquires a special role in this final part. Very cleverly, Igor Legarreta wanted to put a break on this prominence a little bit, and find equilibrium, because one of the problems that we could have run into was giving to much significance to the music. I remember that in the final mixtures one of our main intentions was that the music is not too excessively present so that in the end it does not overwhelm the rest of the film.

In the music and the tone of the short film, one can appreciate the influence of *E.T.*

Emilio Pérez: The reference was very clear. The music that we had in mind in certain aspects, especially in the simplest ones, were certain passages of the soundtrack of *E.T.*, by John Williams. I remember that Igor Legarreta was very reluctant that everything should be too explicit when it came to marking for Fernando Velázquez the guidelines about what the soundtrack should be like. We were afraid, but Fernando Velázquez has an amazing capacity to, with the reference on his mind, compose his own music. He perfectly understood the concept of magic, of fantasy, and what we were looking for. The result was magnificent.

Igor Legarreta: In *El gran Zambini* the influences are more nuanced. They are not so evident as in *El trabajo*. Nevertheless, one can feel the shadow of Spielberg. But I think that it is owing to, mostly, the soundtrack. There is also a shot in which the boy appears and watches the trajectory of the canon that points at the moon, which is very typical of Spielberg's cinema. I love *E.T.*, and I admit that this look is there in the short film. But, for example, an influence that is not manifest at the level of staging is *Paris-Texas* (Wim Wenders, 1984). The idea of the story comes from this movie. With David Abia, the co-screenwriter, we spoke a lot about the moment in which Harry Dean Stanton goes to pick up his son from shool, and the child is ashamed of him. This scene was the origin of the idea of the short film. We also had on mind the way Aki Kaurismäki portrays the rootless, and the losers.

What is the lesson that the end of the story provides?

Emilio Pérez: The father travels to the moon, and brings back the flag that the American astronauts planted there. The father, through this gesture, aims to show his son that he is capable of doing whatever he sets out for. This is a little bit the moral of the story. No matter how disabled we are, no matter how "different" people may consider us, we should be able to achieve what we set out to achieve. The message is very utopistic, very idyllic. Father and son are confronted. The son is ashamed of the father because he is a dwarf. The father, in turn, severely punishes the son. But, even if the father is right, the law of the strongest is not the solution. And in this situation, the mother intervenes to channel the situation. They are two positions in such confrontation that they end up converging by this third one that intervenes: the necessity of dialogue and understanding.

There exists empathy between the two characters and the viewer, something that is not present in *El trabajo*.

Igor Legarreta: El trabajo is a more uncomfortable story. The main character has a great existential conflict. He leads a very precarious life, and he lives his last days. It is difficult that this should penetrate the audience, because it is a more abstract story, more hermetic, more uncomfortable. Robert McKee says that we don't go to the movie theater to avoid ourselves, but so that they explain reality to us. For me, it is revitalizing to see a film that tells me a harsh story, which explains to me why things are the way they are, or that it should be a perspective that complains about what you complain about. *El gran Zambini*, however, is different; there is much more light. And for that reason, the identification of the spectator with the characters is simpler.

Emilio Pérez: In *El trabajo* it was very complicated to empathize with the main character. In *El gran Zambini*, in turn, the identification is possible. We can understand the boy, the father, and the mother; the third leg of the tripod who sometime turns into spectator, who is there from the outside, who does not get entangled with the conflict between father and son until there is nothing else left to do. Inevitably, the spectator empathizes with all of them. Because, in the end, they understand the embarrassment of the boy, the pain of the father, and the conciliatory attitude of the mother. It is a very universal story, which reaches directly the heart of the viewer.

Is *El gran Zambini* a fairy tale?

Emilio Pérez: It has a lot of tale elements, for the fact that one of its main characters is a child. It is precisely his perspective that leads the story. But also, because it's a fantasy. A father who sails through the skies, arrives at the moon, and returns with the American flag is something very imaginative. The viewer doesn't know for certain if he had really done it or he had invented it all, and had bought the flag in the nearby store.

Igor Legarreta: Ultimately, we wanted to do a more open story that does not lose interest, a story that leaves the doors open to different interpretations that reach the depths of the spectator, but without insulting their intelligence. *El gran Zambini* is a story that is very rich in nuances in spite of the fact that it is a tale.

Emilio Pérez: Although it is a tale, its outcome is not the typical happy ending. Nevertheless, the viewer assumes the final look of the child: "perhaps my father is right, and he just showed me that I was wrong." In this sense, it is true that it ended with a ray of hope, a new dawn, a new day that is born. Therefore, the final outcome could have some relationship with the fairy tale with a happy end, where these values are present—often detested or outmoded—which they inculcate in us since we were children. But without falling into obvious interpretations, or excessively plain explanations.

Oskar Santos (Bilbao, 1972)

Santos earned his degree in Audiovisual Communication at the Complutense University of Madrid. He carried out direction tasks in the television series *Urban Myth Chillers/Petits Mythes Urbaines* (coproduction between France, United Kingdom, Germany, and Canada, 2004), *Crematorio* (Crematorium, 2011, second unit), and *Hispania. La leyenda* (2012). He directed the making of the movie by Alejandro Amenábar *Mar adentro* (The Sea Inside, 2004) before releasing his own feature film titled *El mal ajeno* (For the Good of Others, 2010). The two short films that he made until now have been selected by Kimuak: *Torre* (2000) and *El soñador* (2004).

Filmography as Director

2013. *Zipi y Zape y el club de la canica* (Zip & Zap and the Marble Gang, feature film)

2010. *El mal ajeno* (feature film)

2004. *El soñador* (short film)

2000. *Torre* (short film)

In spite of the disparateness of their form and content, both *Torre* and *El soñador* speak of the pain of loss from the perspective of the fantastic. In these films, the subjectivity of the main characters gains great importance, and the border between dream (or hallucination) and reality never gets to be defined in a clear way. The register of one and the other, however, are completely different. *Torre* fits fully with a type of horror film whose references are some of Roman Polanski's films, such as *Repulsion* (1965), *Rosemary's Baby* (1968), or *Le Locataire* (The Tenant, 1976), where an apartment building turns into the site of a person's madness. In *El soñador*, on the other hand, the gloomy and sinister face of his previous work is dyed with hope, allowing its main characters to find ways to escape their desolation, and reach, even if through a dream, a certain happiness.

The Innocent Face of Evil

As its title indicates, an enormous apartment block erected around a patio is the main character of *Torre*. In its center resides evil. Following the pattern of classic films in the horror genre such as *Village of the Damned* (Wolf Rilla, 1960), *The Innocents* (Jack Clayton, 1961), or ¿Quién puede matar a un niño? (Who Can Kill a Child?, Narciso Ibáñez Serrador, 1976), evil is incarnated in a group of children with candid faces.

Clara (Sonia Almarcha) is murdered by an elderly neighbor (Carmen Balenciaga), who immediately afterward kills herself. Before the tragedy, the woman phoned her husband Pablo (Chete Lera), who was on a business trip, and desperately asked for help because the devil had taken the shape of an elderly woman and wanted to kill her. At that moment Pablo ignores her, as he thinks it is only her imagination, a result of the depression that she suffered. However, Clara's is not the first case that happens in the building, and the man suspects that something strange is going on. Pablo starts having hallucinations, in which he receives phone calls from his deceased wife, warning him that he would be the next victim of the devil. He becomes obsessed with a sinister man in black (Kepa Hernández), who he thinks he can see constantly around the building. Pablo ends up murdering the man, convinced that he was the cause of the crimes, although he later dies at the hands of the authentic responsible persons: the evil children who play every day on the patio, and who manipulate the minds of the residents, pushing them to kill one another.

Although the film, written by the filmmaker himself and Javier Sánchez Donate, suffers from an excessive running time (25 minutes), Oskar Santos's competent direction proves his talent in the management of the conventions of the genre, and his ability to create disconcerting atmospheres.

The patio around which the tower of apartments, converted into a prison for its inhabitants, rises with threatening verticality is the center of gravity for this story. In the interior of the building there opens a labyrinth of straight corridors, whose symmetrical horizontality, with the character located at the point of escape, evokes the disturbing compositions of *The Shining* (Stanley Kubrick, 1980). Nevertheless, the geometrical form that dominates as the representative of evil is the circle. Clara goes down the winding staircase toward the apartment of the old woman, where she will meet death. Later a neighbor with mental handicap (Javier Tirado), who is the only character able to perceive with unsuspected insight the real origin of the murders, warns Pablo that evil surrounds the building, and will not allow anyone to leave: "evil is outside, and goes in circles."[118]

From Clara's funeral scene, the camera connects her sepulture with Pablo's close-up in a single movement, the staging makes it evident repeatedly that the main character will meet the same fate as his wife. For that end, Santos's mise-en scène introduces us, as he already did with Clara in the previous scenes, into the psyche of the character to give expression to his gradual hallucinatory process in images and sounds. Thus, the camera penetrates his mind, and illustrates the internal perceptions of Pablo, who relives in his hallucinations the subjective shot of Clara approaching in the corridor the apartment of the old woman. In his case, it is his own wife who opens him the door, given that it is Clara's voice that the devil uses to introduce the idea in Pablo's head that the man in black is the source of evil. Each time Pablo sees this strange young man in the middle of the patio, the passer-bys are out of focus, the camera slows around him, and the sound atmosphere disappears (as it happened when Clara approached the place of her death), transmitting the viewer the delirious perception of the man.

Therefore, only Pablo's subjective visions and hearings, dominated by an evident paranoia, seem to capture the threat that this sinister character represents, and they push him to kill him. In reality, everything is product of the perverse manipulation of these heirs of Damien from *The Omen*

---

[118] Circle is associated with the devil through the pentacle, a symbol used in the invocations of Satan.

(Richard Donner, 1976), who as a genuine diabolical incarnation have poisoned his mind.

The children appear (visually and sonorously) for the first time stalking as shadows out of focus, in the foreground of a panning shot that followed Pablo on his way home. The soundtrack featured the innocent chants of their games, as a referent of the voices that the murderers hear before killing themselves, and above all, the disturbing children's choirs of Fernando Velázquez's music which, with its tone of a sinister tale resembles, to a certain degree, the compositions of Danny Elfman and Tim Burton. At this moment, Pablo did not think of them, as he was only able to discern the recurring figure of his suspicious man in black observing the patio. Only when the satanic design of getting rid of the neighbor is fulfilled does he manage to exit the disturbing vision that guided the story. He finally sees the authentic face of evil: the circle of children that appears over his injured body in an extreme subjective low angle shot. As Pablo has used all bullets in the murder, he is left without ammunition for his own suicide, and the treacherous creatures finish him off by shooting him with his own weapon. The camera flies in circle over the body of the man and, after a dissolving fade-out, links the silhouette of the cadaver drawn in chalk on the floor with the ring of children who, re-united in a witches' Sabbath, get down to choosing the next victim of their macabre game.

The Romantic Dream

El soñador is a production of Carmen Rico (Himenóptero S.L.) presented by the Nescafé brand which, on occasion of its fiftieth anniversary, promoted and financed various filmic projects by various acclaimed directors, in this case Alejandro Amenábar.

Set in the nineteenth century, the film stages another script by Javier Sánchez Donate on the basis of a tale of his own, and it is narrated through the voice-off of one of its main characters, the psychiatrist Guillermo Rivas (José Ángel Egido). Rivas is contracted by Don Álvaro Robledo to determine the real psychological condition of his brother Diego (Dritan Biba). After the death of his young wife, he moved to his quiet country home to seek ailment for his grave insomnia. There, he does not only find sleep, but also starts to sleep for long periods of time, which take even days. Ready to put him in a mental hospital to avoid the growing rumors of his madness, Don Álvaro asks Rivas to observe his brother so that it is him who makes the last decision. What the doctor discovers is that Diego wants to sleep because while he sleeps, he dreams with an ideal world in which suffering doesn't exist, and can continue to live with his wife.

The film is centered on Rivas's stay in Diego's home, and how the strange case of the dreamer affects the life of the psychiatrist, who ends up identifying with his patient. The annotations of the case that he makes in his diary guide a narrative that is exempt from direct dialogue. The careful artistic direction of Vicent Díaz, the elegant photography of Josu Incháustegui, and above all the enwrapping musical composition of Fernando Velázquez contribute to the creation of a melancholy atmosphere that impregnates the story of an evidently romantic trace.

> The romantic implies a very special state of the spirit—dictated by the untranslatable *Sehnsucht*, longing, yearning, nostalgy—for what man, extracting creative energy from his disillusionment and desolation, searches. Through the imagination and the dream, the path of plenitude and infinity. [119]

---

119 Argullol, *El Héroe y el Único*, 34.

Love as a force capable of overcoming death, and the evasion through dream of a world that is painful are typical themes of Romanticism. One of its most frequent archetypes is the sleepwalker who, just like the main character, "*lives the dream-like life.*"[120] In the words of Argullol, "*the romantic discovers in sleepwalking, in dreamlike action, an itinerary of liberty and creativity that he or she is denied in real life.*"[121] This is the reason why Diego feels happy while he dreams, because he is able to construct his own world that is impossible in the sphere of conscience. This is reflected in the fabulous buildings of his drawings.

Although Rivas indicates in his diary the concrete date of his observations, in Diego's world time is not a clearly delimited dimension, which is also suggested by the elaborate Oskar Santos's elaborate mise-en-scène. The camera remains static in only a few shots, and it slides in space in constant movement, while the profuse dissolves that link the images seem to want to capture the continuity of temporal flow.[122]

These two formal elements, the camera's mobility and the linked transitions do not only help create this climate of melancholy, but also visually strengthen the parallelism that the story establishes between these two persons who have suffered a terrible loss: Diego lost his wife, and Rivas his little daughter. The mise-en-scène relates both characters for the first time through a mirror, showing one as the reflection or double of the other. When Diego explains the psychiatrist the nature of this dreamlike world where pain doesn't exist, Rivas' face stays focused in the foreground of the frame, while Diego's figure, whose physical body does not appear on the screen, is reflected unfocused on the specular surface. If the confession of the patient seems to prove his madness, the camera immediately changes the focus to show with total clarity the image of Diego, and blur in change the face of Rivas. Both share the same wound, and the immaterial reflection of the aristocrat through the figure of the doctor seems to give body to the crouching phantoms of the latter's unconscious.

---

120 Ibid., 291. Italics in the original.
121 Ibid., 288–89. Italics in the original.
122 The obtained effect is similar to what we can see, with similar objectives, in *The Age of Innocence* (1993) by Martin Scorsese.

What this visual effect allows to show is that the young man possesses in fact an understanding of what the doctor suffers from, given that ever since the death of his daughter, he has been tortured by his impossibility to dream. Before the happiness that the world of dreams brings Diego, the psychiatrist is immersed in the darkness of pain. That is how he himself writes in his diary, and the sentiment is visually illustrated by the movement of the camera from his person to the detail shot of a candle that goes out completely.

At the end of three months without getting a diagnosis from the psychiatrist, Don Álvaro decides to put his brother in the hospital. But Rivas now understands that Diego is blessed with a peculiar lucidity, which must be preserved. While he thinks about what measures to take, the camera connects in a single and rhythmical movement the flame of a burning candle with the face of Rivas and the portrait of his dead daughter, foretelling what the final outcome of the films also corroborates: that Diego has given Rivas the clarity and light of his dreams so that he once again meets with his daughter.

Rivas writes a letter in the name of Diego communicating to Don Álvaro that he would cede to him all his property, and would leave forever in order to avoid the prejudice that his state could cause him. The country house where he lives, nevertheless, would be left on the name of Guillermo Rivas as an appreciation of his services. Rivas lets Diego go to bed, and seals the door of the house with a padlock before leaving it forever.

The face of the dreamer closing his eyes melts with that of the psychiatrist, who does the same inside of the carriage. A third fade-out leads to the content of the dream: his daughter runs until the iron gate of the entrance of the mansion, and her eyes penetrate with a vertiginous subjective shot to Diego's bedroom, who is now an old man, still sleeping with a smile on his face. When the little girl goes away from there, the camera rises in order to show the marvelous buildings that Diego recreated in his drawings, towering now as *real* over his home. Thus the absolute identification between the dreamer and the psychiatrist is confirmed. He is finally able to dream with Diego's world, where lost love comes back to life, and he smile while he sleeps.

Interview

Did the short films facilitate your way to feature films?

Torre and *El soñador* have been two very important works in my career. And, in effect, they do have value as part of my path toward feature film. It's like a letter of introduction. Nevertheless, I wouldn't dare claim that short films are indispensable to get someone to produce you a film. In fact, I know few cases—that of Daniel Sánchez Arévalo is one of them—where the short film reflects that there is a great director behind them. There are cases of directors with excellent short films, like that of Igor Legarreta and Emilio Pérez with *El gran Zambini*, which show that the short film in and of itself is not decisive. I also remember a lot of meetings with producers where they didn't ask you about your short films at all.

Then, what does one need to do to be able to shoot a film?

You have to have a good script, choose the right moment and, above all, you need someone to trust you. I was lucky because that Alejandro Amenábar—in the production—and Daniel Sánchez Arévalo—in the script supported me in my first work, *El mal ajeno*, and now I can continue to work. Alejandro Amenábar and I have known each other since college, and his help was fundamental in both *Torre* and *El soñador*.

Javier Sánchez Donate wrote the script of your two short films.

Javier Sánchez Donate is another friend from the university. We were flat mates for five years, and we wrote two feature films that could not be materialized. Afterward, I entered in the project of *El mal ajeno*, in which the scriptwriter was Daniel Sánchez Arévalo. Although after *Torre* and *El soñador* I didn't have the opportunity to work with him, I am sure that we will work together again. Javier Sánchez Donate is a torrent of ideas. I would also like to work with Igor Legarreta.

Locations have great importance in *Torre*.

The building is the story itself; a small microcosm where the majority of the neighbors doesn't know one another. It's a giant space, tremendously impersonal and dehumanized. I remember that I looked for one, and didn't find the right building in Madrid for *Torre*. Besides, the producer—Norberto Ramos del Val—told me that for him it was easier to shoot in the Basque Country for various reasons. And, in the end, I found the building in question in Leioa, close to my cousin's house. When we went to see it, I didn't think much of it because it was only three storeys high, and I needed one of eight or ten, a piece of gigantic cupboard. Nevertheless, I knew the applications of digital effects, and I decided to amplify the scale of the building digitally. We found that the building was very appropriate, but the interior was not good for us. Luckily, my brother—Jorge Santos—and his girlfriend built some impressive sets.

But even so, we still needed the hallways. We had in mind the hallways of *The Shining* (1980) by Kubrick: symmetrical, cold, impersonal, with a lot of light... Finally, we found it in a convent school in Amorebieta. The building had a very important character, which is why we gave it the attention it deserved.

You have mentioned Kubrick, who is an obvious reference. But the short film also has something of Polanski.

I am a fan of Polanski. Nevertheless, whom I like most is Kubrick, because in his work I always find something different. From his third film on, whatever he does is a masterpiece one after the other. Besides, I lived and could see his latest films in the movie theater. He is an absolute influence. But then so are Spielberg, Coppola, Fincher, the Coen brothers... Shyamalan, without going further, had a tremendous influence on my first feature film. But with regards to Polanski, I hadn't seen *Le locataire* (The Tenant, Roman Polanski, 1976). I saw it not too long ago, and I realized that Álex de la Iglesia's cinema, and that of very many other filmmakers, owe a lot to this film. Mine was an induced influence. If I had seen the film, surely it would have impacted me more. Certainly, I was impacted by *Rosemary's Baby* (Roman Polanski, 1968). But my inspirations are diverse. Television, for example. The structure of *Torre* is like that of an episode of *Alfred Hitchcock Presents*, or *The Twilight Zone*. They are thrillers of half an hour, and you never quite knew what was going on until the final turn. I always aim that at first viewing, the spectator does not know everything, but perceives elements that in the end will be revealed. I don't like to either cheat, or betray the spectator. The central theme of the short film is something purely metaphorical. It talks of the devil as the evil represented that comes from this dehumanization that is very present in every big city.

Why did you decide that the children were the evil?

We liked the idea of turning around the idea of innocence, and reflect that purity is able to punish with more force than impurity itself. There is also the character of the mentally challenged, who in a way is a clairvoyant, and intuits something that the rest of us don't see. We enter, therefore, in the terrain of the fantastic. I love the fantastic, although I am a totally skeptical person. Nevertheless, one thing I will always avoid in anything I do is the word message. All my generation has seen the same cinema. The culture of the spectator is a skin that we wear, and we will never be able to take it off. As a viewer, I can't stand it when they give me moral lessons. I don't like either moral lessons, or immoral ones; I like amoral ones. It is what Kubrick does in a certain way. This distance that no morality represents, the fact of not judging the characters. Kubrick was an extraordinary dissectionist of the dark aspects of the human soul. And I am very much interested in all this. I even try to bring it into the cinema I make.

Why is it that you have such a negative attitude to cinema with a message?

I like to tackle an issue, but never in an exemplary way. I prefer presenting it, and leaving it there, and that later the spectator decides. I can't stand political correctness. It is the new censorship. I prefer people to say of my film that it is somewhat arbitrary rather than that they say it is pretentious, and has an interior motive. In fact, I won an award in Venice with *Tower*, and then I found out that the president of the jury, Fernando Savater, had said that it was a marvelous metaphor about the sociopolitical situation of the Basque Country. I was astonished. There was never an intention. We shot the short film in the Basque Country, but the script was written by a man from Madrid. It was a purely ludic short film. But oh well, as a famous saying goes, "I make the films, and then come the critics and they explain it to me." I stick to this sentence, and that of Billy Wilder, who said: "When I want to send a message, I go to the post office, and not make movies." The day I want to make a film about the sociopolitical situation of the Basque Country, I will do it. But before that, I will inform and document myself, and will try to do my best. I will also make an effort to give it the distance mentioned before, although achieving this distance in something that is so politicized is extremely complicated.

The two short stories are of the fantastic cut, although the tone is very different. There is a universe that is a bit obscure, human pain, loss ...

El soñador has an encouraging aspect but, to a certain degree, this is an illusion. The story was inspired by a friend who has suffered a lot in life, but who never stops smiling. I am amazed by how she endures the blows that life gives her without losing that smile. Once she told me that she was happier in her dreams than in life. And that made me think. It reminded me of the story of Javier Sánchez Donate about a character who renounced life because he was happier in the dreams than in real life because there he met again with his lost love. I never lived very clung to the past, but yes, I have been told that all my work has some pain in them. Yes there is a certain nostalgy of past times, of lost loves, but I was never obsessed with this theme.

El soñador also has a romantic aura.

When Javier Sánchez Donate wrote the story, it wasn't a period film; it was the story of someone who had lost a loved one, and took refuge in his dreams. There was a friend who helped, who was a doctor, but he wasn't a psychiatrist. This we added afterward. Everything changed with the setting. The mise-en-scène has a close relationship with the literature of the end of the nineteenth century, and the beginning of the twentieth. I grew up with Julio Verne, Edgar Allan Poe, Bram Stoker, Arthur Conan Doyle ... they are fantastic writers, and they had an absolute influence on me. The turn of the twentieth century was the end of the Romantic man, and the beginning of the modern, scientific, industrial man, who starts to quit dreaming. He starts to no longer think about utopian love. I was very much interested in this contrast between the end of an era, and the beginning of another. I like this contrast between the dreamer and the psychiatrist a lot. With whom do I identify as a director? With the psychiatrist. But who would I like to be? The dreamer. In the end, the person learns to dream, and does not allow himself to be consumed by bitterness over the loss of his daughter. But the final dream, really, is the dream of the psychiatrist. There is a moment when he doesn't know what to do in order to save and protect the dreamer, because he thinks that this man doesn't do any harm, and he is happy the way he is. The psychiatrist takes an effort, safeguards the dream of the dreamer, and learns to dream. Obviously, it is a very optimistic ending. With this ending, I suggest that I would like to overcome reality, because deep down, yes, I have this way of being. There was, therefore, a certain homage to Romanticism in the short film. I didn't want the short film to have a devastating ending.

The production work and the technical quality are excellent.

In this short film, I told myself two things. On the one hand, I wanted that everyone who worked would make some money, even if only a little. And, on the other hand, I insisted on spending the money well. The setting is extraordinary, but it is the exclusive merit of the team. Without them, I am nothing. They could work for better directors but, sometimes, people sometimes prefer to work with directors who make them feel important, and owners of their work. Encouraging creative liberty had magnificent results. The artistic direction, the actors, the photography, the make-up, the hair styling, the costumes, the voice-off, the production work ... they are admirable. I felt that I had found a team that understood me perfectly. Many of them worked with me again on *El mal ajeno,* and they will work with me again.

Why do you use the voice-off?

The main reference, this time, was not cinematographic. The more significant cinematographic influence was *The Age of Innocence* (Martin Scorsese, 1993). It inspired the use of the sequence shot. I decided that almost everything should be filmed in sequence shot. I wanted narrative logic to always predominate, not mere aesthetic brilliance. I can't stand that the camera moves if it doesn't bring you anything. What I most like in *El soñador is,* precisely, the use of the camera: it supports the music and the setting, and flies as it tells the story. Nevertheless, I was told that nothing that the voice-off told went beyond what is seen in the image. I don't think it is so. I think that the image rules, and that the voice-off functions as support. The most obvious reference is *Dracula* by Bram Stoker. It is a novel that I like a lot, although I like much more Coppola's film, because the American director went way beyond it. In fact, the film is impregnated by Romanticism. I took as reference above all the epistolary part. The first version of *El soñador*'s script was based on the correspondance between the main character, his brother, the doctor, and the butler. As a consequence, we focused the story on the diary of the psychiatrist. His voice-off is what tells us the story.

What is the significance of the city that appears in the final shot of the short film?

In the first version, the dreamer drew his wife, but he never managed to draw her well. For this reason, he ended up drawing buildings. Buildings are a representation of the world of dreams. This thing that is impossible, but which is born from something plausible by the current of constructivism, and the futurist vision of the end of the nineteenth century. We got inspiration from *Metropolis* (Fritz Lang, 1927), and this marvelous world to create the city. I never wanted to show the world of dreams, because it is something very intimate that belongs to each person. The building means that you are in the world of dreams. What I wanted with the final shot was to show that we were in the world of dreams, and that it was a dream within the dream. It was the dream of the psychiatrist who made a certain decision because he wanted to believe that the dreamer will grow old dreaming, and will live happily. This is impossible, but who knows, maybe in the world of dreams it can be possible.

Koldo Serra (Bilbao, 1975)

He earned his degree at the University of the Basque Country (UPV/EHU) in the Audiovisual specialization of Fine Arts. His intensive professional activity covers almost all areas of the audiovisual sector. He has carried out direction tasks in diverse programs (*Muchachada Nui*, *La hora de José Mota*), as well as television series episodes (*El comisario*, *Gominolas*, *Karabudjan* or *La fuga*). He has also worked in advertising, and has directed the music videos of such different groups like Extremoduro, El sueño de Morfeo, and Estopa. In his phase as draftsman/cartoonist stand out the posters of Fant (Bilbao Fantasy Film Festival) between 2000 and 2004, and the publication of a compilation of cartoons titled *La Bestia del día*. His first feature film, *The Backwoods* (2006), was created in coproduction between Spain, France, and the United Kingdom. He has two short films in Kimuak, *Amor de madre* (1999) and *El tren de la bruja* (2003).

Filmography as Director

2006. *The Backwoods* (feature films)
2003. *El tren de la bruja* (short film)
1999. *Amor de madre* (short film)
1996. *Háchame!* (short film)
1995. *La noche de autos* (short film)

According to Gérard Lenne:
> Laughter and fear are two simple, visceral, fundamental emotions that come from instinct, not reflection. Opposed between each other, and in consequence similar, they make up a reciprocal double. Both correspond to a reflection of liberation: thence comes their possible subversive power.[123]

Koldo Serra devotes his two Kimuak short films of metalinguistic flavor to the exploration of these two visceral emotions that are linked so intimately.

Study of Laughter

Amor de madre, written and directed by Koldo Serra and Gorka Vázquez, is a funny homage to horror cinema from a manifestly loutish and humoristic perspective, a narrative strategy that has become almost a sub-genre since the foundational *Young Frankenstein* (Mel Brooks, 1974). As José Luis Rebordinos indicated, the authors take as reference the tone of movies such as *Creepshow* (George A. Romero, 1982), or the comics series created by William Maxwell Gaines *Tales from the Crypt* (brought to television in the 90s),[124] in order to make a parody of Alfred Hitchcock's *Psycho* (1960). This pastiche crammed with cinephile references is, moreover, flavored with a visual style that is very much in line with horror/humor *grand guignolesco* of the first Sam Raimi, close even to the cartoon (the trilogy *The Evil Dead*, 1981 or *Crimewave*, 1985).

---

123 Lenne, Le cinéma "fantastique" et ses Mythologies, 155.
124 Angulo, Rebordinos, and Santamarina, Breve historia del cortometraje vasco, 178.

Iurii Tynianov conceives of parody as a text of two fields, through which the original text becomes visible:

> In parody, the lack of concord between both fields is obligatory, a gap between them: the parody of a tragedy will be a comedy (it doesn't matter if it is through the emphasis of tragicness or through the corresponding introduction of the comic), and the parody of a comedy may be a tragedy.[125]

The parody of a horror film, therefore, must provoke laughter, which in the words of Lenne continues to be a reciprocal value of fear. In spite of its comic tone, *Amor de madre* allows without dissimulation that the original Hitchcockian text may show through in its filmic fabric[126] at a narrative level, as well as in the elaborate and Baroque compositions, clear debtors of the aesthetics of comics.

The short films starts with the confession of a man, John Merrick (Jon Ariño), sentenced to death for killing several old ladies in the town of Castle Rock.[127] The man explains that the real murder is his mother Bedelia (Mariví Bilbao), whom he simply tried to protect. On the basis of this testimony, the crime story presents itself through a flashback that opens with the shot of the Merricks' mansion situated on a hill. It is an almost exact replica of *Psycho*'s Motel Bates.

---

125 Tynianov, *Poetika*, 201. Cited in Iampolski, *La teoría de la intertextualidad y el cine*, 11.
126 In fact, Serra also emulates Hitchcock himself by appearing in a shot of the short film, half-hidden under a cap and motorcycle glasses.
127 Fictitious place Stephen King uses in his novels.

The images of the flashback develop, as expected, in black and white, and shamelessly rely on the extremely well-known shots of Hitchcockian cinema: stuffed birds decorating the house, the murderer in the bathroom, the detail shot of the hand lifting a knife, the close-up of the woman yelling, and the inevitable drainpipe where the victim's blood escapes. Allusions emphasized by Fernando Velázquez's music rather than inspired by Bernard Herrmann's chilling string composition.

Bedelia devotes herself to the murder of her bridge friends for sheer pleasure, while it is his deperate son John's task to clean the traces of the crimes, and hide the cadavers. Just like Norman Bates, John Merrick[128] is also a weak man, and submitted to the power of a powerful parent. While in case of Hitchcock's main character, however, it was he himself who committed and covered up under two distinct personalities the crimes of her deceased mother, here Bedelia is a flesh and blood person who carries out her atrocities in all their perverse materiality.

It is precisely the formal and narrative structure that governs the construction of the story: the manifest representation of all the mechanisms and conventions proper to the cinema of horror on the basis of the very rich material offered by a classic so recognizable as *Psycho*. The filmmakers deliberately reveal their intentions from the same starting sequence. When one of the mother's invitees says that John is "very strange," Bedelia comically guts the internal traumas that often afflict cinematographic psychopaths: "You know, the mysterious death of his father is the reason why he is the way he is, when he was only twelve years old. Then I had to be both mother and father. That is why he is like that. The human mind is so strange ..."

Serra and Vázquez exploit massively and without squeamishness all the aesthetic processes characteristic of horror cinema: subjective tracking shots, doors and windows that are blown open by the wind, shots from outside of the house through the window,[129] lightning that illuminates human figures in the window, playing with the depth of the field, shadows projected over the walls, and even a little reference to the *soft gore* in the shots where John cuts up the cadavers. The abusive and manifest profusion of these formal resources implies another way to generate conversations about a genre, whose mise-en-scène is

---

128 The name of the main character is an obvious homage to *The Elephant Man* (1980) by David Lynch.
129 Allusion to one of the most impactant scenes of the film *The Innocents* (Jack Clayton, 1961).

based precisely on "stressing the occult character of what is filmed, the relationship of what appears on the screen with that which does not appear, or that which does appear, but in an almost implicit way." [130]

This exaggerated show of generic assets definitely leans toward parodic comedy in sequences like the one at the beginning, when John finds his mother dragging the corpse of her invited friend in the hallway of the house, and scolds her for her irresponsible attitude. On this occasion, it is not as much the image as the markedly quotidian and casual dialogue that lends the scene a humorous aspect, besides the evident features of horror:

> - "But mom, what have you done! Didn't we agree that you will not do it again this week? And it is the third person that you murder in like a month. Look what a mess you've done. And I know who will have to take care of the corpse . . ."
> - "But son, it's that these things . . ."
> - "Enough, mom! What do you want, to set a damn record?"
>
> Bedelia forcefully slaps her son.
>
> - "How many times do I have to tell you to watch your mouth. Is this how I raised you? Look, I'd rather you helped me with this, I have enough trouble with the arthrosis lately."

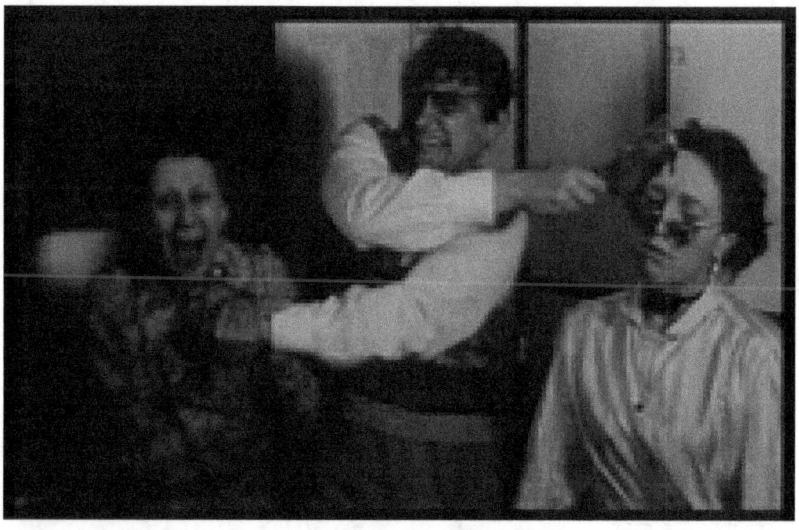

---

130 Losilla, *El cine de terror*, 53.

The caricature rises to its maximum expression in the grotesque image of John, who seems to intend to kill his mother and her friend Mrs. Bates (Loli Astoreka), after a succession of bizarre coincidences that would lead him to the electric chair.

As it could be no other way, the closure of the short film recovers the ending of *Psycho*, with the victory of the mother over her son. The sinister smile of Norman Bates now completely dispossessed of his identity is substituted by the image of Bedelia, who observes in the execution chamber the lifeless body of her son while she marks a new notch in her macabre count of victims.

Study of Fear

The writer H. P. Lovecraft had the clear perception that the fantastic story has its roots in fear: "a profound and elementary principle whose appeal, if not always universal, must necessarily be poignant and permanent to minds of the requisite sensitiveness." [131]

This seduction inherent to human beings is manifested in an ingenious way in the ghost train, a typical attraction in which every child tests, perhaps for the first time and voluntarily, their own reactions before unexpected terror. Incapable of escaping from his chair, the child explores almost unconsciously the scope of their courage, and the limits of the irrational experience of fear. This is also the premise of the short film *El tren de la bruja* directed by Koldo Serra, and written together with Nacho Vigalondo on the basis of an idea of the latter.

A man (Manolo Solo) accepts twelve thousand euros in exchange to be a guinea pig in a strange scientific experiment that aims to study human reactions before extreme fear. The man, who shows constant skepticism about the capacity of scientists to cause him to feel real fear, hears a voice (Héctor Alterio) give him the necessary instructions for the development of the experiment: he must remain seated for fifteen minutes in the middle of an empty hall, and endure whatever event that takes place around him without either getting up, or participating in the action.

---

[131] Howard Phillips Lovecraft, *Supernatural Horror in Literature*, 1927. http://gutenberg.net.au/ebooks06/0601181h.html

Serra competently handles the challenge of sustaining the mise-en-scène in three elements, which reduce the essence of the genre to its minimum expression: an immobile man on a seat, a conversation in which one of the interlocutors does not even appear on the screen, and an intensive focus that demarks the visual field of the man, and keeps the greater part of the scene in absolute darkness. The game between light and darkness, visible and invisible, which is key in the genre, plays a fundamental role in this experiment with horror, given that the most ancestral fear is precisely that of the unknown, and there is nothing more unknown than that which cannot be seen. The limitation of the scene to this luminous circle lends enormous expressive value to what is outside of the field, with which the sudden irruption of elements that come from it strengthens the effect of surprise, which is the principle narrative mechanism on which the story is based.

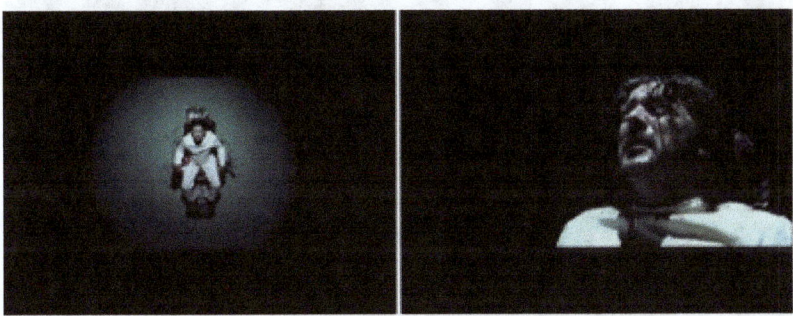

The filmmaker relies on all the visual resources at his reach (circular tracking shots around the chair, shots taken from the back of the main character, top-down shots, alternation of open and closed shots) to construct a disturbing climate of tension *in crescendo* as the frights and the events that surround the human guinea pig increase in danger and cruelty.

Close to the end of the fifteen minutes stipulated for the realization of the experiment, the voice of the person in charge reveals a terrible confession: the organizers of the study do not belong to any team of investigation; rather, it is a group of wealthy individuals who have created this joke to enjoy the spectacle of seeing the torture of a human being. A man dressed as executioner emerges in the room, and throws on the lap of the main character the head of the previous gullible person who fell in the trap. His sarcastic initial skepticism becomes authentic panic until the executioner executes him at cold blood by sending a bullet in his head.

With the body of the guinea pig on the floor, the lights of the industrial warehouse turn on. Two men remove the hood of the executioner, revealing the disconcerted face of the man (Jon Ariño), who can only murmur in astonishment: "I have killed." When the workers take the body outside of the room, the supposed corpse of the main character gets up from the floor, and calmly lights up on a cigarette.

"In the broadest sense, artistic reflexivity refers to the process by which texts foreground their own production, their authorship, their intertextual influences, their textual processes, or their reception."[132] Thus, *El tren de la bruja* is a short film of a reflexive character, not only because it explores the mechanisms of the workings of fear in a human being, a pillar on which a whole cinematographic genre rests and where the short film itself belongs,[133] but also because it brings into being a fiction within another fiction, which reveals itself in the surprising final turn.

The experiment orchestrarted by the voice of Héctor Alterio was not destined to the apparent guinea pig, but to his supposed executioner,

---

[132] Stam, Burgoyne, and Flitterman-Lewis, *New Vocabularies in Film Semiotics*, 204.
[133] It won the Best Short Film Award at the International Fantastic Film Festival of Catalonia (Sitges), and the Méliès d'or to Best European Fantastic Short Film.

which is why it did not ultimately aim to explore the depths of fear, but the more sadistic impulses of humans: a sentiment that is also among the very essences of the genre of horror.

> The reader-spectator feels horror because they see themselves obliged to watch or imagine the figurative representation of their own phantoms. On the one hand, they try to keep themselves within the limits that social education imposes on them, that is, the superego, which emphatically orders them to abhor evil and violence . . . . On the other hand, they cannot avoid feeling fascinated by all the events that develop before their eyes, given that in reality they come from this part in themselves, the id, which unconsciously pushes them to let themselves be dragged by any kind of passion, no matter how inconceivable or aberrant they are.[134]

The horror film provokes in the viewer a contradictory reaction that swings between repulsion and fascination: "the ideal lies in that the viewer intensely penetrates in the universe of the film, in order to end up with the same emotions that they would have had if they had lived these fictitious adventures."[135] In *El tren de la bruja*, the ficticious adventure seems to become true for the executioner, convinced that he had committed real murder. Nevertheless, the different levels of representation that make up the narrative fabric have superimposed themselves on one another, and configured a complex structure that ruins that conviction, and reveals the means on which horror films are constructed. The fiction that the short film stages coincides first with what the false research team recreates for the first guinea pig; this, in turn, forms part of an even greater farce destined to sadism. A lie on top of another with the objective of uncovering a truth, given that the fact of leaving open the artificiality of the horror film's mise-en-scène lends the spectator a knowledge that is often shielded from them. It is a knowledge that offers reflection on the mechanisms of emotional and psychological manipulation, which the genre affects on those innocent spectators ready to let themselves seized by the attractions of fear.

---

134 Losilla, *El cine de terror*, 22.
135 Lenne, *Le cinéma "fantastique" et ses Mythologies*, 56

Interview

Do you think that short films are appreciated in Spain?

Maybe not as much as in the United States. In Spain, above all, people appreciate awards. With twenty-five awards, you have a letter of introduction for the producer, and you can take the lead. The short film opens you doors and, besides, sometimes, the awards lead to more the awards. For me, before Gary Oldman and Paddy Considine, the short film was a wonderful letter of introduction. I don't know if it is determining for someone to give you a project in Spain, but having a successful short film will always help so that people pay more attention to you.

There are short films to win on festivals or open doors, and there are true short films, short stories that they tell what they want to tell.

I have always believed in the short film as a short piece, with its beginning and end. It is an element where you can experiment with things that you will never be able experiment with in a feature film. If you don't take risks in a short film, you will certainly not take risks in a feature film of 90 minutes that costs three million Euros. I think that in a short film you have to shoot the story that you want to shoot, and shoot it well; without thinking about the awards or the doors that it can open for you. A producer may see a much-awarded short film, and this may serve to get you to show him your feature film project. But when the American actors see it and realize that it is a trick, or designed to win awards... In some cinema schools they prepare students to make successful short films by following certain parameters. Some of them have been very much awarded, but I would never defend a short film that is pure aesthetics, or a mere joke...

Amor de madre was your first short film selected in the Kimuak catalog.

I codirected it with Gorka Vázquez. We were in the fifth year of our studies at Fine Arts, and we decided to get make a short film of the expensive kind, a 35mm one. It is the worst filmed short film in terms of planification. We shot 80 percent of the night scenes during the day, and the day ones during the night... Our idea was to shoot the flashbacks in black and white, and the present part, the interrogation, in color. But the audio tracks of the black and white and the color are not the same, and we had to develop everything in color; to turn the black and white into strange colors. Now we would film it all in color, and we would turn what we wanted digitally into black and white. But unfortunately, there was no money at that time. We put together the short film at the university, and it was a nightmare.

What was the main lesson that you learned?

The truth is that in *Amor de madre*, I devoted myself too much to the image, and very little to working with the actors. I found that people laughed at places where they shouldn't have laughed… The short film was too explicit, and there was little work put into the actors. I also learned a lot in the technical area with the problems that we had with the black and white, and I got convinced that one had to have a detailed filming plan. It is from this auto-criticism that *El tren de la bruja* came: a work in which I didn't focus so much on the aesthetics of the film. Besides, *Amor de madre* was a wonderful filming with Mariví Bilbao at her best, and a colossal Jon Ariño, who played her son. I have known Mariví Bilbao since *La noche de autos*, and I wanted to work with her again.

It is surprising how explicit the dialogues are, and the seriousness with which Mariví Bilbao recites them. They fit very well with the parody.

The fact of emphasizing everything has its explanation, because I thought: I bet they don't understand it! Seeing Mariví Bilbao with a machete in hand, sharpening it and saying something very obvious, it functions. We recently showed the short film in Colombia, and the people laughed a lot. I also thought that Mariví Bilbao should appear on *The Backwoods*, but due to the series *Aquí no hay quien viva*, she couldn't be there. Mariví Bilbao, Álex Angulo, Ramón Barea and Paco Sagarzazu are the actors that have made the greatest number of short films in the world! For me, it is incredible that Mariví Bilbao should love making short films so much, and that she should throw herself into it like that. It was funny to dress her the mother of *Psycho* (Alfred Hitchcock, 1960), with the hairdo of Dracula by Coppola. In the short film there is an amalgam of references. For example, there is a funny homage to *Creepshow* (George A. Romero, 1982). There are also references to *Ed Wood* (Tim Burton, 1994), which is one of my favorite movies.

The compositions are overelaborate.

Sometimes we lost focus. Instead of worrying about whether what we were telling was all right or not, we were too preoccupied so that everything is very aesthetic. All the issues with the lights and shadows was very much emphasized. The photographic references that we gave to the director of photography were proper to markedly expressionist movies. We told him that we didn't want that much gray, but a lot of shadows. The references to cartoons are also tremendous. We had the vignettes of horror cartoons on mind, but in the language: a thousand spiderwebs, details... Like I said before, we were too preoccupied with the aesthetic aspects of the movie.

What was work like with Gorka Vázquez?

The part of horror is more mine than Gorka's. At that time, he preferred the world of Tarantino. There came a moment in the set where we couldn't cope, and one of us had to take care of the composition, and the other manage the actors. There was another moment when we had to rent a second camera, and divide the functions between us. Nevertheless, we got on very well to direct the short film, although I wouldn't repeat it. It would be very difficult for me to direct a film with another person. Direction is something very personal, very partial, very individual. It is difficult to share it. Sometimes one gives out an order, and the other the counter-order. Even in the films signed together by the Coen brothers, there is surely one who is the leading voice. Directing has more to do with seeming you know what you are doing, than actually knowing what you are doing. You have to bring security to the team; if you doubt, they will doubt. And the moment they no longer value you, they will stop following you, and that is terrible.

Why did you call the character in *Amor de madre* like the elephant man?

The Elephant Man (David Lynch, 1980) is no doubt one of my favorite films. The son is called John Merrick in clear reference to the elephant man. The mother is called *Bedelia*, like the character in *Creepshow*, and there is also a Mrs. Bates who alludes to *Psycho*. In *The Backwoods*, in turn, Paddy Considine is called Norman Blake after the vocalist and guitarist of Teenage Fanclub. In this case, Norman Blake seemed to me a very British name. Among my philias is also the world of circus, and I have been for year trying to launch a project about a circus of phenomena. I like *Freaks* (Tod Browning, 1932) frankly. I am incapable of hiding my influences. Nevertheless, although many people have commented to me, there is no influence from *Arsenic and Old Lace* (Frank Capra, 1944). I hadn't seen it when we shot *Amor de madre*, but the production company is called Arsénico PC as a small homage to it. Amor de madre *and* El tren de la bruja *are different, but only relatively.*

In *El tren de la bruja*, you keep the tendency toward horror.

I have always liked the fantastic, the cinema of horror. We finished *Amor de madre* in the fifth year of the university, we presented it as a class project, and after that, Gorka Vázquez and I we went to Madrid with the short film under our arms. Nacho Vigalondo, Borja Crespo, Gorka Vázquez and I also tried to sell there a story in the style of *Creepshow*, which was titled *Historias horripilantes*. We even got so far as to make promotional photography with Alaska. After a lot of failures, the project went down the drain. My chapter within the film was *El tren de la bruja*—an original story of Nacho Vigalondo—and, finally, I decided to shoot it as a short film. I intended to do something diametrically opposite to *Amor de madre*, but only relatively, because there is also black humor there. Given that the original idea was to make a film of episodes of horror, it had to happen. But I wanted to do something much more sober, and strengthen the interpretive section. A short film without spiderwebs, thunder, or tarantulas. Something much more minimalistic. In sum, to maintain suspense with the minimum elements. The whole short film is a conversation of shot-reverse shot with someone who isn't there.

The two short films, besides being horror, contain multiple references to the genre.

Amor de madre refers to a concrete collective imagery (*Creepshow, Psycho*…). *El tren de la bruja* is also about horror; it has a lot of meta-references. It is called *El tren de la bruja* because it is a trip to the Ferris wheel, a trip to the roller coaster. Everyone gets on the roller coaster; they are very much afraid, but its fascination is precisely being afraid, and knowing that nothing will happen. You scream continuously, but this is what adrenalin produces. In horror films, the same happens. People go to the movie theater to suffer, and they know that this suffering will last two hours. From Vigalondo's start to the final script that we wrote together, there is a process that goes through all the mechanisms of horror cinema. At the beginning, verbal fear; then we turn off the lights; we arrive to gore, and finally to bleeding. I watched many horror films to see which mechanisms we could use. It is not a film designed for effect, it has a lot of substance beyond a few scares. What was good is that we could film chronologically to see the evolution of the character, to help him and support him with regards to sensations and reactions. When we filmed, we didn't know that it would be in voice-off. We thought about Álex de la Iglesia, but we didn't have so much faith. In the end, Nacho Vigalondo did the voice-off in the set, above all due to the question of time. In postproduction, I used the voice of an actor friend Pablo Viar; but in the end I used the voice of Héctor Alterio. It came out very well, because he gave the character a touch of the manipulating Argentine psychoanalyst. What would have been best is to do it with Chicho Ibáñez Serrador. He always spoke from the heights, like in *Un, dos, tres* (a famous Spanish TV program). Besides, he would have given more play to the meta-language. Voice is fundamental for a short film. I never wanted the face of the voice to be seen, I didn't want to give it a face.

Are you a director of horror films?

I like the genre very much, but I don't think that I categorize myself only in horror cinema. What's more, after shooting *Amor de madre* and *El tren de la bruja*, I was sure I didn't want to make a horror film. *The Backwoods* has a disturbing tone that suggests that something will happen, but it is not a horror film. It is more similar to the thrillers of the '70s, the crude violence of Peckinpah, than to a horror film. It is not *The Texas Chain Saw Massacre* (Tobe Hooper, 1974) at all. There is an unhealthy, strained atmosphere, and one can cut tension with a knife. In spite of that, I don't play with the codes of horror. Nevertheless, I know for sure that I am not a director of comedies. What I like a lot about Arsénico PC is that Nacho Vigalondo, Borja Cobeaga and I are very different. I don't know if I will ever be able to make a movie like *Pagafantas*, because I do not master the codes of comedy the way Cobeaga does. In fact, I have been offered to make a romantic comedy, and I didn't accept it. I feel more comfortable in other courses. Which doesn't mean that I solely limit myself to making horror films.

Begoña Vicario (Caracas, 1962)

Vicario earned her degree in Fine Arts at the University of the Basque Country (UPV/EHU) in Audiovisual specialty (1985). She started out with animation in the studio of the production company PIOT in Moscow. She continued her formation at the Center of Design in Vitoria-Gasteiz, where she made *Geroztik ere* (1993), followed by *Hara-Hona* (1994) and *Zureganako grina* (1996). This same year she established her own production company, and made *Pregunta por mí* (1996), with which she won the Goya Award for Best Animation Short Film in 1997. Together with *Haragia* (1999), this film forms part of two short films selected by the Kimuak catalog. She is Professor of Animation at the Department of Fine Arts at the University of the Basque Country (UPV/EHU).

Filmography as Director

1999. *Haragia* (short film)
1996. *Pregunta por mí* (short film)
1996. *Zureganako grina* (short film)
1995. *Geroztik ere* (short film)
1994. *Hara-Hona* (short film)

Begoña Vicario's experimental animation addresses social themes such as organ traffic or common graves. Her stories are born from personal experience that push her to tell a story. She relies on the voice-off of a female narrator in first person, who explains the meaning of the images. In this way, the spectator focuses on contemplating her work. The visual imagery is characterized by a search for constant movement, textual metamorphosis, and is combined with an intense soundtrack. The objective of her work is to explore emotions.

S.O.S

Pregunta por mí is a socially involved short film that denounces organ traffic, where she uses the technique of sand animation. The anxious cry for help that an immigrant woman sends to her friend through a letter is the main thread of this story. The voice-off of the main character tells her anxieties in first person. The narration in internal focalization allows this voice to assume an *informative* function with regards to the visual content of the animation. Its objective is to explain the viewer the meaning of the images and sounds, and allow them to enjoy the text without having to decipher it. As a consequence, the voice-off becomes redundant and imprescindible at the same time.

The logical narrative of cinema is not valid for experimental animation, whose process of creation is artistic. It manipulates very different materials from filmic image, in this case sand, to give free rein to visual motives that succeed in an imprevisible manner, depending on the desires of the creator. There are no clear images; the objects and elements represented reveal themselves through the forms drawn in red sand against a white background. Without supporting text, without a voice-off, it becomes very difficult to figure out the story. Using this resource gives free way to the creation of images that are combined with sounds to tell a story, and move the spectator. It constructs the story of a terrified woman, in whose nightmares the same obsession repeats itself: the idea that someone snatches the heart of another person, and the suspicion that this person can be the main character herself. Far from her home and without anyone that could help her, she tries to send a desperate message to a friend who lives in her home country. Nevertheless, it is not guaranteed that the letter would ever arrive. The animation becomes the message, the missive thrown in the air, the viewer stays in suspense, waiting for the resolution of the account that never arrives.

We must highlight that, majorly, the images are detail shots, or rather, drawings that center on showing parts of the body or objects. The tracking shots over the illustrations in sand also contribute to this attention to detail, and are characterized by partially exhibiting the body of the woman, or the bodies of the lovers at the beginning. There are no general shots; the only panoramic reference is that of the wire fence of hawthorn that puts an end to the story. The story is constructed around metonymy, and the sum of the parts alludes to everything terrifying. Not for nothing, it juxtaposes the two nightmares of the main character, in which the same anxious obsession is repeated.

The story takes shape through recurrent motives and images that link and mutate constantly. With regards to this question, the relationship that exists between each figure between the sand and the background notably contributes to the construction of the mutant text. Sometimes the silhouettes of the sand impose themselves over the white background, and other times, the same motive is represented in reverse, that is, the white silhouette against the sand. This play lends the film great visual richness. The dynamism is marked by the rhythm and the transition between images, the brusque cut, the fades, and above all, the metamorphosis.

 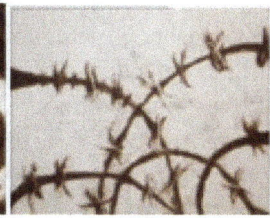 

In this letter that juxtaposes images of nightmare, the episode of the organ robbery is repeated as many as four times, where the same themes occur obsessively: the body, the scar, the hand that grabs the entrails and the heart. The body of sand always presents a white footprint that indicates the lack of something, the absence of the organ that will be removed. The scar or injury presents itself as a stripe that opens in the organism, or in the sand, and it is the path through which the predatory claw enters. In the final part, the scar transforms into hawthorn wire: symbol of the wound suffered by those who are on the other side of the border of the "first world." The hand appears negative, when its fine silhouette on white background grabs a circle of sand, or positive, when it turns into a sucking tongue. And finally, the heart. This may assume two different aspects: in one dominates the form, and in the other, the background. In the first one, the sand draws the outlines on white background, and in the second, the hole that the organ occupies and occupied in the body grows and grows. In both cases the image always changes size, and is accompanied by the metallic sound of heartbeat. Nevertheless, heart and bird are two symbols that are already present in the title credits, whose objective is to illustrate the fear of losing life, and the main character's desperate call for help.

Generally, the interventions of the voice-off are accompanied by silence, although sometimes the metalized echo of the sand appears in the background. In effect, the sounds move away from naturalist representation, and seek stimuli that are difficult to recognize at times because it alternates everyday echoes, and other times because it creates new and disturbing sounds. A good example of this is the songs of the ancestral ritual that are reproduced backwards; the metallic buzz that resembles the flight of a fly, and accompanies the heart; or the muffled sound of the unbridled flapping of the bird's wings. The combination of these with the drawings in sand creates an intensive sensation of anxiety and unease.

Ultimately, the text establishes a metonymic relationship between the themes and images that succeed in a mutant and agile way. They complete a kind of visual and sonorous stimuli chain through which the film aims to move the viewer, and call their attention to the problem at heart.

Without Even Saying Goodbye

Haragia is a short film of experimental animation, whose content is centered on a social message. It gives voice to the lifeless bodies of disappeared persons, whom no one could rescue from the common graves in which they were buried. For both the living persons that seek them, and the dead ones who have lost hope to be found, without a dead body there is no death. There is no goodbye. Only the nothing.

The succession of a series of home videos in Super 8, and the mechanic sound of the handle serve as introduction to the story. They start with the bath of a baby, and continue with brief scenes of happy girls and boys playing in the water. The rattling stops with the shot of a middle aged couple who walk with their arms around each other's shoulders. They smile and greet the camera, turn around, and walk on. This fragment brings up the ontology of the photographic image to which André Bazin refers,[136] and which equally affects cinema. That is, it is a metaphor of cinema as a ghostly and eternal medium. The film goes beyond splitting and the mechanical reproduction of reality, and just like memory, turns the images of reality into a magic universe outside of the reach of death. Cinema has beaten time; or in other words, the time of its images is always the present time.

---

136 Bazin, ¿Qué es el cine?

This initial fragment shows the immortality of the images of those who are no longer alive, but whose memory is eternal. Besides, it is about home videos, which is why evocation is not collective, but refers to a familiar and intimate universe[137] of those who are no longer with us, and those who do not forget them. They present the families of each body buried in common graves; they are the memories of their happy moments. There is no doubt that this resource adds emotional intensity to the drama.

From this moment on, the death theme invades the animation, and it does so by combining three elements: the photographic animation of the corpses; the vertical tracking shot that comes from the depths of the earth in order to, for a moment, show the exterior and submerge again; and above all, the cello solo music of *Khana per a violoncel* by Albert Sardá, played by Gheorghe Motatu. This is the most expressive element when it comes to transmitting the profound pain of the corpses abandoned to their fate. The sound of the cello corresponds to the cry of the dead, and each time the camera ascends, their accords recognize the impotence caused by not being able to get out, and be rescued. Like in the previous case, the voice-off belongs to the corpse of a woman who offers her testimony in first person. The narration in internal focus explains and gives meaning to the images. Once again, this voice leads the spectator, and liberates them from the necessity to interpret so that they may enjoy the animation, and face the emotions that this produces them.

One of the characteristic features of the image band is that it constructs a fabric in constant movement thanks to the alternation of the two resources cited before: the tracking shot, and the photographic animation. This movement of text is directly related to the theme, shows the internal agitation of the corpses who, over the years, have tried to escape to the surface. The technique of photographic animation reproduces a similar effect to the horizontal tracking shot, just as that of movements in other directions. Besides, in some scenes the corpses turn around their axis. Obviously, there exists a little leap between one image and the next one that together yield a more compact, more detailed appearance to the movement.

---

137 These domestic films belong to the director, and are linked to the emotional and intimate universe of her family. The pain over the death of her father is one of the themes that push Begoña Vicario to create this animation.

Each tracking shot marks the passage of time. The change of vegetation, or the birds' sound is witnesses to this development. During the impasse that is produced on the surface, the focus corrects itself to make the landscape visible, and creates the visual effect, the illusion that the camera will emerge from the earth. This image reminds us of the moment when the people that are drowning stick their head out of the water for a second, but then they sink again. The stratum of the earth creates an agonic sensation, which brings the spectator back to the beginning. This movement is a metaphor for the impotence and frustration of the bodies without life; they are close to the surface, to their families and friends, but it is impossible to meet with them again. The image in black gives way to a new fragment of photographic animation. Obviosuly, the development of events has a limited time. As the end approaches, the vertical tracking shot is more vertiginous. The camera moves out from the earth in an almost horizontal position, as if it was turning around its own axis. It is evident that this formal unease makes the anxiety of the dead persons visible, who do not rest in peace. They have suffered torture, violent death, and what is worse, the secret burial of their bodies without goodbye. Nevertheless, in the final outcome the voice-off allows us to understand their resignation: they lost hope of being found.

The representation of corpses is also eloquent. The naked bodies appear photographed from the other side of the glass, which is why part of the flesh gets squashed against the transparent surface, and highlights the hair, the genitals, or the face of the persons, while it evokes the idea of oppression. It is as if the earth that enveloped them was transparent. The lights focus on showing only some parts; the rest is shadow and darkness. Their posture is usually very similar, the hands are intertwined

or tied with ropes, which is also often present on the feet, and highlight their condition of prisoners, and the violent circumstances of their death. A bracelet around the wrist or some earrings are the only personal items that distinguish one from the other. There are corpses of both sexes and all ages. They killed indiscriminately. They are bodies that stretch out or, as it happens with the girl, assume a fetal position. When they appear on sheets, they resemble the corpses of autopsies; as if they weren't entirely dead. In fact, the sound of respiration accompanies these images, and reminds us that they are still there.

Interview

Pregunta por mí and *Haragia* are experimental animations that center on social issues. Where does this preoccupation come from?

The films come to me through my own experiences. The process is always the same. I live a personal thing, this turns on certain switches inside, and everything that I see touches these switches. I find stimuli with those things that happened to me, in the newspapers, on television ... They make me see that it is a universal theme that does not only concern me, and it is something that can be shared. These two parts, one very subjective and the other very objective, results in that I work them with a lot of enthusiasm. The result is work about a general theme, although in fact I am talking about myself. It seems like my films have a social message, but in reality this was not my intention. I have never had the intention of denouncing anything, because I don't think it serves anything. On the other hand, having lived through the Transition, I have seen a lot of documentary cinema. It is something that is inside of me. My intention is to talk about my own experiences. *Pregunta por mí* was born at a time when I had a lot of relationships with people who came from countries of the East. You go making links, you feel the same anxieties, and you see that they have a bunch of terrible problems, such as organ trafficking. In that time, they killed a journalist in Mallorca who was studying the traffic of organs. In *Haragia* there is also personal experience. My father died suddenly. The death of a father or mother is always painful. In that time I saw documentaries about the common graves in Argentina. It was when they brought the bones of Lasa and Zabala and they gave them clubs in the cemetery itself, and in Argentina they were working with Historical Memory. It was about understanding and appreciating this suffering of persons who cannot say goodbye. While you cannot say goodbye, everything is considered alive, and now with the Historical Memory, even more; the subsoil full of corpses, and the ground full of the pain of people who couldn't say goodbye.

In both short films, the ending is sad.

It is realistic. I do not intend to make a speech about something that I know. I keep on doing things, and they bring me a conclusion. If I thought: "I will do something about this topic that ends like that," I would be doing a speech about something that I had thought about previously. I have of course reflected, but not about something that premeditatedly brings me to this. In *Haragia* I documented mortuary rituals in the world, and I have a few texts of a couple of inspired nights that I had about gastronomy and death. There is a text in which I talked about someone that ate the fruits of a fig tree near the cemetery, an image that is so rural and so normal, the recycling of energy. Among the rituals that I have seen, there was an Indonesian one where the corpses were put into the hole of a tree, and each time the tree flowers it is like this person returned. It is something that also has to do with the recycling of energy. It was one of the endings that I considered, lifting the camera from the ground to a flowering cherry tree, but I couldn't do it, it was an overly documented and rational ending. What came out was something much more realistic. The end is that nothing happens, and the character says: "I hope someone finds my tomb, although I do not think so because it's been a long time that the grass has grown." In *Pregunta por mí*, she asks her friend help through a letter, and nothing happens either. It is a very everyday situation and there is no reason why it should be real, but it is only the anxiety that a person may feel who has no one around her to call her. She asks that someone go to the embassy to ask for her. It is the transmission of something withour having a solution, because it doesn't. I considered various possibilities for the ending, but I realize that they are more related to a story than something that I have lived. Nothing happens in the films, it is about transmitting a sensation. If I knew how it would end, I wouldn't do it. What I want is that the story tells itself. Personally, the films serve me to learn. These types of works require from the viewer that they stop self-censoring, and think that what they see is what they have to see.

In both, you use the voice-off as a resource to explain the story.

There is a voice-off that allows you to work empathy and put yourself in the place of the person who suffers. I think that it is basically an explicative text, to facilitate the things, to make the film more accessible. I am aware that it is a production that costs money, a lot of effort and distribution, it has to be public, go to festivals, they have to be admitted at these places. For all these reasons, I chose to distribute the least radical work that I have. In these two cases, the texts were previous to the image, because they have to do with personal experiences, and they were already done. I write a lot, and these texts were "there," and when the film was made, I used them to put them in voice-off. It is like you describe a still life with words, and you also paint it.

The objective of using this voice-off is commercial?

Pregunta por mí was the first movie that I made as a producer. I put it together, asked for a subsidy, I got it, and I learned how to produce. When I finish the films, they don't interest me in and of themselves. I want that people see them; it is not for nothing that I put so much effort in the work. But what interests me is making it, and seeing how it will end; this I never know, this is what makes it interesting.

The cello solo acquires a specific weight in the dramatic charge *of Haragia*.

In *Haragia*, with this camera that rises and sinks, the theme is rather evident. Then there is the cello. It was difficult for me to find the cello solo; it is brutal. I spent a year looking for it, because I knew that it was the cello; the vibration of this instrument has something to do with human desperation, its screams, weeps, moans . . . In fact, orginially, the film had to be five minutes, but in the end it lasted eleven because this is the length of the cello piece. I decided that I had to have image while the cello lasted. I found the piece of music when I already had the images collected. It turns out that the composer, a professor at the Municipal Conservatory of Barcelona, had worked with a Catalan experimental animation artist, and when I called him, he knew what the thing was about; he had already made a piece for animation, and he gave me this one as a present. Something like that changes the whole movie in a moment, because you find the right music, and the rest you adapt to this. There is the cello that speaks, there is the image, and that's it. You only have to decide if you put there a voice-off or no. I ususally wait until they give me the answer; I never know if I am mistaken or not. It is much less dramatic with the text, it makes it more palatable for us. I have nothing planned, this is my methodology. If not, I lose interest.

In spite of the fact that you won a Goya Award in Best Animations Short Film, and that you are a renown person for you work, it seems like you have left behind the artist's life. Why?

When I had my fourth child I decided to leave it. My classes cover the creative space, this satisfies me, and that's it. I help a lot with the work of the students, I don't need to produce, nor that I get recognition. When I do the next one, which I will, it won't be for these reasons.

Presenting my film at the Goya was a thing of my friends. It was nominated by Emilio de Rosa, historian of cinema and animation from Madrid, and a friend. I gave him the copy, and it was selected. And one day, another filmmaker that was selected told me that I was nominated. I didn't have my head around this, because I was arranging the paperwork for the adoption of my third daughter. I have a very funny memory of all of it, and besides, they gave me the award. I would almost say it was a wasted Goya. People use the Goya Awards to pursue a career, but I never wanted to make a career with this, and the next project I presented to the Ministry was so artsy, a porn film with fruits, that they didn't give me the subsidy. The Goya Award didn't mean anything.

Nacho Vigalondo (Cabezón de la Sal, 1977)

Vigalondo started his studies in Audiovisual Communication at the University of the Basque Country (UPV/EHU) the first year the program was launched, together with his friend Borja Cobeaga. Besides his work in advertising and television (as scriptwriter in the programs *Big Brother*, *Vaya semanita*, *Campus*, *MuchoViaje* or *Muchachada Nui*), he is responsible for the script of the short films *Pornografía* (Haritz Zubillaga, 2003) and *El encargado* (The One in Charge, Sergio Barrejón, 2008), and has co-written with Koldo Serra *El tren de la bruja* (Koldo Serra, 2003). His first feature film *Los cronocrímenes* (Timecrimes) was awarded in 2007 at the Fantastic Fest in Austin (United States), and at the Trieste Film Festival (Italy). It gave him a candidature for the Goya Awards for Best New Director. In 2011 he shot his second feature film

Extraterrestre (Extraterrestrial). He has three short films in Kimuak: *7:35 de la mañana* (2003), *Choque* (2005) and *Marisa* (2009).

Filmography as Director

2013. *Sins of the Father* (segment of *The Profane Exhibit*)
2013. *Carlota* (short film)
2012. *A Is for Apocalypse* (segment of *The ABCs of Death*)
2011. *Extraterrestre* (feature film)
2010. *Tres relatos de ciencia ficción* (short film)
2009. *Marisa* (short film)
2007. *Los cronocrímenes* (feature film)
2005. *Choque* (short film)
2005. *Domingo* (short film)
2003. *7:35 de la mañana* (short film)
2002. *Código 7* (trilogy of short films)
1999. *Una lección de cine* (short film)
1997. *Snuff movie* (short film)

A Musical Fright

The story narrated in *7:35 de la mañana* is a grotesque, comical, absurd and devastating time, a bitter but entertaining tragicomedy that is offered under the wrapping of an unusual musical performance. A woman (Marta Belenguer) goes to the same café every morning to have breakfast when, suddenly, a young man (Nacho Vigalondo) starts to sing and dance crudely, accompanied by the waiters and the other patrons in the bar. In his song, the young man confesses that he has fallen in love with a woman whom he sees having breakfast every day in the same place and the same time (7:35 in the morning), but he doesn't dare approach her for fear of offending her, scaring her, or "looking like a fool." The woman is astonished when she realizes it is about her, but her surprise turns into authentic terror when she realizes that the young man wears a charge of dynamites attached to his body, which he used to threaten the people present to collaborate in the incredible staging. The woman manages to call the police with her cell phone, and soon we can hear the sirens. For a moment the young man considers talking directly to this woman that fascinates him, but in the end sings the last words of his song and goes out to the street carrying a bag full of confettis. When the police order him to stop we can hear an explosion, and inside of the café a shower of confettis falls on the stupefied face of the woman.

It is undeniable that in the strict sense, we stand before a musical; nevertheless, if we abide by the characteristics established by Jane Feuer in his book *The Hollywood Musical*,[138] it becomes clear that what Nacho Vigalondo offers us in his bitter sweet tragicomedy is the deformed inversion of the classical conventions of the genre. It is a subversion of the mise-en-scène of the story, its filmic staging, and above else of the genre's idiosyncratic spirit of optimism and happiness par excellence.

As it happens in classical musicals, the clientele of the café where the story develops actively participates in the perfoemance of the leading role, a representation perfectly governed by a director with orchestra, live music, and intended for an audience (the woman), who is present in the screen. Nevertheless, when in Hollywood musical the body of extras starts to sing together with the leading role, they do so apparently infected by the irresistible happiness transmitted by him or her. In the case that interests us, on the other hand, the young man threatened to detonate an explosive charge if the extras don't accompany him in his unusual declaration of love.

The performance perpetrated by Vigalondo and his coerced troupe is opposed to musicals' apparent improvisation and spontaneity as it visibly underlines, instead of masking it, the preparation of the staging. The clients of the establishment follow the lyrics of a song that they don't know, thanks to the notes in the palms; they are out of tune, their movements are uncoordinated, and they obstruct one another in search of their positions in the choral choreography. The leading role himself interacts crudely with the set and the *atrezzo*: he bumps into the tables, he drops the spoons, and executes in a convulsive and grotesque way some childish dance steps to the sound of a coarse melody played by an improvised guitar and keyboard.

---

138 Feuer, *The Hollywood Musical*.

With regards to filmic form, Vigalondo first rejects the effect of voluptuous exuberance that characterizes the fantasy world recreated in musicals, and uses photography of a contrasted black and white dirty texture. The shot that presents the show's leading role is a veritable declaration of intent to this end. In a genre where the essential objective of the director is the exhibitionism of artists, to provoke in the spectator the greatest visual pleasure possible, and to offer in each shot the most spectacular perspective of the show, Vigalondo starts his performance by hiding behind a column that hides his image. From that point on, the camera will always situate itself before some kind of obstacle that inhibits the spectator's comfortable vision of the performance.

In general tems, the spectacularness proper to the genre remains annulled by an aesthetic mise-en-scène that does not adjust itself to the mobility of the action. Vigalondo's camera does not *dance* like that of Vincente Minelli or Stanley Donen; in the few cases when the movement is clearly ostensible, and goes beyond mere re-composition to follow the action, the camera does not move from its axis. Its ultimate goal is always distancing, given that it adopts the point of view of the woman inspecting the scene in search of an escape route. Vigalondo therefore follows Minelli's lesson of mobilizing the camera in function of the subjective desires of the diegetic audience (the woman) and, by extension, of the spectator,[139] although here also with a subversive intention: this subjectivity pushes one to move away from the drama embodied by the leading role of the musical.

This idea of distancing takes us to the first transgression exercised by Vigalondo. The director subverts the mise-en-scène and the form of conventional musicals, but above all, he betrays their spirit.

---

139 Ibid., 29.

> Musicals are unparalleled in presenting a vision of human liberation which is profoundly aesthetic. Part of the reason some of us love musicals so passionately is that they give us a glimpse of what it would be like to be free.[140]

On the other hand, *7:35 de la mañana* is not a portrayal of freedom, but of human misery. The marvelous world of musical in which all dream may become true is substituted by the reflection of a hostile society where contact between human beings is difficult to tackle, where distrust reigns, and loneliness drives us crazy. In such a world, only a lunatic would be able to start dance and sing with no reason.

In a last alteration of the classic pattern of musical, his song is not directed in second person to his beloved who is present in the scene. The lyrics of the song refer to her in third person, in a way that the woman is never addressed directly. Without a clear destination, the composition of the young man may only fall in a hopeless void. The typical final musical song that celebrates the happy union of the couple, and serves as an ode to the spectacle, has its gloomy counterpart in *7:35 de la mañana* in the macabre shower of confettis, through which we can barely see the petrified face of the woman.

---

140 Ibid., 84.

The tone of what is shown up to this point could suggest that *7:35 de la mañana* is a parody of the Hollywood musical. However, it would be more appropriate to say that what Nacho Vigalondo carries out is an *esperpentization* of it. In the words of Pedro Salinas, "the *esperpento* . . . is essentially a deformation."[141] It is deformation practiced from a grotesque perspective, in a sense that Victor Hugo gave the term in his preface to *Cromwell* (1827) as an element that "pervades the whole thinking; it generates deformity and horror on one side, comedy and clowning on the other."[142]

As it is well known, Ramón del Valle-Inclán elevated the *esperpento* to the category of a theatrical genre, and an artistic vision of the world[143] in his work *Bohemian Lights*, constructing "a parodic redefinition of the tragic sense of life, and a new, grotesque manner of giving shape to traditional tragedy."[144] From the destroying perspective of a concave mirror, Vigalondo also reviews a classic genre of cinematographic discipline, the musical, and offers us, the same way as the great Spanish author, a kind

---

141 Salinas, *Literatura española*, 88.
142 Hugo, *The Essential Victor Hugo*, 26.
143 A vision inherited from the literature of Quevedo or Gracián, the paintings of Goya or El Greco, and the parodic and caricaturesque theater of the late nineteenth century, which had their filmic counterpart in some works by Luis G. Berlanga, Marco Ferreri, Fernando Fernán-Gómez, Álex de la Iglesia, etc.
144 Cardona and Zahareas, *Visión del esperpento*, 31.

of tragic farce where they link the laughable and the absurd with the terrible and the painful. Even if *7:35 de la mañana* betrayed the canons of the musical both in spirit and in form, it stays absolutely faithful to the absurd in both aspects.

Salinas emphasized the background of the social complaint and protest that dwells in the first *esperpento* of Valle-Inclán, as well as his quality of the portrait (not so deformed as could be expected) of an epoch. In a lesser scale, *7:35 de la mañana* is also a caricaturistic reflection of a society lacking in solidarity, and frightened by that, which emanates. Desperation is "the heart of psychological motivations from which the new art of Valle-Inclán emerges;"[145] it is also, together with loneliness, the atrocious force that pushes the leading role of the short film to act the way he does.

With regards to aesthetics, the *esperpento* usually "presents the deformed image and the ridiculous features of the human figure . . . And the grotesque figures par excellence are the puppet dolls . . . because they suggest in a ludic way a radical and disturbing deviation of the things that are familiar to us."[146] If in the musical the world is a stage, it becomes a dance floor of marionettes in the grotesque, where humans are nothing but ridiculous puppets at the hands of a creator who watches from a distant and alienated perspective.

We have already highlighted the distancing effect that moves the formatting of *7:35 de la mañana*. Besides, in this case the demiurge splits into two, given that the puppeteer (a puppet, too) who orchestrates the pathetic spectacle in the diegetic stage is himself the great demiurge who, incarnated in the figure of the director Nacho Vigalondo, controls the threads of this puppet theater captured in celluloid.

Duel Under Madrid

The next short film of Vigalondo, *Choque*, is not a portrayal of loneliness, but of human stupidity in the tone of a comedy. A couple, Diego (Nacho Vigalondo) and Lorena (Bárbara Goenaga), discover a dodgem arena in a Madrid underground. When they start enjoying the attraction, a group of young men joins them. The young men start to bump into Lorena's car, and Diego confronts them when he sees that they make

---

145 Salinas, *Literatura española*, 99.
146 Cardona and Zahareas, *Visión del esperpento*, 49.

obscene gestures as they imitate the movement of his girlfriend's breasts when they bump into her car. A security guard rushes to make order, but Diego has lost control, and ends up breaking the cashier's window. Lorena tries, without success, to calm him down, but when she sees Diego buy tokens for fifty euros, she gives up, and leaves the place. The young man, deranged, challenges one of the boys to a duel: their cars will crash frontally until one of them diverts. In the last attack, Diego stands up ready to leap on his adversary like a beast, and the boy diverts his trajectory. The main character is brutally smashed against the wall. Covered with blood and his own vomit on his clothes, he abandons the place, limping before the silent look of the adolescents' gang. He meets with Lorena in the car.

Vigalondo once again enters in the terrain of the grotesque with this "neighborhood Western."[147] As had already happened in *7:35 de la mañana*, the action happens in real time, and in a single place where the neon lights that break the semi-darkness help create an atmosphere between kitsch and amazement.

Situated in the underground of a big city, the rink presents itself as an anachronic space, an out-of-place, a kind of border in the middle of nowhere, which seems to return to the past with the attractions, machines and songs[148] that populated the childhood of these thirty-something main characters in the 1980s. In this place, Diego suffers a regression not only temporally but also mentally, to his childhood brain capacity. The track thus becomes the proper location to stage a stupid confrontation between a villain who is barely sixteen (Christian Nájera), and a righteous man, even more dangerous, ready to protect the honor of a defenseless victim, who by the way does not seem to be particularly offended by the boys' gesture of the boys, and who hasn't asked him to protect her.

After a dynamic scene charged with camera movements that follow the cars' trajectory, Vigalondo uses the slow camera in the purest style of Peckinpah in the peak moment of the duel, when Diego climbs on top of his car. Nevertheless, what in the work of the American master implies a styling of violence with the objective of making the climax more spectacular, it becomes at the hands of Vigalondo a new, parodic use of the conventions of a classic genre, with caricaturistic aims.

---

147 Angulo, Rebordinos, and Santamarina, *Breve historia del cortometraje vasco*, 19.
148 *You're the only one* by Transvision Vamp and *Fotonovela* by Iván.

Our hero wins, in effect. Nevertheless, the long camera movement that accompanies him in a general shot from the other side of the rink as he abandons the place of the duel, strengthens the absurdity and pettiness of his war scars through distancing. In the foreground are the shadows of the viewers of the ridiculous spectacle, while in the background the small figure of the young man ascends on the stairs. When Diego gets in Lorena's car in such a deplorable state, the young woman does not even look at him. In a display of pathetic pride, however, he formulates a question that closes the story with sharp irony: "you want to know who won?"

The Spatial-Temporal Paradox

The last short film of Vigalondo selected by Kimuak is *Marisa*, a production of Arsénico P.C. in collaboration with Notodofilmfest, which is an online competition of compressed cinema. On the basis of an almost paranormal phenomenon, and in barely three minutes and a half, the filmmaker offers an interesting reflection about the passage of time, and the changes that this provokes in humans.

A man tells us in voice-off the story of his complicated relationship with Marisa, a woman whose face and personality vary according to spatial-temporal coordinates. In spite of appearing a short film that lacks action, and is closer to the semi-experimental story, the script of *Marisa*, work of Vigalondo himself like in the two previous cases, abides by the classic narrative structure, and includes all the essential dramatic junctions for the construction of a story. The detonation happens unexpectedly, when the leading role discovers that Marisa changes her appearance depending on her position in space. The man pursues a solution, and takes two years and ten months to localize the place where *his* Marisa may be found. It is the moment when the turning point emerges, which gives the plot a new direction: Marisa's pathology has become more complicated, and in order to be with her, he has to be not only in the right place, but also in the exact moment. In the climax, the main character once again meets with her after many years of searching, only to discover in a bitter ending that at this point nothing really matters, because for Marisa he is now another person.

In spite of such a complex premise, Vigalondo's mise-en-scène is extremely simple, and is based on the repetition of identical placements of the camera in the same locations in order to highlight the paradox that Marisa's face modifies with the slightest spatial sliding.

The principal aesthetic value of the short film is no doubt the smart montage carried out by Jon D. Domínguez, who was also director of photography. Among the shots of the diverse Marisas situated in the same place, different female photographic portraits are inserted with great speed in black and white, which break the monotony of the continuous reiteration.

This rhythm, nevertheless, slows down when the camera softly halts on the image of the man who thinks he has found his version of Marisa. Although the cuts are perceived on the same shot, its visual content does not change, emphasizing the changeability of woman before the constance of the anonymous man, who persists throughout the years in his fruitless search. It is not strange, therefore, that the shot of greatest duration is that which closes the short film: the sad image of an aging man following into the depths of a forest a woman whom we are never able to ascertain was *his* Marisa, if she ever existed at all. In search of this woman who continuously mutates, time also changes him. The man then understands that it wasn't a question of space or time only, but he kept looking for Marisa.

"The nostalgic magnitude of melodrama comes through a reiteration, in images, of special realms that were occupied by a certain sensation of affective plenitude, and which are now seen, through the relentless passage of time, under a new and devastating light."[149] It does not result, therefore, all that crazy to qualify as melodrama, *sui generis* and with fantastic undertones, this metaphor about the changes that space and time exercise over humans, thus deteriorating their relationships. Vigalondo visits once again a classic genre and changes its form (like it happens to the main character of the story), but keeps faithful to its substance; not for nothing, as "everything in melodrama pivots around the loss of the amorous object," and what gives "its unmistakable melancholy tone consists in that the loss, in spite of everything, impregnates its fate."[150]

Interview

Why did you choose the musical to tell a story about human misery so sad as that in *7:35 de la mañana*?

There *are* bitter musicals. *Pennies from Heaven* (Herbert Ross, 1981), *All that Jazz* (Bob Fosse, 1979), series like *The Singing Detective*... Bitter musical is not something new. Lars Von Trier has made the bitter modern musical par excellence. What attracted me was not adding bitterness to an initially happy genre. My point of departure was much more vulgar, it was the formal joke of saying what would happen if we added realism to the key features of musical. Realism is giving a reason, an excuse, or coherent logic to the fact that people sing and dance at the same time. From that point on, the bitterness of the story emerged as a consequence of the mechanics that I imposed. There came a moment when I discovered that the story was very bitter, but it wasn't the point of departure but the logic of the elements that I wanted to put in play, although it could have been influenced by the bitterness that I had at that time.

---

149 Company Ramón, "Dulces prendas por mí mal halladas," 20.
150 González Requena, "Escenografía de la herida," 39.

The film has a work of analysis of the conventions of musical, but also a subversion of the genre. Was it something premeditated, or it simply emerged that way?

From the first joke on, everything else emerges as a consequence of it. I don't know if they are occurrences or consequences of the first thing that you imagine. From the moment you say that we are not in a musical but a reality that imitates a musical within certain limits, it is funnier if the musical turns out half bad rather than brilliant. If the musical becomes brilliant, we are doing the same thing as always. Why do they sing badly? Because it is people who are in this café by chance, they were not previously congregated. Why do they know the lyrics? Because they have it written down on a piece of paper in their hands. From that point on, it becomes exciting that they should read something that is written in their palm. More than a *pack* of occurrences, they are the logical consequence of starting the script. With the passage of time, you acquire a kind of intuition and know what kind of ideas, whether they are good or bad, will generate more good ideas. This idea seduced me because I saw that there would be a bunch of entertaining things afterward.

It seems that there is double suspense. The spectator tries to discover what is happening and, once it is revealed, they are intrigued by how it will end.

There exists an analogy with literature. There is something the writer Philip K. Dick said once, which I very much believe since I first saw it. In a novel you talk about the character, while in a short story you talk about the situation. I can't go into a character very profoundly, but yes I can go into a situation. As in eleven minutes I can't explore the psychological complexities of a person, when it comes to capturing interest about something that is abnormal, I have to play with the geometry of the situation. One of the most difficult parts of script writing was the question of where to put the turning point, which is the appearance of the bomb. It would have been too *short filmish* to drag the revelation along until the ending. What I don't like is when the turning point is also the conclusion of the film. The turning point is a purely formal element; it tends to be less significant than what the consequence of this turn may bring in the characters, or the perception of the viewer. For me it was important that after a great surprise-explanation/crazy turn, there would be a posterior conclusion that gives it some meaning. What the short film tries to be about is what happens after the surprise. There is suspense, but for me suspense may never be the conclusion of the movie. I have to maintain interest, but this interest cannot go until the end. There has to be something there before it functions as a dramatic and important conclusion of what we see. If the film ends with a surprise, it would approximate the joke a little. I prefer transcending surprise.

What did the Oscar nomination mean to you?

It was a tremendous surprise. In and of itself, the short film did not predict any of this. Although we had had success at important festivals—Clermont Ferrand, Gijón—you never think that you may be nominated for an Oscar. If for nothing else, you don't imagine that you ever reach this category of recognition for the film's technical quality. The five short films nominated for an Oscar were dazzling in all aspects, but mine wasn't. If it outshined any of them, it outshined them for a conceptual reason, for its black humor, or its hidden values. But not for its visual sparkle. Besides, if we compare my short film with the other nominations that year, the other four were minor super-productions. The nomination has only brought me benefits at an incalculable level. If I hadn't been nominated for the Oscar, I would have never made *Los cronocrímenes*. I am very positive about this.

What role do short films have in the cinematographic industry?

We should examine the cases one by one. There is no direct correspondence between being a well-known short filmmaker, and not being one. I do not believe therefore that there are a certain percentage of filmmakers who became well known for the fact that they were successful short filmmakers. I think that what influences more is the tenacity and feature film vocation of each filmmaker. Sometimes it seems like we are all directed toward the feature film, but experience shows that no, that for many short filmmakers their natural destiny is television, or making more short films, or the documentary. It is not such a clear, direct path. Sometimes it is perceived as a background career in which you have to win more awards than the next guy in order to obtain the opportunity to shoot a feature film. We allow ourselves to be contaminated by this perspective, but it is not the case at all.

You have moved from the short film to the feature film, but also from the feature film to the short film. It gives the sensation that you have not abandoned the short film.

I have not abandoned the short film, but I resist the repetition of the routine of going to festivals, winning or not winning awards, being selected or not... All this ritual is too much for me. What I do like is making short films with more arbitrary ends, short films for example that immediately spill over in Youtube. I feel more fulfilled when I do minimal experiments instead of shooting a short film that has a life at festivals. I don't mean to say that I have less ambition, or that I don't care. Right now the model of the perfect short film is *Marisa*, which was selected by Kimuak. For me it was a gift. Because it has no vocation as a festival short film. Nevertheless, I have learned as much with this short film as with any other. The mere fact of working with documentary image instead of narrative mise-en-scène is to widen the horizon. There are no orchestrated shots, nor am I directing anyone; it all happens through the montage, and the voice-off converted in a story. None of the girls receive any direction. I had problems with the actresses who came to the application, because they wanted to act, and the trick I used was build up the expectation of the girls as they were waiting for instructions from me, which never came. It may seem something cruel, but it would have been crueler to ask them to act, and then they see themselves in only ten frames in the short film. The male main character is the musician Miguel Ángel Ruiz; the only thing he does is lift the right hand a few centimeters, and lean forward.

In many contemporary short films like **Éramos pocos** by Cobeaga, there is a kind of comedy with a bitter tone.

Borja managed to prolong it in *Pagafantas*. You don't seek all of this. I would say that with the passage of time, you realize that you have been seeking it. A little while ago I recognized that I had never written anything with a happy ending. I suppose that someone should diagnose why we give our comedies a tone of bitterness, or whether in fact we take bitter stories and add them a comic tone on the way. I do not wake up thinking: "I will make a comedy with a black background," for example, but yes, it is something to value as many do it. In any case, it is not our task or authority to investigate what is happening. I almost feel more inclined to explain the reverse: Why does such a black story have so much comical flavor? For example, in *Los cronocrímenes* I see it more clearly. On paper, it is nothing but a criminal drama with a mechanics of science fiction, but why does it have so many moments close to ridicule, to explicit comedy, when it wasn't in the script? It is because, in a certain way, I do not see myself as someone solemn who is transmitting some truths to the public. It is something like a question of modesty; I feel more certain and honest if you can laugh with the film that I make, besides the fact that I am telling something very serious.

Your short films seem to be based on silly things, but deep down they have a lot of substance. They hide authentic human and social portraits.

I do acknowledge that they are based on silly things. Besides, they are formal nonsense. In *7:35 de la mañana* the idea was to make a musical, but in a way that everything makes sense in the end. In *Choque*, in turn, the origins were the fascination that I feel for films like *Vanishing Point* (Richard C. Sarafian, 1971) and *The Driver* (Walter Hill, 1978), where metal takes precedence over flesh. I love vehicles in cinema, but since I don't have the possibility to film a production of this caliber, and I happened to discover a dodgem car track in the center of Madrid . . . well, I'll do a film about dodgems! The original idea is as silly as this, but we think of dozens like this a day. The ones that we fall in love with are the ones that promise something more: those which have a certain emotional, or dramatic touch. It is not as much knowledge as a sensation, an intuition that there might be something there. Artistic creation has more to do with falling in love than knowledge. This also governs good films. Formulaic films have a problem: they end up not functioning. I don't like those very ambitious films in which the characters themselves are formulating the meaning of the film. This is what happens lately with some high budget films, which are already born with the condition that they are a masterpiece. Movies have to deserve that label. I feel closer to the directors and films that aren't trying to convince us of the importance of what they are telling us, and their framed pomposities.

It shows that you like genres, but you end up deforming and ripping them open.

I think that we do this for two reasons: because it tends to be more entertaining, and because we are genetically condemned to fall in these dynamics. Something prevents me from doing pure genre. I should go to Hollywood and work with them. Here I don't think it is possible. Not for me, not for others. Even devotees of genre like Enrique Urbizu, what they do is weaken the genre in their films. We are very much influenced by directors who have never respected genres: Álex de la Iglesia, Julio Medem, Enrique Urbizu . . . Alejandro Amenábar, who seems to be a canonical director, does not respect the rules of the genre, either; except when he is corrupting them.

You are very close to the grotesque, to monstrosity.

I would say that this is something genetic, a personal option; they are philias and obsessions that I share with everyone around me.

Why is *Choque* a western film?

Choque is completely determined by its location: an underground dodgem track. The dodgems evoke an open space, but this place is flanked by cement walls, painted as such, and with an emphatic and brutal ceiling. It is marked by a contrast with the luminosity of the August fair, and the cement tomb underground. On the basis of this crash of elements, there is the emotional crash of a person who is both an adult and a child. I fell in love with western at the university thanks to Patxi Urkijo, and it ended up very present in me. It is impossible not to think of western when you establish an antagonistioc duel between two characters. The short film plays with a perversion; starting as a romantic comedy in which it appears that the girl has an important role, and the male character continues to oust her, until she disappears from the plot. The fight for her also means that she completely disappears from the story, until she forms part of the background, and disappears even from that. Sometimes it is violent; in our careers as filmmakers we are in an environment that is over-determined by the masculine.

The wretchedness of the main character stands out. Instead of defending the honor of his beloved, he defends himself.

It is a game in which he creates all the rules, and what makes him angry is that someone else should propose the rules, no matter who. The man is not protecting anything; he only justifies his pride. What bothers him most is that his girl would want to continue playing with the boys who have broken his rules. This is an absolute failure that cannot be admitted. In this sense, it reminds me of *Straw Dogs* (Sam Peckinpah, 1971). Because the toughest part of the film is when she starts enjoying the guys who are harassing the couple in the ramshackle house.

One of the main values of the short film is its photography.

It was rather tough work, especially because of the limitations of space. It was also the first time that we worked in panoramic format, in 35mm. The trick in *7:35 de la mañana* is that the whole film is a shot—reverse-shot sequence. If we could shoot it in two nights and a half, it's because there are no sideways movements, nor any tracking shots, nothing ... In *Choque* we changed the camera's place. I worked with the steadycam for the first time and, therefore, we made shots with tracking shots in a car. The truth is that I have the sensation that in the world of cinema, I progressed step by step. Until *Choque*, really, I had not moved the camera from its axis, and until *Los cronocrímenes*, I hadn't dared use the crane. In *Extraterrestre*, I backed down because I relinquished the crane, although there is a lot of lateral tracking shot. I like to mark spatial-temporal limits in the scripts, within the margins of a single localization and in real time. I also like formal limitations—there will be no crane here, here one will never shoot with a hand camera, here the camera will be fixed every moment ... These limitations in one area help propel energy in another. I think I have always imposed such limitations on myself.

In *Marisa* there is no humor. It is a very pessimistic drama.

I was collaborating with the festival Notodofilmfest, and my work as jury obliged me to do a piece to act as a patron to the festival. I am very much a fan of the work of Adolfo Bioy Casares, and I was inspired by his literature in this little short film. Borges brought his story to pure metaphysics. Bioy Casares, in turn, on the basis of similar wickerwork, brought everything to a romantic terrain. *Marisa* is like a story by Bioy Casares, inasmuch as it converges pure romantic sentiment, and then an infinity; it can be, in this case, a science fiction story about a woman who receives some influence that brings her into the situation where she finds herself. I was attracted by the idea of describing a mental state through an exercise of absence and montage. Just like in the next short film—*Tres relatos de ciencia ficción*—it is about constructing stories through documentary fragments that are not composed, but robbed. *Marisa* is an eternal story about impossible love. The content is rather classic, but not its formal design. I don't think that I will once again make traditional narrative short films. *Marisa* is like a turning point in my cinema.

Sometimes you play the main character of your stories. Does knowing how actors work help you with direction?

The last story in which I acted the leading role was *Choque*, and since then I haven't played in any of my films. Now it is more comfortable for me to act in other people's short films. In the end, it is a journey. My first stories were monologues before the camera and, little by little, I fell in love with visual planification, with composition, and montage. For me, acting was more attractive than directing, but in *Los cronocrímenes* I started to enjoy the days when I didn't act. I understand the fears and insecurities that an actor has during a shooting because I had them too. I am against the theories that say that the actors have to go through almost ritual phases of suffering so that their acting would have quality. The actor has to be in a state of pleasure so that the result is pleasant for others. It is a conclusion that I arrived at as I was directing, and also acting.

Haritz Zubillaga (Bilbao, 1977)

Zubillaga graduated in the first class of Audiovisual Communication at the University of the Basque Country (UPV/EHU), where he met his friends and also filmmakers Nacho Vigalondo and Borja Cobeaga. He worked as advertising director, and film editor of various feature films. Kimuak has selected three of his short films: *El método* (codirected with José Antonio Pérez in 2001, and winner of the Grand Award of the Basque Cinema in Zinebi), *Las horas muertas* (2007), awarded with the Méliès d'argent in the Ravenna Festival (Italia), and *She's Lost Control* (2011).

Filmography as Director

2011. *She's Lost Control* (short film)
2007. *Las horas muertas* (short film)
2003. *Pornografía* (short film)
2001. *El método* (short film)
2000. *Autoestigma* (short film)

All of Haritz Zubillaga's short films operate within the margins of fantastic thriller. They follow the lines of what Carlos Losilla called "postmodern horror film," which emerged around the end of the 1970s, in the final stretch of the historical evolution that Losilla defines in his study about the genre of horror. In this era, the monster ceases to be the main figure that in the classic period served as the external projection of evil. Instead, filmmakers like John Carpenter, one of Zubillaga's main inspirations, substitute it with the psychopath, which

> "corresponds to an advanced stage of the genre in a sense that by now, every defensive position is destroyed, and the virus of evil has penetrated even the last cracks of the human condition, transforming it into something else, into absolute unhinging, into the demon of madness, into a pure encarnation of the diabolical, without any necessity to appeal to any sign of the supernatural."[151]

The archetype of the psychopath, and the decomposition of the human psyche are very much present in the three short films by Haritz Zubillaga. In all of them there is an external, invisible and indefinitive threat, whose origin always remains in the terrain of ambiguity, which puts the main character on the edge, and ends up unchaining their suppressed impulses, whether they are violent or sexual.

---

151 Losilla, *El cine de terror*, 163.

We Are Watching You

El método, codirected with José Antonio Pérez, is the first short film that Zubillaga shoots on celluloid after a few previous incursions in the fantastic genre realized in videographic medium (like *Autoestigma*, with Nacho Vigalondo). Luis (Alfonso Torregrosa) and Andrés (Ramón Ibarra) have to stay in the office and work late. Soon, Luis receives an anonymous phone call, which orders him to destoy certain pages of a report, and forbids that he leaves the building under the threat that all his movements are watched. Luis obeys, and the telephone voice tells him to locate a secret hearing aid in the phone under the table of the office in order to receive the following instructions: put all the papers that are kept in the boss' safe into a suitcase, and simulate a robbery by causing havoc in the office. When Andrés sees his colleague's strange behavior, he tries to stop him, and both start fighting. Luis wins over Andrés, and ties him to a chair. He nevertheless manages to escape, and kills Luis by hitting him on the head with a coat rack. The moment Andrés remains alone in the office, the telephone rings again.

In spite of the competent mise-en-scène, adjusted to the canon of films of suspense, it is in the script where the film's greatest weakness lies, especially in the unlikely lack of resistance with which the character of Luis accepts the blackmail of the telephonic voice without ever questioning its purpose or origin, or without searching for a way to escape its harassment. All in all, *El método* anticipates, like a rehearsal, some of the narrative and formal lines that Zubillaga will develop in a more purified manner in his later titles.

On the one hand, we find the recurrent irruption of this external threat in the form of an immaterial voice, whose source maintains itself outside of the field. The ambiguity of the outcome prevents us from determining if it is about something real or simply the fruit of a perturbed person's paranoid mind. On the other hand, the mise-en-scène of the story revolves around a double articulation of viewpoint, which fluctuates between the objective and the subjective perspectives, and which is precisely one of the formal strategies that Zubillaga will again exploit in *Las horas muertas*. The shot that opens the short film establishes this division through a zoom that approaches toward an enormous office building, directing the attention of the viewer to a specific window from which the figures of the two workers show. This shot, a modest inspiration by the beginning of *Psycho* (Alfred Hitchcock,

1960), alerts the spectator that an external look may observe the actions of these two men. In any case, like a classic Hitchcockian turn, some spying eyes seem to emerge surreptitiously in the scene of the action.

The following scenes develop inside the office. Everything happens in a conventional way until Luis receives the first call, and the caller warns him that they are watching him through a network of cameras, whose physical location inside the office is never detected (with perhaps the only exception of the camera that, like the montage suggests on many occasions, could be located on the coat stand used as homicidal weapon). They however appear ubiquitous given the diversity of angles that their images offer. In the beginning, the content of the security cameras is projected on the screens of the computers, reframing the action in the shot itself, and only Luis is able to perceive it. But as his madness progresses, the black and white images in low resolution, as well as the sound that accompanies them (a distorted buzz that cancels all natural noise) start to completely seize the screen. The spectators thus put themselves in the position of the subjective look of the voyeurs, while the character remains trapped in the representation of his own paranoia, registered by some ghostly images that we never know if exist only in his perturbed mind. When Andrés finishes with the torment of Luis, hitting him with the coat rack that seems to hide one of the cameras, the security camera's signal is abruptly cut, coinciding with the death of the man. Everything seems to regress to the initial normality. Nevertheless, another phone ring abruptly closes the story, leaving all questions open.

The Gaze of the Voyeur

> Cinema is an art of scopophiliac nature, which—like the art of the horrible throughout the ages—simultaneously causes pleasure and discomfort in the viewer. The pleasure comes from an erotic base: the satisfaction that is experienced through looking at the other, that is, in Freudian terms, through converting them into a sexual object. Discomfort, on its part, is based on the very essence of this same operation: the male spectators, for example, look at the women who appear on the screen with a clear desire of possession, which unveils their primitive and even murderous instincts through a process that we could call "visual violation." ... From this intransferable characteristic of cinema procedes one of the most popular and debated slopes of the horror genre: the so-called *psycho* movies, films whose main roles are occupied by murderous psychopaths who engage in serial massacres, more or less ritual crimes that are offered before the spectator under the most sadistic and cruel appearance."[152]

---

152 Ibid., 26–27.

Losilla's words perfectly define the unraveling conflict in *Las horas muertas*, homage to those horror films whose greatest representative is *The Texas Chainsaw Massacre* (Tobe Hooper, 1974), in which terrorized groups of young people are assassinated through the attack of a violent psychopath that exterminates them one by one. A notorious sexual component is inevitably there in his bloodthirsty fascination with flesh, which sometimes borders on gore.

The short film, written and staged by Zubillaga himself, starts with a rifle shot pointed directly at the camera and, by extension, at the spectator. It is at them that the threat of this man seems to be directed, whose blurred face through the hole of the weapon remains invisible. The next shots, nevertheless, situate the spectator again in the place of this dangerous voyeur by showing from a subjective perspective the object of his telescopic look: two youngsters, Toni (Zoe Berriatúa) and Laura (Nydia García), preparing a barbeque in the countryside, and Ana (Marian Álvarez), Toni's girlfriend, sunbathing topless on the roof of an adjacent trailer.

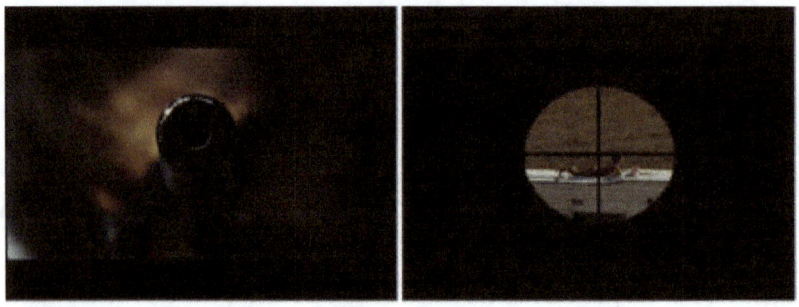

The image of the rifle unites references to both masculine and feminine genitalia: on the one hand, its long shape evokes the shape a phallus; on the other hand, the end of the channel suggests the vaginal hole. This latter one is the only element focused in the frame, and is situatied right at the center of the shot, in perfect correspondence with the circle that shows the look of the weapon. But, besides, Ana's naked body is followed by a detail shot of the phallic finger of the murderer penetrating the hole of the trigger, in a way that the young woman is converted, through the mise-en-scène and the montage, into a sexual object that the psychopath, and the spectator identified with him, desire to possess by force. Even in the presence of his girlfriend Laura, Samuel (Andrés Gertrudix) also watches with shameless desire; he doesn't like the camping plan at all by the highway, and prefers to hide inside the roulotte.

The whole mise-en-scène is articulated around the spatial division between general views of the desert exterior, and the suffocation of the claustrophobic frames inside the trailer. In the first ones, we may observe the vehicle parked at the edge of a highway, where traffic circulates incessantly without suspecting what is happening there. The wide compositions strengthen the barrenness of the surrounding, the isolation of these young people without telephone signal, at the mercy of a demented man who shoots at them mercilessly from an invisible distance, and whose presence is suggested through a horrifying whistle as a leitmotif. But besides that, the immensity of this plain that seems to engulf the small trailer suggests the material impossibility that this psychopath stalking them should hide nearby. In reality, this apparently incorporeal murderer is nothing but the projection of Samuel's unconscious, and his brutal action is the representation of the impulses repressed by the youngster.

The shooting starts precisely when Smauel leaves the roulotte and goes away from the group to look for water.[153] The first one to be taken down was Toni, who went to urinate into the bushes. The girls manage to take shelter in the motor home, but Laura gets out for a moment,

---

153 When he sees him, Toni asks him, surprised: "What happens with the beers?" to which Samuel responds: "You stick the beers up your ass." At this moment, a furtive shot, which neither of the men seems to perceive, makes a beer can burst in the motor home, which is the first sign of the correlation between the young man's desires, and the actions of the psychopath.

and becomes the next victim. Once the two persons who obstruct his desire for Ana, their two partners, are thus removed, Samuel returns whistling (another sign of his identification with the psychopath), and takes shelter with the girl in the motor home.

The interior of the vehicle is the space of Samuel's subconscious. A place full of remote nooks with their lights and shadows, reflected by the chiaroscuro of Ibon Antuñano's photography in the interior, as opposed to the sunburned images of the exterior. The couple hides under a table, and from this moment on, already immersed in the subconscious of the character, the subjective shots of the hole of the shotgun disappear. Samuel does not manage to close the door well, and she keeps hitting the frame, underlying the violent friction between the exterior and the interior world, where Samuel is free to unleash his instincts. Ana falls asleep curled up next to him, and Samuel takes advantage of the moment to reach into her cleavage. The woman feels the touch of his fingers on her breast, and moves away from him. It is then when one can hear the fearful whistle that foreshadows that the rejection of the sexual advance will be her sentence. Effectively, the next morning when Samuel gets up, he discovers the dead body of Ana. The door is left wide open, allowing the exterior space of the psychopath, and the internal subconscious of Samuel meet in the same frame: "evil has not only invaded the ego of contemporary man completely, but has also proceeded with its absolute disintegration." [154] Even if the young man finds the ignition key that Toni had hidden in the sunshade, he will not be able to start the car to escape from there, which is why his desires once again remain frustrated.

At the end of the short film, the fantastic component overtakes the plot, insinuated by the invisibility of the sniper. The disintegration Losilla discusses becomes literal. Time has passed, the cars continue to pass by the roulotte without stopping, and in it, the flesh of Ana and Samuel's bodies (who is still alive) have rotten. His mind has stuck in the interior of a completely broken unconscious that continues to listen to the shots of the tireless assassin.

The extreme violence that the short film exudes is derived not only from the narrated facts, but also from the aesthetic aridity of the story: the abrupt montage that turns each cut into an ax blow; the instability of the hand camera; the exaggerated grain that makes the film dirty,

---

154 Losilla, *El cine de terror*, 162.

and highlights the texture of the legs tainted by blood; the contrast and the chromatic saturation; and above all, the forceful sound effects that in the enclosure of the motor home seem to make a reference to an oversized reality: the horrifying whistle that announces the action of the sniper, the shots, the constant smashing of the badly closed door, the buzzing of the fly on Samuel's face, the horn of the vehicle . . . Images and sounds are exacerbated in a short film of carnal physicalness that appeal to some senses that are always on edge.

She Takes Control

The identification between the monstrous and the main character abandons the terrain of metaphor, and is ultimately accomplished in *She's Lost Control*, a film written by Haritz Zubillaga together with Aitor Eneriz. The short film, which is in English, starts with the mixed voices of diverse radio newscasters who, against a black background, find out about a series of crimes. Their author uses a drug called Reynold in order to annul the will of his victims, and thus rape them and quarter them. Immediately afterward, the image that opens the film evokes, as in *El método*, one of the most emblematic stills of *Psycho*: the close-up of Marion Crane's eye after she was assassinated in the shower. In this case, the eye from which a backward tracking shot starts, revealing the face of a woman, belongs to Amanda (Paola Bontempi), who lies in the back seat of her car, while her assassin is sleeping over her inert body.

The difference between Amanda and her previous victims is that she is still alive, as her voice-off indicates, addressing herself in second person: "Don't move. Not even a hair. Not even a blink."

Once the situation is presented, the story moves backward in flashbacks to show the events that lead to this situation through the woman's voice-off. After she caught her husband cheating on her with a young woman, Amanda stopped her car by the highway with the intention of killing herself. She just finished putting in the cylinder of her gun the only bullet that she had, when suddenly a man parks a car behind hers. He offers her a cigarette, and she accepts it, although she had heard on the radio that the assassin normally gives his victims cigarettes soaked in drugs. Amanda's will and muscles remain gripped by the substance in the cigarette and, after raping her, the man falls asleep on her motionless body.

The plot seems to be inspired by the medium-length film *Breakdown* by Alfred Hitchcock (1955),[155] in which Joseph Cotten plays a man who, after suffering a car accident is sent to the morgue. The Hitchcockian main character, nevertheless, did not die, he is only paralyzed, and the anxious narration, through the man's voice-off, revolves around his desperate attempts to show that he is still alive. Through the explanatory flashback, *She's Lost Control* also centers on Amanda's attempts to move her hand, and clumsily reach the pistol that she left in her bag. When she manages to reach it and she sets out to eliminate her aggressor, an untimely call from her husband wakes up the assassin. He uses the effects of Reynold to prompt Amanda to use the weapon against herself, in spite of the fact that her own voice-off orders her to perk up and turn against him, in a terrible dilemma that constitutes the climax of the story.

She's Lost Control presents, therefore, obvious concomitances with *Las horas muertas*: the entire action takes place in the interior of the car, and the life of the main character is in an extreme situation as a result of the acts of a psychopath whose face, covered by a hood, and always immersed in semi-darkness, remains hidden from sight all the time. The indefinite figure of the psychopath becomes once again the projection of the internal conflict of the character embodying the two values in battle: on the one hand her weakness, the masculine weight that she carries on herself and which, just like her husband, aims to oblige her to end her

---

[155] Prepared for the first season of the television series *Alfred Hitchcock Presents* (1955–1962).

life; on the other hand, the representation of the most obscure side of Amanda, the alibi to unleash her most violent instincts.

What distinguishes both short films, nevertheless, is their contrary aesthetic appearance. Before the aggressiveness of the montage and the dryness of the first one's photography, the images of *She's Lost Control* stand out for their cleanness and sober elegance. The scene is bathed in the faint light of a rainy night in which the only points of illumination come from the lights of the cars, and the streetlights on the edge of the road. Without getting to black and white, the colors are extremely palid, and the continuous movement, slow and maintained, of the camera yields the scene a soft cadence. Given that Amanda can't move, it is the camera, surprisingly agile in such a small space, which moves in its place: it flies over her body, slips by the car's floor while she feels her way to the gun, enters the most hidden parts of the vehicle, and offers impossible close-ups and high angles.

The shot of the woman's eye announced at the beginning of the plot that it was Amanda's point of view that the camera would adopt in every moment, but if she is unable to move physically, this constant movement of the machine can only obey the subjective impulses that dwell in her mind. The final shot of Amanda, which puts an end to the dilemma that the psychopath sets out, stays outside of the frame, while one can observe that car beaten by the rain, in oblique high angle shot, and from a point of view that is external to the woman. This change of perspective suggests that Amanda has liberated herself from the internal conflict that perturbed her so much, which is supported by the posterior movement of this camera that until now has reflected her subjectivity. In the initial shot, a backward tracking shot departed from her eye to show her face completely. Now, in turn, the camera advances toward the face covered with blood to stop at the eye of the woman who, contrary to what her own voice told her at the beginning, blinks. Amanda thus shows who the real victim of the shooting was and, above all, that her muscles are no longer paralyzed, that she got rid of what immobilized her, and has taken control.

The inverse path of the camera shows the metamorphosis of Amanda, her own passage from weak victim on the verge of suicide to a vindictive murderer. The woman puts the lifeless body of the psychopath in the trunk, in a hidden corner of her unconscious dominated by her dark underside. The aggressor now fulfills no function, and she herself adopts the physical form of evil that invaded her, with the face hidden under the hood snatched from the man. Seated in the front seat of the car she holds, like at the beginning, the pistol in one hand and the cell phone, whose screen reads the name of Tony, in the other. In that moment, the camera departed from the phone, as a sign of the wound inflicted on the woman, to show the pistol with which she meant to heal it. Now, the camera makes an identical move, but in the other direction: it starts from the pistol to finish in the next objective of the weapon, the screen with the name of Tony, her husband's voice message is asking her pardon.

Not only the aesthetics of *She's Lost Control* is manifestly more obscure than that of *Las horas muertas*, but also is the narration, given that the assimilation between the main character and the psychopath is now final. The conscious reflections of the main character conveyed by the voice-off disappear, and the new Amanda only speaks again to respond ironically to the pleading language of her husband: "Yes darling. I'm coming home."

Interview

You always move around in the genre of the thriller, and verging on the fantastic. What are your inspirations in this terrain?

Finally you end up, at least in my case, watching a great number of films, but when you see yourself in a fix and you have to put your mind to working on something, of having to create something, you systematically end up resorting to all those movies that you saw before you were seventeen or eighteen. I grew up above all watching American movies of the 1980s, and while I later saw a lot of wonderful films, I think what remains indelible is what you saw as a young guy, the American fantastic cinema of the 1980s, ranging from the most mainstream to the B list: Spielberg, Lucas, Zemeckis, Joe Dante, Sam Raimi, and John Carpenter, who was possibly the most fundamental of all. All of these things end up appearing here and there, screened and reinterpreted later in a more conscious manner when you see movies by David Lynch, Cronenberg, or classical cinema, for example.

Why do use the figure of the psychopath so frequently as an external and indefinite threat that destabilizes the main character, and unleashes his or her repressed impulses?

The more basic question is why I find this interesting. It is very gratifying to use this type of characters, who act in such a clear way for the story, and who are very comfortable to manage because of the way they make the plot progress. They allow you to arrive very quickly and clearly to situations where you want to arrive. After this first phase of enjoyment there comes another one in which I try to rationalize the story, not too much only a little bit; the objective that it becomes clearer, and I try to prearrange these points of connection between the figure of the main character, and that of the psychopath, who in fact is the classic figure of the monster. This is a classic trick in horror cinema, an archetype, the way the monster appears to disturb the initial status quo of the main character. I think it is these points of empathy that exist between the main character and the monster that allow the story to become a bit more uneasy, beyond pure emotion or scare, which for me are also necessary and fundamental.

With regards to this point, both in *El método* and *Las horas muertas* you play with the point of view, combining objective and subjective perspectives.

I don't like movies where there is a clear distinction between dream and reality. It seems much more interesting to me when things are more ambiguous, when this frontier is more diluted. I like double-dipping. For me, the supernatural fact is always objective, it is always there, and what interests me is that the peculiarities of the main character, all those internal pulsations, coincide with what the monster is doing in such a milimetric way that it is then that the supernatural element emerges. In this sense, there is a writer that I like a lot, who is called Richard Matheson; also the *Duel* (1971), Spielberg's film, who always perfectly achieves this strange and sinister thing that the main character and the monster function as an absolutely symmetrical mirror.

How did the idea of *El método*, your first Kimuak short film emerge?

More than anything else, *El método* is a learning process. José Antonio Pérez brought the producer Carlos Juárez a story that we had in our hands, a short film that in principle we were going to make in video, in Super VHS. He saw the possibility to shoot in 16mm, and both Jose and I were very much interested. For me, the exercise of shooting for the first time in film was very useful. It was in this moment that I had the obligation to plan everything very precisely, because we had a ridiculously low budget. There was money only for the negative, and very little of that. It became a kind of tour de force, an obligatory exercise, in quotation marks, to learn something absolutely fundamental, which is not only narrative economy, but also the economy of work at shooting a film. In the first short films, especially when you are confronted with shooting in 16mm, it's a little bit like losing your virginity; when you get through the shooting alive, it is already a success.

There is an important qualitative leap in the technical work of *Las horas muertas*.

A lot of time passed since *El método*, and there were a couple of other short films, among others *Pornografía*, which I shot in video. One of the things I realized as I was doing *Las horas muertas*, which perhaps caused the qualitative leap, is that beyond the intellectual and even creative processes, the work of the director consists in resolving problems in order to get to the most essential thing, which is that the story works for the audience, and that the viewer understands what you want to say.

The mise-en-scène is articulated around the contrast between general shots of the exterior, and short shots of the interior of the motor home.

The interior of the motor home was obviously very important, because that is where the whole story took place. But I very much wanted, from the perspective of the script, the motor home to be parked like in a ditch, close to a highway, and that there is traffic on the highway. It seemed to me that it was one of the elements that could be more disturbing, as the cars pass and the motor home is parked there in these general shots, when only the spectator knows what is going on inside the vehicle. I find this rather interesting, that in a more or less everyday image there should be a detail or element that only the main character and the viewer perceive, which on the one hand implicates the viewer in the story, and on the other achieves that this detail or element distorts this everyday image.

Ibon Antuñano's cinematography is fundamental for the atmosphere of the short film.

I wanted that, in general, the whole aesthetics of the film should be rather dirty, for the type of story that it was. Contrary to *El método*, in which the decision to shoot in 16mm was a question of budget rather than anything else, in *Las horas muertas*, yes there was an aesthetic decision to have more grain and dirt . . . I also very much wanted that the camera is not only inside the motor home, which was a very small space, but also inside the nooks and crannies of the vehicle, when they were hiding under the table. In this sense, managing a camera of 16mm, and for purely practical reasons, it helped a lot that it would be always close to the characters. When you locate the camera, what you do is put the spectator to the physical space where it is most interesting to observe the events, and this is one of the most important decisions that a director has to make. On the other hand, I also found it funny that this dirty image should resemble a bit the image that we all have from movies such as *The Texas Chainsaw Massacre* or *The Hills Have Eyes* (Wes Craven, 1977), which would approximate the dirtiest aspect of fantastic cinema in the 1970s. I was always fascinated by the filth of *The Texas Chainsaw Massacre*, by its texture and atmosphere rather than what we can actually see, because in reality it is not that gore or violent. This is also what I was looking for in *Las horas muertas*.

The design of the sound is also very important to insinuate this invisible threat, and is elaborated with a lot of care.

We devoted a lot of time to the sound. In these types of stories, atmosphere is fundamental, and the sound is 50 percent of the story. When you want to keep the camera inside the motor home and close to the actors, the sound has to be very suggestive. The whistle, for example, was something I liked to do, to apply a sonoric letmotif to the psychopath that can be only identified with the sound, which is a very classic move in psychopathology in movies. One of the fundamental influences for *Las horas muertas* is *giallo*, the Italian horror cinema. At that time I was watching a lot of these movies. In fact, *Las horas muertas* was a script that I had written a long time before. I wrote the first version little after *El método*, and I didn't decide to make it for various reasons; the factors of resources did not come together... But above all, perhaps for motivational or creative reasons. Until I discovered the *giallo*, especially the movies of Mario Bava, of Dario Argento or Lucio Fulci, who were the ones who focused and gave me the certainty to make *Las horas muertas*. The whistle is related to this type of cinema.

Why did you participate in the production of *Las horas muertas*?

It was by necessity, and it was a tough experience. Being a director, it is very difficult to be also a producer, and I think that in fact it is even counterproductive, at least for me. In a certain way the director and the producer have to move toward different places, which is okay. In *Las horas muertas* I could use more my director half than my producer half. If there is a good producer, you can have the same result and even better, because they will contribute and besides, they will do it in the most economical way, which is something fundamental in cinema, because everything is so expensive...

What was the shooting like?

It was really tough. The decision to shoot it in Monegros, for example, was an unquestionable decision for me, because it was exactly the location I had in mind. But having twenty or thirty people put up in a hotel for a week sent things a little out of control. It happened like it did with *She's Lost Control*, that they are tricky scripts: you read them and they are the type of story you like, with few elements, very enclosed, you need only one location... But then if you want the story to be minimally stylized, or to have certain aesthetics, it becomes very complicated. In the end it wasn't as bad as with *She's Lost Control*, but in *Las horas muertas* we also had to go and cut parts from the motor home, making space, with the added complication that it was shot entirely outside. It was expensive, but even so we recovered the money, and we gained something almost symbolic. It was a relief that we recovered the money, which is the most you can hope with short films. There are a lot of urban legends about how you can make money with short films; in my case, breaking even is already a feat.

Why did you decide that your last short film *She's Lost Control* should be in English? Is it related to the geographical coordinates of the story?

I suppose that this ties in with what I said before about the type of movies that I grew up with. On the one hand, I had wanted to shoot something in English for a long time. I would have liked to shoot *Las horas muertas* in English, but there was direct dialogue, and the complications were great. *She's Lost Control*, on the other hand, is with a voice-off and that was very fitting. Working with this genre, with references of American fantastic cinema and thriller all my life, and doing it in English gave me the adequate atmosphere and texture, so that it resembles what I had in mind at the beginning. I didn't want it to be a re-creation of any specific epoch, but I did want that all the elements of the story point toward a certain decontextualization. I knew that I wanted a story that takes place in the films. Where does *She's Lost Control* take place? In a thriller; there is no concrete geographical localization, there is no concrete epoch.

The fact that all this happens at night, and inside a car implies a challenge of staging and photography.

The first idea I had for this short film, before working with the coscriptwriter Aitor Eneriz and focusing it more, was very different from what it turned out to be. I even planned doing it with a 5D, with a much smaller camera, in a much more immediate way, without complicating it so much. But it is true that when I started to write more seriously, and started to plan, I quickly saw that what the story demanded was a greater, or at least different, styling. Even different from *Las horas muertas*—not to play so much the trick of this dirty and aggressive aesthetics, but that it would be cleaner, more stylized, more expressionist...That is, it occurred to me that we have to have tracking shots inside the car, and this triggered everything. In this sense the work of Jon D. Domínguez, who is not only the photographer but also the producer of the short film, was fundamental. When I told him about the planning, and I showed him the storyboard and the animatic that I made, he searched for the concrete form of making each thing that I planned for him. And there was of course also the artistic direction (Idoia Esteban), which made an incredible work of fragmenting the whole car to be able to shoot inside, and make the tarvellings. The truth is that it was cool seeing the car broken up.

How did you tackle the shooting after your previous experience?

She's Lost Control had a thorough preproduction work on part of everyone. I am happy because later things fell into place during the shooting. Contrary to *Las horas muertas,* in which the killing was the shooting in and of itself, in *She's Lost Control* there was all this process of preparation. It was very hard work, because we had to fragment and deconstruct everything in every sense, moving toward the planning that I made previously. I think that it closes the circle of what I started to learn, not in *El método* but in *Autoestigma,* or in the first video short films: that the type of cinema I want to make is based on the thorough and millimetric planification of every element, and that the objective is that the shooting is an execution of the things that I had planned. It is what Hitchcock invented, who is for me *the* film director, and he is a reference that I had not cited before, but who is evident in *She's Lost Control,* and I think he is in all the things that I have done.

You shot *El método* and *Las horas muertas* in cinema and in *She's Lost Control* you used Red One. On the basis of your experience, how do you see the transit to digital cinema?

I was one of those who said that I didn't want to make video. My experiences with video had been rather frustrating, because it was very difficult to get the texture that I wanted my movie to have: this pictorial fabric of unreality. In *She's Lost Control* I was rather worried, because for economic reasons it was impossible to make it in 35mm, and I was not only surprised by the result, but I now see clearly that I will continue to shoot with the Red One. The 35mm is insuperable, this is evident, but these digital formats have now reached a level of quality from where, given all their advantages and how easy they make your life during filming, there is no return, and this helps me a lot as director. It also gives you the ability to manipulate after the images. In *She's Lost Control,* 70 percent of the images are retouched in some way. Besides, if distribution now happens over the Internet, if the product ends up in 0 and 1 formats, it is very absurd that at one point you should convert it into the most analogic thing in the world.

What do you think about specialization in a given genre? What seems to be your case?

Making fantastic films comes to me naturally; it is absolutely not premeditated. Within the process of making short films, which is a learning process, what I have learned or I am learning is to make thrillers, fantastic stories, or put them on stage. And I'd like to put this in practice in a feature film, which is in the end what I would like to make. I like short films, I make them because I want to direct, and they can be done on the short or medium run. But now what I would like to make is a feature film. You can't make a living on short film, and even if the festivals and Kimuak do a great job of distribution, they will never have the diffusion that a feature film with media success does. Cinema needs to be industrial, and I think it is very interesting that the directors specialize themselves. I do not consider it pigeonholing. In the United States, for example, you see it clearly that a director makes a movie in a certain way, and it is not only that he or she has projects in this line, but also that the producers push them into this direction, because they have demonstrated that they know how to do it. I wish it were like that in Spain too. That they pigeonhole you in a genre? Well, that's all right. You do something well, and if it is something you like doing, as it is my case, what else can you ask for? In the end, a director of esteemed authors becomes more enslaved to their own universe than directors adhering to a genre, because they have the liberty not to spend so much time re-inventing themselves. Even the creativity and the formal conclusions of these directors who have very clear frameworks may be more interesting than those of a premeditated or militant authorship, as the history of cinema shows.

4

Most Important Short Films

Love Beyond Death: *Muerto de amor* (Ramón Barea, 1997)

Muerto de amor entered the Kimuak catalog of 1999 after being selected at the Semaine de la Critique in Cannes. It is a beautiful love story with a bittersweet tone, a result of the inspired combination of some of the most important talents of Basque cinema in the past years. It was directed by Ramón Barea, prolific actor and director (theatrical and cinematographic), who has worked with filmmakers such as Montxo Armendáriz, Imanol Uribe, Álex de la Iglesia, Julio Medem, Pablo Berger, Enrique Urbizu, and Gracia Querejeta, besides directing diverse theatrical works and two feature films *Pecata minuta* (1999) and *El coche de pedales* (The Pedal Push Car, 2004). Besides, *Muerto de amor* is written by Michel Gaztambide, script writer of *Vacas* (Cows, Julio Medem, 1992), *La caja 507* (Box 507, Enrique Urbizu, 2002), *La vida mancha* (Life Marks, Enrique Urbizu, 2003), *Un poco de chocolate* (A Tram in SP, Aitzol Aramaio, 2008) and *No habrá paz para los malvados* (No Rest for the Wicked, Enrique Urbizu, 2011), which won the Goya Award for Best Original Script in 2012. The photography was carried out by Kiko de la Rica, a habitual cameraman of Álex de la Iglesia, and its main character is the always impeccable Paco Sagarzazu who, together with the tireless Mariví Bilbao, is the actor who had greatest presence in the Kimuak short films ever since the program's first editions.

The short film starts with a view from a window of a Bilbao rooftop, where the skyscraper of the Plaza Circular stands out. The camera retreats until a cage enters the frame, in which a couple of lovebirds groom each other. The following detail shots, accompanied by a children's song that seems to take us to a singing lesson, present with elegant subtlety the main character of the story before we get to see his face. As we deduce from the perfectly ordered pile of clothes, and the recently folded quilted table cloth, someone is ironing with meticuous care. A vertical general view of the whole body finally reveals the features of an elderly man dressed in perfectly clean pajamas without a single crease, focusing on his domestic chore (Paco Sagarzazu).

The doorbell rings, and the man leaves the living room. The camera, however, does not follow him; it stops for a moment on the cage with the two birds in order to later approach slowly the piano on which a series of photographs rest. A brief conversation offscreen They were same motifs and the same obsessions tells us that the postman rang the bell with a registered letter. The main character starts to read out loud the content of the letter, which tells him that, following the rules that come into effect after the tenth year of his spouse Amparo's death, her remains have been extracted from the burial niche, and were passed on to the ossuary. The words of the man, still outside of vision, are illustrated by a general view from left to right, which covers the photographs on the piano, which show diverse images of the marriage, as well as a snapshot of his wife seated by the piano, surrounded by children.

> If the field is the dimension and the special measure of the frame, the offscreen is its temporal measure, and not only in a figurative sense: it is in time where the effects of offscreen unfold. The offscreen as a place of the potential, of the virtual, although also of disappearance and fading: a place of the past and the future, much before it is a place of the present.[156]

Jacques Aumont gives us the key of these images that belong to a happy past. The words that come from the off-field bring this woman to the future, a woman who was once flesh and beloved, but who is now, faded forever and perhaps more than ever, has become just another cold heap of bones destined to be lost in a common ossuary.

The camera returns to a close-up of the man to capture his grief-stricken face before the news. Shaking, he takes off his glasses, which fall on the floor. They crack. The man remembers Amparo through the music that she taught the children and, above all, from her photographs. Her wife has stayed alive in his memory, visual and sonorous but intangible, and now that she has been un-earthed and her loss is made visible and palpable through its material evidence (the bones), one of the components of this inseparable pair of glasses breaks, making the idealized vision impossible.

The main character goes to the cemetery with the letter. An emphatic low-angle shot shows the man threatened by the arch of the entrance to the cemetery, and starts the nightmare he has to suffer to localize and recover the bones of his beloved wife. From this moment on, the action developed in the cemetery is tainted by black humor in each one of its minor detail. Proof of it are the images of the man picking up a boquet of flowers that fell off a funerary car to bring it for his wife; the coffin that hits him because the negligent funerary workers let go of it to light up on a cigarette; the children who rob bones for science class; or the familiar tone the ossuary manager (an excellent Álex Angulo) uses when he talks about the remains of the deceased, referring to them as "fishbone," and commenting that the man's wife was "a delicate woman, the kind that calls attention," while he weighs the bones wrapped in a garbage bag.

---

156 Aumont, L'oeil interminable.

The widower refuses to leave there the remains, and the ossuary manager takes pity of his pain. He accompanies him to the exit with the bag in hand, and tries to convince him that he forgets about the episode. However, they run into a couple of adolescents: the daughter of the operator and a friend of hers, who got hurt by a robbed bone. The character of Angulo asks the widower to hold the bag for a second, while he accompanies the boy to the medicine cabinet. The widower grabs the opportunity and escapes with the remains of his wife.

At home, he spreads one of the knitted tablecloths that he just ironed on the bottom of a suitcase, and deposits the bones of his wife one by one. The man takes the pieces with care, he attentively observes and cleans them before putting them in the immaculate coffin, with the same care and order that he displayed in the opening sequence. The meticulous operation, illuminated by a fearful chiaroscuro, alternates with the shots of the cage, home of the lovebirds, which alludes to the time when the married couple was happy. It impregnates the macabre situation with romantic tenderness.

At night, the widower sits on a bank in a park with the suitcase on his lap, and watches a couple of adolescents seated on the adjacent bank. Contrasting with the sequence in which he slides the scarf over his beloved, the camera now takes pleasure in the caresses of the young man, which in a suggestive detail shot travel around the young and feminine flesh of his girlfriend, touching with his fingers her perturbing knee bone. The half smile of the man before this lovely vision is shadowed by the inevitable wave of nostalgy. But romanticism is once again cruelly replaced with black humor when a dog, excited by the appetizing delicacy that the man guarded in the suitcase, starts to bark at him insistently. The owner takes the animal away, and the man realizes that the couple is also gone. He takes out the tools, and digs a pit where he carefully places the suitcase. He buries it, and a low angle shot analogous with the one in the cemetery shows the entrance door of the new cemetery, where Amparo will rest eternally: the skyscraper of the Plaza Circular in Bilbao.

The closure of the story reveals its circular structure, reestablishing the state of harmony and peace that characterized its beginning. A panoramic view scanning from left to right traverses the photographs on the piano in reverse order. We once again hear the children's song that the main character himself hums as he sews, and watches the lovebirds.

The camera moves from the cage toward the window, and it is then that the shot that opened the film assumes all its symbolic value: what the window allows to see is the omnipresent skyscraper, telling our man that, although his glasses are broken, he will always have his beloved Amparo next to him, within the scope of vision.

The Strange Couple: *Hombre sin hombre* (Michel Gaztambide, 2001)

Two years after *Muerto de amor* was selected into the catalog of 1999, Kimuak took another story by Michel Gaztambide, *Hombre sin hombre*, produced and directed by him, and written together with Roberto Cibrián, coproducer of the film together with Mireia Lluch. The film narrates the unclassifiable sentimental story between two men, Paco (Paco Sagarzazu) and Saturnino (Saturnino García), but as opposed to *Muerto de amor*, it makes no concessions to any romanticism. Rather, it is about, as José Luis Rebordinos points out, "a descent to material and human misery... A rough short film, not gratifying at all,"[157] whose principle values rest on a solid script and the excellent performance of the lead actors.

Paco is an infantile man, and probably also a mental disability. He lives in a small hotel with Saturnino. The latter man is sick, and Paco takes great care of him in spite of the fact that his surly and bitter companion treats him like a slave. Paco's mother (Teresa Gastón), who lives alone and is unable to understand his son's adoration for such an unpresentable man, suddenly passes away, and leaves him the apartment, and some money. The two move in there, but Marina (Marina Shimanskaya), the Russian woman who runs the shop in front of the house, starts to approach Paco with the objective of appropriating the apartment. The poor devil sees no harm in the woman's intentions, but Saturnino considers Marina a threat for the stability of the couple. He confronts her with the aim of throwing her out. She resists it, and upon seeing that Paco defends her, Saturnino abandons the home. On his own and in the street, the man decides to kill the woman. Saturnino thus eliminates the reason of discord, but also provoques the final separation of this eccentric masculine duo.

---

157 Angulo, Rebordinos, and Santamarina, *Breve historia del cortometraje vasco*, 186–87.

In spite of constructing the nucleus of the story, it is definitely difficult to define the insane relationship between these two colorful characters. They both behave like an old married couple that has lived together for very many years. Paco does the shopping; he takes charge of administrating Saturnino his medication on time, and does not hesitate to ask his mother money when this latter man needs it. On his part, Saturnino constantly yells at Paco, and shows little respect for him. He is demanding with him, and becomes jealous like a macho husband; he reprimands him for being late when he talks with Marina, while he was waiting for lunch. In the sour discussion that confronts them, Marina calls Saturnino a "fag," a word that offends him terribly to the point that he tries to hit her. It is also true that in spite of their behavior and almost marital routines, we see no sexual component in the bizarre relationship that unites these two men, who are of different temperament, but their behavior is childish all the same.

There are various indicators that suggest that for Paco, Saturnino could be the substitute of an absent father figure. The sequence of surrealist tones that precede the title of the film, and which seems not to fit with the rest of the story, shows in a general shot his mother in the middle of a beach, as she shouts into the camera from the distance: "Call your father. Tell him it's you." Paco looks in a frontal close-up to the side, but only sees a dog walking about on the sand. When he looks toward the place where his mother was, she is no longer there. This dreamlike episode implies a certain trauma related with the deceased father in Paco's subconscious. The possibility that Saturnino occupies this role is later confirmed. When once again they move back to the old house, Paco allows him to sleep in his parents' bedroom, while he retires in the room of his childhood; he invites his ragged companion to use his father's clothes, which were left in the drawer after his death.

The harmony between these two strange individuals is broken with the arrival of the woman. Her irruption casts doubt on the initial impression that Saturnino's interest in Paco is solely utilitarian and egotistic, and Saturnino's attitude shows the existence of authentic affect and emotion between the two men. In spite of this, the man can't resist his mean nature, and the exit that he seeks from the triangular conflict will lead the couple to its disintegration. Gaztambide stages this whole outlandish game of relationships without any grand allure, but with sober efficacy, reflecting the distinct phases of the relationship between Paco and Saturnino thrugh their respective positions in certain fundamental framings.

At the beginning of the film, the two men share the bed in a frontal shot that shows Saturnino lying on the left side of the composition, with Paco on his right. The first night Marina comes for dinner, nevertheless, it is her figure that is placed before the camera, physically separating the two men, who are seated on the two sides of the table. The characters thus visually reproduce the vertex of the fateful triangle that will emerge from this evening, and which will change the life of the couple.

That alteration is confirmed when Saturnino, defeated by Marina, leaves from home, and she occupies his place on the right of Paco, in a frontal shot that shows them seated on the sofa. Paco preferred that it is Marina who stays, but as the events unfold, neither of the men is happy without the other. The composition of the short shot of Paco in conversation with the woman situates his face in the place that was Saturnino's before, whose face, split in two by the chiaroscuro light, appears pushed toward the right of the frame in a composition that is symmetrical to the one before. Both are separated in different shots; their positions, nevertheless, continue to be complementary.

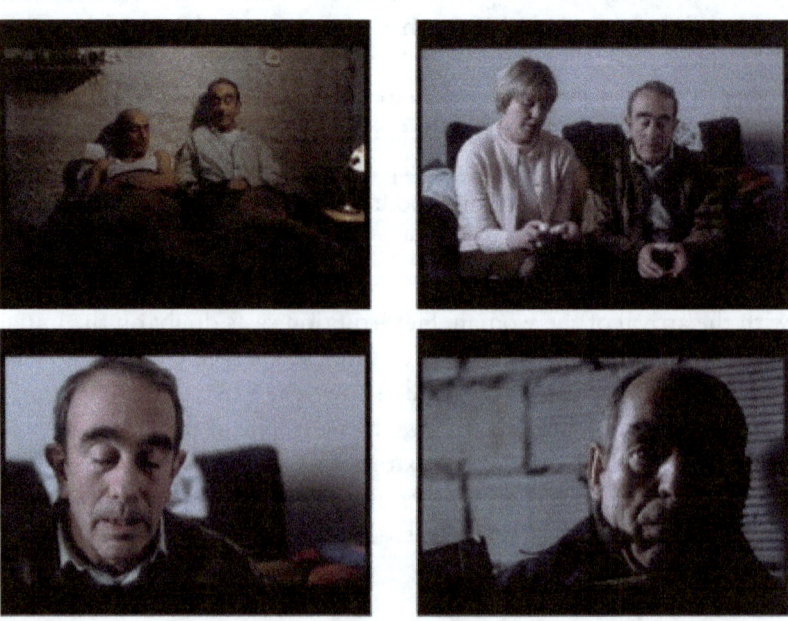

Marina is eating an apple[158] when Saturnino stabs her offscreen. The man thus eliminates this evil Eve who has perverted the stability of his world, obliging him to take the path of perdition. Paco returns home, and finds Saturnino seated on a chair in the middle of the room. He declares categorically: "I killed her." Paco sees the mess, and calls the police. Afterward, he sits down on another chair next to Saturnino, exchanging their positions with respect to the initial shot: Paco on the left, and Saturnino on the right. Everything has changed and they know it; although they are together again phsyically, they can no longer share their lives like before. Saturnino says in a tone of reproach: "now you will know what it's like to be alone," and the camera, which marks the pathetic image of these two men sitting still on their chair, retreats in a tracking shot, and abandons them to their loneliness.

Looking the Other Way: *Terminal* (Aitzol Aramaio, 2002)

Aitzol Aramaio is the director and scriptwriter of this short film based on the short story *La chica de la terminal* by the Bilbao-based musician and journalist Roberto Moso. *Terminal* was selected in the Kimuak catalog of the same year, and earned many recognitions among which stand out the Best Short Film award at the Berlin International Short Film Festival, Interfilm (Germany); the award for Best European Short film at the La Cinema Fe Film Festival (New York, United States); or the audience award at the Venice International Cinema Festival Circuito Off (Italy). Before devoting himself to fiction, Aramaio made various documentaries: *Bosnia vive* (1995), *Immigration* (1998), or *Guggenheim Museum* (2000). In 2008 he switched to feature film with *Un poco de chocolate* (A Tram in SP), a cinematographic adaptation of the novel *SPrako tranbia* by Unai Elorriaga, with which the Basque writer won the National Narrative Award in 2002.

Terminal is an unhappy love story spoiled by the prejudices of its main character, a man who works at the ticket booth of a bus company (Miguel Ángel Solá), and who falls in love with a young junkie (Blanca Oteyza), whom he runs into every night on the bus that takes her from work a hostess bar, to home. This story is full of tenderness and subtlety.

---

158 Throughout the story, the apple functions as an object of affective circulation. Paco's mother offers an apple for his son for dessert, and he gives it to Saturnino. Afterwards, it will be Marina who enjoys Paco's fruit.

It is centered on the profoundly human, kind-hearted and transparent character of the drug addict, when at the same time it shows the cowardice of the man, who gives more importance to the woman's past than the possibility of being happy with her.

The film divides the events in distinct episodes separated by a brief black screen, and it presents them chronologically. This structure facilitates the articulation of the mise-en-scène, as it is a short film without dialogues whose material are the images and sounds. There are no conversations or voice-off. The text uses the expressive devices that allow it to halt by details to show, on the one hand, the relationship that is established between the two persons who occupy a very unequal position in society, and on the other, the evolution of the female character, who overcomes difficulties and goes forward. Each fragment is articulated as a link in this chain, but in all of them the same devices are repeated: a descriptive look in which the tracking shot has a specific weight, when it halts on two important aspects. The musical leitmotif that accompanies the female character throughout the story, and the mise-en-scène of the couple's relationship on the basis of the look.

The woman's transformation becomes visible through her physical appearance. The film introduces her in her worst moment: haggard and shaking before passing out. A paused vertical tracking shot halts to show her sandals and the red handbag, objects that always accompany her. This device is repeated on the last trip where the girl has a much healthier appearance. The handbag and the sandals attest that she continues to be submerged in the world of prostitution, but she has decided to put an end to this life. For this reason, when she breaks with the past, and presents herself at the ticket booth, she has a totally different appearance. She wears a modest coat, and she is without her usual accessories. The surgical collar is the only visible sign of tough experiences. The physical wounds imply the violent blows that her pimp gave her before letting her go. In this last scene, the mise-en-scene does not use the vertical tracking shot given that this tool, the same way as the handbag and the sandals, belongs to the past.

On the other hand, the musical leitmotif irrupts throughout the story to narrate the steps of the main character, and evoke her absence. It is a sweet music which contrast with the tough reality of the young woman's life, and highlights her innocence. This soundtrack composed by Bingen Mendizabal also accompanies the relationship that she establishes with the man, and makes it evident that it is a romantic encounter with clean intentions. The sound of heels, beside the music, is the only thing that marks her presence. The rest of the noises refer to the motor of the bus, and the street. We may claim that the short film is rather quiet in its atmosphere, which yields greater subtlety to the story, as it erases the miserable connotations of Bilbao's Palanca district. After all, the musical theme is like a woman's perfume that invades the image, and leaves a trace of the real nature of the woman hidden under a false appearance.

But without a doubt, the look is the backbone of the relationship between the two characters. During the first trip on the bus, amidst the depreciative looks she receives from all the passengers, the girl offers her seat to an elderly woman. No one made this gesture. In that moment, the secret looks of the two characters cross for the first time. He tries to hide his interest when she catches him looking at her tenderly. But it is too late, the man's gesture has made her smile again. The music and the rain that starts to beat against the glass mark a turning point in the existence of the main character. The water serves like a healing element that cleans the stains of the past. Next, the bus route becomes a trip in which she tries to recover her faith in life, and the possibility to love and be loved. She becomes interested in the man who has been able to see her, for a moment, as a person, and not a prostitute.

The girl's innocence and the freshness contrasts with the world around her. From this moment on, she takes the initiative, and she delicately approaches the man. The mise-en-scène works to show the ephemeral gestures of mutual approaching. In spite of the fact that the man turns his look away at the beginning, he ends up yielding, and accepting the touch of the female body. In their second encounter she situates herself before him. The man looks at her and then looks away for a moment. She grabs the bar of the bus, and puts her hand on that of the man. Then he looks at her hand, and looks at her somewhat disconcerted but happy. The tracking shot describes with detail this moment where their hands are on top of one another. As a climax, she looks at him and sweetly smiles at him. The melody continues during the whole trip. On the next encounter, the woman stands right behind him, and takes advantage of the passage of people to gently rub herself against his body. He recognizes her presence, and the music marks the moment when the man turns his head as if he wanted to look at her, but finally he doesn't do so.

Nevertheless, when the young woman shows up before the ticket booth where he works, the man rejects her, and denies the look. What is more, he quickly shuts the blinds, although he leaves a little strip open through which he sees her leave. He looks at her for the last time, and when she discovers him, he closes the blinds entirely. To emphasize the harshness of this moment, the careful mise-en-scène uses a shot in which the figure of the young woman is projected on the red background of the glass; the same color as that of her sandals and the handbag that linked her with prostitution. The negation of the look is the equivalent of the depreciative looks that the young woman received in the past: the look of the mother and daughter who see her fall at the station, that of the passengers on the bus, and even that of the old woman to whom she offers her seat. This one, however, is crueler than all the previous looks because this time the man, instead of looking at her like the person who she really is, reminds him of who she used to be in the past. The attitude of the box office clerk inverts the meaning of his first encounter with the girl on the bus. Obviously, his behavior has to do with his incapacity to give a step forward, and take advantage of the opportunity to be happy with what life offers.

The ticket booth of the station symbolizes the immobility of the masculine character, who looks at the world from behind a window that protects him. This observation tower turns him into a judge and executioner of what takes place before his eyes. He is incapable of crossing the border, of feeling empathy, of facing his emotions. He does not want to either risk, or expose himself to an amorous relationship, and much less with someone who has a dubious past behind her. The two occasions that he appears watching from behind this barricade prove it: the first at the beginning, when he observes impassively how the ambulence carries her away, and the second when, nervous, he looks at the bank where she used to sit, but is no longer there.

But while the masculine character does not evolve, the young woman undergoes a profound transformation throughout the story, which associates her with the idea of movement and progress. This is a concept that is materialized through the bus trip. The vehicle represents the crossroads of everyday existence in which everyone takes a direction. In case of the woman, it symbolizes the path toward redemption, and the struggle to be happy. The ticket booth marks the turning point of this personal pilgrimage: the initial hell, and then that of the arrival, of the man's rejection. Fortunately, the ending makes it clear that in spite of the pain, the young woman embarks on a new journey by herself. She is a young woman who faces the challenges of life. He however is anchored to a station from which he will never move. His existence is limited to observing the journeys that people take every day. And like everything in life, this choice has a price: loneliness and melancholy. Under the day's light, the bus runs around the city, and we hear the leitmotif of the short film. Taciturn, the clerk grabs the bar with both hands, and his little finger keeps searching for the woman. But it is now too late. His incapacity leads him to regret things twice. The first time, at the beginning, when he thinks that she is dead and he regrets that he didn't help her before, and the second time at the end, when he realizes that he lost her forever.

Ultimately, beyond the tender story of impossible love, the short film reflects about the distinctive positions people take before life. It criticizes a society in which those who are stagnant look at the world from behind a watchtower, and do nothing to help others. Their inaction turns them into an example of virtue, when in fact they are cowards and egoists who feel nothing, and suffer from nothing.

The Myth of the Vagina Dentata: *Máquina* (Gabe Ibáñez, 2006)

The Basque production company Aprieta Fuerte, lead by Emilio Pérez and Igor Legarreta, produced the first short film of the Madrid-based director Gabe Ibáñez: *Máquina*. Ana Vázquez wrote the script of this work, and it was shot between Mexico and Madrid. It relates a terrifying science fiction story in which a young girl is attacked by a strange being, and is submitted to a sinister operation that will change her life. The short film lasts sixteen minutes, and was selected in the 2006 catalog.

In 2007 it won the special award of the jury at the Clermont-Ferrand International Short Film Festival. Gabe Ibáñez moved on to feature film with the psychothriller *Hierro* (2009).

Máquina is a short film that mixes horror and science fiction, and whose staging presents various characteristics proper to postmodern cinema. The filmic texture mixes animation, television, video, the ultrasounds and x-rays with cinematographic image. It relies on all these visual forms in order to create a futurist universe without the necessity of great special effects. It lacks dialogues, which is why the articulation of the soundtrack becomes fundamental. On the one hand, the music of Johann Sebastian Bach and Dimitri Shostakovich leads the events in a harmonious way. And on the other hand, the metalic sounds combine among one another, either with instruments or with musical compositions to transmit the anxiety and unease that revolves around the only main character of the story. We must highlight the disturbing role of an almost omnipresent sound in the story, that of a motor that resembles the cold mechanical world in which the young girl lives. In sum, the soundtrack is always characterized by minimalism: that is, it uses only the necessary sounds for every instant.

The main character (Iazúa Larios) lives alone in a big city. She is scared, and she watches out attentively for everything that happens around her. One night she is attacked by a stranger, a being from another world, who inserts a grinding machine in her vagina. Next, the young woman enters a spiral that consists of six phases: the search for a clear diagnostics; the discovery of the device; the suffering and fear of what she hides inside her; the decision to face life and enjoy sex; the horror of discovering the consequences of her actions; and finally, the pride of accepting and assuming her power. Throughout this process, the girl goes on to experiment a successive transformation that implies four feminine images. First, she is shown as the inversion of the Virgin Mary. Later, she represents the birth of Venus; then she turns into a jovial Eve, and finally she assumes the role of Lilith, the castrating woman. Besides being a personal attribute, the girl's long hair has a symbolic charge[159] with regards to her symbolic and demonic power. It goes on and turns from a protecting layer[160] that covers her body into a long and sensual mane that leads man to his perdition.

---

159 Bornay details the erotic symbolism of women's hair. Bornay, *La cabellera femenina*, 56–68.
160 At the beginning, the girl is very shy, and covers her naked body with her hair. It resembles the image of Santa Inés. Her attitude refers to hair as an element that

It is obvious that the myth of vagina dentata[161] lies behind this terrifying story, which symbolizes man's anscestral fear to succumb to the sexual desires of a powerful woman who is at the same level as he is. That is, the vagina represents female power, and its toothed character alludes to masculine castration. But in *Máquina*, it is the main character who, at the beginning, lives terrorized and anxious as she intuits the power of her vagina, until she accepts and uses this power in a conscious and proud manner. The story may be understood as a kind of metaphor of female empowerment, in which the main character not only knows and accepts her sexuality in a way that it is no longer a cursed device that someone inserted in her, but also decides to enjoy it beyond the consequences that it may cause to men. Besides, in this case, the girl is an inverted image of the Virgin Mary. Just like the mother of Jesus Christ, she receives the announcement in the form of a premonition that something extraordinary will happen. It is the only thing she notices from the strange signs that come from the sky. But as opposed to the immaculate conception of the Virgin, in place of a child, the alien inserts in her a malign artifact that gives her pleasure and power, and above else, freedom. A machine substitutes the womb that in the figure of the Virgin symbolizes the maternal and reproductive function traditionally assigned to women. This is both destructive and pleasurable at the same time. The redundant shot of the X-ray where we can see the machine in the place of the baby strenghtens this inversion, alluding to Maria's womb where her son Jesus developed.

The mise-en-scène creates a futurist universe of the short film on the basis of relatively simple visual effects against an austere set that evokes the style of the 1970s. The house and the hospital stand out for having almost empty rooms, with only the most indispensable furniture, and the white walls. They are old spaces, and somewhat abandoned. The streets' shop windows display clothes that look like clothes for work, and which take us to another place. There are no daytime scenes in this strange enclave where the loudspeakers, located on the ceiling of the streets closed by fibre cement walls, reproduce the chirping of birds. The only living beings are the enigmatic insects of great size, which hide under the pillow, and the mosquito that agonizes in the glass of milk that the girl drinks. This shot is repeated twice, before the aggression and after the orgasm, and symbolizes her destructive power.

---

hides sexuality, and protects women from men's lecherous desires. Ibid., 32.
161 Paglia, *Sexual Personae*.

As if it was about a prophetic warning, *Halt im Gedächtnis Jesus Christ* by Bach accompanies the unbridled movement of the aerial images of the city at sunset, which starts the short film. They contrast with the impeccable high angle tracking shot of the city that precedes the nighttime escapade of the woman. The shape of the highways and squares resembles the earth drawings that were dicovered in England, and attributed to extraterrestrials. But they are both shots in movement, which work like a supernatural sign that announces that something extraordinary will happen.

The mise-en-scène highlights that she is the chosen one, and uses two simple visual tools: the quick camera, and the close-up of the eye. In the presentation, the images of the metro show her being isolated in the middle of a multitude that moves around her with great speed. The velocity of the obstruction and reproduction of these shots was manipulated in order to achieve an effect that resembles the urban aesthetics of the documentary *Koyaanisqatsi*[162] (Godfrey Reggio, 1982). The close-up of the girl's eye scrutinizes the space, and describes her fear before the sign; nevertheless, she is the only one who realized it. The shot of the scrutinizing iris is once again repeated when the woman wakes up in the garbage dump after the attack, and symbolizes her rebirth: a new look from a new reality. This scene corresponds with the birth of Venus, and implies a new step in feminine transformation.

The way it happens with the insect in the glass of milk or the scrutinizing eye, there are three elements that the mise-en-scène emphasizes to mark her evolution in a symbolic way: the television, the bathroom, and the X-ray of the machine. The television tunes in to the dirty images of the building's CCTV video in order to show first the arrival of the aggressor in a kind of obscure announciation, and afterward, to wake up the main character to alert her that her suicide attempt did not work out. The bathroom, as well as the rain, is a symbol of purification related with female transformation. The first time she baths, unaware, she realizes a cleansing ritual that prepares her to receive the strange visit of the aggressor. On the second occasion, it is about cleaning up the marks of suicide, and implies the beginning of a new relationship with her metallic vagina.

---

162 In this documentary, Reggio locates the camera in the neurolgic spots of great cities in order to portray modern life, and its frenetic rhythm. The accelerated reproduction of these images is a metaphor of contemporary society, which functions as a giant machinery. The short film recovers this iconography in order to emphasize the rhythm of a futurist, and profoundly dehumanized world.

The X-ray of the woman's womb in which, as if it was a baby, they observe the movements of the machine, is repeated three times. It appears for the first time after the attack, and for the last time before she goes out at night when the machine is totally developed. The second appearance coincides with the judgement that the doctor has been unable to clarify. The look of the girl connects the photographs of the footprints the extraterrestrial has left in her body, the scar and the drawings of dolls, with the final X-ray. We can hear the sound of the motor in the soundtrack. There is no doubt that the machine implanted by the alien is alive. No one gives a solution to her problem. In spite of the fact that the sinister nuns of white habit tried to delete the marks of her sin, she carries it in her womb.

After the unsuccessful suicide attempt comes the discovery of the device, which is produced in two consecutive scenes. In the first one the girl contemplates the reflection of her vagina in a mirror. She thus discovers her sex, something she hadn't done before, in a kind of ritual of self-discovery. Then, she tries to explore the vagina with her finger, which hurts her. The second scene exposes masturbation, and experimentation with pleasure. She inserts a carrot, an evident reference to the penis, and excites herself; but again, her vagina quarters the vegetable. The experimentation with sexual pleasure for the first time is materialized through an allegorical image: the girl appears in an artificial setting seated on the mountains, together with a tree and a bird. It symbolizes the primitive Eve that laughs loudly, making Paradise tremble. She is a new woman, aware of her body, which marks the starting point toward a definitive transformation.

The birth of the fragile Venus gives way to Eve's security, and after the final test, she undergoes the final transformation into Lilith: encarnation of the sexually powerful woman who devours men, and who also stands for the anti-mother. She is a model opposite to the Virgin and, in general, to the image of the maternal woman. The metaphor of the vagina dentata is precisely the most powerful symbol of this terrifying power.

An orchestra from the '70's plays on the stage of an immense, semi-empty dance hall, lit by the sparkle of the spotlights. The sound of the place has been substituted by the melody of a music box, and the young woman seems like a lovely doll. When she finally dances with a man, the motor of the machine becomes audible, and connects with the sound of the drums. In her bedroom and to the rhythm of the battery, naked, she smiles and seduces the immobile man, who is stretched out on the bed like a doll. Next day she wakes up only to discover in horror the blood fest of the previous night. The great red stain stands out in the clarity of the room. Scared, she decides to escape, but the sound of the rain keeps her back. In a gesture that resembles the opening of the curtain, she opens the curtains, and her face is seen from the raindrop-covered glass. This new ritual of purification by water has worked magic: the woman decides to assume her power, and exploit it.

Finally, we must emphasize that in this short film, violence is represented in two totally different ways in function of the nature of the attacker. Thus, the violence exercised by the woman is explicit, while when it's she who suffers from it, it is distorted. Proof of it is the stylization of the violence of the alien's attack. This is made visible through nice cartoons in black and white, which lower its intensity. The color of blood cannot be percieved, and the naive character of the designs lends them a charm that resembles a children's universe. Besides, the soundtrack alters the voices of the characters reproducing them at great velocity, which creates an unreal effect that testifies the supernatural phenomenon. This mise-en-scène contrasts with the sequence of the orgasm, where the images of her naked body moving on the man are shown with the cry of pleasure of the woman and the rumbling of the machine.

A Vital Impulse, Curiosity Leads My Path: *Hezurbeltzak, una fosa común* (Izibene Oñederra, 2007)

Hezurbeltzak, una fosa común is one of the Kimuak short stories that forms part of the current of pure animation experimentation; that is, it clearly situates itself in the terrain of artistic creation. For this reason, when we approach a work of this tendency, it is necessary to assume a different point of view than that of the textual analysis of the narrative character. It becomes indispensable to situate ourselves in the place of the creator in order to understand the process, and analyze the object with an adequate perspective. As a consequence, the analysis of *Hezurbeltzak, una fosa común* is accompanied by the reflections that are extracted from a conversation with Izibene Oñederra.

Besides the cited short film, the filmography of this artist from Azkoitia consists of a contribution to the *Berbaoc* collection, and a piece with which she participates in *Diario Instantáneo* (2011) with the artists Miguel Aparicio and Adrián Orr. It was a project proposed by Krea, Expresión Contemporánea, and its theme was the capital of Álava. Although obviously, artistic liberty does not know borders.

This short film was born in the classes of Bego Vicario. Oñederra's drawings kept repeating themselves. They were same motifs and the same obsessions of a tough, but intimate universe, which had to be expressed. "Here you have your storyboard" said Vicario. From this moment on, all the artist had to do was follow what the drawings suggested her, that is, identify the characters, know what is happening to them, what their relationship was, how they move, and where this movement leads them. The creative process of this artist is circular, and has nothing to do with the development of the audiovisual production of other short films. In fact, the function of the drawings and the relationship that is established between them in the animation is to express the artist's sentiments, her interior world; that is, to provoke the same sentiments that drove her to draw them. For this reason, it doesn't matter how terrible the drawings, or the tough situations that the animation represents, may be. What matters is that they express the artist's feelings.

Oñederra draws forms of very fine stroke, and they are messy and fast as they impose themselves on the white sheet. Sometimes the ink stains fall on this background, or on the silhouettes. To a great degree, it is the spontaniety and carelessness that create the intensity of her drawings. They respond to the creative impulse that is behind her work. The language of this animation moves away from that of cinemaography. For that reason, the use of a voice-over, or an explicative voice-off, or a text makes no sense. The objective is to generate emotions. What's more, first the animation had no sound, as it needed none, until Xabier Erkizia composed a piece that gave body and space to what was presented. The constant movement of the shapeless forms and the mutations gains even more life thanks to a sound of an editing projector, which repeats itself cyclically from beginning to end, and creates a disturbing sensation of agony. Thus, the soundtrack matches what the drawings aim to transmit. We also hear other sounds like the whistle of a train, the rattling of the tracks, the sound of a dog's tongue, or the words that can never be pronounced; and they always accompany the images.

The main character of this short film is a mutilated woman. She has neither arms, nor hair. She has an androgynous face, and her naked body suffers mutations and aggressions throughout the work. There exist elements that insistently return, such as the windows that appear next to the image. Sometimes we see characters who repeat what the main character does, that is, the sign of silence; or figures that try to walk by the railway tracks. Other times, naked bodies appear and display male or female genitalia. The letters that fall like a fog on the main character, and what her vagina expulses more than once after sexual aggression are also a constant. The relationship between these two motifs creates the sensation that there exists a terrible secret that cannot be revealed. There is a taboo here, of which no one can speak, but everybody knows. Given the rest of the motifs that are reiterated, and the crude way they are done, the taboo is either about an abnormal sexual aggression, or a sexual perversion. Something very tough that, for one reason or the other, is prohibited to talk about.

Without a doubt, this taboo has to do with the central theme that is repeated time and time again: a savage animal, a kind of big dog, attacks the mutilated woman. Sometimes it has a long tongue, other times sharp denture, and it licks the woman's vagina. And always, the violent sexual relation ends when the animal enters her body. Among all these aggressions, that of Mickey Mouse stands out. This cartoon character turns into a brutal rapist of the woman; he ends up putting his head in her, and gobbles up her body.

The image of the animal who maintains an ambiguous relationship with the woman is a recurrent motif that reminds the viewer of scenes of sexual bestiality that has populated the imagery of painting throughout the history of art. From the point of view of mysogenous ideas and biological sexism, man and woman are not equal. Her primitive and indomitable nature puts her on the level of beast. Sex is the greatest expression of this impulsive nature, which is why man must protect her, and therefore put a break on her sexual impulses. One of the most extreme scenes that come from mysogonous ideas is that of sexual bestiality. That is, the image of the woman who has sex with an animal and enjoys it. In case of this animation, the illustration clearly refers to a sexual relationship between an animal and a woman. And effectively, this theme, repeated in different ways and with different intensity, creates a disagreeable sensation in the viewer. The soundtrack notably contributes to this sensation with its rattling and occasional whistles. In sum, it is for this reason that these images are interpreted as a savage rape, and produce discomfort and repulsion.

On her part, the artist confirms that the terrible acts that the tape suggests are ambiguous. According to her, the story has tenderness and love. The presence of Mickey Mouse strengthens this ambiguity. On the one hand, it is the blackest character of all. It is a big stain of ink, which gives him greater presence than the rest, and also a more sinister charge. On the other hand, this character forms part of the global imaginary of

Disney cartoons, and acquires a fond closeness. But at the same time it is also a figure with an important symbolic and ideological charge, which corresponds to the moral discourse and the conservative vision in the whole world that Disney spreads through its productions. In this sense, Mickey Mouse represents a masculine model that one must follow, which is why the violent irruption of the animated mouse may be interpreted as criticism to the intent of adoctrinating the childhood of the entire world.

The treatment of the female character is very aggressive; the violence to which the woman is submitted is extreme. It is not only noticeable in the explicit sex scenes, but also through the fact that the representation of her body carries within it a latent burden of self-destruction. Her body is dismembered, and suffers constant mutilations. Its androgynous appearance, which is stripped of all feminine features, is a clear example of abuse done to her. Oñederra denies that there should be a conscient or purposeful discourse behind her work. The fact that she is a woman influences, nevertheless, this treatment. As she suggests, there is aggression done to the woman, and she remains passive; but at the same time there is pleasure before the aggression, and this is something that puzzles the viewer.

In conclusion, the animation's sexual violence and bestiality provoke anxiety and rejection. It doesnt matter if it is about a bestial violation, or the contrary, we witness pleasurable passion. What matters is that the mutation of forms and sounds synchronize into a chain of stimuli that stir the viewer, disturb them, and generate unease. In the end, they provoke the same emotions that the artist felt before her impulsive drawings at the beginning of the creative process. In this moment, there was no ambiguity between suffering and pleasure, between violence and tenderness, as the artist said. These ideas are a result of a posterior interpretation that is born from the final text. And as it happens with all artwork, the search for meaning is a free process where our subjectivity intervenes. Nevertheless, what remains unquestionable is the internal agitation that watching this short film generates.

Even in the Best Families: *Traumalogía* (Daniel Sánchez Arévalo, 2007)

Traumalogía, directed by the Madrid based Daniel Sánchez Arévalo, and produced by Koldo Zuazua was selected in the Kimuak catalog of 2007. It is the work of a recognized director who arrived at the program with an important cinematographic career behind him. Besides this, he counts with seven short films to his credit, which earned him numerous recognitions such as ¡Gol! (2002), *Profilaxis* (2003), *Exprés* (2003), *Física II* (2004), *La culpa del alpinista* (The Mountaineer's Guilt, 2004), *Pene* (2007) and *(Uno de los) primos* (2010). In 2006 he directed his first feature film *Azuloscurocasinegro* (Dark Blue Almost Black). The film earned three Goya Awards that year, among which stands out the Best New Direction Award, and numerous international awards. His second feature film *Gordos* (Fat People, 2009) was awarded with a Goya in the category of Best Supporting Actor. *Primos* (Cousinhood, 2011) is his latest comic feature film.

This film presents a family drama with comical elements, and with a deep well of bitterness and resignation. The disagreements, the hidden passions, the dirty secrets and pious truths of a family come to light while they are waiting at the doors of the Emergency Care Unit. The father (Héctor Colomé) suffered a heart attack at the wedding of his firstborn child Antonio (Antonio de la Torre), and is between life and death. The bride and bridegroom Antonio and Esther (Natalia Mateo) confront the void of their life together, and the crisis of their relationship. Joaquín (Quim Gutiérrez) and Ángel (Jorge Monje), Antonio's brother, on the one hand, and Carla (Estíbaliz Gabilondo), Esther's sister, on the other, are trapped in an insane love triangle. And last, Miguel (Raúl Arévalo) and Carlos (Javier Pereira), the other two brothers of Antonio, are pathetic and unstable persons who confess their homosexuality and their sordid Oedipic perversions.

Sánchez Arévalo creates an impeccable mise-en-scène that recovers the key features of classic cinema. Its objective is to portray the three situations in a minimalist way, and on occasion, almost theatrically: that is, he uses expressive devices to center attention on the relationship that exists among the characters. Each frame is milimetrically elaborated, and the rhythm is slow. The dialogues acquire a fundamental importance in the soundtrack, and a kind of silence is produced during the conversations, where the music and the sound occupy secondary importance. The montage continues to alternate the three situations, and drives them to a final scene in which all the characters of the plot converge in a false and ironic happy ending, where also the mother participates (Carmen Arévalo)—who years before had abandoned the father and her five sons.

The waiting room close to the Emergency Care Unit is the scene of disagreement between the bride and the bridegroom. The heart attack interrupted the ceremony that Antonio had agreed to in order to satisfy his father's will. He thinks that it is a sign that they shouldn't continue, and brings to light the profound relationship crisis that is developed in four scenes. The director plays with the proximity or the distancing of the characters. When coldness sets in, and Antonio and Esther blurt out painful truths into each other's face, the mise-en-scène suggests the reconciliation of the couple through the juxtaposition of the first scenes that call attention due to their unusual composition.

On the one hand, in the frame of the bridegroom's first close-up, the air leaves a great empty space between the left margin and Antonio's face. He is positioned in the far-right end of the picture, from where he turns toward Esther, who is offscreen. The composition of Esther's close-up is the same, except in the reverse order; that is, the bridegroom's face is situated exactly on the left side of the frame, from where she turns toward Antonio, who is offscreen. The air leaves an empty space all the way to the left end of the frame. This combination gives the sensation that the two are very close, practically next to each other. Nevertheless, a general view reveals that they are seated at the two far ends of the waiting room, and a few chairs separate them. Finally, this mise-en-scène makes it clear that the fear of loneliness, and the security that marriage offers, condemn Antonio and Esther to live together, although their relationship is as empty as the space that separates them.

The same way, the siren of the ambulance car that follow their harsh words during this conversation stops abruptly, when the general view appears. The alarm is a metaphor of the lack of communication that exists between the couple, and it contrasts with the images that suggest their contiguity. Thus, the words of the conversation are a strident background sound that will always accompany them, and evokes the lack of their connection. Also, the silence highlights the emptiness of the final image, which turns into the reverse of a wedding story, and reveals what hides behind appearances.

The scenes of the love triangle take place in the ladies' room, which makes reference to Clara as a vortex of the relationship. The scenes in which the two brothers make love with the same woman in a few meters of distance from one another reveal that sordidness, morbid pleasure, transgression and envy are the motor behind this triangle. In the last one, scene, Ángel confesses to his brother that he is "the other," and that his desire for Clara was born in a dirty way: he masturbated when he heard them making love in the room next door.

There isn't a single, pure sentiment that should unleash the events. They are three immature characters that act in function of the basest instincts; their relationship is a sick addiction to pleasure that fascinates them. The composition of the final scene refers to the idea of an endless loop. The mirror on the wall re-frames the couple, whose reflection is infinitely repeated, and evokes the insane character of this passionate relationship that needs morbid attraction to nourish, and repeat itself incessantly.

Now, the most obscure and deprived story of the three, and also the most comic one, is that of Miguel and Carlos. The younger brothers are two failed characters who drag along the trauma of their mother's abandonment. The mise-en-scène condemns the sick person, unconscious and immobile, to having to listen to the most obscure confessions of his sons without the option to respond to them. They talk freely because they think that he is asleep, anesthetized.

Miguel's confession uses a tracking shot to frame the father and the son, but maintains the shaking until the end. This vibration contributes tension, and allows us to see that, in reality, the father is listening to him. Seated by the bed of the ECU, the boy starts his testimony while we can hear the ubiquitous sound of the machine that controls the father's heartbeat. First, he confesses his Oedipal obsessions for his mother, which he could only satsify by continuosuly masturbating with his father's pornographic magazines, in which the father had substituted the face of the models with that of his wife. Then he goes on to reveal his homosexuality, a sexual condition that has nothing to do with the deprivation and abnormalcy of the previous one, but which is a hard blow for a conservative person.

With the objective of doubling the emotional charge of the first declaration, the staging resorts to a theatrical tool: the plastic curtain opens, and there appears Carlos. Mute witness until now, he breaks his silence to openly confirm, between sobs, that he too shares the dirty practice of masturbating while thinking of his mother, and that he is gay. Once again, the tracking shot serves to approach the brothers' embrace, when the whistles, until now constant, stop. The music adds to the anxiety of the viewer. The camera movement proves the suspicions, and shows the father mumble, with open eyes; so many emotions ended up hitting him hard, and worsening his state.

In the final scene, the hospital priest officiates the marriage of Antonio and Esther, with all the persons united around the bed of the agonizing father. Like in the best families, the parents hold each other's hands, and look at each other fondly, the homosexual brothers tie together their index fingers and exchange a complicit look, the trio stretch their hand, and the couple put their arms around each other's waist. Once again, all the painful truths and the poisonous secrets remain hidden. A tracking shot out moves away to show this false photograph of the harmonious and traditional family, who all want to say goodbye to the father, and above all, want to keep appearances. Thus, the circle closes with the ceremony, although the comical tone with which this 22-minute short film starts gives way to the sadness of the ending. The ironic presentation of the family singing Hallelujah turns into a bittersweet drama when the trio's glimpses meet, and the high angle view shows the father collapse when the priest says "because you will have moments in life when you'll have problems."

Tragedy and Frivolity: *La gran carrera* (Kote Camacho, 2010)

La gran carrera is Kote Camacho's first short film. He earned his degree in Fine Arts at the UPV/EHU, and worked as a scriptwriter and cartoonist in Napartheid. He made storyboards for feature films such as *Caótica Ana* (Chaotic Ana, 2007) by Julio Medem, or *28 Weeks Later* by Juan Carlos Fresnadillo (2007). He did animation (traditional and 3D) as well as post-production. His debut with this unusual film of 7 minutes can't have been more satisfactory: to the more than 60 awards that it has won until now, we must add other merits like selections at prestigious festivals such as Clermont-Ferrand or Tampere, or its candidacy to the European Cinema Awards.

The short film was produced by Asier Altuna and Marian Fernández through their production company Txintxua Films, and although the script is signed by Camacho, [163] the story is based on an original idea of Altuna himself. In fact, the shadow of his creative universe hangs over this film notoriously which, from a metaphorical perspective, and on the basis of a small and unsuspected anecdote, proposes a reflection about the stinginess of certain human behaviors.

It is 1914, and there is great expectation in the Lasarte race track before what promises to be a historical achievement: the Half Million Grand Prix. The eight best horses of the world will run 2100 meters to win the 500,000 pesetas, the greatest prize ever awarded in a racetrack. When everything is ready for the start of the race, the jockeys suddenly stay hung in their starting gates, while the horses fling out to run the race.

Kote Camacho aims to visually reconstruct the atmosphere of the epoch. To achieve this, he combines archive footage (which come from the collection of the Filmoteca Vasca/Euskadiko Filmategia) with images shot by himself. Thanks to an excellent production design and the decisive intervention of digital effects, these images are montaged with the real archives in an almost imperceptible manner. The short film starts with documentary images of Donostia-San Sebastián, and of the Lasarte racetrack at the beginning of the twentieth century. The viewer may detect even the presence of the then King Alfonso XIII. The previous shots, staged and registered by Camacho himself, mask their fictitious origins by simulating the same perspectives and texture as the archival materials.

The negative seems to have deteriorated through time (stained with lines, spots and hair), and displays the typical lack of focus and shaking of old projections. The audience's faces and attitudes coincide with the portraits of those who were really present, and the signs emulate the typography and design of silent film captions. Against music of festive tone, the soundtrack maintains a constant background buzz that aims to show the imperfections that come with the passage of time. Even the

---

163 He is also responsible for the photography, animation, editing, and sound.

announcer's voice, who relates the events through loudspeakers (played by the director himself), acquires the old intonation of other times.

Camacho's strategy is very similar to that employed by Basilio Martín Patino in the documentary *El grito del sur. Casas Viejas*, which belongs to the television series *Andalucía, un siglo de fascinación* (1997). In it, Martín Patino deliberately used the aesthetic conventions inherent to archive footage to recreate a film presumably shot by some Soviet cameramen during the tragedy of Casas Viejas. The invention of a discourse properly argued around the discovery of false film, as well as its own quality, adjusted to the visual codes of archival materials, may at the beginning make the viewer fall for the filmmaker's trick. The complexity of the mise-en-scène, however, ends up purposefully revealing its fictitious origins: the abundance and diversity of points of view to show situations that are apparently spontaneous and unrepeatable make it clear that, either the Soviets had entered the riot with several cameras (which is a rather unlikely scenario), or it is a reconstruction prepared and directed by Martín Patino himself, which is in fact the case.

The same happens in *La gran carrera*. The moment the jockeys stay hanging in their gates, the fictitious character of the story imposes itself over its documentary content. The broadcasting disappears, and silence takes over. The shots of the hanging jockeys from unusual perspectives (in low angle from the ground that show their bodies balancing in air, or extreme close-ups showing their agonizing features) alternate with the images of the astonished countenance of the participants shocked by the Dantesque spectacle. It seems like the race will be cancelled, but suddenly we hear the faint murmur of the horses running the track. One of the spectators follows the evolution of the race with binoculars, and the animals continue to race in spite of their missing jockeys. He starts to cheer them. The rest of the audience follows his example, and the sound of the track mixes with the shouting and yelling of the spectators to the point of completely dominating the soundtrack. Although the announcer tries to pick up the narration again, his voice remains buried by the uproar of the voices, and the gallop of the horses.

In this moment, when the narration fully enters the terrain of surrealism, and the race gains all attention, Camacho's staging also gives away its fictional nature. In spite of the fact that he repeatedly shows us the shot of a cameraman shooting the events with his camera, there are several signs that make it clear that we are witnessing a prepared and constructed mise-en-scène. First, the camera insistently stops at certain members of the audience, who end up having some importance for the short film, and whose reactions are captured as the events unfold; the old woman with the scarf and the woollen bonnet, the gentleman with a pipe and his spouse, the man with the binoculars, the child whose eyes his father covers, etc. Second, the mannerism of some shots does not correspond to the composition's simplicity, nor the scarcity of the tools that newscasters of the time had at their disposal to shoot the events of the historical world. The image of the racing horses reflected in the lense of the binoculars; the change of focus of the announcer's shot to the reflection of the animals in the mirror of their booth; the fast lateral tracking shot that covers the terraces from the tracks; or the aerial movements of the camera that flies over the race track approaching the steeds in battle, could not have been taken by a static camera in the middle of the crowd.[164]

In the frenetic final outcome of the race, the rhythm of the montage ostensibly accelerates in order to emphasize the excitement of the moment. The images of the vigorous run of the animals, sometimes taken from the sand itself, alternate with the increasingly closed shots of the spectators, who cheer on their favorites to the victory. When the winner crosses the finish line, those who put their bets on him yell triumphantly. The happy music returns and, finishing the spectacle, the audience dissolves and goes home, as if the spectacle had promptly fulfilled previous expectations. *La gran carrera* thus offers us an allegory dressed in the robes of a gone-by era; however, it illustrates a social attitude that is invariable through time: the ease with which human beings forget tragedies in order to succumb to frivolities.

---

[164] And even if it could, to whom should we attribute the shots that show the camera itself?

Take My Hand: *Zeinek gehiago iraun* (Gregorio Muro, 2011)

This moving family drama, which under its simple appearance as children's animation hides a devastating story of mother-son love, is the second short film of Gregorio Muro selected by Kimuak, after *Tras los visillos* (co-directed with Raúl López) formed part of the 2008 catalog. Cartoon author, scriptwriter and film and television director, Muro has great experience in the terrain of animation: he debuted as scriptwriter in the animation film *La leyenda del viento del Norte* (The Legend of the North Wind, Maite Ruiz de Austri and Carlos Varela, 1992), and his debut as director was also with a feature film of this genre, *El rey de la granja* (King of the Farm, 2002). *Zeinek gehiago iraun*, written and produced by himself, was a candidate for the Best Animation Short Film award of Goya in 2012.

The title of the film refers to the dangerous game that a group of children play by the railway tracks. When the vibrations of the tracks tell them that a train is approaching, two of them stand in the middle of the tracks holding hands, and the one who longer endures without jumping out of its way is the winner. One day however, Ander's shoelaces get stuck in the steel, and the boy is run over by the train. He recovers, but the neurological damage is grave and irreversible. The short film describes the difficult existence of the boy and his family throughout the years: the tough rehabilitation sessions that he has to complete, and the incomprehension of the rest of the world before Ander's difference, who will never be a normal child again. Thanks to their efforts, the child starts to move about by himself, but then his father dies suddenly. The mother devotes herself to the care of his child for decades, but while she is growing old, Ander never ceases to be a big child. When the woman becomes ill and she understands that she will no longer be able to take care of her child, she decides to end their lives by taking his hand and bringing him to the railway tracks. Ander thinks that they are playing "who lasts longer," and the same instant the machine hurls them away, he retreats. The train runs over the old woman leaving the son unhurt, but alone.

The toughness of the story contrasts with the extreme visual simplicity of the cartoons that illustrate it. The forms and the stroke of the figures of the characters are extremely elemental, and refuse to make the impression of realistic volumes. The colors are clean, and the backgrounds remit, both in color and indefinition, the effects of watercolor.

Before this almost elementary aesthetics, the narration stands out for its density, just as the spatial treatment, the craftful use of the rhyme, and the elegant and subtle dominance of the ellipsis, essential resource because this is a story that condenses in twelve minutes an extensive period of time that covers a whole life.

The ubiquitous train is the axis around which the narration pivots, given that it is the channel that connects the two localities where Ander's life takes place: the hospital, and the farm house where he lives with his family. This train, which caused the family's misfortune (his own cerebral injury and the death of his mother) is also a space of sadness. The passengers' black silhouette reflected through its windows are the only reference point that Ander has of an exterior world reduced to these continuous trips back and forth. The interior of the train harbors the parents' affliction when they come home after leaving their son for the first time at the hospital; their painful return with Ander in a wheel chair; the desolation of the father's absence when mother and son go to therapy by themselves; or the brief alusion to social rejection that the main character undergoes when a girl rebukes him, or later a boy mocks him.

The concept of the journey always seems to be associated with a certain idea of movement and change, but Ander's life is limited to covering time and time again the distance between his home and the hospital, without any possibility of progress. The route of the train, eternally repeated by the inalterable itinerary that the rails signify, thus becomes a symbol of repetition only modified by the inevitable passage of time.

The beautiful ellipses, supported precisely by the reiteration of certain iconic actions and compositions, reveal the changes that the passage of time provokes in the life of Ander, and it is in the sequences of the hospital where we find its most refined examples. The first time that the parents wait in the waiting room for the doctors to tell them about their son's state, the broom of a cleaning lady crosses the frame in the foreground, intermittently blocking the image of the couple. After the death of the father it is the mother who accompanies Ander to the rehabilitation sessions, and her motionless figure seated in the waiting room is blocked for a second when the cleaning lady walks across the hall with her trolley. The worker disappears in a corner, and when we recover the mother's image we notice that, without inserting any cut, time has passed in the same frame: the clock on the wall is now digital, and the woman's face has aged visibly. Only her position and sad waiting remain invariable.

A little later, the traditional rag doll that at the beginning of the story served as a scarecrow in Ander's farmhouse, is now substituted by discs that hang from a wooden cross. The change to a modern system to scare off unwanted birds reveals the temporal leap before we get to see the now older face of Ander, and that of his mother, completely aged. She says that they have to go to the hospital, and once again a cleaning tool, now an electronic machine of the latest technology, temporarily occupies the frame before showing us the figure of those waiting in the hall. The passage of time has provoked the ultimate alteration in the life of the main character, and now it is Ander who waits for his mother to exit the door as he used to do before.

Waiting is not, nevertheless, the only situation that is repeated in Ander's life; there is also the double encounter in the train with the friend who accompanied him in the dangerous game. When still an adolescent, Ander was observing a couple of punks kissing inside the train. The girl turned toward him agressively, and the boy timidly asked her to leave Ander in peace. Years later, a boy sitting in front of Ander in the train makes fun of him by sticking out his tounge at him. The mother scolds him, but the father, ashamed, hides his face behind the newspaper. In both cases a recognizable birthmark on the cheek allows us to identify the man as his old friend. With the passage of years, the appearance of the boy changes the same way as that of Ander, but while his existence and circumstances vary, the life of the main character came to a halt in the same moment. Therefore, the presence of this friend who embodies the usual phases of growth (the rebelliousness of youth, the first love, making a family) presents with painful clarity what misfortune denied Ander.

Loss and abandonment penetrate Ander's sad story, and they materialize in a visual rhyme that is both beautiful and dreadful, which cuts across the story from beginning to end: the close-up of two intertwined hands that let go of each other. We see this image for the first time in the moment of the tragedy, and it is repeated twice more: when the parents happily observe Ander's advancement, just before the father drops dead; and in the decision of the mother to take his son on her final journey. The separation of these hands in close-up always reminds us of the rupture of a connection, and foreshadows a terrible loss for Ander: his health, and the love of his father and mother.

This latter is no doubt the more devastating loss. In a story marked by ryhme and reiteration, it is not strange that the final outcome of the story should refer back to its beginning, as if seeking some kind of circular meaning. Ander, who never grew up, remembers in his broken mind the chants of his friends little before the accident, and the similarity of the situation (the walk by the railway tracks and holding hands with his mother) makes him think that once again, he is playing. This time it is her that endures more and, unable to understand what happened, Ander happily proclaims the victory of his mother. When moments later he calls her in trembling voice, his words in off have no response. The screen turns black, dresses in mourning the loneliness that awaits Ander.

5

Final Words: Assessment and Challenges

If the objective of Kimuak was to achieve the maximum national and international diffusion of Basque short films, the data that we have from these first fifteen editions show that the results went beyond expectations. Between 1998 and 2012, the program has put 109 films into circulation, which, according to data from 2001 to 2014, have achieved 10,389 selections at festivals, of which 4,287 were state competitions, 3,625 were European, and 2,477 from the rest of the world. These indices confirm Kimuak's increasing openness to the international market, while presence at state competitions has progressively descended. The Kimuak short films have crossed the borders of five continents, arriving at such different countries as Nigeria, Taiwan, Iran, Australia, United States, Brasil or South Korea, and have accumulated a total of 1,862 awards.

Besides the numbers, another incontestable manifestation of the success of the formula that, just like its promoters José Luis Rebordinos and Amaia Rodríguez who were inspired by similar international initiatives, Kimuak too has prompted eight Spanish regional communities to imitate its model, turning it into the predecessor of successive diffusion programs in several autonomous communities: Catálogo de Cortometrajes Andaluces (2002), Programa Curtas in Galicia (2003), Hecho en Castilla La Mancha (2004), Madrid en Corto (2005), Catálogo Jara in Extremadura (2006), Canarias en Corto (2006), Short Cat (2008) and Curts Comunitat Valenciana (2008).

Kimuak works, and the directors themselves who participated in the program think the same. According to Koldo Almandoz, for example, the filmmaker who has most short films in the catalog, Kimuak is "the best thing that this country has done for audiovisual works in the last twenty years." Everyone agrees in their very positive assessment of the program and, above all, the management of the program for two main reasons. First, because directors and producers save a lot of money, time and effort by being able to delegate distribution works to a managing body established precisely for that purpose. Bego Vicario, who included his works *Pregunta por mí* and *Haragia* in the first two editions when the catalog was not yet consolidated, remembers that at that time it was often normal to "leave production on the side for the sake of distribution for a whole year or two." Koldo Serra's experience was similar: "When I made *Amor de madre* with Gorka Vázquez, we spent a lot of money, a lot of our parents' money, and little of institutions, because we didn't have subsidies. Sometimes, even as we were filling out the paperwork, we preferred that our works would actually not be selected at American festivals, because if you are selected you had to send a copy in 35mm, which are some reels that weigh a lot, and its cost was impossible. When you can save this, and Kimuak does it, it is marvellous. All you have to do is go to the festivals where the short film was selected. What is wonderful about Kimuak is that it only has good news for you... They don't tell you which festivals they sent your film to, and where they didn't select you."

The second great benefit Kimuak offers its directors, and which all of them consider essential, is the exhibition of their work in places where it would have been impossible to arrive in any other way. The fact that, after all the work the team invested in the film it will not be kept on the shelf and will be projected in various parts of the world, motivates directors to continue working. Some of them like Luiso Berdejo, Borja Cobeaga or Koldo Serra even draw a direct connection between the efficient international distribution Kimuak has done with their short films, and the professional opportunities that emerged thanks to those successes.

José Luis Rebordinos, one of the creators and promoters of the program, highlights four factors that explain in his view the success of Kimuak. The first one, without a doubt, is the quality of the short films. To this one should add the help of the Basque Government, whose confidence in the project never wavered at any point. The entrance in the market of Clermont-Ferrand was decisive, as it is the most important festival in the world of short films, and a meeting point for all buyers. And above all, the management of Txema Muñoz established contacts and personal relationships with buyers through his professional, serious and attentive attitude. A good part of those directors who made up the successive catalogs corroborate his opinion, especially those who participated in the first phase of the program before Muñoz took charge of it, and witnessed its spectacular prospective evolution. The total commitment of Muñoz to a project he believed in was, according to the filmmakers, the key for the consolidation of Kimuak. In their words, Muñoz "protects," "gives confidence," and "counsels" short filmmakers, with an interest and an attitude that Borja Cobeaga summarized this way with forceful clarity: "Txema Muñoz cares about your film more than you do."

As a consequence of Kimuak's success, there has been a continuous increase in the production of short films in the Basque Country. Although it wasn't a primary objective, it is also true that it served as a quarry of Basque cinema, and spread new values: an effect that was implicit in the very name of the program, which alludes to sprouts from which the future plants of the Basque audiovisual sector grow. Besides a great staff of technicians who collaborated in the realization of short films and now work in the audiovisual industry (cinematography, commercial or television), we must mention a total number of twenty-four Kimuak directors who got to shoot at least one feature film: Tinieblas González (*ASD. Alma sin dueño*, 2010), Joxean Muñoz and Txabi Basterretxea (*Karramarro uhartea/La isla del cangrejo* [The Island of the Crab], 2000), Asier Altuna (*Aupa Etxebeste!*, 2005; *Bertsolari*, 2011), Telmo Esnal (*Aupa Etxebeste!*, 2005; *Urte berri on, amona!*, 2011), Mercedes Álvarez *(El cielo gira*, 2004; *Mercado de futuros*, 2011), Koldo Serra (*The Backwoods*, 2006), Ramón Barea (*Pecata minuta*, 1999; *El coche de pedales*, 2004), Pablo Malo (*Frío sol de invierno* [Cold Winter Sun], 2004; *La sombra de nadie* [Nobody's Shadow], 2006), Oskar Santos (*El mal ajeno*, 2010), Ione Hernández (*Uno por ciento esquizofrenia*, 2007), Gorka Merchán (*La casa de mi padre* [Black Listed], 2008), Borja Cobeaga (*Pagafantas*, 2009; *No controles*, 2010), Luiso Berdejo (*The New Daughter*, 2009), Maru Solores (*Camera obscura*, 2011), Jose Mari Goenaga (*Lucio*, 2007; *80 egunean*, 2010), Jon Garaño (*80 egunean*, 2010), Aitzol Aramaio (*Un poco de chocolate*, 2008), Nacho Vigalondo (*Los cronocrímenes*, 2007; *Extraterrestre*, 2011), Safy Nebbou (*Le cou de la giraffe* [The Giraffe's Neck], 2004; *L'empreinte de l'ange* [Mark of an Angel], 2008; *L'autre Dumas* [Dumas], 2010; *Comme un homme* [Bad Seeds], 2012), Gabe Ibáñez (*Hierro*, 2009), Gregorio Muro (*El rey de la granja*, 2002), Miguel Ángel Jiménez (*Ori*, 2009) or Mikel Rueda (*Izarren argia* [Stars to Wish Upon], 2010).

From this perspective, we may observe an interesting and unusual phenomenon, which contributes to the re-assessment of the short film itself: the return of directors to short film after debuting in feature film. This is the case of Asier Altuna, Telmo Esnal, Jose Mari Goenaga, Jon Garaño, Nacho Vigalondo, Borja Cobeaga, Gregorio Muro, Miguel Ángel Jiménez, Mikel Rueda or Daniel Sánchez Arévalo, who entered in Kimuak with *Traumalogía* after his first work *Azuloscurocasinegro* (2006) received three Goya Awards, among them Best New Director.

Kimuak is no doubt something more than a quarry of future feature film directors. In a cinematographic industry like the Basque (weak or straight inexistant), where it is so difficult to make a feature film, Kimuak provides a showcase for the work an evolution of those Basque audiovisual creators who find the short film the most accessible expressive channel for their artistic interest. As the interviewed filmmakers noted during their tour at festivals, this showcase has gained international renown for its quality, to the point of turning Kimuak into what they themselves called a "brand", "seal", "label", or "certified quality." Film festivals look forward to receiving the annual collection of Basque short films, because they know that they are a result of a pre-selection, which is already a guarantee that the work is more than presentable.

It appears therefore that the initial objectives of Kimuak are for now fulfilled. Nevertheless, its leaders are aware that there is neither time nor space to relax. Among the future challenge they set for themselves is the maintenance and increase of Kimuak's prestige all over the world, and searching for new ideas that allow them to renovate and develop the program.

Another one of the great challenges Txema Muñoz mentioned is that the catalog, as well as the short films that it distributes, should be more well known within our borders. They paid more attention to international rather than national distribution, and there are few occasions where the Basque audience can enjoy the films that often gain fame abroad before they do at home.

As far as the improvement of distribution work is concerned, Kimuak aims to increase its presence in the Internet, and tries to exploit with greater efficiency the opportunities of diffusion that the net offers. One must also add the possibility of establishing stable collaborative agreements with EITB in order to get the autonomous television involved not only in featuring the short films, but also in their production, through the previous purchase of emission rights.

Finally, it remains to be seen how Kimuak will respond to all those high quality Basque short films that are too locally focused, or do not meet the program's selection criteria. Koldo Almandoz and Jon Garaño warn us that there exist Basque short films outside of Kimuak, and the fact that the program does not select a film means that it can't reach considerable diffusion, or develop a successful trajectory. Txema Muñoz considers that there should exist a more extended and stable structure or organism that integrates the Kimuak program itself. What they need is a kind of Basque short film agency that serves as a reference point for anyone who wants to make a short film in Euskadi, facilitating them consultancy, information, support, and collaboration.

These are questions and projects that still need to be clearly defined. But there is no doubt that planning new challenges implies a future vision that wants to continue to improve, and this is the best proof of the good health of constantly growing sprouts.

Bibliography

Altman, Rick. *Film/Genre*. London: British Film Institute, 1999.

Angulo, Jesús; José Luis Rebordinos and Antonio Santamarina. *Breve historia del cortometraje vasco*. Donostia-San Sebastián: Euskadiko Filmategia Fundazioa–Fundación Filmoteca Vasca, 2006.

Argullol, Rafael. *El Héroe y el Único: El espíritu trágico del Romanticismo*. Madrid: Taurus, 1999.

Aumont, Jaques; Alain Bergala; Michel Marie and Marc Vernet. *Aesthetics of Film*. Austin: University of Texas Press, 1992.

Aumont, Jacques. *L'oeil interminable: Cinéma et peinture*. Paris: Librairie Séguier, 1989.

Bazin, André. *What Is Cinema?* Berkeley: University of California Press, 1967.

Bettelheim, Bruno. *The uses of enchantment: The meaning and importance of fairy tales*. London: Penguin Books, 1991.

Bordwell, David and Kristin Thompson. *Film Art: An Introduction*. New York: McGraw-Hill, 2008.

Bordwell, David; Janet Staiger and Kristin Thompson. *The Classical Hollywood Cinema: Film Style and Mode of Production to 1960*. London: Routledge & Kegan Paul, 1985.

Bordwell, David. *The Cinema of Eisenstein*. New York: Routledge, 2005.

Bornay, Erika. *La cabellera femenina*. Madrid: Cátedra, 1994.

Buccheri, Vincenzo. *Sguardi sul postmoderno: Il cinema contemporaneo: questioni, scenari, letture*. Milán: Isu Universitá Cattolica, 2000.

Burch, Noël. *La Lucarne de l'infini: Naissance du langage cinématographique.* Paris: Nathan, 1991.

Calabrese, Omar. *Neo-Baroque: A Sign of the Times.* Princeton: Princeton University Press, 1992.

Cardona, Rodolfo and Anthony N. Zahareas. *Visión del esperpento: Teoría y práctica de los esperpentos de Valle-Inclán.* Madrid: Castalia, 1987.

Castex, Pierre-Georges. *Le conte fantastique en France de Nodier à Maupassant.* Paris: José Corti, 1951.

Company Ramón, Juan Miguel. "Dulces prendas por mí mal halladas: El objeto en el melodrama cinematográfico." In *Acerca del melodrama.* Coordinated by Vicente Ponce. Valencia: Conselleria de Cultura, Educació i Ciència de la Generalitat, 1987.

Eco, Umberto. *Postscript to the Name of the Rose.* San Diego: Harcourt Brace Jovanovich, 1984.

Eliade, Mircea. *The Myth of the Eternal Return.* New York: Pantheon Books, 1954.

Feuer, Jane. *The Hollywood Musical.* London: BFI, 1982.

González Requena, Jesús. "Escenografía de la herida." In *Acerca del melodrama.* Coordinated by

Vicente Ponce. Valencia: Conselleria de Cultura, Educació i Ciència de la Generalitat, 1987.

Hugo, Victor. *The Essential Victor Hugo.* New York: Oxford University Press, 2004.

Iampolski, Mijaíl. *La teoría de la intertextualidad y el cine.* Valencia, Episteme, 1996.

Jullier, Laurent. *L'écran postmoderne: Un cinéma de l'allusion et du feu d'artifice.* Paris: L'Harmattan, 1997.

Kellogg, Rhoda. *Analyzing Children's Art.* Palo Alto, California: Mayfield Publishing Company, 1969.

Lenne, Gérard. *Le cinéma "fantastique" et ses Mythologies, 1895–1970*. Paris: Henri Veyrier, 1985.

Leutrat, Jean Louis. *Vida de fantasmas: Lo fantástico en el cine*. Valencia: Contraluz libros de cine, no. 5, 1999.

Losilla, Carlos. *El cine de terror: Una introducción*. Barcelona: Paidós, 1993.

Lovecraft, H.P. *Supernatural Horror in Literature*. 1927. Available at http://gutenberg.net.au/ebooks06/0601181h.html

Luque, Ramón. *En busca de Woody Allen: Sexo, muerte y cultura en su cine*. Madrid: Ocho y medio, 2005.

Nichols, Bill. *Representing reality: Issues and concepts in documentary*. Bloomington: Indiana University Press, 1991.

Paglia, Camille. *Sexual Personae: Art and Decadence from Nefertiti to Emily Dickinson*. London: Yale University Press, 1990.

Palacio, Manuel and Santos Zunzunegui. *Historia general del cine. Volume 12, El cine en la era audiovisual*. Madrid: Cátedra, 1995.

Ríos Carratalá, Juan Antonio. *Lo sainetesco en el cine español*. Alicante: Universidad de Alicante, 1997.

Salinas, Pedro. *Literatura española: Siglo XX*. Madrid: Alianza, 1980, first edition, 1970.

Schrader, Paul. *Transcendental Style in film: Ozu, Bresson, Dreyer*. Berkeley: University of California Press, 1972.

Stam, Robert; Robert Burgoyne and Sandy Flitterman-Lewis. *New vocabularies in film semiotics: Structuralism, post-structuralism and beyond*. London: Routledge, 1992.

Truffaut, François. *Hitchcock*. New York: Simon & Schuster, 1967.

Velázquez, José Martín and Luis Ángel Ramírez. *Una década prodigiosa: El cortometraje español de los noventa*. Alcalá de Henares: Festival de Cine de Alcalá de Henares, 2000.

Weinrichter, Antonio. *Doc: Documentarism in the 21st century*. Donostia-San Sebastián: Festival Internacional de Cine de Donostia-San Sebastián, 2010.

Yáñez, Jara, ed. *La medida de los tiempos: El cortometraje español en la década de 2000*. Alcalá de Henares: Festival de Cine de Alcalá de Henares/ Comunidad de Madrid, 2010.

Zunzunegui, Santos. *La mirada cercana: Microanálisis fílmico*. Barcelona: Paidós, 1996.

———. "Lo viejo y lo nuevo: La reinvención de la tradición cinematográfica en el final del siglo XX." *Letras Deusto* 25, no. 66, ref 12 (1995): 59–74.

www.ingramcontent.com/pod-product-compliance
Lightning Source LLC
Chambersburg PA
CBHW050328230426
43663CB00010B/1777